Along The Med
on a
Bike Called Reggie

Andrew P. Sykes

A <u>CyclingEurope.org</u> book

First published in Great Britain in 2014

ISBN: 9781849145053

Contact details for the author can be found at
CyclingEurope.org

Typeset in Georgia.

Printed & bound in Great Britain by
Lightning Source UK Ltd, Milton Keynes, UK

Along The Med on a Bike Called Reggie

Also by Andrew P. Sykes

Crossing Europe on a Bike Called Reggie

"It's by riding a bicycle that you learn the contours of a country best..."

Ernest Hemingway

For more information about Andrew P. Sykes and his travels, visit his website at CyclingEurope.org

Follow the author on Twitter @CyclingEurope...
...and his bicycle @ReggieTheBike

Visit the *Cycling Europe... on a Bike Called Reggie* Facebook page to see the full set of photographs from the journey.

Cover illustration and design by Andy Mitchell / custard4gravy
custard4gravy@btinternet.com

Acknowledgements

Writing the follow up to '*Crossing Europe on a Bike Called Reggie*' has been far more challenging and rewarding than I ever imagined it would be. In the back of my mind has been the feedback I received from the people who wrote reviews, or who contacted me directly as a result of reading that first book. I feel that it is you whom I should thank first. If you hadn't been so encouraging with your comments and criticisms, I would have never set out for a second time to cycle across Europe, let alone write about my experiences of doing so. I am especially grateful to those people who, in late 2011, were brave enough to take the plunge and invest their time in reading a book by an unknown author with no writing credentials to his name.

While travelling, all of those mentioned by name in this book deserve to be thanked; without them, the story would be very much diminished. I will mention certain people here, however, as they were not only helpful, but they went out of their way to be so: Maria, Manos and Katerina in Athens, Aida in Tirana, Simone in Venice, Diego, Luciana and Tiago in Cornovecchio, Carla and Luigi in Pragate, Lucia in Cherasco, Nicolas, Christel, Nolwen and Raphaël in Provence, Eddy in the Pyrenees and Dave and Pauline in L'Estartit. I also need to thank my cousin Richard, who was particularly helpful in Spain (although I didn't necessarily show my appreciation at the time).

On a practical level, I must thank Catharine, my boss, who allowed me to take some extra time off school (in addition to the normal six weeks that a teacher receives) and to my friend and colleague Stéphane for his logistical support at the start and end of the trip. Thanks also to Andy Mitchell who has created some fantastic artwork, not only for the cover of this book but also for the first one. I will also mention the unknown person who mis-sold me payment protection insurance many years ago; the refund was extremely well-timed and helped considerably in financing the trip.

Finally, two friends and colleagues who have done an excellent job in proofreading and editing my words: Faith, who has helped with an updated version of the first book and Zoë, who through her dedication, good-humour and frankness, has done an excellent job with this second book. Any errors that remain are entirely down to me.

Andrew P. Sykes, August 2014

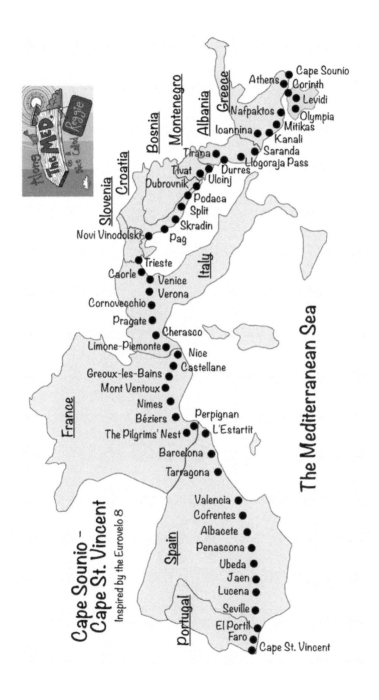

Along the MED on a Cafe Reggie

Cape Sounio –
Cape St. Vincent
Inspired by the Eurovelo 8

The Mediterranean Sea

Greece
Cape Sounio
Athens
Corinth
Levidi
Nafpaktos
Olympia
Ioannina
Mitikas
Kanali
Saranda
Llogoraja Pass

Albania
Tirana
Durres
Ulcinj

Montenegro
Tivat

Bosnia

Croatia
Dubrovnik
Podaca
Split
Skradin
Pag
Novi Vinodolski

Slovenia
Trieste
Caorle
Venice
Verona

Italy
Cornovecchio
Pragate
Cherasco
Limone-Piemonte
Nice
Castellane
Greoux-les-Bains
Mont Ventoux
Nimes
Béziers
Perpignan
The Pilgrims' Nest
L'Estartit
Barcelona
Tarragona

France

Spain
Valencia
Cofrentes
Albacete
Penascona
Ubeda
Jaen
Lucena
Seville
El Portil
Faro
Cape St. Vincent

Portugal

PROLOGUE

Shortly after my arrival in Brindisi in the late summer of 2010, at the end of my first continental crossing of Europe by bicycle, I told myself that should I ever decide to repeat the exercise at some point in the future I would do so along a route that guaranteed cloudless skies and temperatures that would make me wilt. The cycle from southern England to southern Italy had been a soggy and at times cold affair for most of its 3,300 kilometres; indeed the month of August 2010 has since been recognised as the wettest month on record in northern Europe. At the time however, such exploits were only very distant thoughts. I had accomplished what I had set out to achieve and was more than comfortable in the knowledge that, despite what some of my cynical friends had thought about my chances of success, I had done it. I returned home from Italy with a smile on my face and looked forward to settling back into my ordinary little life as a secondary school teacher in the Thames Valley.

Writing and publishing a book about what I had done was very much an afterthought. Ironically it was a friend who had once scoffed at the thought of me successfully cycling across Europe in 2010 who encouraged me to put pen to paper (or indeed finger to keyboard) but after much procrastination and given a few free days afforded me by the Easter holiday away from work, I started to type. Three months and many sips of wine later I had turned my small-time adventure into a book, *Crossing Europe on a Bike Called Reggie*.

Would this be the end of my temporary escape from the world of education? I wasn't sure. The motivation for writing about what I had accomplished was more in the desire to avoid forgetting what I had done, rather than to make a business out of being a cycling, travelling author, but the book sold well and the question started to be asked, *where next?* I cast my mind back to my thoughts upon arrival in Brindisi and looked once again at the map of the lattice of routes that make up the *European Cyclists' Federation Eurovelo* network. The cycle from southern England to Italy had been along the rough line of the Eurovelo 5 from north to south, passing through Kent, skirting along the Franco-Belgian border before arriving in Luxembourg, where I headed due south following the line of the Rhine in the direction of the Swiss Alps and then Italy beyond. *Cloudless skies... temperatures to make me wilt...* There was only one other *Eurovelo* route that could potentially give me what I was looking for, as it stayed well clear of anything that could be remotely described as being in 'northern

1

Europe'. *The Eurovelo 8.* The official description explained how, after leaving Cadiz in Spain, I would travel through Andalucía '...*known for its white villages and huge fields of olive trees'* from where the route would guide me along disused railway tracks towards the Pyrenees, through the French regions of Languedoc-Roussillon and Provence, across the length of the Po Valley in Italy, at the end of which I would turn the corner to head south along the Adriatic coast through Slovenia, Croatia, Montenegro and Albania, before finally arriving in sun-drenched Greece. I was even given the option of continuing the route onto the island of Cyprus. It wasn't difficult to see why the *Eurovelo 8* had been given the less prosaic subtitle of *The Mediterranean Route.* Not one word in the description evoked thoughts of anything but heat and blue skies; it was a long-distance cycling route designed with a sun-craver in mind and after my earlier experiences of the *Eurovelo 5,* I was that craver of sun.

It was also, rather conveniently, a west to east route taking me through areas that would, in the main, contrast starkly with those through which I had cycled in 2010. If I wanted to cycle across Europe again, but avoid simply repeating my earlier experiences it would be difficult, if not impossible, to choose a route that was so different in nature to that of route 5. There would even be a nice crossing point somewhere in northern Italy – the point of intersection of Eurovelos 5 and 8 - where I would be able to sit and ponder what I had achieved and what was yet to come. But hang on! When I cycled to Puglia in southern Italy I had a purpose in mind; my good friends Basil and Liz had moved to live in the region some years previously and I was able to look forward to seeing friendly faces at the very end of my trip. Who did I know in Greece (or indeed Cyprus) who could welcome me, celebrate with me, reward me with good food and wine and generally look after me for a couple of days before I returned home to the UK? I didn't. I did, however, know people at the other end of the route near Cadiz; an uncle and his wife in the coastal town of Estepona and a cousin in Portugal. I could flip the route 180 degrees and have my starting point in Athens. The thought of travelling from the unfamiliar countries of Greece, Albania, Montenegro, Croatia and Slovenia – all places that I had never previously visited - to the much more familiar Italy, France and Spain – all of which I had already travelled through quite extensively – was also much more appealing. The Internet forums warned me against such a decision due to the prevailing winds, but I parked such trivialities to one side.

There was one further issue that I was keen to address. Despite the name of the book – *Crossing Europe on a Bike Called Reggie* – it hadn't really been a point-to-point crossing at all. In the *Eurovelo 8* I did, however, have an opportunity to achieve such a worthy feat. Athens to Cadiz wasn't quite a continental crossing, but should I extend my journey by a few hundred kilometres (which at the planning stage can be so easily brushed aside as insignificant!) from the very south-eastern corner of Greece at Sounio to the south-western corner of Portugal at Sagres, I would have completed a true crossing of the continent. Digging a little deeper, I discovered that each of these European extremities had iconic structures from which to depart and arrive and so it was that my cycling journey along my version of the *Eurovelo 8, The Mediterranean Route*, would start at the Temple of Poseidon at Cape Sounio in Greece and end at the lighthouse at Cape St. Vincent in Portugal. I had a plan. Kind of.

-

I was still, at the heart of things, an inexperienced touring cyclist. Through my book I had become a little more widely known and appeared to have been promoted to an elevated status in the long-distance cycling world. All I had done was cycle to Italy and write about my experiences in what had become a popular book. I only had two long-distance trips under my belt (the other being a 2009 pre-Eurovelo 5 shakedown travelling the *Pennine Cycleway* along the spine of England from Berwick-upon-Tweed to Derby in the English midlands), was overweight and certainly not worthy of any accolade other than perhaps being described as 'plucky'. My knowledge of how a bicycle worked, and more importantly, how to mend one remained woeful. When it came to bicycles, I had always taken the view that if a job is worth doing it's worth paying someone to do it for you and my local bike shop had certainly done good business by me over the few years since I had sold my car and adopted the lifestyle of a full-time, cycling commuter. What the 2010 trip had given me, however, was confidence. Confidence to say *'what the heck!'*. Confidence to leave the detail out of the planning. Confidence to take the aspects of the trip that took me outside my comfort zone – cycling through Albania for example – and ignore them. Confidence at least to try and masquerade as the experienced cycling tourist that I wasn't.

I could also talk the talk when it came to equipment, route finding, camping (and hotel finding if needed) but essentially I was still a naïve 'adventure cyclist', as the Americans so positively call anyone who sets out on their bike and heads for the hills. Perhaps it would be more accurate to call me *faux-naïve* in that yes, the 2010 trip had clearly given me a few more arrows in my cycling quiver, but there was plenty of space left for more, many more. Robin Hood would not have been comfortable heading out into Sherwood Forest with my little armoury. To be perfectly honest, naivety is a quality that I find wonderfully appealing and one which had already stood me in good stead on my previous forays along the cycle paths of Britain and Europe. Better that than an over-confident, arrogant traveller who lacks curiosity and the willingness to go off and explore because he thinks he knows it all. I certainly didn't and in the few areas where perhaps I did, I was more than happy to give the impression that that wasn't the case.

-

As the months became weeks and the weeks became days, a plan, albeit a vague one, started to coalesce. When I looked at the map I could see that my route was about a third longer than my route in 2010. The official distance from Athens to Cadiz via the *Eurovelo 8* was listed as 5,388 km. With my additional bits at the beginning and end of the ride I had added perhaps 200 more. Averaging 110 km per day over a period of 50 cycling days with another 10 'rest' days factored in would make a trip of exactly two months. The problem was that my long summer holiday away from teaching was barely six weeks. I wasn't sure what the reaction from the school would be in the ever money conscious, target driven educational world of the 21st century, but I asked for the whole of the month of July as unpaid leave and was delighted that the answer was *'fine, go ahead!'*. In fact I could have been a little offended that the decision-making process wasn't more drawn out and arduous; was I not a key member of the middle-management team without whom the place would collapse? Evidently not. I immediately purchased a one-way flight to Athens and started to look forward to a summer cycling in the sun. Detailed route planning was not for me, although I did manage to plot fifty dots onto a map at roughly equidistant spaces between Cape Sounio and Cape St. Vincent. Dot 25 was close to the Italian-French border so I knew that if I arrived in Nice by the start of August I would be on track to finish in time to get back to work on the 1st September. If I didn't, well, would my employers miss me for a few extra days? (Probably not.) I was keen to meet some interesting people as well as visit some interesting places along the way and more time was spent arranging those meetings than expended working out how to get from A to B to C. Much of the equipment that I had used in 2010 to cycle to Italy could be reused, although I did buy a new tent; my one man, ultra-lightweight adventurer's tent was replaced with a heavier but roomier one. I could, however, afford to add a few kilos of equipment, as one thing that I had managed to do in the twelve months leading up to the cycle was shed some 20 kilos from my own body. On occasion, as I glanced at my figure via the reflection of a shop window (and if the angle was just right), I could have passed for one of those lean, lycra-clad machines that I had long since dreamt of becoming. My new tent – a Robens Osprey 2 – weighed in at 2.7 kilos which was an additional 1.2 kilos compared to the old Vango Helium 100, but with my body mass reduced, I was still carrying 18.8 kilos fewer than I had been in 2010. Other than that, most of the equipment simply required a dusting down. And of course my main piece of kit, the bike, would be just as it was three years earlier. He had a good service courtesy of the local bike shop and we were then almost ready. Almost ready to once again head out to cross Europe, on a bike called Reggie.

-

I was still wide-awake at 1am on the morning of Sunday 30th June. My flight was due to leave Heathrow at 7am – just a short 30 minutes drive from my home in Reading – and a colleague from work had offered to drive me, Reggie and our equipment along the M4 at the uncivilised hour of 4am. I had initially asked another friend whose car was large enough to hold a bike if she could give me a lift and she was more than happy to do so. However a week or so before I was due to fly to Greece her car had developed some kind of technical issue. I remain curious about the coincidence between this mechanical problem and my revelation that I would need to be picked up at 4am. There was also an issue with the M.O.T.. Of course there was! My colleague Stéphane, a hardened Breton, made no such excuses and seemed to revel in the challenge of an early start. He was even on time and quite jovial (both of which did make me question his credentials as a Frenchman) as we eased Reggie into the back of his people carrier. I had purchased a large plastic bag that had been specifically designed for transporting bicycles by plane. It was possible to wheel the bike into the end of the bag before sealing the whole thing with what seemed like kilometres of masking tape. Or rather it would have been possible to do so had Reggie not first been wrapped like a gentle flower in 25 (yes, twenty-five) metres of bubble wrap. It was almost guaranteed that his flight to the Hellenic peninsula would be considerably more comfortable than my own. I was quite proud of my packaging efforts and was fairly confident that despite the combined efforts of the British and Greek baggage handlers, I would have a bike that was in one piece on arrival in Athens. Well, almost one piece. Minor panic had ensued on the Saturday afternoon when I attempted to remove the pedals. They just wouldn't budge and even after I had bought a new 15mm spanner (that a frantic search on the Internet told me that I needed), they were staying put. I cycled back to the bike shop where one of the mechanics produced a long tube of metal; the increased torque finally started to move the nut. It was all a little worrying so close to departure and a none too subtle reminder that my own skills were not quite where I would have wanted them to be immediately prior to such a long cycling journey.

Heathrow Terminal 5 should win awards for its design. Ah yes, I see it has. Well, apart from the spectacular building itself, it is such an easy place at which to arrive, check in, deposit your bags and fly away. I balanced Reggie on a trolley and with the bright lights of the airport terminal in front of him and the bubble wrap tightly against his frame he could just be seen through the plastic haze that surrounded him. I shook Stéphane firmly by the hand – I can't imagine Bretons shake hands in any other way – and he was gone. I would not see a familiar face until I arrived in Italy; Greece, Albania, Montenegro, Croatia, Bosnia and Slovenia all lay ahead and unless I was to be paid some impromptu (and probably unwelcome) visit by a friend or relative, every face would be unknown. A sobering thought for me to ponder as I pushed the trolley towards the British Airways check-in desk.

Earlier in the year I had been on a walking holiday with a couple of friends to the Tatra Mountains of Slovakia and we had flown Ryanair from Stansted. It had also been a very early flight but 5am at Heathrow Terminal 5 couldn't have been more different to the frenzy of activity of Stansted at 5am. I'm not the greatest of flyers and need to be soothed somewhat before take off. Terminal 5 was able to do that in a way that Stansted could only dream about. The airport was busy but calmness abounded. Even the arrival of hoards of children en route home after what looked like a shopping visit to Britain couldn't elevate the level of (almost) tranquillity. I was a little anxious that my packaging efforts would be derided by the check-in staff and that I would be told to start again from scratch in order to fulfil stringent size guidelines (that I had never actually bothered to check to see existed) but the smart chap in the blue uniform in front of me was more interested in the extra payment that had to be made. Clearly I hadn't infringed any packing guidelines, so what about a compliment then? It took a couple of anxious moments for Reggie to be eased through the tunnel at the over-size baggage counter; I couldn't help but think how the whole set up of a vertical shutter opening to reveal a dimly lit square tunnel was reminiscent of a crematorium. That said, the process lacked the decorum of a funeral with the conveyor belt juddering backward and forward as the operator tried placing Reggie at different angles to ensure that he squeezed through the gap in the wall. If I was presented with an urn of iron filings in Athens I would know that what remained of the baggage handling process hadn't gone well.

I had been allocated a window seat that allowed me to look west as the plane headed south. The plane wasn't fitted with electronic maps enabling the passengers to see where we were at any given moment so I had to try and guess what river that was or what mountain range it could be. It was, however, more obvious when we started to travel along the fractured Adriatic coast of Croatia. Hundreds of bits of rock, some large, some small, many tiny, blurred the transition between mainland and sea. I wondered which of them, if any, I would visit. But I didn't want to know. Although this was a trip along the coast of the Mediterranean, my routes would be worked out from day to day. I didn't want to veer too far from the sea but the plan was never to follow the coastal road. Apart from anything else it would be clogged up with every other Mediterranean tourist, his car, his family and far too often his caravan. I didn't really fancy spending two months battling that kind of traffic although I knew that at times it would be difficult to avoid. Even the fifty dots on my map were mostly very nominal. With the exception of a few fixed points along the way – Sounio, Athens, Olympia, Tirana, Dubrovnik, Venice, Nice, Mont Ventoux, Barcelona, Valencia, Cadiz, Seville and Sagres – the remainder of my dots would be jostling for position along my route at the most appropriate, hopefully most interesting points. Some I could probably guess, but for many others I was gleefully ignorant as to where I would be pitching my tent or finding a hotel. It wasn't quite a voyage into the unknown but it certainly was a trip along the *unknown to me*. This would definitely be the case for much of July before I cycled into the more familiar territories of Italy, France, Spain and Portugal.

BA0638 touched down in Athens at around midday local time; my journey was about to begin...

PART ONE: GREECE
Sunday 30th June 2013
Athens

I had tucked into a hearty breakfast on the flight from London to Athens in the expectation that I would be burning it off later in the day cycling under the Mediterranean sun. My plan upon arrival was to reassemble the bike at the airport and then cycle on an inland route from the airport to Sounio. Athens airport was about 20 km to the south east of the city centre, which was very convenient for anyone who wanted to cycle from the very south-eastern corner of the country back to the capital itself. I would spend Sunday evening at the campsite – promisingly named *Camping Bacchus* - which I had located at a place called Lavrio on the coast. An early start on Monday morning might even allow me to see the sun rise over the Aegean through the ancient columns of the Temple of Poseidon. Sufficiently motivated by this stunning sight, I would then head north along the coast towards Athens where I had booked a hotel room for two nights. My first rest day would be Tuesday, allowing me time to acclimatise and explore the ancient ruins of the capital. As you can see, this first bit of the trip I *had* thought about in detail. Unfortunately it didn't work out quite as I had planned.

Athens airport arrivals hall was more reminiscent of hectic Stansted than cool, calm and collected Heathrow Terminal 5. People buzzed around in all directions, chatting predominantly in a language that was alien to me. To my shame, I hadn't even taken the time whilst on the plane to practise any basic phrases of Greek such as *'excuse me'*, *'can you help me?'* and *'where is my bike?'* All three would have come in handy as I stood in the middle of the baggage reclaim area, wondering from which hole in the wall or conveyor belt or desk or door would appear my bubble-cushioned travelling companion. My panniers were easy to locate as they came along the conveyor belt with all the other assorted luggage from the plane. I placed them on a trolley and made my way towards what looked like the information desk to join a queue of sorts. It was really more of a gathering but I parked my English desire to form an orderly line to one side and hoped that I would make progress towards the desk shortly. After a few moments of shuffling on the spot, I noticed a door to my right open wide and a man appear carrying a large plastic bag; it was of course Reggie. I deserted my fellow gatherers to be reacquainted with my 'abnormal' package and on first glance he seemed to be in good shape (the bike, that is, rather than the man carrying him, who in fairness could have done with losing a few pounds). I thanked him in English (I hadn't even learned how to say '*thank-you*' in Greek), placed Reggie on the trolley and made my way into the baking midday heat outside the building. I needed to find a quiet, preferably shady spot where I could rebuild him. As I hadn't really done any dismantling back in the Britain, this wouldn't be a difficult job; I just needed to reattach the pedals with my recently acquired 15mm spanner, turn and secure the handlebars in position, lift the seat a little and pump up the tyres. I would be heading for Lavrio quicker than you could say *Presta valve*.

Now, when I was first acquainted with the concept of riding a bike back in the late 1970s, it soon became apparent that certain mechanical skills were, from time to time, essential. The most essential of these essential skills was that of mending a puncture. Everyone had a little kit. It came in a small metal box containing three levers to prise the tyre away from the rim, chalk to mark where the puncture was (but which nobody ever used), sandpaper (that was also ignored), rubber patches to place over the hole itself and glue to secure the patch to the inner tube. The most difficult thing about the whole process was getting the tyre on and off the rim of the wheel, but once that had been achieved the tube could quickly be inflated again through a valve – that I now know to be called a *Schrader* valve - onto which you were able to screw the connecting tube and pump away merrily. When you did get a puncture, you sighed at the thought of fiddling around with the levers; the rest was plain sailing. Fast forward three decades and the levers no longer phase me. In fact there is a certain enjoyment in stretching the rubber slightly to the point where it pops over the rim and the tyre sits securely once again around the circumference of the wheel. What does cause me a considerable amount of stress at the mere thought of having to do it, is the inflation of the tyre using a *Presta* valve. Reggie has Presta valves and this depresses me somewhat. The Presta valve was invented by Etienne Sclaverand, a Frenchman of 6, rue Caffarelli, Paris. I give the man's full name and address so that anyone with deeper financial pockets than my own and who wishes to take legal action against him has at least a starting point. Unfortunately, they might also need a medium of some kind as the patent was lodged in London on the 9th April 1897 and accepted the following year, so I fear M. Sclaverand has long since departed this world. I'll leave it to you to decide whether it is fair or not to burden his descendants with the legal responsibility of the folly of his invention. The valves have caused me much anguish in recent years and outside Athens airport in the early afternoon of Sunday 30th June 2013 that anguish was about to reach its pinnacle.

The tyres had been deflated for the flight due to the low pressure of the aircraft hold. Pumping them back up on arrival should have been a straightforward affair, but it never is with a Presta valve. I unscrewed the fiddly bit that allows air to enter the inner tube, attached the pump, locked the pump and started - you guessed it - pumping. Nothing happened of course. I tried again. And again. And yes, once more. And quite a few more times after that. The fiddly bit that I had to unscrew on the Presta valve was screwed more and then less. The pump and the valve didn't appear to be in any kind of romantic mood, as no coupling could be formed between the two. I investigated the pump. Why was it not working? I dismantled the pump - bad idea - and came to the conclusion that I had broken it. This was not good news.

Reggie's rear tyre was inflated to about 80%, the front tyre to about 10%. I had a broken pump (or so I thought) and a bike that wasn't going anywhere. I stood back from and took a few deep breaths. I was at a foreign airport in the very first of the ten countries I hoped to visit, it was getting late in the afternoon and I had about 40 km to cycle before I found the bar of Camping Bacchus, a place where I could relax and laugh off the trials and tribulations of my first day on the road, if I ever managed to get there.

I find that the best strategy in these situations is to ignore the situation, at least for a few moments, so I busied myself by tidying up and disposing of the large plastic bag and the 25 metres of bubble wrap (in itself not an easy task), loading the panniers and tent onto the bike and checking that the other basic bits and pieces of Reggie were working correctly. The good news was that everything seemed fine. Apart from the tyres. I needed a working pump to inflate them. How difficult can it be to find one at a major international airport? I looked around but couldn't see any bicycle racks so I wheeled Reggie back into the terminal and found the main information desk. The woman behind the counter spoke good English but showed only bemusement when I asked if she knew anyone who cycled to the airport to work.

"Everybody drives or takes the bus. The roads are too dangerous to cycle!"

"Thanks."

"The nearest bicycle shop is in the city centre and you will need to take a bus. The buses leave from just outside the terminal. You must buy a ticket from the bus office."

I was still hopeful of bumping into a cyclist who had decided to defy convention, risk life and limb and cycle to work at the airport, but if he or she existed they certainly weren't in the vicinity of the arrivals hall. Instead I found the bus bay, just as the woman had said, immediately outside the terminal. Once again I stood and stared gormlessly at the things around me; several red bendy buses, another 'gathering' of people and a small plastic office. One man stood out from the crowd as he had a badge and (more importantly) a clipboard. I assumed that he was in charge and indeed he was. His English was limited but it was markedly more proficient than my Greek, so I tried to explain my predicament. He initially indicated that it wouldn't be possible to put the bike on the bus so I bent down and attempted to explain what the problem was. He too bent down and started to examine the valve, which was in perfect working order. The issue was with my pump. If he understood my dilemma he would surely take pity on me and allow me to travel to the centre of Athens on one of his flexible friends. He fiddled with the valve and I watched hopefully. He fiddled a little more. Something fell to the floor. What was that I wondered? We looked but couldn't find it. Although initially a little alarmed that something, perhaps a vital thing, had now been removed from the bike, this was good news. The man in charge of the buses had broken my bike (I had only managed to break the pump) and moral obligation would surely dictate that he allow me on one of his buses. Bingo! It worked.

I bought a ticket - €5 - and I was soon en route to central Athens courtesy of the X95 bendy bus. More excitement was to come, as not only had I found the correct bus, I had also found Stellios Moss (Stirling's Greek cousin) and he was driving the X95 in which I was travelling. Clearly brakes are things that need to be punished in Greece and boy! did this driver punish those poor pads. It was a more or less straight route along the suburban highways of Athens from the airport to the centre of town, but clearly the driver was on some kind of bonus scheme that stipulated that he would be paid in direct proportion to the average speed he was able to record over the distance of the route. I hung on for dear life. Reggie hung onto me for dear life as momentum attempted to fling us in all directions around the busy bus. I smiled apologetically in the direction of those who I thought might have been the victims of one of Reggie's limp tyres or my less limp torso. Eventually, we arrived in the centre and, with much relief, I alighted the bus in a square that looked more than just a bit familiar.

This was my first ever visit to Greece but in recent years the country has been a regular fixture in television news bulletins as a result of its financial woes. As the bendy bus screeched away into the distance, I turned to my right and could see a three-storey beige building at a slightly elevated position. Just below the porticoed entrance were two white sentry boxes and next to each of these boxes was a solider in traditional Greek costume, carrying a more contemporary gun. It was the Greek parliament building. The only thing that was missing from the scene, compared to the images we see in television news broadcasts, was a demonstration or indeed a riot taking place in the middle of the square itself. At least, I thought, my racing bus driver had managed to deposit me at the very heart of the capital.

I had a reservation - albeit one only for the Monday and Tuesday night, not the Sunday night - for the Hotel Tempi, a two-star establishment just north of the Acropolis on Eolou Street. I found the place on my map and it wasn't too far to push Reggie along the narrow road (and even narrower pavement) from the square in front of the parliament. I hoped that upon arrival the hotel would have a room available for that night, in addition to the two I had already booked. As I pushed I looked around at the unfamiliar city and it struck me immediately how low rise it was. Few buildings were taller than six or seven storeys, which, for a capital city, seemed somewhat modest. However, as I arrived at the junction with Eolou Street I glanced to my left and there before me was something that could never be described as modest; the ancient Acropolis and one side of the iconic Parthenon. I paused to take in the scene. I had never imagined that it would be so prominently positioned in the very centre of the city and for the first time I had a real sense of having arrived. Airports are airports, suburbs are suburbs and even parliament buildings are all too often much of a muchness but here was a mound of rock and a building of which there was only one. Welcome to Athens!

The Tempi Hotel was easy to locate on Eolou Street. It was tall (although clearly not too tall) and thin. Outside the entrance a man in his early fifties was giving instructions to a workman who was washing the area in front of the hotel with a hose. He didn't need a badge or a clipboard to show everyone he was in charge, he just clearly was. Once again I asked the question that I would be destined to repeat many, many times as I travelled north along the Adriatic coastline;

"Excuse me, do you speak English?"

"Yes, of course."

"I have a bit of a problem. I have a reservation for Monday and Tuesday but not for tonight..."

"You want to stay tonight? No problem!"

I didn't even have the chance to explain what my problem was. The owner's name was Yiannis and he was to prove to be an invaluable source of help and information during the first three days of my trip. Once he had given me a chance to explain why I needed an extra night of accommodation, he offered to bring in his own pump the following morning. He also reassured me that if our combined efforts couldn't solve my mechanical problems then there was a bike shop in the next street. It was almost as if Yiannis had been planted in Athens by a kind benefactor who wanted me to have a trouble-free start to my trip. Within minutes of meeting him, my mood had changed from one of considerable anxiety to one of delight that things were actually working out fine. I locked Reggie to the railings directly in front of the door of the hotel. A long corridor ran through the building to a short flight of stairs and a small office, where Yiannis could sit behind the counter and keep an eye on my deflated bike. My room was on the fourth floor of the building and there was no lift, but it wasn't too much of a challenge to carry my four panniers and my tent up the stairs. It was a rudimentary room for €35 a night, with a toilet and shower shared with the other residents of my floor and a less than inspiring view from the window; just a wall and a rusting skylight. I could see nothing of ancient Athens. But the room did have one thing that made me smile broadly; air-conditioning. I picked up the remote control, switched it on, let the cool air descend to my level and lay on the bed to relax. Despite the problems I had encountered rebuilding the bike, things had worked out pretty well overall. OK, I wasn't at the bar of Camping Bacchus and I didn't have the prospect of waking up to see the sun rise over the Aegean, but I had found a base for the first three nights of my cycle and I had some interesting plans for the next three days. I was a happy man.

I hadn't abandoned the idea of starting my cycle at The Temple of Poseidon, the very south-eastern point of mainland Europe. Yiannis explained that there were buses from Athens to the temple and he was fairly confident that they would allow me to take my bike on board. The priority for Monday morning, however, would have to be finding a working pump to inflate Reggie's tyres. That surely couldn't be too difficult, could it?

Monday 1st July 2013
Cycling Day 1: Sounio to Athens, 70km

White rabbits. It was, after all, the first day of the month. I had
exactly two of them in which to travel the length of the continent, so
that would be two white rabbits, perhaps three if I ran over schedule
before I would be heading for home. I hoped to run over no rabbits
themselves. It seemed a long way off. The early start of the previous
day had at least made me tired and I slept well in the cool air of the
room. I had been woken from time to time by the buzz of the air
conditioning unit (or was it the students in the room next door?) but
had soon nodded back into the land of dreams and the result was that I
woke up refreshed and ready for my next challenge. Once again it was
a logistical one.

Yiannis had forgotten to bring his pump to the hotel, so it was
option B; find the local bike shop. He explained that it was on a street
only 300 metres away and, using the wi-fi connection provided by the
hotel, I was able to watch a short video on YouTube telling me just how
good the shop was. I had high expectations. The shop was due to open
at 9am, so I wheeled Reggie down Eolou Street and found a café where
I was able to take in my first morning coffee of the trip. I was so
relieved to have found a part of the city centre that was so welcoming
and relaxed. For all I knew, this could be said for the whole of Athens,
but I preferred to think that it was my good luck and judgement that
had brought me here to this little corner of the capital.

The bike shop was called *'Podilato'* (which I was later to discover
means 'bike') and was housed behind a modern two-storey shop front.
As I stood waiting for a member of staff to arrive, I had time to
examine the items on sale and it wasn't radically different to any bike
shop back in the UK. In fact, it was perhaps a little too familiar, as they
seemed to specialise in London-made Brompton folding bikes and
above me, on the second floor, I could see a pristine butcher's delivery
bike, complete with a sign in English. It was now past 9am and no one
had arrived to open up, so I double-checked the times on the website. I
also checked that the shop hadn't closed for the summer holidays; it
didn't appear to be the case. I stood and shuffled on the spot. It was an
activity that I was getting quite used to.

After about fifteen minutes, a guy in his early thirties sporting a
full beard appeared on a motorbike and greeted me in Greek. I
apologised and he immediately started speaking fluent English. He in
turn apologised profusely for not having arrived on time, explaining

that there had been an issue with the train. He introduced himself as Alex and he told me that he didn't have a key. At this point the story became quite complex, involving the son of the man who owned the shop not having been at a particular place at a particular time... I nodded sagely as if I was following the thread but was struggling (it included, amongst other things, the tax office and a bad back). The upshot was that we would have to wait for the key to be driven over. It did at least give us time to chat. He was young and Greek; just the kind of person that we are told is bearing the brunt of the financial crisis in Greece. Alex, however, was a very positive man. He worked two days in the shop where we were standing and another four days a week at a second branch of the shop in the outskirts of the city. He was a university-trained, mechanical engineer but seemed happy that he had a job, despite it not making the most of his no doubt considerable technical abilities.

"*The economic situation is bad but not that bad*", he explained. "*People need to be more flexible but at the end of the day most people are happy. At least if you don't have a job in Greece you can always sit in the sun. You can't do that in northern Europe!*"

I found it difficult to fault his logic and we continued to chat over the sweet espresso coffee that he bought for me from a bar down the street. It wasn't until nearly 10am that a key was finally located and the shop was opened. Alex promptly hoisted Reggie onto a stand, changed the inner tube, checked everything else was working on the bike and, rather embarrassingly, refused to charge me for anything but the cost of the tube – just a couple of Euros. I tried to protest but he wouldn't change his mind, citing the fact that I had been forced into waiting for the shop to open, so I resorted to giving him a €5 and refusing to take any change. He even inspected my pump and declared it to be in perfect working order. What a nice man he was and what an idiot I had been. Perhaps all this could have been avoided back at the airport if I had simply managed to use the Presta valve properly. Alex wished me good luck with the trip and, for the first time since arriving in Greece nearly twenty-four hours earlier, I cycled off down the road.

Back at the hotel, Yiannis had been busy. During my absence, he had phoned the bus company and had asked if they would allow bikes on the bus to Cape Sounio. "*Was it a folding one?*" they had enquired and he had told them he didn't know. I winced slightly as he recounted the conversation, as I couldn't help but recall the issues I had had with the bus at the airport. Yiannis did seem more optimistic than me, however, and he handed over a street map of Athens upon which he had scrawled various circles and lines indicating how I should find the bus that I needed to catch.

"There is one every hour and it will say 'Sounio' on the front", were his last words as I set off downhill in the direction of the Parthenon, before turning left and retracing my steps back to the parliament and up a hill to a point opposite a multi-storey car park, where Yiannis had indicated the bus would stop. I was travelling light with just one of the small panniers on the back of the bike containing a few essentials for the day. I was ready for my first day of cycling, but where was the bus? No one around the bus stop spoke English or indeed wanted to help me out in any way, shape or form. Perhaps, after Alex and Yiannis, I had had my quota of nice Athenians for the day. Yet again, I stood looking gormless hoping that something would happen to help me on my way. Bus after bus arrived, but none of them said 'Sounio' on the front. I tried to work out from the list of destinations posted on the wall of the bus shelter, if one of the buses that didn't say 'Sounio' on the front would get me there just as well. It didn't seem that they would. More hanging around looking anxiously up and down the busy street ensued.

I then noticed something about 100 metres from the bus stop. It was an orange coach (not a bus – perhaps there wasn't a difference in Greece) but it did have the word 'Sounio' displayed brightly on the electronic display above the driver's head. The coach was on my side of the road but the four-lanes of traffic between me and the other side of the street prevented me from crossing the road and cycling. The pavement on my side of the street was too narrow and busy so I clutched Reggie firmly and started to run in a way that only anyone who has ever tried to run whilst pushing a bicycle can imagine; not very successfully. *"Please don't go, please don't go..."*, I pleaded under my breath as I tried to run and much to my relief, when I did arrive, the driver and his coach/bus hadn't moved. The good news with the bus being a coach was that I was able to place Reggie in the luggage compartment underneath; I just prayed that the driver didn't have the same love of high-speed driving as his colleague who had been (almost) in control of the bus from the airport. This time there was no 25 metres of bubble wrap to protect poor Reggie.

It was a two-hour drive along the coastal road to Sounio and mercifully far more pleasant than the ride into central Athens from the airport. The coach was full of elderly women, so I did feel as though I had gate crashed an outing of the Athens Women's Institute, but they ignored me as they chatted and, at times, argued. I do like listening to languages I don't understand; it's the equivalent of giving your brain a good massage. The coach would occasionally deviate from the main road to enter a small village along the coast. The land was rocky and treeless, with just a few bushes, mainly around the sporadic settlements of whitewashed houses. The sky wasn't quite cloudless and occasionally the sun would spend a few minutes hidden from gaze, no doubt to the relief of those outside. The air-conditioned coach was keeping the old women and me cool, however, and at times I dozed, dreaming of the sun-drenched days that lay ahead of me as I made my way along the Mediterranean coastline to Portugal.

I had seen many pictures of the Temple of Poseidon at Cape Sounio, but just as I had been by the elevated position of the Parthenon back in Athens, so too was I taken aback as to how prominently the temple was positioned on a high cliff at the very corner of the European mainland. Despite having only three of its four sides remaining, the building shouted its elegant presence across the Ionian Sea. It was built from white marble in the 5th Century B.C. as a sanctuary in honour of Poseidon, the god of the sea. In times gone by, animal sacrifices would be carried out here in the hope that the sailors doing the sacrificing would have pleasant onward journeys. I had no animal to sacrifice (and it would no doubt have caused all kinds of problems if I had tried), but I did have to sacrifice one thing; Reggie was not allowed past the ticket office, so there was no opportunity for man, bike and temple to be immortalised in a pre-trip photograph. I didn't fancy trying to explain the sentimental value of such a picture to the stern-faced woman who sold me the ticket. Perhaps she should have been in charge when Lord Byron paid a visit to Sounio and the Temple of Poseidon back in the early 19th century. It is alleged that he carved his name into one of the pillars of the temple during his grand tour of Europe in 1810, but there is no evidence that he was actually guilty of the crime. For a man of art and letters, it does seem a little incongruous that he should have developed such a skill as a stone engraver.

The temple was quite a busy place, so I moved away from the main structure towards the cliff where I found a spot that gave me a clear view towards the west. I pondered the days, weeks and months that were ahead of me, the places I would visit, the people I would meet and the problems I would encounter. Most of the places and people would be new to me, but my mind could dream about how fascinating and how uplifting they might be. As for the problems, I didn't like to dwell upon what *they* might be, but, as my first 24 hours of the trip had already thrown up some interesting situations for me to overcome, I was at least confident that I would approach everything that life could throw at me as a puzzle waiting to be solved. Unless, of course, it involved Presta valves.

I recorded a short video of my thoughts over the sound of the cicadas, hidden away from view but ever present in the ears, asking those watching via my website to wish me luck, but hoped that I wouldn't need it. With that done, it was finally time to start cycling, so I returned to the ticket booth, unlocked Reggie, filled up his bottles with water and my stomach with a sandwich from the nearby café, and set off down the hill to the main road to retrace the route back to Athens.

It was a tentative start to the cycling. The journey back to the capital would only be 70 kilometres, well below the average that I needed to cycle over the next fifty days of cycling if I wanted to be in with any chance of arriving at Cape St. Vincent before the end of August, but compared to the 12km daily commute that I was used to completing each day back in the UK, it was a significant step up. I tried to ignore the perils of cycling on a coastal road in an unknown country in the heat of the afternoon, but the road was at least quiet; just the occasional coach heading back from Sounio interspersed with a few cars, mainly locals, but few lorries. I don't suppose that there is much to carry to that extremity of the continent. And so it continued over the next couple of hours. I paused for a snack at a point that I judged to be about halfway to Athens; I was using a cycling app for my iPhone to track my route, but it wasn't always easy to see exactly where I was as the 3G signal was sporadic along the remote coastline. My back up map was of some use, but the scale – 1:300,000 – didn't give sufficient detail to allow me to work out with great confidence where I was with any kind of precision. There was, however, only one direction of travel and I knew that if I kept the sea on my left and the rugged, sparsely populated land to my right, I would be just fine.

Conditions on the road did begin to change after my short pause for sustenance. I could see in the distance the sprawling suburbs of Athens as they spread along the coast like treacle along the edge of the tin. The traffic was becoming much, much heavier and at times the road became a six-lane highway. It was at these points where I questioned whether or not a bicycle was allowed on the road, but there was nothing either on my map or on the chaotic signage around me to indicate that I shouldn't be there. I did, however, feel increasingly uncomfortable as I made my way closer and closer to the capital. When I was about 10 km from the city centre, I decided to quit the main coastal road and discovered a parallel road past the old, eerily deserted airport. The problem was that I couldn't turn right towards the heart of the capital, presumably because of the existence of the old runway. I was eventually forced back onto the main coastal road, but as soon as I thought that I had passed the end of the runway, I once again returned to the quieter roads and tried to fathom a path towards the city centre. With most of the signs being written in an unknown alphabet, let alone an unknown language, it was just as much a mental challenge as it was a physical one to work out a route in the heat of the day, but eventually, after much turning left, then right, then left again, I found myself in front of the Greek parliament. There can be few people as glad to see that building in recent times; for me it was nothing political, just the knowledge that from that point I could easily navigate my way back to the hotel.

Yiannis welcomed me like an old friend. I glossed over the issues with finding the bus and the later tribulations finding a route back into the centre. I was just delighted and relieved to have completed my first day of cycling, albeit a modest one. I rested for a while in the hotel and could probably have simply stayed horizontal until the following morning, but that wasn't an option as I had arranged to meet local journalist and cycling blogger Manos, for what turned out to be a wonderful introduction to Greek nightlife.

We had exchanged emails prior to my arrival in Greece and text messages earlier in the day. The rendez-vous point would be outside the Tempi Hotel at 9.30pm. Back in the UK, I consider such a time in the evening as the beginning of the end of the day. That's not the case in Athens of course, so after a couple of hours of snooze I was obliged to put aside my northern Europeanness and join my southern continental compatriots for a slice of Athenian nightlife. Manos, who was born and educated in Athens, arrived by bike, indeed one of the folding bikes that I had seen being sold back at the bike shop earlier in the day; they had clearly taken off in these parts. After a day in the saddle, I preferred to walk to our destination – a roof top bar on the other side of the city – and he was happy with this. It was a long walk, but it gave us the time to chat and get to know each other. Manos works for Greece's largest circulation newspaper, *Ta Nea* or *'The News'* as a journalist specialising in religion and education, but as part of the newspaper's website he runs a cycling blog, hence his interest in meeting me. I don't suppose it's everyday that some bloke from England rolls into town with the crazy idea of cycling all the way along the Mediterranean coast to Portugal, and it got me a short mention on the website if not in the newspaper itself. Manos had worked for the newspaper for around 15 years, but he explained that the economic situation was proving challenging. Circulation had halved compared to pre-crisis levels and many jobs had been lost. We continued to walk through the busy Plaka area at the foot of the Acropolis, where every street was lined with bars and restaurants. Each establishment seemed to be a busy hive of eating and drinking and was in sharp contrast to the comments that Manos was making about the state of the economy in general. We were heading for a bar 'with a view' however, and we didn't stop until we finally arrived at a point just north of the Kerameikos ancient cemetery. If I hadn't just spent a good three-quarters of an hour chatting with Manos, I could have been a little disconcerted as he led me down a backstreet with not a bar in sight. On our left he opened a non-descript door and I followed him along several flights of stairs and through an equal number of abandoned rooms. Eventually we climbed one final flight of stairs onto a roof terrace bathed in green light, which was apt for a bar called Bios or 'life' in ancient Greek. Above the bar itself, the gable end of the building next door was being used as a screen upon which to beam advertising. And then, as I turned to my left, I immediately understood the reference to it being a bar 'with a view'. In the near distance was the mound of the Acropolis and the Parthenon, bathed in light that made the pale yellow of the stone shine bright across the Greek capital. My breath was momentarily taken away.

We sat on the deckchairs that had been set up to admire the view and chatted more as we sipped Greek beer. Manos' girlfriend, Katerina, joined us and the conversation once again turned back to life in Greece in 2013. They were both well-educated and, despite the economic problems, happy and positive about the future. In many ways their views mirrored those of Alex back at the bike shop earlier in the day. Both Manos and Katerina were conscious of how their hometown was being depicted internationally, with riots outside the parliament and right-wing fringe groups grabbing the headlines; having seen no evidence of either since my arrival, I sympathised with their concerns.

In the early hours of the morning – perhaps about 1am (time didn't seem to be an issue for the Greeks after dark) – we left the bar and headed to an area of the city which had once been a sprawling electricity generation plant, but which had now been converted into a cultural quarter called *Technopolis*. We ate *souvlaki* (pork sausage in a pitta bread with chips) - which went down extremely well after 70km of cycling and three beers - before wandering back across the city, passing as we did an open-air salsa class that was taking place beneath the colourful, graffiti-strewn walls of the cemetery. We made it back to the hotel at 2:30am, where I said my farewells to Manos and Katerina, and went to bed. I had a distinct feeling that many in Athens weren't quite ready to do the same thing.

Tuesday 2nd July 2013
Rest Day 1: Athens

It seemed like almost cheating to have a rest day after only one modest day of cycling, but I was determined to make the most of my visit to Greece and I couldn't continue without exploring the jewel of the capital, the building that is arguably the birthplace of modern civilisation: the Parthenon.

Now if you are one of those people who struggles when it comes to finding your way in foreign capitals, Athens should perhaps be on your list of destinations to visit. Sitting as it does in its lofty position as part of the Acropolis complex, the Parthenon is almost impossible to miss. Indeed, it had been almost a constant in my eyeline since arriving in the capital almost 48 hours earlier. I didn't really need a map to seek it out; it was just a case of wandering around the base of the Acropolis in a clockwise direction until I stumbled upon the New Acropolis Museum on the opposite side of the mound to my hotel. Prior to my trip, I had contacted an organisation called *Marbles Reunited* and had received an email from Maria, their campaign manager, offering a guided tour of the museum, as well as the ancient monument itself.

Marbles Reunited, as you may have guessed from its name, campaigns for the reunification of the Parthenon sculptures and friezes currently housed in the British Museum - commonly known as the 'Elgin Marbles' - with the remaining surviving sculptures and friezes in Athens, Greece. Its campaign is based upon the belief that the Parthenon sculptures *"...are best seen and studied as a single archaeological collection in sight of the monument they were once an integral part of, namely the Parthenon."* If Maria had any concerns prior to our meeting that she would have to argue her point vociferously, she had little to worry about. She would be preaching to the converted.

The Parthenon sculptures and friezes were removed from the building itself in 1803, on dubious legal grounds, by Thomas Bruce, the 7th Earl of Elgin and the then British ambassador to the Ottoman Empire which controlled Greece at the time. Lord Elgin had a passion for art, so much so that instead of commissioning a few paintings of the Parthenon and its sculptures and friezes, he removed 70 metres of them and shipped them back to Britain. Even Lord Byron – the alleged chisel-wielding graffiti artist back at the temple in Sounio, so perhaps no saint himself when it came to a bit of cultural vandalism – was shocked by the removal work that he witnessed. It can't have been an easy job removing the statues and the friezes, and saws had to be used to prise them from the building. Once 'safely' on Elgin's ship, the marbles started their journey to Britain only for the ship to be wrecked and for the stones to lie at the bottom of the sea for two years. They were eventually recovered by divers and finally made it into a gallery of the British Museum in 1816 following a Parliamentary Select Committee enquiry which, according to the leaflet that is now distributed by the museum to curious folk like me, *"...fully investigated and approved the legality of Lord Elgin's actions"*. I'll bet it did! I had purposefully made the short pilgrimage down to London to see the marbles prior to my trip to Athens, to remind myself of the context in which they are displayed. It's difficult to describe room 18 of the British Museum as anything other than drab and uninspiring.

Maria had agreed to meet me at 11am outside the far-from-drab and very architecturally-inspiring New Acropolis Museum, but I was early so spent some time reading about the history of the Acropolis, Parthenon and the new museum in my guide book. The word 'acropolis' refers simply to the highest point in a town or city and as such Athens is not unique in having one. The cluster of buildings on top of the Athenian acropolis, of which the Parthenon is but one (albeit the most magnificent and recognisable), were built in around 500BC as temples to the gods. That's what they remained for about 1,000 years until they were converted for use as Christian places of worship. When the Turks arrived, the Parthenon was once again converted, this time for use as a mosque. In the 17th century, the Venetians, while trying to oust the Turks, managed to cause an explosion which blew the roof off the Parthenon and set the whole place on fire. Then Lord Elgin turned up (along with his French counterpart ambassador Fauvel who was up to the same light-fingered activities) at the start of the 19th century and started to pilfer what remained. It's a miracle that there is any of it left standing today, but it does perhaps explain why the building is currently shrouded in scaffolding and has been for the last 40 years.

Maria arrived precisely on time. Half British, half Greek, my guide had a British mother and Greek father and spent most of her childhood in Greece before returning to London to study. She came back to Athens a few years ago, where she now works as a freelance graphic designer, teacher and manager for Marbles Reunited. After exchanging a few pleasantries (of which one was to reassure her that I wasn't about to argue the case for the British Museum), we decided that the best place to start the day would be on the mound itself, so we wandered along the wide, traffic-free road leading from the museum, towards the collection of crumbling temples that sit on top of the Acropolis. Our entrance tickets bought, we joined the tourist throng and gradually edged our way into the complex for a wander and a chat. Maria didn't claim to be an expert on the history of the site, but she was very good and informative company as we stood, stared, wandered and occasionally stumbled on the rough ground in between the main points of interest. Despite the on-going restoration work, scaffolding and cranes that sporadically cover much of the building, the Parthenon is a breath-taking edifice. The sheer scale of the thing would be impressive enough, but then the precise symmetry of the architecture... OK! I know... It isn't symmetrical, but it certainly appears to be, which, apparently is one of its many splendours. *It is not symmetrical in order to look symmetrical!* You've got to take your hat off to the ancient Greek builders.

Wilting somewhat under the midday sun, we eventually headed back down to the museum for some air-conditioned respite from the heat and the crowds of tourists. The museum opened in 2008 and is a wonderful monument to early 21st century architecture, although I somehow doubt that in 2,500 years time its concrete pillars will be adorned with notices asking visitors not to touch the concrete. But you never know. The upper floor is the museum's showpiece. It is built to the same proportions and upon the same axis as the Parthenon and houses, in the places where they would have been were they still stuck to the monument itself, the statues and friezes that still remain in Athens. In place of the ones that are in the British Museum (and the Louvre and several other museums across Europe), there are crude plaster casts of the originals (*'how did they do that?'* I asked Maria but she was equally bewildered – those British Museum security attendants are pretty sharp operators!) with a discrete note underneath each one indicating what they feature and diplomatically explaining that the original is in the 'BM'. On the northern side of the upper gallery you can turn your head to see the glorious remnants of the Parthenon itself high above the museum, and whatever arguments the British Museum puts forward for keeping hold of the statues and friezes, they can certainly never claim to be able to house them in a more dramatic and spectacular fashion than they would if they were all sent back to Athens. The New Acropolis Museum awaits their return and in my humble opinion, one day justice will be done. It usually is.

For the record, the British Museum takes the following position:

"The British Museum exists to tell the story of cultural achievement throughout the world, from the dawn of human history over two million years ago until the present day. The Museum is a unique resource for the world: the breadth and depth of its collection

allows the public to re-examine cultural identities and explore the complex network of interconnected world cultures.

Within the context of this unparalleled collection, the Parthenon sculptures are an important representation of the culture of ancient Athens. Each year millions of visitors, free of charge, admire the artistry of the sculptures and gain insights into how ancient Greece influenced – and was influenced by – the other civilisations that it encountered."

My day with Maria ended with lunch in the extremely reasonably-priced restaurant that is part of the museum – much cheaper than the one at the British Museum I would guess, and with a wonderful panoramic view of the Acropolis rather than the traffic on the Tottenham Court Road - and we chatted about Maria's work for the association, as well as modern day life in Greece. Like many Greeks of her generation, she finds the current economic situation a struggle, but she was in no rush to head back to England. In such a stunning location it wasn't difficult to see why. We descended three floors to the entrance of the museum and braced ourselves for a plunge back into the stifling heat outside where we parted company with sincere promises to keep in touch. I headed back to my hotel for a late afternoon snooze and to contemplate the thing that I had almost forgotten: the cycling.

Wednesday 3ʳᵈ July 2013
Cycling Day 2: Athens to Corinth, 98km

So far the trip was feeling like a short city break involving just a little bit of cycling. I had spent many more hours wandering around ruins and museums and drinking in bars than I had actually cycling. I was at least acclimatising to the Mediterranean climate, but with only 49 cycling days to go, I needed to escape the capital and start making progress along the coast.

The Eurovelo route that I was nominally following – route number 8 – would have kept me cycling on the Greek mainland all the way to the Albanian border. I had other plans, however, due to my desire to visit the small town of Olympia and its ruins. Olympia sits on the western side of the Peloponnese, the large mountainous peninsula in south-western Greece. I had made contact with a Peloponnese cycling enthusiast via the Warm Showers website which I had used successfully back in 2010 during the cycle to southern Italy. The site allows touring cyclists to hook up with fellow touring cyclists who are able to offer accommodation in their home or room for a tent in their garden. No payment is required, just a willingness to reciprocate the arrangement to other touring cyclists when you are back home. Some areas of the world are packed full of Warm Showers people, other areas less so and the Peloponnese was in the latter category. The four or five people listed on the website were all located along the southern coast of the peninsula and the person I had contacted was in a place called Astros, some 160km from Athens. When planning the route back in the UK (to the extent that any detailed planning took place), I thought it would be a nice challenge to get me into the swing of cycling long distances. On the ground in Greece, I groaned to myself at the thought of the effort involved on only the second day of cycling, had a rethink and decided to take a more direct route towards Olympia, with an overnight stop in Corinth, not far from the famous canal. I sent an email to my Warm Showers contact, apologising for the change of heart and he graciously emailed back explaining that he could understand perfectly why I had done so. The cycle to Corinth would be a more modest 90km, slightly more than the 70km on cycling day 1, but still less than the 110km I needed to average per day if I was to be within a fighting chance of arriving in Portugal on time.

I had packed my panniers on Tuesday evening and it had taken some time as a result of my inability to remember in which of the four bags the item I was searching for was located. Invariably it was as the bottom of the fourth bag I looked in, by which time everything else had been removed. I resolved in future to look for what I wanted at the bottom of the fourth pannier first. The plan never quite worked. However, my efforts of the previous evening did at least afford me an early start in the morning, so it wasn't long after having woken and freshened up, that I was having a chat with my new friend Yiannis. He gave me detailed directions as to how I could best make my way through the north-western suburbs of Athens to find the coastal road out of town to the north, and once again it involved lots of lines, squiggles and crosses on my map. He was clearly a visual learner and indeed explainer.

I still hadn't managed to learn any words of Greek, but as I was now leaving the comfort of the cosmopolitan capital, I thought I had better make a small effort at least.

"Yiannis, how do you say 'thank-you' in Greek?"

"Don't bother; it's too complicated. Just say it in English, the Greeks won't mind."

"No, really, I'd like to be able to thank people in their own language rather than mine."

"Efharisto."

"Efharisto."

With that, I shook his hand and was gone.

I followed Yiannis' instructions to the letter, or rather the squiggle, on my street map of Athens and it worked. I navigated my way through the Athenian suburban streets and back onto the coastal road which, unsurprisingly, was a continuation of the monster coastal road I had tried to avoid two days earlier when making my way along the coast from the south. Six lanes of traffic confronted me. Had Yiannis momentarily forgotten that I was travelling by bicycle? I had to work hard once again to convince myself that I wasn't cycling on a motorway; only the existence of shops, cafés, bus stops and mopeds with riders who never seemed to be wearing helmets was evidence that I was cycling on a 'normal' road. My own helmet was securely attached, although how it would have fared should it have come into contact with one of the juggernauts thundering past Reggie and me didn't bear thinking about. In fairness to the drivers, most of them stayed well clear. Indeed the car that came the closest to ending this trans-European bicycle ride even before it had barely begun was not Greek but Italian registered. I had the joy of cycling with the Italian drivers to come, if, that is, I survived the ordeal of the coastal traffic between Athens and Trieste. One thing that did work in my favour was that the

27

Greeks seemed to have built their roads far too wide for the needs of driving a car, bus or even lorry along them. Most of the routes had a wide band of spare tarmac to one side of the carriageway, where I tried to cycle whenever it was possible to do so. My only concern about doing so, was that I had noticed that very slow vehicles tended to use this thin lane as a space along which to trundle in order to avoid the ire of the speedier vehicles behind them. I hoped that my decision to wear a bright yellow t-shirt would be useful in this regard. Indeed Yiannis had said as much before I had left the hotel. At the time I just thought he was being reassuring, but the more I cycled along the coastal motorway that wasn't a motorway, the more I could see why he had commended me for my sartorial decision.

I scoured my map for reassurance that the horrors of the road would soon come to an end and I found some just north of a place called Elefsina, where a motorway that *was* a motorway – the E94 – approached the coast after having curved an arc around northern Athens. Logic would dictate that at this point much of the heavy traffic would leave the road I was then on and join the motorway. So much for logic; it would be another 20km before the big boys finally had the sense to abandon the twists and turns of the coastal road in favour of the E94.

Prior to leaving home and embarking upon the trip, I had exchanged many emails and had had the occasional face-to-face chat with other cyclists who had cycled in Greece and Albania. Their experiences were many and varied, but they all tended to warn me of one thing; wild dogs. One of my contacts had been attacked so badly by a dog that she had had to be repatriated back home and abandon her cycle. Some cyclists had gone to the length of taking with them on their travels a small pepper spray canister, but warned that customs regulations could be difficult. Others carried juicy morsels of meat that were easily accessible while cycling, should they be required to be thrown in the direction of a fast-approaching mutt; but surely the whiff of a nice sirloin steak hanging from the frame would have any self-respecting carnivore speeding towards the bike, no? One person suggested small packets of butter be thrown, but in the heat of summer that strategy clearly needed to be thought through just a little more. There was another solution to the problem and I was about to put it into practice.

Climbing out of the town of Elefsina required me to cycle through a large industrial area consisting mainly of docks, warehouses and an oil refinery. It was now around midday and there was not a soul to be seen. If the security guards were on duty at the entrances of the various establishments, they were cowering from the heat behind the mirrored windows of their huts. The only life to be found was in the form of two dogs that were lazing in the shadow of a gate. As I approached, carefully, my heart started to pound just a little more quickly. In the back of my mind I started to question the wisdom of ignoring the pepper spray / meat / butter options but I cycled on. As I passed the gate I purposefully looked away so as to avoid eye contact (although whether that has any effect on a hungry dog who sees human lunch cycling by is open to question). One of the dogs stood up and its head followed me but its body didn't move. I *was* being sized up however. Suddenly it leaped into action and started to run in my direction. This had two knock on effects. Firstly his mate - who up until this point had been happily ignoring me - also sprang into life and, probably without having had time to think why, also started galloping after me. Secondly, I started to pedal in a manner in which I had rarely pedalled before. I looked straight ahead and to my horror the up-until-that-point flat road suddenly started to climb. The dogs had this planned out! I ignored the gradient and put every effort into my escape without daring to look behind me. My heart was racing, not just because of the extra effort involved, but also because of the terrifying thought of being leapt upon by the potentially rabid creatures that were pursuing me. I was a wildebeest racing frantically away from the ravenous lions, but this was no slow-motion wildlife documentary... My solution was simply to flee as fast as I could.

After perhaps thirty seconds I dared to glace behind me and... they had stopped. In fact they had not only stopped, they were nonchalantly sloping off in the opposite direction, heading back to their place in the shadows. I clearly just wasn't worth the effort required. I could have been (but wasn't) offended.

The remainder of the cycle towards the Corinth Canal was not quite as picturesque as that from Sounio to Athens on cycling day one. It was punctuated with the occasional strip of closed shops and what appeared to be abandoned business premises. I paused for a long lunch in the garden of a modern but rudimentary restaurant under a canopy of leaves. I was very conscious of avoiding the sun of the early afternoon, especially in the very early stages of the cycle. Factor 50 sun protection cream could prevent me from getting burnt, but it couldn't stop the sheer heat of the sun sapping away my energy.

I could see from my maps – electronic as well as paper - that I was approaching the Corinth Canal, but it was a little frustrating not being able to see anything remotely grandiose on the horizon. The Temple of Poseidon in Sounio and the Parthenon back in Athens had both shouted their presence well before I was able to get anywhere near their fine Doric columns. This wasn't the case with the Corinth Canal. My final destination of the day, the town of Corinth itself where I hoped to find a campsite, was on the northern end of the canal, but my cycle from Athens had brought me to the southern end where there didn't appear to be anything apart from a large bay. I had expected to see something that wouldn't look out of place in a Cecil B. DeMille movie. The first clue that I had indeed found the canal was when I noticed a luxury yacht in the distance that appeared to be crossing the road. I cycled towards the point at which I had seen the yacht, but a barrier across the road prevented me from approaching the edge of what I assumed was the start of the canal. A large yellow sign to my right indicated that there was a bridge ahead, but when I peered ahead there was no bridge to be seen. Further evidence that the sign was right and I was wrong was in a second notice, this time just for cyclists, which stated in Greek and in English "*Do not ride when crossing the bridge.*" What bridge?

A third and final sign – this time electronic – simply stated '16 MIN', which I assumed was the period of time I would have to wait for the moment that the bridge would finally appear. Perhaps Cecil B. DeMille was involved after all. In anticipation of the spectacular sight that awaited me, I parked Reggie under a tree and sat on a nearby bench to watch the sign tick down to zero. By the time the sign read '5 MIN', a small queue consisting of a motorbike (and rider without helmet), a moped (same again) and a car had formed. Both the motorbike rider and the moped rider had ignored the barrier in the road and approached the edge of the canal where the 'bridge' wasn't. I followed suit and looked over the edge into the canal. There was still no sign of a bridge, but by this time I had figured out that it must be submerged somewhere, ready to appear from the depths at the push of a button. And so it eventually did, slowly and with a quiet whirring of a heavy-duty mechanism somewhere hidden on the side of the canal. The shimmering length of the two carriageways of the bridge, separated by a pedestrian gangway, gradually came into view under the water. After a minute or so, it broke through the surface and the water bubbled away into the gaps of the planks of the road. A few moments later, there was an audible locking in place of the bridge and the whirring stopped. The motorbike and moped zoomed across, before the barrier had lifted to allow the few cars that had now gathered to approach the canal. A cyclist on the other side of the bridge cycled down the pedestrian strip, so I let him finish his crossing before doing the same myself. I was getting the distinct impression that what was written on the road signs in Greece seemed to have the status of guidelines rather than rules.

Glancing to my right as I crossed the bridge, I could, for the first time, see the glory of the Corinth Canal, a lockless passage barely 20m wide but cut deep into the rock. Its 6km length is what in effect makes the Peloponnese Peninsula an island, joined only to the mainland by the submerged bridge that I was cycling across illegally, and several high bridges some 90m above the surface of the water. I had plenty of time left in the day, so I turned off the main road and climbed to the height of the bridges in order to take in the view. The first one I came to was the motorway bridge, but fortunately I was able to cross the E94 in order to access the second, much older bridge, where I could see many people peering over the edge and down towards the blue surface of the now distant water below. I joined them for a while, although pushing Reggie along the narrow caged-in pavement didn't make me many friends amongst the crowd of people that had just piled off a tourist coach that was parked at one end of the bridge. I smiled and tried in vain to remember the word for '*thank-you*' that Yiannis had taught me earlier;

'*Af... Affri... Affa... Eff... Sorry, excuse me... Thank-you.*'

Once back on the Greek mainland, I had a nosey around the tourist-related attractions. A gift shop, an opportunity to bungee jump off the bridge and a modern marble monument to the memory of two Hungarian gentlemen, Istvan Turr and Bela Gerster who '*planned, organised and directed the construction of the Corinth Canal, a masterpiece of 19th century engineering*'. Indeed it was, but I couldn't help but wonder what Messrs Turr and Gerster would have made of the bungee jumping.

I chose to cycle with the traffic back onto the peninsula, rather than fight through the crowds of pedestrians. The journey into Corinth was quick and downhill for most of its length. Corinth isn't a town to put on your list of must-see destinations; I cycled through it and nothing enticed me to stop pedalling. I was on the lookout for a campsite, as I had noticed a little tent sign on a roadside map that I had seen back at the bridge over the canal. I also knew of the existence of a place called *Blue Dolphin Camping* following a quick Internet search when back in Athens, so when I saw a sign for the campsite in the place where it should have been, I yelped a little in joy (but only a little as I didn't want to attract the attention of any stray dogs).

I was looking forward to my first night in the tent and just hoped that the campsite had room for me. I needn't have worried. At the reception of *Blue Dolphin Camping* I was greeted by a smiling woman:

"Do you have space for one person with one bike and one small tent?"

There was a slight pause. I sensed that had she been able to say it in English, she would have replied:

"Are you taking the piss?"

She explained that they were so quiet that only one small part of the site was open. I paid my €10 for the night and headed off to pitch T116, where I erected the tent before taking a quick swim in the sea that was only a few metres from the perimeter wall of the campsite.

There was only a handful of other people on the site including an Englishman in a camper van. I asked him if he had a mallet that I could borrow to hammer in my tent pegs (this was to prove an excellent way of breaking ice with the neighbours in almost every campsite I was to use during the trip) and he did, but then proceeded to recount the intricate details of how horrid his trip had been driving across the various countries through which I was about to cycle. I was already anxious about travelling through Albania and this was doing nothing to help allay my fears. I escaped as soon as I could and avoided him for the remainder of the evening.

A far more affable man to converse with was the owner of the campsite. His name was Nikos and we got chatting as I was paying for my food in the on-site restaurant. I complimented him on his excellent level of English and he explained that he had a British passport and that his father used to own a restaurant called (no surprise) *The Blue Dolphin* in Goodge Street, London.

"At this time of the year we would normally expect to have 150 or more people staying at the campsite; tonight it's more like 20."

"The economic situation?"

"Yes, it's that, but also the Dutch and Germans who used to come with their families are getting older. They can't drive all the way to Greece anymore and younger families go on all-inclusive holidays in hotels."

The economic situation will hopefully gradually improve, but it was difficult to see how Nikos' business would be able to overcome the demographic changes in the Dutch and German populations and the modern-day tastes of their offspring.

"We don't employ anyone anymore – it's just me and my wife – and I'm not sure how much longer we can survive. I may go back to London."

After a cycle of nearly 100km, a swim in the Mediterranean, a large pizza and several of Nikos' beers I slept well in the tent. As I dozed off I couldn't help but wonder how long it would be before the *Blue Dolphin* campsite near Corinth would be another one of those deserted businesses that I had cycled past during the day without thinking twice about the reality of the situation for the people who used to own them and those who used to work in them.

Thursday 4th July 2013
Cycling Day 3: Corinth to Levidi, 107km

If cycling days 1 and 2 had been a bit of a mechanical shakedown for my bike, Reggie, cycling day 3 would be a shakedown for me, his rider.

The plan was to aim for Olympia on the western side of the Peloponnese peninsula, and I was willing to put in a long day in the saddle as I had planned for my second day of rest to be the following day, in order that I could explore the ancient ruins at Olympia. I looked at the map in the morning and thought to myself *'yes, that's do-able'*. I don't think it ever was. I had lamentably failed to appreciate just how challenging the Peloponnese mountains could be. Switzerland has proper mountains. Austria does too. France, Italy and Germany share bits of the Alps, and France and Spain have the Pyrenees. Greece? Well, no. Greece is just full of beaches and temples that are falling down... Isn't it?

In the knowledge that I had a good distance to cycle horizontally (if not vertically) and despite the fact that my guide book used the words *'compelling'* and *'stunning'* to describe them, I ditched any idea that I might have had of visiting the ancient ruins at Corinth fairly quickly. I reasoned that if I stopped to reflect in a Byronesque kind of way at every pile of stones in Greece, I would be still be there at Christmas. So instead, I headed for the hills (not, at this stage, the mountains).

There wasn't really a direct road from Corinth to Olympia that I could follow, so it was a case of trying to assemble a route that headed in the general direction of the western Peloponnese without spending too much time heading north, south or even back towards the east. This strategy of cherry picking the best routes was as confusing as it was frustrating, and I seemed to spend just as much time peering at the dim screen of my iPhone while consulting Google maps, or screwing up my eyes to extract the detail from my 1:300,000 map, as I did staring at and admiring the wonderful scenery surrounding me. After the two days of cycling on busy coastal roads, it was such a nice contrast being away from the traffic. Indeed, the further inland I travelled, the quieter the roads became. I didn't even mind when the car drivers beeped their horns to acknowledge me.

I was, however, getting the distinct impression that this part of Greece didn't receive many visits from touring cyclists. I was clearly a bit of a curiosity, although when I paused for a snack of bread and

Coke in the small town of Chiliomodi after around 25km, I sensed that the stares were increasingly from those who thought of me as an oddity rather than a curiosity.

"What's that nutter doing over there?" I could hear the men in the bars mutter in my imagination, before they turned their attention back to more important things in life such as how they could once again justify staying in the café sipping coffee instead of heading home to help the wife water the veg. As I left the bench where I had been taking my short impromptu break, I smiled and waved ironically at the group of men who had been giving me the strangest stares. One of them almost smiled back and made a gesture that wasn't quite a wave, but did indicate a morsel of acknowledgment that I wasn't completely crazy after all.

Already by that point I was surprised and delighted by what the Peloponnese was giving me: beautiful Italianesque scenery, quaint little villages, attractive churches in front of which Reggie could pose to have his photograph taken and, in fairness to the majority, friendly locals who were willing to smile and occasionally wave when I passed them on the road. Out of the towns and villages the vines stretched wide across the valley and every so often a string of brightly coloured beehives would punctuate the otherwise green scenery. In the far distance I could see the ever-increasing height of the land ahead of me, but I reasoned that my yet-to-be-chosen route would weave delicately between the large 'hills' and I would be able to admire them from the valley below.

In Nemea, where I paused to refill with water from a communal fountain just outside the centre of the town, I began to wonder what really lay ahead. The fountain was in a large paved area that formed the pedestrianised centre of an even larger roundabout. I parked Reggie in the very middle of the paving and carefully spun around to examine the 360 degrees of scenery encircling me. The hills had become mountains and when I lined up my map to match the direction in which I was heading, I noticed that whichever of the two, or possibly three routes that I could take, there was no avoiding the yellow squiggles. My map may have been lacking in detailed topographic information, but a road that squiggled was a road that was climbing and there were lots of squiggles on my map.

The climbing was gentle at first, but it wasn't too long before the long switchback roads started to predominate. Switchback roads are obviously designed for a good reason – the alternative would be to have a road straight up the side of a mountain which would have been almost impossible to cycle on a bike – but when you need to get from A to B they clearly make the journey a lot longer, not just in terms of distance but also time. By mid-afternoon I was still climbing and I was becoming increasingly anxious that I needed to find somewhere to sleep for the night. My attitude to such trivialities in the morning tended to be dismissive, but in the afternoon when I began to realise that I didn't have a destination in mind, I always became a little worried. This had suddenly become cycling at the deep end, after quite some time – both back home on the daily commute and on the two previous cycling days in Greece – of mucking around at the shallow end of the pool. The traffic had all but disappeared, so not only did I not have a destination in mind (Olympia itself was now out of the question), but I was in an extremely remote part of the mountains. I did have plenty of (albeit very warm) water but no food. As I neared the pass I stopped for a rest and to reflect upon my situation. I had started at sea level and Nemea had been at around 300m. My cycling app told me that I had ascended a further 900m into the sky to over 1,200m.

I tried to empty my mind of anxieties. All I could hear was an orchestra of natural sounds consisting of the cicadas (string section), the breeze in the trees (wind section) and my heart pumping (percussion). Until a few moments earlier, this had been complimented by the smooth movement of Reggie's mechanism (the brass section?). And then a car roared past me heading towards the pass, interrupting the tranquil scene somewhat but reassuring me that there was something worth visiting in the next valley. A small village with a patch of grass for my tent? A small town with a run-down hostelry? I unfolded the map, lay it on the ground and located where I was. There appeared to be two options. The first was a small place called Kandila. It was quite close but had nothing marked on the map to indicate that there would be anything there apart from a small collection of houses. The second place was called Levidi, larger – it even had a little red building (hotel) on my map – but much further away, probably about 20km. I decided that I would stop at the first place where I could either pitch the tent on a campsite or rent a room. Wild camping? Let's not think about that for the moment.

The other side of the mountain pass revealed a long downward route. There was so little in Kandila that I didn't even notice cycling through the place, but I could see all the way down the valley towards what I assumed was Levidi. It wouldn't be too long – and it wasn't – before I would be once again cycling on the flat across a wide plain. My challenging day in the saddle did appear to be about to have a happy and straightforward ending. Well, nearly. The nearer I got to Levidi the more apparent it was that, rather than being a town on the valley floor, it was perched on top of a hill some 200m above the valley bottom. On a normal day of cycling this might be a mere triviality, but when I looked at the iPhone and it confirmed what my legs were already screaming - that I had climbed almost 2km since leaving Corinth – my heart sank. I hadn't eaten anything since munching through the loaf back in Chiliomodi. If ever a man needed sustenance it was me, as I crawled across the valley in the direction of Levidi. Never again would I set off in the morning without emergency rations stashed somewhere in my panniers (probably at the bottom of that fourth bag just to keep them out of easy reach). As the last 200 metres of ascent started, I tried to stay on the bike but it was all but impossible. I got off, pushed Reggie and dragged myself for the final 500m into Levidi, where I just hoped there would be somewhere for me to stay the night and get something to eat.

A weary traveller stumbling across an abundant oasis of life is a bit of a cliché, but I was happy to be part of the cliché. At the top of the hill I found a large square. On three sides of the square were cafés, restaurants and at least two mini-supermarkets jostling for position. Most of the square itself was taking up with tables, chairs and parasols. On each of the three corners of the square that I could see were almost identical kiosques selling the essentials of life – snacks, drinks, magazines, cigarettes (if that's your thing) – and it is to the nearest one of these that I headed first, rather more quickly than I had been travelling for the previous half an hour or so, to feed my hunger. One large bag of salt and vinegar crisps, one can of Diet Coke and one large chocolate bar later I was still ravenous, but felt a little embarrassed to return to the same kiosque, so I went on a calorie crawl buying almost exactly the same things at the second cabin. I still needed chocolate, so I went to the third and it was here that, once I had established he spoke some English, I got chatting to the owner who introduced himself as Petros.

"Are there any hotels in Levidi?"

"Yes, there are three."

"Which one is closest?"

"Go up the street and just next to petrol station."

"Excellent, eff...aff... thanks!"

That was all very simple I thought, so stomach full of crisps, Coke and chocolate I cycled in the direction of the petrol station. After only a couple of minutes I could see ahead of me a woman waving her arms. I glanced around to see who she was waving her arms at, but there was only me on the road. She was standing just beyond the petrol station and above her was a sign with 'Rooms To Let' written in English at the bottom. Now, don't get me wrong, I'm just as eager to welcome the assistance of the locals as the next jaded traveller, but I don't like it when I get the merest whiff of being stitched up. Was I about to be stitched up? The woman didn't speak English but she did mention Petros by name and indicated that he had telephoned to let her know I was coming. Already?

I indicated that I only wanted a room for one night and she made a sign with her fingers telling me it would be €25. Leaving Reggie outside for a few moments, I inspected the room and, not being able to fault in any way what I was being offered, agreed to take it. She handed over the key but in doing so she seemed rather insistent on me knowing about a restaurant owned by someone called Costas. I wondered how long this chain of hospitality might stretch.

Showered and refreshed I still needed more food, but was now a little wary of wandering into town lest I be accosted by Costas waving his hands madly in my direction. It would be a risk I would have to take, so off I cycled back towards the square on a bike devoid of its panniers. If Costas was looking for me he never found me. I plonked myself under one of the parasols in the square and ordered a hearty meal from, well, whoever it was. I suppose it could have been Costas. He fed me well: pork and chips, garlic bread, two types of melon all washed down with a 500ml bottle of local wine. I rounded off the evening in an old man's café in one corner of the square with two black coffees and even then I found room for a packet of digestive biscuits through which I nibbled when I got back to the hotel.

On reflection it had been a great day of cycling. Yes, I hadn't known where I would end up at the end of the day and I had been woefully underprepared (or stupid) by not taking food with me over the mountains but what a wonderful place to have discovered. It had it all: stupendous vistas, challenging climbs, quiet roads and some great places to eat once I had arrived in Levidi. Just one thing puzzled me: where were all the other cyclists?

Friday 5th July 2013
Cycling Day 4: Levidi to Olympia, 103km

I woke with a full stomach and when I rolled over on the bed I did so through a fine carpet of biscuit crumbs that had been deposited there the evening before. As I lay, occasionally dabbing a moistened finger to collect a few of the crumbs and pop them into my mouth (my stomach can't have been that full perhaps), I reflected upon the previous day's cycling. Had I been adventurous or just plain stupid? The answer was probably both. I'm not sure why I ever thought that I would be able to cycle all the way from Corinth to Olympia in one day, and then have time to have a look around the ancient sporting ruins before setting off the following day for Patras. It was never going to happen and clearly never did. My Michelin map, scale 1:300,000, didn't have sufficient detail to say with any certainty whether the route I was about to follow was predominantly up or down. In some ways this was good; would I have ever crawled out of the tent in Corinth on the Thursday morning if I had known what was ahead of me? Well, yes I would, as I had little choice, but I may have thought carefully about an alternative route, perhaps one that skirted along the north-eastern coast of the Peloponnese. If I had, what a wonderful ride I would have missed.

Dragging myself away from the crumbs and off the bed, I made my way towards the balcony of the room. I was wearing very little – just a pair of swimming shorts – and the balcony was shared with the room next door but I had the distinct impression that I had been the only guest at the *Anatoli Hotel* that night and took the risk of shocking a fellow tourist with my white body. It was a risk worth taking, as the sun had just risen over the top of the mountains to the east and warming yellow rays were cascading down the valleys. I stood for a few moments to allow my body to collect the warmth after a night spent in a cool air-conditioned room, before returning inside, packing and wheeling Reggie out of the hotel without being seen. On arrival the proprietor had indicated that it wouldn't be possible for him to join me in the room but after my night on the town I had ignored her request and placed him inside anyway. To avoid any discussion of the subject in the morning I had to be careful to ensure that none of his metallic parts clanged against the metal railings of the flight of stairs between the front door and the road. Mission accomplished I then searched for the owner who was still in possession of my passport, but couldn't find her in the flat that she lived in on the ground floor of the building. I was forced to wait and watch the juggernauts hurtle past the hotel towards the centre of town. I surmised that they were heading in the same direction as me, which made my heart sink somewhat. Since leaving Corinth and heading for the hills, I had seen so few cars, trucks and buses, that I could have almost imagined that they were few and far between throughout the peninsula, but here they were in number, speed and volume. Once I did have my passport back in Reggie's front left pannier and I had found a gap in the traffic, I freewheeled back into the centre of town where I returned to the old boys' café and ordered yet another espresso. Some of the men who had been there on the previous evening were back again (or perhaps they had been there all night, who knows, and I certainly didn't have the Greek to ask them). One or two of them pointed at Reggie, smiled and said something encouraging about cycling. Well, I presumed it was encouraging. For all I knew it could have been "*Ha! You must be that pillock who cycled over the mountains yesterday without any food and then got fleeced by Petros' family...*"

Logic would dictate that on a two-day crossing of a land mass such as the Peloponnese, if you spend the first day ascending, the second day should surely be spent descending. From the little I knew about that part of Greece, I was fairly sure that it wasn't famed for the monumental size of its cliffs on the eastern side of the peninsula, so I was hopeful that my ride would be a downhill one all the way to sea level. The road to Olympia – just one this time, rather than the myriad of routes that I had navigated on the previous day – did have its fair share of hairpin bends on my map indicating that a gradient was involved and as long as that gradient required me to put in little or no effort on the bike, I would be happy. And so it was to be, eventually.

Initially some climbing was required: about 200m in total over a distance of around 30km but in comparison to what I had experienced in order to arrive in Levidi, it was tame stuff to say the least. Furthermore, most of the lorries that I had assumed would be travelling with me to Olympia, branched off the road after only 10km to take a more direct route north, so once again I was cycling on quiet and I have to say, very good quality roads. Every so often I would see a sign telling me, in Greek and in English, that the construction of the road had been financed with money from the European Union. From the perspective of a European taxpayer, I couldn't help but think that my money might have been invested more intelligently elsewhere, but then from the perspective of a cyclist, it was wonderful that they had decided to carve a wide, high-quality road through the middle of the Peloponnese just for me and the few cars who went by from time to time. Perhaps in future the Eurocrats should consider doing just that: constructing high quality cycle routes spanning the continent, something like the *Eurovelo* routes? It's just a thought.

Then, only a few kilometres short of a small town called Langadia, the descent started and it was to continue for a glorious 30km. I sat back in the saddle, released Reggie's brakes and let gravity take over. Well, at least for a couple of kilometres I did. Langadia itself was too tempting a place to whizz through in a blur of black lycra, so I pulled on the brakes and ground to a halt. Levidi had been a town built upon the gradual slope of a valley. The square in which I had eaten my pork and chips was slightly terraced but only in a way that would cause a person with the most serious of heart conditions to break into a mild sweat. Langadia was also built upon an incline but anyone with a heart condition should stay well clear of the place as it clings to the side of a precipitous slope on both sides of the road. Above the cafés, restaurants and souvenir shops to my right were built houses, and more houses above them, every layer ever so slightly further back than the previous one. Winding between the buildings were flights of steps that would completely invalidate the need for anyone to open up a gym in the town. To the immediate left of the road were the terraces of the cafés and restaurants that were to be found on the right of the road. I chose one of them and spent a considerable amount of time gazing further down the valley and daring to dream that the downhill cycle would continue for many kilometres to come. As I looked around I also wondered where all the tourists were. It was the first week in July! Was this a sign of the economic downturn or simply that the tourists had scuttled off to the beach at this time of the year?

This being the fourth day of cycling, I was now comfortably into my pit-stop routine. It would normally consist of the following actions in the following order: cycle around aimlessly for a few moments deciding upon which café was worthy of my custom (too many customers and I would have to wait an eternity to be served, too few would imply that there was something not quite right about the place), find a table where I would not only be comfortable in the shade and out of the direct sunlight but also position Reggie within arm's distance should I need to access something from his panniers, sit and stare at the buildings or the view or the people around me (if I was lucky, all three) whilst the perspiration on my skin evaporated and my clothes began to feel just a little less damp and then finally catch the attention of a passing waiter or waitress so as to order at least something to drink but very often something to eat as well. Now you would think that in a place like Langadia, which was obviously geared up to cater for passing tourists by the bus load but which had so few of them, I would never get the chance to sit, stare and dry off, as I would have been pounced upon by an eager café employee desperate for the business. But no. I sat and waited, and waited and waited a little more. Each of the three cafés had a waitress on duty and each of them was sitting on the step of the door to the café on the other side of the street. Obviously I had only chosen one of the cafés – the one in the middle – but my waitress didn't move. She occasionally glanced over but then returned to her cigarette and her glancing up and down the street. Perhaps my one drink and small sandwich just wasn't worth the effort. To one side of me was a group of old men playing cards in a gently-animated fashion. It was only when one of them needed a top up of caffeine that the young woman was sufficiently motivated to rise from her semi-squatting position and drift over the road towards the terrace. I seized the moment by raising my hand and smiling. Shortly afterwards I was finally delivered my cappuccino and pork-filled baguette.

The remainder of the afternoon was the delightful, downhill cycle I had hoped for. It was hot, the sky was blue and the views down the valleys were idyllic. The quality road surface, scarcity of traffic, and gradient allowed me to pick up speed and at times I was only one or two kilometres short of 50km/hr. I'm never happy at such speeds however, and whenever I reached the high forties I would quickly apply the brakes. Now I wouldn't want to come across as a cyclist who complains about descents as well as ascents but they do have a, err... downside. Firstly, the constant applying of the breaks can be tough on the hands. I tried to take an ABS approach whereby I would apply my brakes repeatedly off and on; it somehow seemed far safer to do so (as well as being easier on the hands) but I have no evidence to justify why that should indeed be the case. In addition, high-speed descent doesn't mix well with wind and, as I continued my journey towards Olympia, for the first time since leaving Sounio, it became a factor in the cycling. Was this a sign of things to come? I suspected that it was. Perhaps I should have taken heed of those who had warned me of the prevailing direction of the winds. As I turned the corners of the winding roads I was often confronted by a sharp blast of fast-moving air; if I were to be knocked off my bike by the fierceness of the gusts, I would rather be travelling at a speed considerably lower than 40 (or even 30) km/hr. As a direct consequence, most of the journey was at a relatively sedate 20 to 30 km/hr. Many a risk-taker would have scorned at my slow-speed descent, but it wasn't just the wind that kept my mind focussed upon keeping safe. Every single road along which I had so far cycled had been dotted with miniature shrines – mini-churches on a raised platform – identifying the position where some poor soul had lost their life. I assumed that most of them were motorists who had put their foot down on the quiet roads only to find themselves meeting their maker far sooner than they would have preferred. The scant details etched into the walls of the shrines or on plaques nearby mainly indicated that the victims were young and male. According to the *Hellenic Research and Educational Institute 'Panos Mylona' for Road Safety and the Prevention and Reduction of Traffic Accidents* (an organisation in desperate need of a snappy acronym), Greece is the most dangerous place in Europe to be anywhere near a road. It not only has the highest number of road fatalities per capita but you are more likely to die on the roads than by any other method. Forget heart attacks, fatal diseases or strokes. If you want to stay alive longer in Greece, no need to quit the fags, just keep away from the roads. The *International Transport Forum* reports that in 2010, 11.1 people in every 100,000 were killed on the roads in Greece; in the UK it was 3.1. Things are, however, improving. In 2012 the number of deaths dropped by 14%: bad news for the makers of small memorial shrines but good news for the rest of us. I kept applying my brakes, determined not to become yet another statistic.

When things did start to level out a little, I was keen to press on but the heat was beginning to grind both me and some of my equipment down. First to succumb was my iPhone, which started screaming (silently via a red message on the screen) that it was overheating and about to shut down: I moved it into the shade of one of the panniers and, after a period of deciding only to function in Greek, it came back to its senses. I couldn't, or rather didn't want to, turn it off as I was using it to track my route. Soon it was my turn to crave a bit of shade once again, but as I was unable to curl up inside one of the panniers I took the more sensible option of stopping at another café. This time it was a little more off the beaten track, but once again I had a choice of three establishments. The decision as to which one to choose was made for me however, as all three proprietors (all in their mid-twenties) were sitting in just one of cafés sharing jokes (some, perhaps, at my expense) while waiting for customers who never seemed to arrive. I bought three small bottles of Fanta and felt a bit embarrassed to pay only 3€ for the privilege. An older chap who was sitting with them tried to strike up conversation with me but, like most of the other people I had met on my journey across the Peloponnese, he assumed that I was German and started talking to me in German. My shrug of the shoulders and a short explanation that I was in fact

43

English (in English of course), seemed to instantaneously douse any hope of conversation. I found this curious; weren't the Germans first in line to be singled out by the Greeks for having created the conditions that had resulted in the worst economic recession in living memory?

As the afternoon was drawing to a close, I began to see an increasing number of signs for Olympia and its ancient ruins. As I approached the town itself, the infrastructure required for such a world-renowned site multiplied around me. The road had become more like a motorway and there were lanes and signs directing certain groups of people along particular routes. I cycled past an increasing number of hotels, but I was on the look out for a campsite and one in particular; *Camping Diane*. My guidebook described it as being '*set amid a pine forest with a pool, restaurant and good facilities, including wi-fi*' - just what I needed - and it wasn't too difficult to find a few hundred metres to the west of the well-kept town centre, up a steep but mercifully short road. What my guidebook didn't tell me was that I would be welcomed by a spritely chap called Thucydides who was the owner.

"*Hello, do you speak English?*" I enquired.

"*My English is OK but my French is better*", he replied.

Initially this caused a little linguistic confusion, as when I then spoke to him in French he replied in an almost impenetrable hybrid Greek/French accent. It seemed that I would have more chance sticking to just English, so I quickly backtracked and repeated what I had said. He didn't question the fact that I had done so, perhaps he too was struggling with what he perceived to be my impenetrable English/French accent.

We went through the formalities of check-in inside the campsite office. While Thucydides was noting down the details from my passport, my eyes wandered around the room. The many bookcases were full of weighty, and what appeared to be legal tomes interspersed with the Greek classics. I recognised a few of the names but not much else. Thucydides must have spotted my glances and started to tell me about himself:

"*I was born in Olympia – in 1923...*" He clearly had a problem with English numbers but I didn't interrupt him. He spoke softly with an almost constant smile.

"*Before I retired I was an economist working for the government in Athens but I also like to write about the great Greek philosophers*", he explained. I looked more carefully at some of the spines and many of them carried his first name, Thucydides.

"But I also worked in Paris which is where I learnt my French."

He stood up and pulled a book from one of the shelves to show me. I nodded in a way that only a man who has just been handed a book written in Greek can nod.

"Not bad for a 90 year old!" he exclaimed while beginning to chuckle once again. There had been nothing wrong with his English numbers; he really had been born in 1923. I congratulated him on looking so youthful and he smiled. Before me was a fit 70 year old with a bushy white moustache, small white beard and a reasonably full head of hair. His mind was sharp and from what I had seen so far he moved around effortlessly. But this 70-year-old was actually 90. The span of 20th century Greek history – war, occupation, dictatorship, military rule, democracy, economic ruin – quickly flashed through my mind. This man had lived through most of it and I was sure he had some interesting tales to tell. I hoped that during the 36 hours of my stay at *Camping Diane* I would hear a few of them. As there were few campers on site, this seemed a distinct possibility.

Saturday 6th July 2013

Rest Day 2: Olympia

I was dearly hoping that the long detour across the Peloponnese to Olympia would be worth the effort. It was somewhat of a pilgrimage for me to visit the site of the original, ancient Olympics, as it had been the efforts of the modern day Olympians at the Beijing Olympics in summer 2008 that had first inspired me to get off my backside and do something more adventurous with my summer holidays. Five years has passed since I had watched the rain-sodden cyclists at the Great Wall of China, sat up from my horizontal position on the sofa and wondered how wonderful and exciting it would be to do something similar in a far-off land. I hadn't quite made it to the Far East, but one continental crossing of Europe by bike had been completed and here I was embarking upon a second. I was making good progress on my quest towards wonder and excitement.

Just as Yiannis had done back in Athens, Thucydides gave me a map of the town and proceeded to annotate it with squiggles, arrows and a few numbers as he gave me a quick verbal run-down of what I needed to know about visiting his hometown and the ancient ruins on the other side of the river. The map resembled one that might be used to teach children what a town should look like; most streets were arranged in a grid pattern and every street contained coloured boxes or circles labelled, in English (more or less), with the names of the facilities on offer: 'hotel', 'bank', 'butcher's shop', 'tabacos'... There were even three red boxes labelled 'disco'. That might be handy later, I thought.

It was still early, but I wanted to get to the Olympic site as soon as it opened at 8am. Not only was it cooler in morning, but I also suspected that for the first time since leaving Athens, there would be hoards of fellow tourists at the site and if at all possible I didn't want my visit to coincide exactly with theirs. I just hoped that everyone else was lacking in the forethought department.

The main archaeological site was just one part of a larger complex of ruins and buildings on the south side of town, the first of which – the *Museum of the History of the Olympic Games in Antiquity* – was closed. Thucydides had already explained this would be the case, so I headed past the museum, down the road and over the bridge to the parts of the site that I would be able to visit. It was mercifully quiet and there was no need to queue at one of the ticket offices at the entrance. I paid my €9 fee and the guy behind the perspex screen congratulated me on having arrived before the cruise people. I wasn't quite sure what he was implying by this comment, but I smiled and wandered off towards the entrance of the archaeological site. It seemed a good idea to visit the ancient ruins themselves while it was still relatively cool, before heading over to the *Museum of the History of Excavations* - which I hoped would be air-conditioned - later in the day. Having just paid €9 for a joint ruins and museum ticket, I also hoped that this particular museum would indeed be open.

At the gate to the archaeological site half of my ticket was torn off and I was allowed in. A large stone slab, angled slightly at waist level, politely set the scene:

"Dear visitors,

Welcome to the archaeological site of Olympia, one of the most important religious centers of antiquity. Its power and influence was felt throughout the Greek world.

In this place Zeus, father of the Olympian gods, was worshipped, and splendid athletic contests, the Olympic Games, were celebrated. In the cella [sic] of the temple of Zeus was placed the enthroned gold-and-ivory made cult statue of the god, work of the famous Greek sculptor Pheidias, one of the seven wonders of the antiquity. Here too, nowadays the ceremony of lighting the flame for the modern Olympic Games is held."

When I visit sites of great interest to tourists, it never ceases to amaze me how much money has been lavished on creating beautiful, well-designed, long-lasting signage like this, yet how little has been invested in asking a native speaker to check whether what has been written is actually correct. Communication is, of course, the most important thing, but the open letter to visitors continued as follows:

"To enjoy your visit there is no need to:

- *bring animals*
- *climb on the ancient walls and monuments*
- *carry off any object whatsoever from the archaeological site*
- *enter areas that have been temporarily fenced off*
- *pollute the environment"*

You can if you want, there's just '*no need to*'. I made a mental note to bear their very broad-minded attitude in mind.

Putting aside my grammatical pedantry and raising my eyes to see what was beyond the sign, I could see the extensive ruins of ancient Olympia set amongst the equally extensive areas of trees that were growing across the site. The key architectural features visible were the stunted columns of varying heights aligned in neat rows marking out where the buildings used to be. A few were still the size they had been back in ancient times, but their supporting function was now redundant as none of the cornices or pediments remained. I tried mentally to rebuild the view as it might have looked in 776 BC when, *according to tradition* (did that mean that there was no conclusive proof?), the Olympic Games were established. In my virtual reconstruction of the scene I was, of course, assuming that all the buildings had been completed on time and, for the sake of the builders, on budget. I suspect that the sanctions for not doing so were a little more severe in 776 BC than they might have been for the modern day construction firms in London, Beijing, Athens or any of the other host cities since the revival of the games in 1896. Well, apart from perhaps Beijing.

My first Olympics – the first that I remember being aware of – were the Montreal Games in 1976, and ever since I've been a fan. I hesitate to say it was ever a passion. If it had been, I may well have been one of the athletes competing, rather than a mere spectator in front of the television, but I fondly remember spending time as a child watching the Olympic Games, starting with those 1976 games in Canada. Was it the spectacle and the colour? Was it patriotism? Was it the far-off locations? Was it (until more recently) the grainy pictures and crackling commentaries? Was it the fact that all the normal TV programmes were shunted aside in favour of something that those in charge deemed to be more worthy? It was probably all of these. After Montreal, there were the Moscow Games in 1980 when the Americans didn't show up but Seb Coe and Steve Ovett did, the Los Angeles Games four years later, when the Russians reciprocated in kind but we nevertheless marvelled at the spectacle of the astronaut hovering above the stadium, Seoul in 1988 when Ben Johnson tried his best to spoil the party and then Barcelona in 1992. I had been in Barcelona in the summer of 1989 and was amazed by how the city was already festooned in Olympic flags and banners a full three years before the opening ceremony. The 1996 Games in Atlanta – the Coca-Cola Games - are the ones that everybody remembers for the wrong reasons, but Sydney 2000 put the movement back on track with the "*best games ever*". The Athens Games of 2004 had a hard act to follow, but seemed to do just fine after a frantic effort to finish the venues, and then came probably the most expensive games ever in 2008 in Beijing. London could never aim to match the spending power of the Chinese, but proved the cynics more than wrong by producing one heck of a show. And I played my small part in making those Olympics happen by being a *Gamesmaker*, one of the fabled volunteers who smiled, helped out and generally made the whole thing run like clockwork. Well, most of the time. So, mountains or no mountains, my cycling journey through Greece was always going to find its way to Olympia, the home of the original ancient games.

The Olympic Stadium itself seemed like a good starting point for my wander around the ruins, so I followed the signs past *Hera's Altar* (where the lighting of the Olympic flame has taken place for all the games since 1936) and the *Bases of Zanes* (upon which bronze statues of Zeus, paid for by the fines imposed on athletes who had been found to be cheating, were strategically placed as a warning to competitors entering the stadium), before passing under an arch (which I suspected might have been rebuilt) and along what used to be a covered tunnel into the large and very open Olympic arena. The first thing that I noticed was the proportion of the stadium's length to its width: much narrower than a modern-day equivalent which is roughly the same as the proportions of a football pitch. The track itself was also very different. The starting line was marked in the gravel by a line of stone protruding from the surface – clearly health and safety wasn't a big issue back in the 8th century BC – and 192.27m (according to the sign) in the distance was the equally lethal finishing line. There were no curves around which to sweep majestically around in a Usain Bolt-style 200 metre dash. Well, come to think of it there weren't even 200 metres. He would have had to make do with being the 192.27 metre Olympic champion had he been around at the time. On either side of the track were gently sloping banks and a third 'stand' at the far end. There were no seats and the capacity crowd of 45,000 spectators (apart from the small number of officials and dignitaries who did have a somewhere to park their bums in a cordoned off area halfway along the length of the track) would have either stood or sat on the grass. If you hadn't managed to get hold of a ticket for the events (and let's face it, that was quite likely if you were just an 'ordinary' citizen, a slave or, most inconveniently, a woman as they wouldn't let you in to begin with), you could go and take up position on the neighbouring Hill of Kronos, a well-positioned mound, much steeper than the stadium itself, just next door.

I walked to the far end of the stadium to escape the modest crowd that had now congregated at the tunnel end of the track, and climbed the bank to look back at the whole of the stadium. The other tourists must have been part of a group, as they all appeared to leave together and I was left alone to gaze down upon this cradle of sporting endeavour. Again I tried to build a picture of how it must have been to be part of the crowd in ancient times. I took out my camera and started to frame an arty shot of what I could see, eventually squatting down to include some of the wild flowers at my feet in the foreground of my photo, at which point I heard a shout to my left. I turned to see that a man had appeared and he was approaching me at a relatively fast pace from the far end of the embankment. It is never a good sign when someone starts wagging their finger at you, and his fingers were in wagging mode. I had no idea what he was saying of course, but I imagined it to be along the lines of *"Hey you, what are you doing? You can't squat in this stadium and take a..."* Ah! I began to work out why he had an issue with my stance. I stood up and held the camera so that he could clearly see that I was taking an arty photograph and not a crap. He smiled and turned away.

The most striking aspect of my visit to the Olympic Stadium was discovering that it was only excavated relatively recently, during the Second World War, by the Germans on the orders of Adolf Hitler. Perhaps he had ambitions of one day emulating that equally mad dictator Nero who, in 67 AD, came to Olympia, competed and won every event in which he entered. What a surprise...

I returned to explore the other areas of the archaeological site but when I emerged from the tunnel leading out of the stadium, the whole area seemed to be far busier. Groups of brightly-clothed people, many with brightly-coloured orange skin, most with hats and some with parasols, were being herded in groups around the rows of columns, collections of rubble and semi-ruined buildings. The people doing the herding were carrying aloft a white paddle, and as I approached I could see that each person in the group was wearing a badge, upon which was printed a number that matched the number on the paddle. Some of the people were wearing earphones plugged into a small box slung around their neck. The box in turn was linked wirelessly to a microphone clamped to the face of the person with the paddle. It was a scene that I was destined to see over and over again as I made my way around the Mediterranean coast; it was my first encounter with the cruise ship mob.

Now let me first say that, as individuals, I'm sure that every one of the cruisers I encountered had their good points and their bad points, just like you, me and everyone else. I have cruisers in my family; my parents, my brother and his wife, an aunt and a cousin, and they are all nice people. However, put them all together, rig them up with an intercom system and send them off to follow someone with a paddle and they become a menacing swarm. For this first encounter I preferred to observe from a distance trying to follow cruiser-free paths around the ruins, and most of the time I was left alone to my own aimless wanderings and reading of plaques.

By now it was early afternoon and the heat was beginning to bear down upon the cruisers, the ruins and me. It was time to explore the other side of the complex and investigate the *Museum of the History of the Excavations in Olympia* so off I plodded back towards the entrance kiosques and through a separate gate that led along a path in the direction of a modern, flat building whose main attraction was that it did indeed have air-conditioning installed and working. The covered walkway around the perimeter of a square pool outside the entrance was in itself slightly cooling, but the best was yet to come as I walked through the doors and into the cold air beyond. Many people had at this point just given up and found a place to relax, either on benches or simply on the floor. It was tempting to join them and sit out the heat of the day, but ever the person to squeeze the value out of a €9 entrance ticket, I strolled around the museum, albeit with the enthusiasm of a sloth on his day off. There were many exhibits to catch the eye, from miniature animals to full size bronze statues of the gods. Most impressive however, were the reconstructed pediments from some of the buildings around which I had been wandering earlier. The overall flat, triangular shape of the pediment had been maintained in the display, but many of the arms, feet, heads, legs and quite a few bodies had been lost over the centuries leaving curious collage of pieces of statues appearing to hang without the support of a body or arm or leg. I did wonder if Lord Elgin had perhaps paid a visit, but then again, if he had he would no doubt have swiped the lot. Room 8 of the museum appeared to have caught the eyes of the cruisers, so I followed them discreetly and listened in on the talk being given by one of the guides who hadn't adopted the microphone method of communicating with her followers. It was the *"famous statue of Hermes..."* in front of us *"...carved by the sculptor Praxiteles in the 4th Century BC, depicting the god carrying the infant Dionysos to his nurses in Boeotia"*. I began to regret not having paid more attention in Classical Studies lessons back at school. I shuffled off around the back of the statue (lest I be spotted without a cruise ship badge) to admire Praxiteles' efforts and I was suitably impressed. There can be few such smooth arses that can claim to be nearly 2,500 years old. It was certainly a darn site smoother than my own arse after the four days of cycling that I had so far completed.

By the time I had made it back to Camping Diane, a late afternoon storm was brewing. I sat on the covered terrace area outside the campsite office having bought a beer from the small shop that was run by Thucydides' wife. She was just as spritely as her husband, but my guess was that she was a mere spring chicken in comparison. As I was typing up my notes from the visit to the archaeological ruins, there was a sudden loud crack above my head and within a few minutes the rain was falling in such a manner as to have me worried about whether the tent would survive its first dousing. I couldn't see it from the terrace but had no wish to venture through the storm just to check if it was still standing. As I waited for the conditions to change, the terrace became a refuge for the few people who were staying on the site that evening. Thucydides appeared from his afternoon slumber (perhaps that was his secret) and I chatted on and off with him as he read the newspaper and I updated my online diary of the day's events. We were joined by an American guy from Texas who was in his late teens. He too was making the most of the storm to do his online stuff and we got chatting. His name was Rick and he was travelling with his older brother, mother and father around Europe. After a while his brother Danny joined us. They didn't really fit the Texan stereotype of redneck Republicans an observation that I pointed out to them and they laughed. Their parents were both teachers, Danny was a teacher and Rick was about to start his training to become a teacher. It was their sixth trip around Europe as a family and they reeled off the places that they had visited over the years. Both brothers had had the opportunity to travel more extensively in Europe than most Europeans, but it wasn't lavish no-expenses-spared travel. They had always camped and cooked for themselves, seeking out the interesting nooks and crannies of the continent rather than heading directly for the great points of tourist interest. As both brothers were now at the point of leaving home, they thought it would be the last time that the family travelled together as a group. I thought of my own family and how I would have recoiled in horror at the prospect of spending an extended period of the summer holidays in my late teens or early twenties travelling around Europe with them. There would have been blood and I suspect it would have been mine that was shed first. Their situation was in marked contrast to my own, and there was a tinge of sadness as I later reflected upon the downsides of travelling by yourself: the constant searching for things to do, the complete absence of collaboration, the unease felt in restaurants surrounded by couples, groups of friends and families or, come to think of it, sitting alone under the tin roof of a campsite terrace, waiting for the rain to stop.

Sunday 7th July 2013
Cycling Day 5: Olympia to Nafpaktos, 142km

Somewhere back in the UK, probably in south-west London, Andy Murray was no doubt experiencing a restless night prior to becoming the first British tennis player in over 75 years to win the men's singles championship at Wimbledon. As he tossed and turned under his satin sheets (I'm making wild assumptions here but bear with me), he was unaware of the outcome of the day that lay ahead. In Olympia, I was experiencing similar problems, but my night in the tent wasn't so much restless as almost sleepless and it wasn't because I was anxious about the cycle that I would be embarking upon in the direction of the Greek mainland. It was, more prosaically, because next door to *Camping Diane* there was a hotel and it was a night of celebration. What exactly they were celebrating remains a mystery, but this being Greece in the summertime, the festivities were taking place outside and that included very loud music being played and occasionally sung. If ever I am in a similar situation back in Britain, I know that, however annoying such loud music can be when I am trying to sleep, as long as it is an official event that requires a licence (i.e. not just your neighbour having a wild house party), the music will stop at the precise time written by the local council on the licence. If it's not midnight, then the chances are that it will be 1am. With this hopelessly British respect for local officialdom in mind, I was keeping an eye on the clock. Midnight passed and the music continued, as it did at 1am. I had high hopes for a 2am finish and was already fantasising about what I might dream, but it, too, came and went. When the same thing happened at 3am I was very annoyed, but as the music continued to play at volume as my watch struck 4am, I was ready to make an emergency call to the embassy back in Athens. The music did finally stop at around 5am and I managed a couple of hours of Andy Murray-esque restless sleep but it was never going to be sufficient to keep me pedalling enthusiastically through a long day in the saddle.

With the music still ringing in my ears, I didn't sleep at all well and I decided to get out of the tent more through a wish to do something – anything! – that wasn't interrupted every few minutes by being jabbed in the side by an annoyingly-placed stone under a groundsheet. By 8.30am I had packed everything away and was waiting at the campsite reception for Thucydides or his wife to appear and open the long metal gate. The father of the two Texan boys to whom I had been chatting the night before appeared and we were able to pass the time comparing the relative merits of teaching in Texas and England. In terms of retirement, the Texans win hands down. I marvelled over the simplicity and generosity of the '80-year rule' that the state has in place for its teachers. The man in front of me was a healthy-looking, fit and active 53-year-old. But he had just retired as he had been teaching for 27 years and 53 plus 27 makes 80. Bingo! If this man lived a life as long as Thucydides (our still-slumbering host), he could look forward to nearly 40 years of being paid to do nothing but be retired. I had been teaching for 13 years and in order to claim a full pension, would probably have to continue for another 25 years at the very least. I would be retiring at the age of 68 at which point I would probably be dead from exhaustion anyway. I made a mental note to write a letter to the newspapers when I arrived back home and to crack on with writing this book in the hope that it would become an international bestseller. The thought of teaching teenagers at the age of 68 is decidedly alarming.

Thucydides arrived looking as fresh as a 68-year-old who hadn't spent the last 38 years teaching teenagers, and chatted to the Texan and me about our plans for the day. The elephant in the room was, of course, the music that had lasted until 5am but it never got a mention; it wasn't the fault of Camping Diane that someone had decided to celebrate in (loud) song until sunrise, and Thucydides and his wife had been very kind and helpful people. Why burden them with such a complaint? A complimentary coffee perked my spirits, and it gave me the necessary burst of energy to unlock Reggie from his position near the front gate and ride off down the road into the town centre.

The plan for cycling day 5 was to make it as far as Patras, a city near the northernmost tip of the Peloponnese, where a new bridge had been constructed linking the peninsula to the mainland. I knew that there was a campsite just south of the bridge, so the plan was to stay there overnight before crossing the bridge in the morning and continuing northward along the coast the next day. A route following the crow would no doubt have seen me spending another half day climbing mountains, but mindful that my legs were still in recovery from the efforts earlier in the week, I decided to head for the coast and continue in a semi-circular fashion towards my destination. As a result the ride was a long, flat one. It was also quite boring, a fact which doesn't bode well for the remainder of this chapter.

I just had to accept that some of my days were going to be transitory ones spent cycling through nondescript areas from one place of interest to another place of hopefully even more interest. Olympia had been fascinating and Patras with its bridge and, ...well its bridge would hopefully be, at the very least, an interesting diversion. Anyway I like a good bridge and from the photographs that I had seen, the one at Patras – the *Rio-Antirrio Bridge* no less – was in the premier division of such structures.

One of the beauties of long-distance travel by bicycle is that it gives you time to ponder. How often in our busy 21st century lives do we ever get a chance to just look at the scenery and think? Perhaps the opportunity is there when sitting as a passenger in a car or in a plane or train, but in all three of those situations you are under the control of someone else's travelling whims (or the timetable of the airline or train company). You don't normally have the freedom to clench your fists, pull on the brakes and slow down when you see something that interests you and which requires just a little bit more observation and thought. On a bike, travelling alone, you are the master of your destiny, or at least your route. It may not have been the most exciting day along the Mediterranean coast that I would experience over the two months of summer 2013, but there were plenty of oddities upon which I could ponder. The petrol stations for example. I don't think I have ever visited a country which has more petrol stations. Dozens of them, strung along my route at regular (and occasionally irregular) intervals. One that took my fancy so much that I paused for refreshments under its large roof, was run by a company called Motor Oils. There was something Olympic about the building's construction; the bright red roof was supported by four large red columns at each of its corners and on top of the roof was an enormous red sign with the words '*Motor Oils*' emblazoned across it in bright yellow lettering. Above the words was an equally jaundiced stallion, which was larger than the white transit van that was filling its tank just below. Curiously, everything was labelled in English with no Greek to be seen: '*welcome*', '*diesel*', '*parking*', '*mini market*', '*bar*'. Standing against the pale blue sky and the faded green of the scrub vegetation that made up most of the flat landscape, it was a sight that could quite easily have left an indelible impression on the retina had one cared to stare at it for an extended period of time.

Equally colourful, but in a much more natural way, were the fruit and vegetable stalls that had been set up along the road even more regularly than the service stations. The most popular items on offer seemed to be large pumpkins that were stacked high on groaning trestle tables in the open air; more delicate fruit was kept in the shade of wooden shacks with either thatched or corrugated iron roofs. Behind the fruit I could just make out the figure of the stallholders who were invariably reading a newspaper while drawing on a cigarette just waiting for the next customer to come along and interrupt them. Every single stall had a flagpole proudly flying the cross and stripes of the blue and white Greek flag.

Almost with the same regularity as the petrol stations and the fruit and veg stalls were the miniature shrines to the dead of the Greek roads, but for the first time in my travels through Greece I started to pass signs for speed cameras (it's interesting to note that the universal sign that has been adopted for a modern digital speed camera is that of a very old traditional film camera complete with concertina lens), and I wondered as I cycled whether it was the cameras or the frequent shrines that had the biggest impact upon the habits of the motorists.

I was in a relaxed mood as I approached Patras. I knew that there was a campsite called *Camping Rion* along the shoreline just south of the bridge, so at least I didn't have to start stressing about finding accommodation for the evening upon arrival in town. It was a little frustrating trying to navigate my way through the city centre and towards the northern suburbs, but I knew that as long as I could see the bridge in the distance and it was gradually becoming larger, I was heading in the right direction. The streets appeared to have been built upon a grid pattern, so after quite a number of sharp left or right turns I found myself on a semi-pedestrianised street with the Gulf of Patras on my left and a strip of night-clubs, small amusement parks, restaurants and (I hoped) *Camping Rion* on my right. No sign of the latter quite yet, but I remembered that from the map it was quite close to the bridge, so I cycled along the road keeping one eye on the ever-changing miscellany of entertainment venues and one eye on the spectacular multi-span bridge ahead of me. More of that later.

Sure enough *Camping Rion* was just where I thought it might be. As with many of the establishments along the sea front it was far narrower than it was long. The entrance barrier was next to the campsite restaurant and bar, and beyond that I could see the other more rudimentary facilities of a campsite – showers, toilets and the like – and along each side of the strip of land were patchy green camping pitches. It didn't seem very busy but after my experiences at Corinth and Olympia that wasn't much of a surprise. It did look as though the restaurant and bar were closed, however, as I could see stacks of chairs behind the windows rather than set out next to tables. A few people were milling around, most of them wearing cleaning gear and carrying a broom or a vacuum cleaner or at least a cloth. In my now customary fashion I apologised for not speaking Greek before launching into English:

"*Where is the campsite reception?*"

The woman I asked didn't reply but just pointed in the direction of a door, which I entered. Before I had the time to repeat my linguistic apology, a surly-looking woman behind the desk simply said:

"*We are closed.*"

I stood for a moment wondering how I could respond. However logical and water-tight my arguments that the campsite should actually be open (which included the fact that it was listed in my guide book, I had found it on the Internet the day before and – most compelling of all – the sign outside said 'open'), I sensed that the woman in front of me wasn't going to change her mind for anyone, let alone an Englishman with a penchant for apologising for his lack of knowledge of the Greek language. The devil in me wanted to argue the toss or at least persuade her to break the bad news to future travellers in a more gentle fashion:

"*I've just cycled over 100km for you to say 'we are closed' and imply through your tone of voice that it's my fault that your campsite has decided to shut, not yours or indeed Greece's*", I would have loved to say but didn't.

I returned to the long road outside the campsite that was no longer a campsite and stared at the bridge. I had really wanted to cross the bridge in the morning, but it was now looking as though I would have to extend today's cycle as far as the mainland. The bridge itself was about 3km in length and, when I added in the short cycles on either side to get from where I was standing to the bridge and then to another campsite on the other side, it would be more like 10km. My body had already shut down for the day upon arrival at *Camping Rion* and there I was being forced to start the engine again.

Despite its enormous size, I initially struggled to find my way onto the *Rio-Antirrio Bridge* and when I did my cycling was more of a two-wheeled trudge. I really wanted to savour the moment crossing from the Peloponnese back to the Greek mainland along the world's longest, multi-span, cable-stayed bridge (there are probably two many descriptive elements there to be really impressive but I'm easily pleased), but I didn't. I had read that there was a lane just for cycles but I couldn't find it. In fact, no provision whatsoever seemed to have been made for cyclists and I was somewhat alarmed that when I approached the far end of the bridge, each lane – including the one along which I was trudging – had an automated, full-width barrier across its length. Fortunately I was spotted by a security guard who indicated that I should wheel Reggie through the gravel, lift him over a knee-high metal fence and then through more gravel on the other side. This reduced trudging to a new level of lethargy.

So, plan B was to find the second campsite highlighted by the previous evening's online research. It didn't exist or at least I couldn't find it. I located a third campsite (plan C) but it was the kind of place that I *wished* didn't exist or at least couldn't find. *Camping Dounis Beach* with its high fence, dilapidated buildings and dogs (heard but not seen) was, much to my relief this time, also closed. It was time for plan D which could be summarised as *'Bugger this, it's getting late, I need a hotel'*.

Having already cycled a few kilometres in an easterly direction away from the bridge in my vain attempts to find a campsite, it made sense to continue to the town of Nafpaktos. It was about 10km from the bridge and I knew that those 10km would have to be re-cycled the following morning but it looked as though it was a town that was of sufficient size to have hotels and, much to my relief, it did. Later during my Mediterranean odyssey, I was to discover the wonders of booking hotel rooms online. In Nafpaktos I was still in the pre-enlightened days of turning up at a reception desk and asking if they had a room available. This approach has two downsides: firstly, you have no idea how much the hotel are going to charge you and this can lead to that awkward moment when you come up with some fanciful excuse as to why the hotel might not be the one for you (*'You don't have an overnight bicycle-washing service? Sorry...'*) and the receptionist raises their eyebrows in a manner only those in the high-end customer service industries are able to manage. Secondly, it gives the hotel the option of turning you down for looking like the bedraggled cyclist that you are. This was the case at the *Plaza Hotel*, Nafpaktos, which claimed to have no spare rooms. Mmm... After a quick glance across the deserted communal areas on the ground floor, I wasn't convinced. I had more luck at the *NAFS Hotel*, which described itself as 'an oasis of comfort', and it certainly was. Who needs a €10 campsite when you can spend six times that amount and live in luxury? In fact it was €56 which, when compared with the discomfort of the previous night in the tent back at *Camping Diane*, didn't seem unreasonably expensive. I luxuriated on the comfortable bed, sipped the cold Belgian mini-bar beer, stamped unceremoniously on my lycra cycling gear in the slate-lined, hot shower, toasted Andy Murray's victory at Wimbledon while watching the 24-hour news channels and then flaked out in the silence of a sound-insulated room. Wonderful.

Monday 8th July 2013
Cycling Day 6: Nafpaktos to Mitikas, 125km

It really was a very comfortable room and I slept well, although this was probably just as much down to the sleepless night at Camping Diane back in Olympia as it was to the four star conditions that surrounded me. The room had a balcony with a couple of chairs, and a table over which I had draped my cycling gear following my attempts at cleaning them in the shower the night before. They were now dry but before pulling them on I sat for a few moments overlooking the modern interior courtyard of the NAFS Hotel, reflecting upon where I had been and, more importantly, where I was yet to cycle. The bridge linking the Peloponnese back to mainland Greece had been the end point of any detailed planning that I had completed in the UK before setting off. Throughout the first week of the trip, I had had a pretty good idea where I would be finishing the day. It might not have worked out exactly as planned – the previous day's cycle being a good example of that – but I wasn't too far away from where I had imagined I might be. From here on, all the way to Portugal, I really would be making the whole thing up as I went along. I did have towns and cities in mind – the next one being the capital of Albania, Tirana – but as to intermediate stops and the routes between them, well, it would be a case of planning as I cycled. I estimated that it would be about a week of cycling before I arrived in Tirana, so that would be perhaps six intermediate overnight stops, to which none had I yet given a second thought.

I checked out of the hotel feeling very refreshed and smelling just a little sweeter than I had done for quite a few days, found Reggie where I had left him in the underground garage, loaded the panniers and ambled into the centre of town for a coffee. Nafpaktos was a very pleasant seaside resort, the kind of place in which you could quite easily spend a week or so of your holidays and I guessed that that was exactly what the other tourists were doing. I seemed to be the only person who wasn't Greek. This was certainly the case in the main square, where I ordered a coffee and small cake and listened to the chatter that surrounded me. It was a lively Monday morning however, and not everyone had decided to start the week with a leisurely chat over a drink. The streets were busy with cars, vans and mopeds, and the pavements alive with people walking and talking either alongside a friend or colleague or at distance via a mobile phone. The town centre was much older than the strip of modern hotels of which the NAFS

59

Hotel had been just one, and above where I was sitting I could see the long walls of the 15th century Venetian castle that was mentioned in my guidebook. I smiled as I realised that it was probably the first time since arriving in Greece that I had read about something that was clearly very old without it being referred to as 'ancient'. Nafpaktos, as well as being in with a shot at winning the silliest-named town in Greece competition (I'm sure there are many other contenders), was the kind of place where I would have loved to spend a little more time – perhaps not a week but certainly a couple of hours – but as ever, I had lots of cycling to crack on with.

The municipal authorities in Nafpaktos had incorporated a network of cycle lanes – some of them even segregated – into their town centre and as I set off from the main square it was quite a novelty to be treated to such facilities in Greece. I had seen very few nods to cyclists so far on my travels in the country but here was a town that had clearly gone out of its way to welcome two-wheeled travellers just as much as motorised ones. Well, up to a point. Where the local council had seen an opportunity to hold out their arms to cyclists, the local population (and no doubt the tourists as well) had resolutely decided to give one long metaphorical finger to me and Reggie by parking their cars erratically along most of the red strips of cycle lane leading out of town. I was determined to persevere however, and weaved my way along the road, squeezing past the cars even in places where physical contact between Reggie's panniers and the parked cars was inevitable. I like to think I was making a point but my efforts were lost on all but a young pizza delivery driver who had parked his moped across a segregated portion of cycle path. I forced Reggie through the narrow gap between the moped and the segregating curb, lost my balance and ended up in the middle of a bicycle and moped sandwich at a 45 degree angle to the road. He ran over and pulled the ungainly pile of flesh and metal back to a vertical position, apologising as he did so. Well, I assumed he was apologising, as he was smiling while repositioning his moped back in the middle of the cycle lane. I think my point-making efforts may have been lost on him too. For the remainder of the route out of town, I resolved simply to ping my bell loudly at anyone in the process of manoeuvring their car anywhere near the cycle lanes. At least it made me feel better.

Between Nafpaktos and the bridge I was retracing my route from the previous evening. I stopped to take some more photographs of the world's longest multi-span, cable-stayed bridge (if it still doesn't sound that impressive, add the expressions 'earthquake-proof' and 'expanding' – as the Gulf of Corinth is expanding by 30mm per year –

and it does sound much better) and to work out a route. I looked at the map and my eye was drawn to the small coastal town of Mitikas, just to the north of an island called Kalamos. It attracted my attention because it was the first place along the coastline heading north that had both the symbol for a campsite – a small red triangle - and that of a hotel – a small red house. My preference was for the former but if that couldn't be found (or if it could be found but I didn't rate my chances of surviving a night under canvas in the place) I could always resort to the hotel option. I also noted from my Michelin map that much of the coastal road had a green edge. This meant that it would be scenic and, after the drab cycle from Olympia on the previous day, this was too good an option to turn down. I estimated a distance of around 100km and set off.

The one thing that I hadn't noticed from the map was that the motorway heading west along the coast from the Rio-Antirrio Bridge was actually not yet built. As a result, for the first 30km between the bridge and Mesolongi, it was a return to cycling alongside the very heavy traffic that I hadn't really seen since leaving Athens. Had the roads been as gloriously wide as they had been while cycling across the Peloponnese, this wouldn't have been so bad, but they weren't and I felt increasingly intimidated by the cars, lorries and coaches that thundered past me at high speed. I have already quoted the lamentable casualty statistics associated with the Greek roads; cycling along the coast to Mesolongi was providing me with all the evidence I needed to believe them. The driving habits of all but a small - very small - minority were appalling. Speeding (one guy drove past me doing at least 80 km/hr which wouldn't have been too bad if the motorway had yet been built but he was driving at the time through a 30 km/hr zone in town), overtaking habits, tailgating, using a mobile phone while driving (I've just checked and it is as illegal in Greece as it is in most other places) and not wearing a seatbelt were but a few frighteningly common bad habits noticed that morning. We know that Greece is running a large budget deficit; may I suggest that the government has a serious crackdown on bad drivers? It's a win-win solution as far as I can see. Either the driving will improve, or if it doesn't, at least the public finances will benefit from the imposition of fines and the massive income it would generate. My sympathies are most definitely with the Greek road safety minister but, then again, I suspect that Greece doesn't have a road safety minister. If it does, I would advise him or her to take a cycle along the coast from Nafpaktos to Mesolongi to experience life in the fast lane. Or perhaps just get on with building the motorway...

As I neared Mesolongi I was able to peel off from the main coastal road and, as some kind of celebration was required to mark my survival to that point, I headed for the centre of town. At a fork in the road, I was welcomed by a brightly painted green and orange bicycle that had been attached to a short post in the ground. Its tyres had been removed and, in place of pedals and a handlebar bag, it had flower pots in which red and pink geraniums were growing. As I made my way through the quiet streets towards the main square I noticed something that I hadn't seen in Greece before. There were people cycling. I'll say that again. People were cycling. Strangely, there were no cycling-related signs and, so far as I could see, there were no cycle lanes painted onto the road. But people were cycling. The contrast with my experiences back in Nafpaktos earlier in the day was extreme to say the very least. There, it was almost as if the local authorities had tried too hard to force cycling upon the town and as a result the local population had turned their backs on the activity. Here in Mesolongi, apart from the green and orange bicycle-cum-flower pot, there was no nod in the direction of cyclists, yet the locals were doing it as a matter of course. Discuss.

After Mesolongi, as the bit of the motorway that had been built headed north, and I continued west, the cycling was a delight. Having the morning's experiences still fresh in my mind clearly helped, but it had everything that your touring cyclist might want: a gently undulating topography with a few short challenging climbs thrown in for good measure, great coastal views across the southern Adriatic Sea, interesting encounters with humans and animals and a nice pile of ancient ruins. What more could I have asked for? The ruins were at Kalydon, where a 2nd century BC theatre had been discovered. Had a group of university archaeologists (are there any other types?) not been continuing to dig at the site under several large, green sheets of plastic that had been hoisted into the air to serve as protection from the early afternoon sun, I would probably not have noticed the site in the first place. The ruins were just to the right of the road and, as the gravel prevented me from doing anything else, I pushed Reggie down the slip road that connected them to the main highway. One young female archaeologist spoke English and she explained that they were concentrating that summer on the stage area of the theatre complex, much of the other work having been completed during previous digs in previous years. There was a clear distinction between the two groups of people doing the work: some were middle-aged men and they were doing the hard graft, the rest were much younger – students perhaps – or much older with spectacles, and I presumed these two sub-groups made up the archaeologists. They tended to have clipboards, measuring devices or hand-held computers. I watched the work continue for a few minutes and, having never seen such an activity at close hand before, found it fascinating. The only things missing were Harrison Ford, his Indiana Jones whip and a few Nazis. Perhaps they were at the top of the hill where a second group was working under another large, green tarpaulin sheet.

Of equal interest, but in a completely different way, were Isabelle and Samuel. Shortly after leaving the archaeological dig, I had cycled past a tractor that was towing a caravan in the opposite direction. Apart from their progress, which was almost as slow as my own on Reggie, I had thought nothing of it at the time. A few kilometres down the road however, I was on the look out for a garage as I needed to fill up my bottles, and I found one just over the crest of a hill. The garage itself was unremarkable apart from the fact that there were two people in their thirties sitting outside the large echoey café, keeping watch over two video cameras that had been set up on tripods. I assumed that they were travelling in the French-registered van that was parked just to one side. With my bottles filled with ice-cold water from the fridge, I lingered for a moment outside the garage, listening to the conversation between the two French filmmakers. I couldn't work out what they were filming so I asked them. We spoke in French and they introduced themselves as Isabelle and Samuel. They explained that they were working on a documentary for French public television, about two friends who had decided to travel from their home in the Jura region of France to Greece in order to donate a tractor to a group of Greek women. It was never clear why the women in Greece were in such desperate need of the tractor but what was clear was that the tractor in question was the one I had cycled past earlier. On board had been Daniel and Bernard who were making their way, slowly, to Olympia. The documentary would be called "*Une autre histoire vraie - L'amitié à 20 km/h*" or "*Another true story – friendship at 20km/hr*" and would tell the gentle story of the two retired Frenchmen's trip on a tractor through France, across Italy and down through Slovenia, Croatia, Montenegro, Albania and Greece. Hang on! That was my route. I used the opportunity to quiz them about Albania. *Did they feel safe? Had they found accommodation easily? What were the roads like?* Most of their answers were reassuring, although they did allude to an incident in a coastal town where there had been issues with a group of local men. It wasn't the kind of answer that I wanted to hear, so I quickly moved to other, more important issues such as the weather. I did think that they might have wanted to film me as I cycled off in the direction of Mitikas, but they chose not to. Another traveller moving at around 20 km/hr (on the flat with a favourable wind), albeit on a bicycle and in the opposite direction, might have made a nice contrast to the two Frenchmen on their tractor, but that clearly wasn't the case. Perhaps that's why I'm writing a book and not editing a documentary.

Until my arrival in Mitikas, the remainder of my encounters were just with the goats and a herd of cattle that had chosen to spend their time wandering aimlessly along the Greek roads. Had they not seen the statistics? It struck me how much the goats smelled of goat's cheese. This isn't meant to be a stupid comment, but it did keep me thinking for a while as the road moved away from sea level to a much higher position along the cliffs in the final 30km of the day. Cheese from cows doesn't smell like cows so why does cheese from goats smell like goats? I didn't work out an answer to my question and it was soon forgotten as I paused to take in the views across the island-dotted ocean that spanned across the horizon beneath the late afternoon sun. In the foreground were circular fishing pens set out in neat rows of about ten. Large, square, red covers had been placed over a few of the pens and the whole arrangement was organised within an invisible lattice marked out by numerous buoys. I have no idea what the catch would be but it was certainly a well-organised one.

The French TV couple had reassured me about the existence of numerous campsites in Mitikas, but I only found one and it took some finding. It was run by a man who you wouldn't want within a hundred metres of your children and the majority of the other guests seemed to be there for the long haul rather than just an overnight stay. A few of them were gathered around the owner, playing cards and drinking shots, when I arrived; they were still there some hours later after my foray into the town centre to find something to eat. I erected the tent in the middle of a patch of scrubland that passed as the area set aside for tents, but near enough to a lamppost so that I could secure Reggie overnight and keep an eye on him at the same time. For the first time since arriving in Greece, I felt uncomfortable about my own personal security. The campsite was sufficiently quiet not to have immediate neighbours, but those that I did have were better kept at a safe distance. Two girls who were sharing a tent nearby spent most of their time speaking aggressively into their mobiles and when they weren't using them to communicate, the phones were put into service as tinny speakers for alarmingly loud music. It's amazing how quickly you can build up an entire life story for people by simply spending a few moments observing them from a distance. For all I knew, they could have been post-doctoral archaeological fellows who had just had a bad day at the local temple and needed to unwind. I doubted it however. On the other side of my tent, in a caravan-tent complex that had seen better days, was a large family. The children spent most of their time staring at me eerily. Perhaps they were doing the same thing and making wildly inaccurate assumptions about me. It was all very different from the previous night spent at the boutique hotel back in Nafpaktos.

Tuesday 9ᵗʰ July 2013
Cycling Day 7: Mitikas to Kanali, 67km

Despite the dodgy owner, dubious fellow campers and decidedly downmarket facilities at the campsite in Mitikas, I slept well. It was the first night of more or less continuous sleep in the tent and worthy of some minor rejoicing. Reggie was still where I had secured him to the lamppost and better still, when I returned to the same shower cubicle that I had used upon arrival the previous evening, the €2.50 that I had inadvertently left on the shelf and had forgotten about was still there. Perhaps this place had redeeming features after all.

I am most definitely a morning person and never more so than when travelling by bike. Setting off without a care in the world and in the general direction of where I needed to be heading, without worrying too much about the final destination or where I would be sleeping that evening was wonderful. I felt like this on most mornings and cycling the three or four hours before the clock hit midday was by far the best part of most days. After lunch I would start to concern myself with the important business of making a final decision about the destination for the day and then the accommodation situation would start to play on my mind, but the morning was generally a stress-free cycle with my mind full of positive thoughts. I am also an unashamed optimist and leaving a place like the horrible campsite in Mitikas could mean only one thing: the next destination would be much better.

That said, on that morning of the 9ᵗʰ July I did have an interim destination in mind. It was the coastal town of Paleros, about 18km north of Mitikas, where I had arranged to meet fellow cyclist Ed Cox. Ed had contacted me back in the summer of 2012 after having read about my cycle from southern England to southern Italy. He too was planning a cycling odyssey but had no plans to stop when he arrived in Italy; his plan was to cycle from his home in Bristol to Brisbane, Australia.

Now I hate to shatter any illusions that you may have, but when it comes to long-distance cycling, I'm probably some way down the Championship table (at times hovering around the relegation zone). The Premier League of long-distance cycling must surely be reserved for those who have cycled to the other side of the planet, and I suppose the Manchester Uniteds and Chelseas of the epic cycling fraternity are those who continue cycling in order to finish back at the point where they started. In 2008 Mark Beaumont made his name by breaking the record for such a cycle. He set off from Paris in early August 2007 and 195 days later was back celebrating under the *Arc de Triomphe*. His subsequent television documentary and book popularised the idea of circumnavigating the globe on two wheels, but he wasn't the first to do so. In his book *The Man Who Cycled The World*, Beaumont sums up the situation prior to his own attempt as follows:

"I was amazed to discover how many people had cycled around the world by different routes and distances. But only a few had gone for the Fastest True Circumnavigation of the Globe by bicycle. An Englishman called Steve Strange held the record, at 276 days."

Following Mark Beaumont's smashing of the record, it has been broken several times and (why do they always do this when something becomes popular?) the rules have changed. The current record holder is a chap called Alan Bate. Under the old rules he cycled around the world in 106 days (that's excluding 'transit time' i.e. the time it takes you to fly from the edge of one continent to the start of the next one), which is simply astonishing. If you fancy breaking a cycling-related world record incidentally, you may find it easier to attempt one of these (genuine) records: the longest distance cycling backwards on a unicycle (109.4km), the longest distance cycling underwater without oxygen (67.6m, with oxygen it's 3.04km), or (and this one is my favourite) the longest distance cycled in one hour without using your hands (37.4km).

When it comes to cycling to the other side of the world however, I admire those who do it with a bit of panache. In 2010, Oli Broom, a former chartered surveyor from Berkshire, cycled from London to Brisbane with a cricket bat in order to watch the match being played there between Australia and England. He subsequently wrote about the adventure in his book *Cycling To The Ashes*. Ed Cox, my contact in Paleros, was also en route to Brisbane but his reward would be meeting up with his girlfriend who had secured a job setting up a laboratory in the city. His plan was to arrive in Australia in March 2014 (which he did), so he was in no rush. We met in a bar by the sea and chatted about our respective journeys so far: his journey south had followed quite closely my own 2010 trip, but whereas when I arrived in Brindisi I headed home on the plane, he had caught the ferry and arrived in Igoumenista in northern Greece. This was a pity for me as I wasn't able to ask him about cycling through Albania. Before the end of the week, I would be passing over the border from Greece but as yet I still knew very little about what would await me. On his beautiful, albeit expensive, bespoke Roberts bike (I admit it, I was jealous!), he would soon be setting off in an easterly direction towards Thessaloniki, before his onward journey through the southern former Soviet republics of Georgia and Azerbaijan and then Iran, but not before he had spent a few more days relaxing with some former colleagues at a nearby sailing resort complex where he had once worked. One thing he did tell me, however, was that I would have to think carefully about cycling to Preveza, a town some 30km north of Paleros, as it was inaccessible by bike via the coastal road due to a toll tunnel for motorised vehicles only. This wasn't good news, as the only alternative would be to cycle around the shore of the Ambracian Gulf, which I estimated to be a potential 100km detour. Ed had managed to hitch a lift with his bike through the tunnel and I reckoned this strategy to be worth a try. Even if it took me a couple of hours to find someone who was willing and (more crucially) had the space for a bicycle, it would be quicker than a long slog around the gulf.

We bade our farewells and set off in our opposite directions. The cycle towards the tunnel continued to be a flat one and I was able to knock off the 35km in quick time. The roads were quiet but for the first time this was a little worrying. If I wanted to hitch a lift at the tunnel entrance, then a steady flow of traffic would be to my advantage. Or perhaps not. Would a stranded, forlorn, solo cyclist pull the heart strings of the passing Greeks?

On arrival at the wide expanse of concrete that fanned out to accommodate the row of tollbooths – half of which were closed – I parked Reggie in a prominent position by the bus shelter. Had the tollbooths been on the other side of the tunnel I would probably have risked cycling through the tunnel and playing the 'stupid tourist' card at the other end. I might have been given a ticking off in Greek, but was there anything else they could have done? Unfortunately (or perhaps fortunately), that wasn't an option that was open to me. I examined the information on the wall of the bus shelter but couldn't really work out if a bus was due or not. No one else was waiting and the shelter itself didn't look as though it had seen much action in recent times, certainly not of the people-standing-and-shuffling-on-the-spot kind, as much of it was overgrown and the notices were a little dated to say the least. I turned my attention to the passing motorists and started to identify likely candidates who might be able to accommodate Reggie and me. In effect this meant trucks, lorries or large 'people carrier' cars. The traffic wasn't that heavy – perhaps a couple of vehicles per minute – and a few choice candidates just drove by without stopping. Bastards. Then, after around an hour of trying to look like the normal person I was (as opposed to the I'm-going-to-do-something-nasty-to-you-in-the-back-of-your-van type), a Volkswagen van passed and then braked.

I pushed Reggie towards the passenger door and a cheery fellow in his 50s asked where I was going. He turned out to be George, a German and, usefully for me, the back of his Volkswagen Passat was completely empty apart from a bed that was made up on the back seat. I avoided thinking too much about why George should have a bed in the back of his van, as there was ample room for Reggie to stand, fully-panniered, in the area between the back seats / bed and George and me in the front.

Considering that the journey from the toll booths through the tunnel and along the road on the other side to a suitable drop off point was only a matter of five minutes, George and I had a good and surprisingly diverse conversation. He explained how he spent half the year in Greece and the other six months back in Germany, and today he was en route to pick up his son who was arriving for a holiday. George knew his local history and explained that the sea above our heads had been the place of a great battle involving Antony and Cleopatra. At that point I suddenly had images of Elizabeth Taylor and Richard Burton in my mind, bobbing about on the ocean trying to look glamorous. (Go on, admit it; you did too. For those of you who are interested and who probably didn't have images of Taylor and Burton in mind, it was the Battle of Actium that had taken place in the Ambracian Gulf in 31BC and Antony and Cleopatra were, sadly for them, defeated. I bet they still looked glamorous however.) George deposited me at a junction just to the north of the tunnel. He was keen to take me further, but mindful that I was on a cycling, not a camper-van adventure, I alighted just opposite a Peugeot car dealership and thanked George profusely for his generosity.

I knew that I didn't have much further to cycle if I was to make it to a campsite that Ed had suggested earlier in the day, but after having been in George's van-cum-bedroom for five minutes I was a little disorientated. I needed to consult my online map, which gave me much more detail than the paper one clipped to Reggie's handlebars, but in order to do that successfully I needed some shade, so I made my way to the thin strip of shadow generated by the overhanging roof of the Peugeot garage. Shadow was often an elusive thing to find in southern Europe. Trees were usually my best option but car dealerships came a close second. No sooner had I started peering at my iPhone, than I heard a voice that was clearly being directed towards me;

"You want water? We have water! Come inside, come inside..."

"Effra... Thank-you." I still hadn't mastered the pronunciation of the Greek for 'thank-you' and with only a couple more days' cycling in Greece, it didn't seem worth the effort of trying to remember it now.

"My name is Dimitris and this is my son Dino."

I didn't think it was necessary to point out that I wasn't interested in buying a new Peugeot, but was happy to explain that I was travelling north towards Albania, at which point Dimitris guided me over to two panels that had been set up on a stand on the other side of the showroom next to a large BMW motorbike.

"In 2008 I travelled to Aqaba in Jordan on my motorbike and then in 2012 I went to Iran. Each trip took me four weeks."

I looked at the maps on the panels which marked out his route from Preveza to the east through Turkey, Syria, Lebanon and Jordan and then in 2012 through Iran. I sensed that this white-haired, middle-aged man saw in me a kindred traveller and I reciprocated with a short summary of my own travels. Dino, his son, then joined the conversation:

"Have you done much travelling?" I asked

"A little, but not much. I have just finished studying civil engineering at university and I would like to go to England to study for a masters."

"Do you sell many new cars?"

"Only two or three a month but we sell more Vespas and quite a few bicycles."

"Is that because of the economic problems or because people care more about the environment?"

"Probably both. Most of our profits come from the bikes and mopeds."

Dino then ushered me towards a section of the showroom dedicated to bikes, cycling equipment and clothing. It was all presented in the spotless, oil-free way that only a modern car dealership could manage and was a million miles from the bike shops I was accustomed to back home. Had I been at the end of the first month of cycling, I may have been tempted to get out the credit card, but as this was only the middle of the second week, nothing had yet fallen off Reggie or been worn out by me. I picked up and admired a few gleaming items before carefully placing them back where they belonged. I couldn't help but imagine that although the profits came from the sales of bikes, this father and son outfit would much prefer if they sold a few more 208s as well.

Dimitris was eager that the water was as cold as possible and he gave me mineral water from his fridge. I could really have done with a pit stop like this every 50km as I cycled along the Mediterranean coast; not only were Dimitris and Dino interesting company, they worked in a wonderfully air-conditioned environment and were able to supply me with fresh, cool water. Just before I left, I showed them how to track my progress on my website. Dimitris was especially interested and I suspected that I may have sparked thoughts of another adventure in his mind. Perhaps even on one of his pristine bicycles.

The day was turning into a bit of a chat show; first there had been Ed, then the French filmmakers, then German George and now Dimitris and Dino. I needed to crack on, so bid farewell to the Letsios' family and continued my journey north to my final destination: Kanali. Ed hadn't given me the same of a site, just the knowledge that there was one, so when I reached *Camping Panorama* I thought I had arrived. Unfortunately they didn't have a restaurant and as the town itself was still some three kilometres further down the road, I continued cycling. Next up was *Camping Monolithi*, which looked much more promising. I waited for a few minutes at the reception area and yes, there was a restaurant and even better, it would be opening later. I had run out of cash so I asked if I could pay by card. '*No.*' It was going so well... There was, however, a cash machine in town, so I had little choice but to cycle an extra few kilometres to find some euros.

Once back at the site with my tent erected, I headed for the bar-restaurant. I was the only customer and service came without a smile from a young woman who looked as though she wouldn't scrimp on portions and that was certainly the case. I was delivered an enormous heap of energy-giving spaghetti carbonara that I devoured in a manner only suitable for deserted restaurants and washed the whole thing down with a couple of large beers.

Given the time afforded me while I ate my way through the carbonara and given the emotional nudge of a drop of alcohol, I spent most of the rest of the evening thinking about Albania. Just as the sun was setting, I crossed the road in front of the campsite and onto the beach empty of people but full of parasols and chairs, to record a short video:

"It's about 9 o'clock on Tuesday evening: I'm getting towards the end of the Greece parts of the journey and increasingly I'm thinking about Albania. Not sure exactly what to think about Albania. It'll be two or three nights in the country, hopefully one of those nights in Tirana and I've got a contact in Tirana to see, but apart from that it's

the mysterious part of the journey, it's the bit that... I'm looking forward to it but it's certainly the bit which is the most... intriguing, the bit that I don't know anything about... really everything will be new. I've no images in my mind as to what Albania will be like. It'll be interesting to find out... Today is Tuesday so I should be there hopefully at some point on Thursday and then to Montenegro by the end of the weekend... hopefully."

Wednesday 10th July 2013
Cycling Day 8: Kanali to Ioannina, 97km

Sitting in the old man's café just down the road from *Camping Monolithi* at 8am, I wasn't sure which way to go. I had escaped the campsite a little earlier after having spent a second consecutive comfortable night in the tent. For some reason the air immediately next to the coast in Kanali had been much cooler than it had been on previous nights in the tent. I suppose I was forgetting that 'weather' didn't just exist in the changeable climatic conditions of Britain; it also existed in places like Greece. It was just that in the summer, or certainly during the nearly two weeks that I had experienced so far, 'changeable' was not a word that would be used to describe the weather. Apart from the brief and torrential rainstorm that I had experienced in Olympia, it had been blue skies ever since my arrival in Athens and the nights had been stickily warm. The night in Kanali had been the first that could be described as 'comfortable', albeit not 'cool'. Such meteorological musings weren't helping me come to a decision as to which direction to take in my cycle towards Albania however. There were two possibilities. The first one would involve sticking to the coastal road and crossing the border between the Greek town of Skala and the Albanian town of Konispol. On my Michelin map they were linked by a very thin purple (or was it red?) line which the key told me was a '*carriageway*' in English, but a '*chemin carrossable*' in French. (Incidentally, if the line was red, I would need to take a ferry and that, in the circumstances, seemed unlikely.) It was the use of the French word '*chemin*' which worried me. It means '*path*' and didn't exactly fill me with confidence that I would be able to cross an international frontier by following it. Following the border north of Konispol, the next crossing point indicated on my map was at a place called Kakavi, and to get there would require me to cycle away from the coast towards a large town called Ioannina. This second option seemed the better one to choose and so it was that after finishing my coffee with the old men, I cycled north out of Kanali and made a right turn in the direction of Ioannina.

I paused for breakfast in a small town called Louros and sat on the steps of the patisserie watching the trucks and cars hurtle past me. There was another unfinished motorway marked on my map (this time I spotted it before I wasn't able to find it), and resigned myself to another morning of sharing the road with some heavy traffic. I searched on the map for some indication as to how high in the mountains I would have to climb to arrive in Ioannina. My heart jumped a beat when I saw 2014 written in red – that would be a climb more strenuous than even the Peloponnese en route to Levidi – but then I relaxed as I realised that 2014 was referring to the date of completion of the motorway. A little more scrutiny revealed that my destination was only at an elevation of 500m. That said, the first few hours of cycling were very flat. I sensed that I was making some progress vertically but only because, when I turned around to look at where I had come from, I was looking down, rather than up, a valley. In the distance I could see the challenging climbs to come however, and they gradually started to kick in during the latter part of the morning.

The scenery was very different from anything that I had seen so far. It was reminiscent of the lower Alps: very green with the occasional outcrop of white rock and buildings only very sparsely scattered around the valleys. Whereas in more southerly regions of Greece the land had been predominantly uncovered by any kind of vegetation, here in the north it was abundant. When the ascent did start, it was fairly abrupt; unlike in the Alps (or indeed in the Peloponnese), the road seemed to take a straight route up the mountainside rather than following the contours of the land to create switchbacks. At its steepest, I was climbing about 100m vertically for every 2km horizontally, which gave a gradient of around 5%. Not quite *'hors catégorie'* but halfway there, and over a distance of nearly 10km, I began to feel the pain in my legs, especially my right knee, and more worryingly in my lower back. I dismounted Reggie (who seemed to be coping just fine) on numerous occasions to allow my body to recover a little, but also to take in the views down the valley, which by this point had become nothing less than stupendous.

It was just a pity that the places I chose to pause – predominantly large lay-bys where people travelling by car had stopped to do the same thing as me – were strewn with litter. To be fair to the lay-bys, it wasn't just there that refuse had been dropped. Since the start of my cycle in Sounio I had been surprised, at times shocked, by the amount of detritus discarded by people travelling along the roads. Most of my cycling had been through the middle of two bands of garbage, one on either side of the road. At places in the mountains where people had the chance to stop their cars, get out and wander around, the problem had become ten times worse and it was depressing to contrast the spectacular background vista of mountain and vegetation with the foreground carpet of litter that had been left by passing human beings. It is bad enough seeing the urban landscapes of London, Lyon or

Lisbon strewn with litter; seeing the same thing in a fundamentally natural environment was tragic. Many countries, including my own, suffer from a chronic problem of littering but Greece seemed to have taken the art to a whole new level.

I finally breached the final mountain pass (at just over 600m) about twenty kilometres from my destination, Ioannina. I was initially rewarded with a pedal-free descent for about ten minutes, but the road soon levelled off to give me the remainder of the cycle on the flat. I was expecting Ioannina to be an isolated lakeside paradise in the mountains, but I had underestimated its importance big time. It announced itself first with a brand new IKEA store some way out of town. Then followed about half a kilometre of mainly newly built car franchises, most of which were packed full of brand new, polished cars. *Crisis? What crisis?* I was beginning to wonder whether Ioannina was a town immune from the economic downturn afflicting the rest of the country. It didn't stop at the outskirts of town as next up was a freshly constructed – it looked as though it had been finished only a few days previously – six-lane highway leading into the centre of the town. Although not quite as new as the car dealerships, businesses appeared to be booming along this strip of commercialisation. I began to wonder if the town was profiting from its position as a gateway to the Balkans. Whether or not this was the case, it was a certainly a place that was loud and proud of itself in a way that other Greek towns I had passed through hadn't been.

There was a large blue sign on the edge of Ioannina proclaiming a welcome to *'the town of silver art creators'*. I wasn't exactly sure what that referred to but I reckoned that when I went for a wander around the town later in the day its meaning might become much clearer. As I approached the heart of the town the road led me towards the castle on the edge of the lake. I avoided going inside, preferring instead to sort out my camping arrangements. I knew from the map and my guidebook that there was a campsite on the shores of the lake – *Camping Limnopoula* – for which I had high hopes. In my mind I had images of the pristine campsites in Switzerland where I had stayed over the years, either as a campsite courier for a British camping company in the 1990s, or more recently during my trip along the Eurovelo 5 in 2010. I followed the signposts that were distributed along a run-down strip of very un-Swiss-like shops, bars and casinos, before being directed to turn right behind a petrol station. By this point my hopes had been all but shattered. How could I possibly find an idyllic campsite here?

At the end of the path was a three-storey, white, chalet-style building. Perhaps there was some hope after all. In front of the building was a large expanse of car park but there were very few vehicles. I was the only person around, and it didn't look as though anyone was manning the reception area despite the times written on the door indicating that there should have been, so I crossed the car park towards the lake. The view was idyllic. What a contrast with the urban strip of road I had been cycling along only a few minutes previously. I sat on the ground and gazed at the mountains on the other side of the lake while listening the choppy waters of the lake splosh against the concrete edge of the car park. It was a very nice way to end a strenuous afternoon in the saddle.

I may have dozed for a while, I can't quite remember, but I do remember that when I came to erect the tent, there was still nobody at the campsite reception. The camping area of the site was very quiet so I surmised that it wouldn't be a problem for me to erect my tent before having formally checked in. The other people on site were mainly travelling in camper vans and I could see from the registration plates that they were predominantly from either The Netherlands or Scandinavia. As I was fiddling with the poles on my tent a young woman approached me. She was from Denmark and her young son, who was perhaps eight years old, had a question.

"My son wants to know if you are you an Olympic athlete?" she asked on his behalf.

My temptation was to say *"yes"* but then I figured that when she saw me hobbling on my dodgy knee and holding my lower back like a character from *Dad's Army* she may see through my pretence.

"I'm sorry, I'm not. I'm just an ordinary cyclist", I replied trying a bit too hard to be self-deprecating.

"Why does he think that?" I enquired.

"Because you are wearing a London 2012 ribbon around your neck. He thinks it is a medal."

I smiled broadly before explaining that the ribbon was the one I used to hold my accreditation badge while working as a volunteer at the London Olympics. I was using it to hang the key to Reggie's lock around my neck so as not to lose it. Could life get much better? Not only had I found a wonderfully peaceful campsite in a spectacular setting on the shores of a lake in the mountains, but now the other campers (well, one Danish boy) were under the impression that I was an Olympic medal winner. Who needs Switzerland when you can get all that in Greece?

Shortly after I had finished putting up the tent it started to rain, so I made my way back to shelter under the roof of the reception building. To my delight it was now open, so I went in and apologised for having put up my tent before seeking the approval of the owners but... The man behind the counter just stared at me.

"Fill in this form."

"Look my friend, I have just been mistaken for a medal winner at the London Olympics..." I thought, but didn't say. It's a long time since I have worked in a customer service industry and, admittedly, when I did someone once filled in the *'any other comments'* section on a feedback form with the words *'miserable bastard',* but even I know that a smile doesn't go amiss if you are working on a reception desk. You smile at me, I at least have the impression that you are glad to see me, I smile back and pay over my hard-earned cash, you say *'thank-you'* and smile again, I walk away with the impression that you are a nice person even though that's not necessarily the case, I fill in an online form to say your hotel / restaurant / campsite is wonderful, you get more customers as a result, your boss loves you, you keep your job. No? Miserable bastard.

The woman who served me in the Tomouselimi Café later that afternoon couldn't have been more different. Despite the fact that I only drank one €2 coffee in her delightful establishment in the *Kastro*, the walled old part of town that jutted out into Lake Pamvotis, she smiled and was happy to answer my questions about her café and about the town in general. At other times of the year, she explained, it was a thriving university town with some 20,000 students famed for its Ottoman mosques and once home to Ali Pasha, the *'Lion of Ionannina'*. He was a Muslim Albanian who fought against the Ottomans in the 18th century. Our old friend Lord Byron met Ali in the early 19th century and was suitably inspired by the event to write about him in his poem *Childe Harold*. He ended his days by being ambushed, shot and decapitated by the Ottomans. Ali, that is, rather than Georgie Byron who, rather prosaically, died from a catching a cold.

I'm not sure how Ali Pasha, or indeed Lord Byron, spent his final nights in Greece (although the latter's doctors seemed insistent upon draining him of his blood, which I dare say had a significant impact upon his demise), but my final evening in the country during this trip was spent eating pizza at a very pleasant lakeside restaurant while quaffing a bottle of the local wine. I was still trying to blank out the thought of cycling through Albania and the alcohol helped immeasurably. As for Greece, it had been a fascinating trek through the parts of the country that most other people probably don't get to see. Apart from Athens, and perhaps Olympia, I had crawled my way north without having seen anything that would be familiar to a fan of the film *Mamma Mia*. I had met some wonderfully generous and kind people, seen some magnificent sights and enjoyed some fabulous and surprisingly challenging cycling. But no pristine whitewashed houses framed against the backdrop of a deep blue sea. As my mind turned to the journey north through Albania, Montenegro, Croatia, Bosnia and Slovenia, I wondered what people, places and surprises were yet in store for Reggie and me.

PART TWO: ALBANIA
Thursday 11th July 2013
Cycling Day 9: Ioannina to Saranda, 107km

I woke up on that final morning in Greece to the most magnificent sight. As I pulled open the flap of the tent (which I had purposefully erected to point in the direction of the lake and the mountains beyond), a most wonderful vista of morning tranquillity was revealed. The grass was bright green and slightly damp in the dew, the foliage of the trees was equally vibrant and a mist hung over the pristine lake that was gently lapping against the shore just a few metres away from where I was lying. I could hear the calls and oars of early morning rowers on the lake – they were presumably making the most of the opportunity to practise during the coolest part of the day – and in the far distance were the occasional squawks of wide-winged predatory birds. A few kilometres away, the mountains rose out of the water on the other side of the lake but with most of their detail masked by the mist apart from the fine line that distinguished their dull green and brown slopes from the cloudless blue sky. The whole of the scene was drenched in bright morning sunlight. Beautiful, just beautiful.

Had I not promised myself that I would be ticking off the first of my ten countries later that day I would have been perfectly content to sit and watch Lake Pamvotida all day. I think that was what most of my neighbours were spending a few days doing and I could certainly see the attraction. There are strong arguments that travel broadens the mind, but there are also pretty persuasive ones that dictate that from time to time you should just stop and stare. Here in Ioannina, I had found good evidence for doing just that.

I moved from being horizontal in the tent to a vertical position on the grass and stretched in a way that only campers (and some wild animals) will appreciate. The tent itself, just like the grass, was very damp so I unpegged it from the ground and dragged it over to a nearby strip of concrete that was already bone dry. I also released Reggie from his overnight position tethered to a tree, wheeled him onto the concrete, crouched low on the floor and took a photograph of him silhouetted against the sun. He had rarely looked better. His mechanicals were also in fine form, having survived the roads of Greece without any issues whatsoever. The mishap with the Presta valve back at Athens airport was beginning to be forgotten.

Leaving Reggie to guard the drying tent, I packed everything else away and wandered over to the reception area to see if they sold anything for breakfast. They did, but it was limited to processed croissants in cellophane packaging. Not that this prevented me from buying a couple and munching through them as I returned to complete the process of loading everything back onto Reggie for the cycle towards the Albanian border. Everything was done at a slow speed as it was a delight to 'work' in the warmth of the morning sun and I was in no particular rush. Eventually I was ready to depart and pushed the bike back towards the area in front of the chalet-like building at the entrance. In the middle of the car park was a large tree around which had been built a low wall. Sitting on the wall was a cyclist. His lycra shirt contained most of the colours of the rainbow and on his head he was wearing a baseball cap turned so that it faced backwards. I nodded in his direction and exchanged greetings with him;

"Are you going far?" I enquired. It was a bit of a silly question, as next to him was not only his bicycle but also his trailer, piled high with equipment.

"That's a bit of a silly question," he would have been perfectly entitled to reply but fortunately didn't.

"I am going east in the direction of Thessaloniki," he did reply and I detected an accent.

"Are you French?"

"Yes, my name is Jean-François and I'm from Brest."

It turned out that Jean-François was not just cycling across Greece but cycling around the whole of Europe, an adventure that was going to last some seven months and take in most of the continent's countries. He had set off from western France in April and was following a route that would guide him along most of the edges of the continent, both the sea borders and the land borders. He was about 50 years old and had taken a break from being a cycle courier in his hometown in Brittany. It was quite some feat he was attempting and made my own little jaunt across the continent resemble *Les Vacances de Monsieur Hulot*. If Ed Cox and his cycle to Brisbane had been in the Premier League of long-distance cycling, Jean-François Le Strat was certainly leading the Championship.

We chatted about our respective routes but again, as when I had exchanged experiences with Ed earlier in the week, Jean-François wasn't able to offer advice about Albania, for he too had taken the ferry from Brindisi in Italy to Igoumenitsa in Greece. I was so desperate for some recent first-hand knowledge of cycling through the country that still remained a mystery to me. I would simply have to find out for myself later that day. Jean-François was just as keen as I was on keeping tracks of where he was cycling, but instead of investing in some light-weight computer equipment (I had an iPhone and a mini iPad, both of which could easily fit into the pockets of one of the small panniers), he had brought with him his relatively bulky laptop computer. I was beginning to see why he needed the trailer that was attached to the back of his bike. (Indeed the comparison between my efforts to travel light and his less successful ones, was something that Jean-François later commented upon on his own blog: *'Il roule plus léger que moi!'*) He insisted upon showing me the exact route that he had taken and the myriad of statistics with which his Strava GPS track was able to furnish him. It is truly amazing to consider how much data is now available to your average cyclist as he or she goes about their daily commute, or in the case of Jean-François and myself, our continental journeys. Until relatively recently, this information was the preserve of the military or very well financed sporting teams in money-drenched Formula 1. Now it's cheaply accessible to almost anyone who wants it. It's just as amazing how little interest it is possible to have in someone else's statistics. I nodded and smiled without taking in much of what Jean-François was telling me:

"...elevation... moving time... calories... cadence... cuddly toy..."

I activated my own iPhone GPS tracking app at the gates of *Camping Limnopoula* with a promise to myself to use the data only sparingly in conversation should an opportunity arise. I consulted my (paper) map and estimated that it would be a cycle of around 60km to a place called Kalpaki, at which point I would turn left and cycle for another 30km to the border with Albania. From the border it would be a gentle ride back down to the coast at Saranda, where I would be looking for a hotel having long since given up much hope of finding many, if any, campsites in Albania.

The final few hours of cycling in Greece were spectacular as I climbed higher into the mountains. I was travelling through extremely remote and wonderfully verdant countryside. Even the campsite in Ioannina was busy compared to the isolation I was feeling as I moved closer and closer to country number two on my list. I paused at a bakery that I found in a town about half way between Ioannina and Kalpaki and fell into a conversation of sorts with a man who turned out to be Albanian. He spoke no English and I spoke no Albanian or Greek – he was fluent in both – but we somehow managed to communicate the fact that he had lived in Greece for 25 years and that I now needed to turn left towards the border with Albania.

'*No, no...*' I insisted while pointing straight ahead.

'*No, no...*' he retorted while pointing down a road branching off to the left.

I smiled and thanked him for his useless insistence that I turn left. I knew that I needed to arrive in Kalpaki before considering turning off the main road. That's what my paper map said, although it wasn't something I could confirm via an electronic map as there was no 3G signal available to me in the remote mountainous area. But something wasn't right. There was something about the road itself, which, as I cycled out of town, degenerated somewhat. It was still very much a proper road and there were no issues with cycling along it, but it had suddenly been downgraded significantly. In addition, the traffic that there was along the road had more or less stopped, and most cars and lorries were turning along the road indicated by my Albanian friend. I asked a passing pedestrian the direction to Kalpaki by simply saying the name of the town and proffering my hand in the two possible directions.

"*Here Kalpaki,*" she said while pointing to the floor. What? I was in Kalpaki already? Surely not!

There are times when, for some unknown reason, you take on board a fact and never question its validity. '*Crime is rising*' (no it isn't), '*GCSEs are easier than O levels*' (no they aren't), '*Kalpaki is 60km from Ioannina*' (err... no it isn't). All morning in my mind I had been cycling towards a town that was 60km away when in fact it was a mere 30km away. I must have seen signs along the road that told me that, or at least hinted at that, but I had clearly chosen to ignore them. I was indeed standing in Kalpaki and the Albanian had indeed been correct. Why did I have the temerity to think otherwise? An Albanian who had lived for the past 25 years in Greece would surely be someone who knew the direction to the border.

I doubled back and, rather sheepishly, turned along the road towards the border, the road that the Albanian chap had told me I should be following. He was still sitting outside the bakery and I couldn't help but glance towards him. He smiled and waved. I have no idea what the Albanian word for 'idiot' is, but I'm sure he was thinking it.

In those last couple of hours of cycling in Greece, my mind wandered between the fear of entering the unknown and the occasional distractions that I found along the way: reminders of fighting from the early 1940s with the word '*Οχι*' (Greek for 'no' and a message to approaching Italian forces) still visible in big letters on the side of one of the valleys, a modern fighter jet parked by the side of the road on an embankment with its long pointy nose, complete with even longer, spear-like radio antenna jutting out above the heads of any passing road user, and the idyllic Lake Zaravina which, according to the information boards along its shore had been puzzling travellers for centuries:

"Holland, a physicist and a doctor that passed by the lake just before 1820, reported flammable gas released through a hole in the ground... [a] passerby reported dark stones that smelled of petroleum or tar and that burned when placed in fire."

Had I stopped reading there a shiver may have passed along my spine but I continued and was informed that *"in the eyes of modern scientists"* the stuff about flaming gas and burning stones was complete tosh (although it took a couple of paragraphs to explain why).

Finally, after a welcome few kilometres of freewheeling downhill, I climbed a kilometre or so to the border crossing. From a distance, the small cluster of modern buildings looked like a shopping centre and to a certain extent that was what they were, as there were opportunities to be deprived of your last euros or first leke – the Albanian currency – on either side of the border. But above all this was a proper border crossing, the kind of which is increasingly rare in our Schengenised continent. I had visited the town of Schengen during my 2010 cycle to southern Italy, a place where Luxembourg melts into France and Germany almost seamlessly, but here in one of the further reaches of the Schengen area there were no such informalities. My passport was checked first by the Greeks then, after a short cycle through no man's land, by the Albanians. All this will no doubt be swept away when, as it inevitably will, Albania joins the European Union, but for the time being I gloried in the rare opportunity to feel as though I was a proper international traveller.

Greece had now ended and Albania had started. A large, white signed proclaimed *"Miresevini ne Shqiperi"* which was usefully translated underneath to *"Welcome to Albania"* and just past the border buildings themselves was a semi-circle of what appeared to be closed shops and money exchange outfits. To the right was a large metal communications tower – there were no problems with the 3G signal here – and a fenced-off car park with vehicles that had seen better days. Many of those days I guessed had been in the 1970s.

I cycled a short distance away from the border to a point where the road curved to my left and I was able to look down upon a long valley with a wide plain at its bottom. I pulled on the brakes and dismounted to take in the view and to work out my bearings. The first thing that I noticed was how abruptly the landscape itself had changed. Gone were the valleys of deeply wooded slopes; this land had been stripped bare of almost anything that could be used for fuel on a fire, or so it seemed. It was possible to follow the line of the border behind me, as it was the point where the trees were no longer standing. I aligned my map of Greece with the line of the border running north to south and it too reflected the fact that vegetation was abundant to the east – it was shaded green – but there was very little to the west where, apart from a few isolated patches of green, the map was white.

Not that my map would continue to be of use for much longer. I was about to hit the edge of the paper and having forgotten to purchase a map of Albania before I left home, I was now reliant upon the far less detailed black and white maps contained within the Bradt guide to Albania that I *did* have with me. The journey from the border into the valley before me, over the mountain on the other side, and then down towards the coast at Saranda would be about 30km. I remounted Reggie and took the plunge, freewheeling around the curve in the road and towards the flat valley bottom.

I would eventually become accustomed to experiencing regular changes in the style of the road paraphernalia around me, but this was the first of those changes: different signs, different fonts, different markings on the road. Within a few minutes I was cycling along the flat, wondering at which point to turn and once again head out of the valley. There were a few candidates for routes but as I followed them with my eyes up the bare hill opposite me, all but one petered out and disappeared. The one that didn't was first signposted Jorgucat and then, much to my relief, to Saranda. That wasn't too difficult.

I stopped to buy some water in Jorgucat itself. It was not so much a town, as a collection of buildings spread along the road that by this point was a few tens of metres above the valley bottom. Lots of the buildings appeared to be abandoned but one most certainly hadn't. It was a brand new betting shop but, reasoning that it wasn't the best place to buy water, I ventured a little further along the road to a shop that was set back from the road. The woman who served me was a delight, asking me where I was going and indicating with her angled lower arm that it would be a bit of a climb. She wasn't kidding. It was a steep crawl of 300m over a distance of just 5km, with the final couple of kilometres along a bendless road straight to the top of the hill. I paused occasionally to take in the views and they were just reward for my toil.

I was in urgent need of food and just over the crown of the hill I found my oasis in the form of a petrol station. I was the only customer around and the two likely lads who were running the place initially looked towards me with suspicion and I reciprocated. Both sported bright yellow t-shirts that I assumed passed for a uniform of sorts, and both looked and sounded as though they had been knocking back beer since lunchtime. They were also chain smoking, but it didn't seem appropriate to point out the potential risks of doing so in their current environment.

"Hi. Do you speak English?"

"You are English or American?"

"I'm English. Do you have any food?"

"Why you come here? Albania is shit country. No money, no jobs... Everyone leave to work in England, Germany... Money, money... Drugs..." one of them said cryptically.

These two were clearly not on message when it came to welcoming foreigners to their country. Despite the harsh words towards their own country, they were in fact affable company for the few minutes that I spent at the petrol station eating some more of the pre-packaged croissants I had enjoyed earlier at the campsite in Ioannina. I had only been their second customer of the day, although the wad of euro notes that one of them pulled from his pocket in order to give me change implied they weren't on the breadline just yet.

From there, it was a long glide down towards the sea at Saranda. An attraction called (in English) 'Blue Eye' was being regularly advertised as I descended from the petrol station – 15km, 10km, 8km... - so when it came to the point where I was invited to turn right to visit the 'Blue Eye' it seemed too good an opportunity to turn down. Advertising does work. It was some way from the main road, or rather it seemed that way as I meandered past the potholes in the road towards a large lake. At the edge of the water a better quality road started and, under a rusting overhead sign saying 'Welcome to Blue Eye' there was a man wearing what looked like an army uniform. He was in charge of the barrier across the road and was also responsible for collecting the money. I had no leke on me, just euros, but he opened the barrier anyway and let me through without charging. I still had no idea what I was about to visit. The road once again deteriorated to the point of being comically potholed, but after a few minutes I arrived at a cluster of buildings in the woods. There was a bar, a restaurant and quite a few families milling around. There was even a large coach parked up outside (how did that manage to negotiate the route I had just taken?). A man indicated that I should leave the bike by the side of one of the buildings and when I went to find my lock he wagged his finger indicating that it wouldn't be necessary. Warily I did what he said and walked further along the path into the deeply wooded area, leaving Reggie at the mercies of any passing thief. It was a pretty little spot with a fast flowing river and a couple of bridges over the water, but after five minutes or so following the arrows, I was back where I started, still none the wiser as to exactly what the 'Blue Eye' was.

For the remainder of the afternoon I kept my eyes wide open taking in as much of this new country as I could and resisted any temptation to deviate from the path I had chosen. At times I passed sights that surprised me – a large shanty town on the outskirts of Saranda for example – but many others that reassured me that this was just as much part of 21st century Europe after all, the enormous signs advertising Vodafone being the prime example.

I had expected Saranda to be a quiet fishing port but what I found was a large seaside resort that wouldn't have been out of place had I been travelling through any other Mediterranean country. I found a bar and ordered a beer, opened up a browser on my phone with no connection issues whatsoever and within a few minutes I had booked myself a room at the three star Hotel Palma. It was all a far cry from the kind of Albania I had thought I was about to visit only a few hours previously and as I sat on the balcony of the hotel overlooking the crescent of shoreline in front of me, complete with high rise apartments and hotels, a pristine beach, a smart outdoor swimming pool and yet another large advertising hoarding for Vodafone, I was a bit confused. Albania wasn't meant to be like this.

Friday 12th July 2013
Cycling Day 10: Saranda to The Llogoroja Pass, 89km

The Hotel Palma probably dated from the 1970s but for a three star hotel it was in good nick. It was clean and spacious and all the fixtures and fittings seemed to work. What the owners hadn't yet discovered, however, were pastel shades of paint. Immediately after waking up I walked towards the window and threw back the curtain. Bright sunlight almost knocked me over as it flooded into the room, at which point the rays bounced around the stark white walls, plunging me into a scene from the film *2001: A Space Odyssey*. I quickly closed the curtains lest my retinas not recover before my arrival in Portugal, found some sunglasses and wandered out onto the balcony to face the full force of the rising sun but this time with protection.

I really never imagined I would be standing in such a place on the first night of my trip through Albania. I'm not quite sure where I thought I would be standing, but it was certainly somewhere a little more low key, grim, dated, poor and probably unfriendly. Preconceptions can be funny things and here was the proof. So far (and admittedly I had only been in the country for a matter of 20 hours or so) I had not felt uncomfortable with my surroundings and the people with whom I had interacted had been friendly and helpful. Even the two guys at the petrol station on the hill had been comically charming in their own way. Their negative sentiments towards the society in which they live could quite easily have been echoed by any pair of disgruntled school dropouts from across the European continent.

Reggie had spent the night attached to the railings of the balcony on the ground floor of the hotel and I could see him through the (white of course) net curtains as I ate my very un-Albanian continental breakfast in the restaurant of the hotel. Before heading back to the room to pack, I paused at the reception to pay the bill and to ask if my clothes were ready for collection. I had dropped them off in a plastic bag shortly after arrival and was promised an overnight laundry service. The girl on reception looked puzzled and she called over one of the cleaners who just happened to be walking by. A conversation ensued that I couldn't understand but which I tried to fathom through facial expressions and body language:

"Hey, Lindita! This cyclist asked us to wash his clothes last night. Do you remember? They were crumpled up in an old Sainsbury's plastic bag. I'm more of a Waitrose woman myself in this new Albania but there you go..."

87

"We haven't had a laundry service since the communists were in charge."

"It was Majlinda on reception last night. She'll promise to do anything!"

"OK. Don't panic. I'll pop downstairs, dampen them a little, fold them neatly and spray them with Febreze. He'll never notice"

At this point the receptionist turned to me and reverted to English;

"No problem sir. They'll be ready for you when you come back down."

I returned to the reception area a few minutes later with the panniers and collected Reggie from his sun-drenched position on the balcony. I was duly presented with my Sainsbury's plastic bag full of neatly folded, slightly damp clothes. Lindita had forgotten to spray the Febreze and as I looked inside the bag I noticed that the tidemark on my cycling shorts created by my perspiration was still visible. In true British style I smiled in Lindita's direction:

"Thank-you. That's perfect."

It would be a return to cycling by the coast today and I was looking forward to a bit of flattish cycling all the way to the town of Vlora, a place whose main attraction was that it was roughly halfway to the capital Tirana. A few years ago *The Guardian* newspaper had described the Albanian Riviera as '*the new undiscovered gem of the overcrowded Med,*' so I had high hopes for a very nice day in the saddle as I cycled past the pristine beaches, waving at all the Guardian readers who had taken their favourite newspaper's words to heart and had booked themselves a cheap holiday in the sun.

I was expecting the biggest challenge of the day to be my departure from Saranda itself. On arrival the previous evening it had been a short and very steep descent into the town centre and when I examined the map there was only one road in and out of the coastal town. I gritted my teeth, found a low gear and pedalled up the hill. My slow speed allowed me to see at close quarters the extent to which there was a building boom taking place. Almost every other building was either brand new or in the process of being constructed. I wondered to what extent this urban expansion was actually planned, as the overall impression could best be described as 'eclectic'.

Once over the crest of the hill, it was a short cycle downhill to re-join the main road and head north along the coast, although at this point the coastline itself was well hidden behind the long coastal mountain that I had just climbed. At least the cycling was nice and flat, or rather, it was for the first 10km.

I am told it is possible to go onto the Internet, plug in your start point and your destination, and the magic of the digital age will provide you with a detailed topographical profile of the cycle that you are planning to undertake. I can see much merit in this if you are in some kind of competition and you want to know how to outwit your rivals. The cyclists in the *Tour de France* must spend hours poring over such detailed printouts prior to their mountainous climbs. I can also see the merit if you have a one-off challenge in mind and perhaps out of curiosity, perhaps out of a desire to plan like a professional cyclist, you furnish yourself with a detailed route profile. Me? Well, I take a rather different approach. I prefer to see my route profiles *after* the cycling has been completed, once all the hard work, the anguish, the shouting, the crying, the straining of every sinew in your body is over and done with. Why do I take this radical approach? Well, I fear that if I did give myself the option of not starting the cycle because of the climbing that would be involved, I would never set off in the first place. It was a tactic that had worked well during the 2010 cycle to southern Italy allowing me to successfully navigate Reggie over the Alps via the Gotthard Pass, and I had already benefited on this trip when naively setting off from Corinth in the blind hope of arriving in Olympia on the same day. Ignorance really can be bliss and here I was again, ignorant of the extent of the climbing that would be required to get anywhere near Vlora.

The first few climbs were mere pimples compared to what was to come later. I gritted my teeth and cycled up them, taking regular stops for coffee, crisps, chocolate bars, sugary drinks, more chocolate and ice cream. It was one of those grazing days but each pause gave me a boost of energy that was much needed. The hills made progress very slow, as did the frequent stops and by early afternoon I had barely dented the 130km I would have to cycle to get to Vlora by the end of the day. My final pit stop came at a service station where the owner asked me in which direction I was heading. He laughed knowingly when I revealed that I was heading north and indicated with his hands that in terms of climbing, the most strenuous effort was yet to come.

I was getting the distinct impression that whoever was responsible for the Albanian road system lacked some fundamental civil engineering qualifications. Don't get me wrong, there was much positive to say about the roads; they were in generally good condition (apart from the occasional, and frankly bizarre, 10 metre strips of gravel) and, just like the Greek roads, they were very wide. However, their gradients left much to be desired. In Britain we have mainly hills and when the road builders of yesteryear started, they did so at the bottom, pointed to the top and built a road along the more or less straight line that they had created. They got away with it as the hills were never very high and the roads never very long. In alpine areas the switchback road was of course the favourite, whereby the steepness of the road was moderated by having the roads criss-cross the side of a mountain. I'm generalising of course, and there are many examples of roads that take a hybrid approach, but bear with me. This is, after all, a travelogue and not a textbook for road construction in mountainous areas. Along the Albanian Riviera, despite there being some very large hills, which many would describe as mountains, the tendency was to adopt the British rather than the alpine approach to road building, resulting in very long and very steep climbs. On several occasions I had little alternative but to get off and push. During these off-bicycle experiences I wasn't a happy man and was audibly cursing myself (for having chosen this road in the first place), the Albanians (for having built them) and even the man at the garage (for having told me about them). Even the few cars that did pass me were straining in second gear. Every so often, inevitably, there was an equally steep downward section, which although it came as welcome relief to my legs, was no time to rejoice as it would have been suicide to simply release the brakes and let gravity do the work. As if to prove just how treacherous the roads were, just north of Himare was a tragic monument marking the point where, in May 2012, a bus carrying university students on a pre-graduation trip toppled off the side of the mountain killing twelve people and injuring another twenty-one. Albanian media reports from the time of the accident do say that the bus '*had been going very fast*', but even a bus travelling at normal speed up and down such gradients can't have been the safest method of transport to be using.

On at least half a dozen occasions I was brought back to sea level as the road passed through the small towns and villages it was serving, which were predominantly on the coast. This of course meant that more climbing was necessary as I continued my journey north. As always, such terrain offered some stunning views, as well as a good selection of diversions to take my mind away from the physical efforts required just to keep moving. Along one stretch of particularly remote coastline, I could see a large tunnel that had been dug into the cliff. Its entrance was heavily protected by a thick concrete arch and scattered around and about were numerous abandoned military buildings. I wondered what secret activity had taken place there during the height of cold war tensions. Had I be so inclined, there was nothing stopping me making my way down to the tunnel and poking my head inside. Only a few decades ago, such an activity would surely have seen me pay for my curiosity with my life. In one village that wasn't on the coast, where the donkey count rivalled that of the human population I spotted a small plaque dedicated to Koste Aleksi whose short life lasted from 1820 to 1848. The inscription, in Albanian and English, noted that he was *'sacrificed in the fight against the Turkish invaders'*. I had already seen signs of how this part of Europe had been fiercely fought over on my travels through northern Greece and here was another snippet of history to add to the mix. Away from the relics of past wars, I was beginning to learn just a little bit of the Albanian language. The building boom had not stopped since my departure from Saranda and every town had its fair share of flats for sale. Well, that's what I assumed was meant by the words *'shiten apartamente'* attached to the balconies of most of the new buildings. More obvious translations made me smile.

The biggest climb of the day was yet to come, however. It would be a 1,000m haul from sea level to the Llogoroja Pass, but this time it came as no surprise as I could see the mountain from quite a distance looming large beside the coast. It was about 5pm and I paused for thought at the bottom. I had just passed through the town of Dhermi and wondered if it was wise to attempt such a long climb so late in the day. I did realise that by this point I would not be making it as far as my intended destination of Vlora and although I would no doubt make it to the Llogoroja Pass before night fall, I had little idea of what was at the top. More crucially, would I be able to find any accommodation up there? My guidebook came to the rescue, promising accommodation at the *Llogora Resort,* which, according to the map, was just beyond the 1027m pass itself. And this wasn't just any old accommodation. It had *'restaurants, pub, tennis court, heated indoor swimming pool, gym… constant electricity and spring water (tested by water authority)'.* Not even the plushest of plush hotels in Park Lane in London promises constant electricity and tested spring water. Perhaps they don't feel such admissions are necessary but it's reassuring to be told nevertheless.

Initially the expressions of the car drivers heading down the mountain were of bemusement but I stuck at it, switchback after switchback – fortunately this road builder had been to road building school – and slowly edged my way further up the mountain. I paused at various points, trying to look as though it was to admire the view rather than to take a breather. In reality it was both. The drivers were using their horns to full effect (were they applauding me or warning me?) and I started to ping them back with my loud bell. It somehow made me feel happier. Eventually after some 10km I arrived, exhausted, at the pass. There was a large wooden building containing a bar and I sat on the terrace for more ice cream and a celebratory beer. In front of me I had laid out the route that I had just taken, zigzagging its way to the top. I was probably the only person that day to have cycled all the way to the top. Perhaps the only one that week, who knows? What I did know was that the glamorous woman standing at the end of the terrace had certainly not cycled up. Her unfeasibly tall, white stilettos would have prevented that. She was posing as if for a photo shoot and to a certain extent this was true, as she was holding a large microphone and talking into a hand-held television camera. I watched her for a few moments as she repeatedly fluffed her lines. She was, of course, speaking Albanian but fluffed lines are fluffed lines. Eventually the cameraman ran out of patience and went to sit with the rest of the crew who were drinking beer on the table next to me, leaving the mini-skirted presenter to try and learn the words. '*Why not turn your camera on me?*' I thought. I had a tale to tell and I probably wouldn't screw up my lines! But then I glanced down upon my attire, my sweat-drenched t-shirt, my tide-marked cycling shorts and my still relatively pale, factor 50-protected skin. I could perhaps see why the woman with short-term memory loss had the job after all.

Thoughts of continuous electricity and spring water tested by the local authorities returned. The Llogora Resort, with all its luxury, couldn't be far away so I drained the last remnants of beer from the bottle and idled over the crest of the pass and down the gently sloping road on the other side. It was a deeply wooded area in contrast to the other side of the mountain and for a few minutes there was no sign of any kind of luxury, unless you were a passing squirrel. Then, to my left appeared a collection of buildings, set back slightly from the road. There was a large car park containing a few cars (including an old British-registered Ford Fiesta), and a modern building painted pastel green. Such shades had arrived in Albania after all! Between the car park and the building was a two-level terrace with chairs, tables and red and white parasols advertising the brand of ice cream that I had spent much of the day eating. Slightly nearer the road was a row of four stone-built huts with bright red, tin roofs. The huts were numbered 1 to 4. At the entrance to the small complex was a modest stone arch announcing it as the Hamiti Hotel. This must be the Llogora Resort. It wasn't called that and I couldn't see a tennis court, heated pool or gym, but it was in the right place and there was nothing else to be seen in the forest. There was one other thing missing: people. I was the only person around but I could see doors ajar and smoke was coming out of the top of one of the buildings. I parked Reggie by the water tap in the car park, went to sit on the terrace and waited.

After about ten minutes a rather earnest young employee finally approached me. He introduced himself as Antonio.

"Do you speak English?"

"A little."

"Are you open?"

"Yes, we are open"

He didn't seem keen on giving me any more information than the specific piece for which I had asked him.

"Can I have a room for the night?"

"Yes."

"Are there any other people staying at the hotel tonight?"

"Yes."

"Are there some British people staying? I noticed a British car in the car park."

"Mmm..."

He seemed a bit cagey on that one. Antonio then gestured towards the sheds and showed me around shed number 2. Everything inside was pine. Pine walls, pine bed, pine table. It had a double bed and bunks and what appeared to be continuous electricity. I said I would take it.

Once showered I was back on the terrace. Alone apart from Antonio.

"Could I order some food?"

"Yes."

"Do you have a menu?"

"Yes."

I looked down through the choices. The dishes were translated into a kind-of English. Everything consisted of some sort of meat and salad.

"Could I have the grilled chicken?"

"The pork is very good."

"Is the chicken not available?"

"The pork is very good."

"OK. I'll have the pork."

I think Antonio had found his dream customer. Fortunately a beer was a beer and no debate was required. After some time, four very fatty pork steaks were delivered. I picked at each one and attempted to prise the meat from them, but much was left on the plate when I stopped eating.

"Did you not like the pork?"

"Yes, it was very nice but... thank-you."

I left it at that. Customer service in this little corner of Albania had a hard edge to it.

I needed my bed and walked across to the hut where I played with a few items such as the TV (it didn't work) and the air-conditioning (it didn't work). Some of the plugs didn't work either, but I finally located one which would recharge my iPhone and another that would do the same for my back-up battery pack. It was very quiet. Too quiet. I was in a glorified shed, in a remote wood in the middle of Albania, in a hotel that had just one customer and at least one creepy employee. The most worrying thing was that I was almost certainly not alone in that dark cabin in the forest.

Saturday 13th July 2013
Cycling Day 11: The Llogoroja Pass to Durresi, 172km

There had already been quite a few epic cycling journeys on the trip to this point (and there would be many more to come), but these had been because of the vertical challenge that they posed. Cycling day 11 would prove to be the first of the truly epic horizontal challenges, but as I woke in the cabin in the woods, I remained oblivious as to the nature of the day that lay ahead. Indeed, cycling was not on my mind at all. I was preoccupied by the sounds that surrounded me. It was difficult to work out if they were above or below me. To the left or the right? Were they coming from outside the shed or inside? The nature of the sounds was initially equally puzzling, but after a few moments of thought, I came to the conclusion that I was sharing my hotel room with a family of mice and a rather active one at that. I don't like mice, or come to think of it any animal that moves quickly in erratic directions. I much prefer the slow-moving inhabitants of the animal kingdom; the ones that look at you with disdain and say to themselves *'just don't even think about it...'* The mice were my main motivation for throwing back the heavy covers of the bed, jumping in the shower and getting dressed. I never saw them, but I knew they were there somewhere.

Breakfast was a minimalist affair served up by Antonio, consisting of just toast, butter and an object that was pickled and tasted sweet. I have no idea what it was. Perhaps he was still annoyed with me for not having eaten the pork chops down to the bone the previous evening and had told chef to lay off on the Shreddies. In fairness, by the time I was ready to leave he did appear to have lightened up a little and he smiled as he waved me good-bye. I cast my mind back to the definition of the *Hamiti Hotel* in the guidebook and began to question the quality of the research that had taken place prior to publication. They hadn't even managed to get the name right! Two minutes later, following a very short cycle through the woods, I stopped the bike and looked at the building in front of me. I could see a restaurant, a bar, a tennis court... Was that a heated indoor pool through the steamed up window? The sign – *'Rezorti Llogora'* – confirmed what I now realised. On the positive side of things I had at least saved myself a few euros.

The first job that Saturday morning was to get back to the sea and away from the mountains of the south. Having climbed the 800m to the pass on Friday afternoon, I was guaranteed a long downhill ride through the forest. It would be about 20km to the coastal town of

Orikumi and then I would continue north to Vlora, before working out a route that might get me as far as the capital Tirana, but more likely to the towns of either Fieri or Lushnja in central Albania. The scenery in those first 20km was simply exquisite and on a grand scale. I had never before had the pleasure of seeing so many picture-perfect views, apart from in the most pristine alpine regions of Europe and wondered how the Albanians had managed to keep such an area so secret. I then remembered that I was cycling through a country that for much of my lifetime had been a closed, communist society and it began to make sense. It's strange how, in building up a picture in my mind of post-war eastern bloc greyness, I (and probably most others) had imposed those preconceptions upon not just the lifestyles of the people who lived in the former communist countries of the east, but on practically all aspects of life, including physical geography. The tectonic forces of the planet had not stopped functioning at the Iron Curtain and neither had Mother Nature stopped painting in colour. However miserable their lives might have been under a repressive authoritarian regime, at least the comrades could be miserable while looking at some very beautiful scenery indeed.

Eventually the road flattened out and my thoughts turned (yet again) to how annoying the drivers could be with their speed, overtaking and horn habits. The bustling street of Saranda aside, the roads were now much busier than they had been at any point since arriving in Albania and I was beginning to build up quite an accurate profile of how your average Albanian gets around on four wheels: quickly. And for the majority it seemed to be that their car of choice to travel quickly was a Mercedes. Those not taking to the roads in a model from the German manufacturer had frequently opted for either 4x4 Toyotas or Range Rovers. It seemed logical that in a country where the quality of the road surface was (to be diplomatic) 'variable', most people had chosen a heavy-duty car that would be able to cope with the rigours of the road. According to the World Bank, the country that famously banned private ownership of cars until 1991 had seen an explosion in car ownership from just a few thousand to 400,000 in 2013. The road network appeared to be catching up only very slowly, so the decision of the vast majority of motorists to go down the solidly built vehicle route could be easily understood. As a cyclist, I think I would have preferred if the nation as a whole had opted to spend more on replacing the road surfaces rather than on a sturdy fleet of cars to cope with the old ones. On a more positive note however, having seen the infamous edition of the popular British motoring show *Top Gear* where the three presenters take a trip through Albania and make thinly veiled suggestions that there is an active market in the country for imported stolen vehicles from the UK, I was on the look-out for right-hand drive cars. Apart from the clapped out British-registered Ford Fiesta I had seen in the car park at the *Hamiti Hotel*, I saw none.

After several kilometres following the coastal road from Orikumi, I could see in the distance the town of Vlora, with its impressive seafront curve around the bay. Palm trees lined the road into town from the south and, as I had been on arrival in Saranda earlier in the week, I was somewhat taken aback as to just how un-Albanian the town was. Once again, there was a building boom taking place with smart apartment blocks being thrown up wherever one could be squeezed in. The central area of town had clearly had some money spent on it and much of the main square had been mercifully traffic-calmed, with a smartly paved pedestrian area and restricted routes for motorised vehicles. There was even an enormous display screen, advertising a varied programme of upcoming cultural events interspersed with the weather forecast. The buildings of historic interest had not been swept away under a carpet of new development however, with the occasional Byzantium church taking pride of place amongst the more modern buildings. Recent history was also being cherished with one particularly striking, communist-era monument celebrating Albanian independence dominating 'Flag Square'. A cosmopolitan, visibly affluent town on the way up I would say, and not a hint of it being the home to Albanian organised crime. The Italian port of Brindisi is under 200km away on the other side of the southern Adriatic Sea, and Vlora has seen much trafficking of people in its recent history, but you would never have guessed this if, as I did, you were to cycle through on a sunny summer's afternoon.

Following the signs for Fieri I continued my journey north, but on the outskirts of Vlora I hit a problem in that the road, rather abruptly, became a motorway. I paused beside the green sign (like the Swiss, the Albanians had defied the general European consensus of indicating motorways in blue), and pondered. From what I had seen so far, this was a country that took a liberal approach to its driving regulations: speeding, overtaking in inappropriate places, driving in the middle of the road, riding a motorbike without a helmet, using a mobile phone at the wheel were all commonplace. The Bradt guide I was using stated that *'there is no stigma attached to drink-driving and practically no attempt is made to check it'*. In front of me I could see a beautiful, silk-smooth road surface with a wide band on the right of the carriageway that would be perfect for cycling. The quality of the out-of-town roads that I had been using since arriving in the country had been gradually deteriorating the further north I pedalled, to the extent that some of them had become comically pot-holed. On occasions the entire surface of the road simply stopped and it was necessary to cycle over an extremely uneven surface of dried mud for a few metres or even a few tens of metres. The speed limit on the motorway sign said 110km/hr. That was probably the average speed of most cars that had passed me in the last few days anyway. *Why don't I continue cycling along the motorway?* It seemed unlikely that by doing so I would bother anyone, less likely still that the police would pull me over. It was a tough call.

I couldn't do it. For me it was a step too far. Cycling on a motorway would be madness, even in Albania. And at this point I did have an alternative road that I could follow, which shadowed the direction of the motorway until at least Fieri. I would perhaps reconsider upon my arrival there. So off I cycled along the woefully poor quality, secondary roads once again. At least now much of the traffic had been syphoned off by the motorway and I was left to cycle on much quieter roads. On the flip side, the cars that hadn't taken the motorway now had much more space to themselves, and it only seemed to encourage them in their attempts to break the land speed record for a 15-year-old, black Mercedes with tinted windows. But overall it was probably a much more interesting ride than if I had chosen to cycle illegally along the motorway. I never tired of the architectural eclecticism of Albania, and new houses under construction in the countryside were particularly worthy of my attention. Many were being built with towers and turrets as if they had been designed for Disneyland Albania. One house, along a quiet road in the middle of farmland, was in the shape of the front half of a large boat, complete with pointy bow, portholes and bridge. More kitsch design than grand design, but it was so monstrous that it was difficult not to admire the efforts of the architect, if indeed they had existed.

Upon arrival in Fieri, I paused at a café just outside the centre of town and again considered the motorway question. The added factor in my internal debate was that now I would be required to pick my way along a much less obvious series of roads that didn't shadow the direction of the motorway. In fact, the deviation from the direct route to the next town of Lushnja was this time considerable. But I still couldn't persuade myself to throw in the towel and break the law, even if I knew that there was little chance of me being caught in the act.

The few hours of cycling that followed must have ranked as one of the most uncomfortable, at times terrifying, experiences of my life. My eyes were being torn in four directions. The tourist in me wanted to look at the pretty scenery, the oddities, the animals and the people. The bike owner and chiropractor in me wanted to keep my eyes firmly on the roads, watching out for the next pothole, crevice, gap, lump or large patch of gravel. The latter, if it went unnoticed, could have a comically disastrous effect as the tyres suddenly sank into a sea of small stones, resulting in abrupt deceleration of the bike and requiring some rapid unclipping of my cycling shoes in order to avoid toppling over onto the ground. My lower back was beginning to feel the pain of the ride and I'm sure Reggie, if he could have complained, would have been screaming. The self-preservationist in me wanted to keep an eye on those coming up behind me (were they really that close or was it just a loud engine?), and those in front heading in my direction, err... on my side of the 'road'. More than one articulated lorry came very close to ending my cross-European adventure rather prematurely. I was in cycling hell.

In my mind I penned an open letter to the Albanian government and people, declaring their country to be incompatible with cycling. I'd come up with a detailed ten-point plan as to how they could start moving in the right direction but lots of little caveats, mainly to do with lack of funding, forced me to rethink each suggestion. In the end, I could only draft one potentially cheap solution to the problem of Albania's roads and that was for everyone to change their driving attitude. It could happen at no cost to the taxpayer, but of course it never would. Should money be available for a driver education programme however, you wouldn't have to worry about targeting your audience. In Albania there wasn't a problem with young men driving or pensioners driving or middle-aged women driving. *Everybody* had a problem with driving.

It was now later afternoon and I was worried. Not only was I particularly disheartened by my experiences of the previous few hours of cycling, I was also conscious that I needed to find a place to stay overnight. There was little chance of making it to Tirana before the end of the day and the only place that looked like a reasonable candidate for having a hotel to stay in was Lushnja. As I approached the town I had made my mind up: I would either find a hotel or, failing that, go to the station and take the next train to the capital. This would be quite some step to take, as it meant that after fewer than two weeks of my journey across Europe, I would have given up on my aim of cycling from one corner of the continent to the other. It was a reflection of just how bad the cycling experience had become.

On arrival in the centre of Lushnja, which wasn't a particularly nice town and certainly wasn't somewhere I would have wanted to hang around for too long, I could see no obvious signs of there being a hotel. It was just a horrid, urban sprawl of drab apartment block after drab apartment block. Apart from being on the map, my guidebook made no mention of the place. I searched on the Internet via my phone for hotels and none were listed by Booking.com, the site that I was now using most regularly as it seemed to have the broadest range of different types of accommodation listed. The nearest Warm Showers host was some 50km away in Durresi, a town on the coast to the north. It was just beginning to get dark. If I couldn't find the railway station, I was in trouble. My online Google map was of limited use. I couldn't find the railway station, but there was a long thin black line that snaked its way through western side of town and which I presumed was the railway, so I cycled off to find it. It was my intention to follow the track until I came to the railway station and then hop on a train. The line wasn't difficult to locate, although it was hidden behind derelict buildings for much of the time. The overhead electricity lines gave the game away and I followed these for a few minutes without seeing anything that resembled a train station. I did find a petrol station and paused to ask a young man in his late teens if he knew where it was. He spoke no English and stared at me in a way that you don't really want to be stared at in the middle of a run down town in Albania (or anywhere else) just as darkness is beginning to fall. He scared me somewhat, so I made my excuses and continued to cycle – a little faster than before - along what I believed to be the road next to the railway track. I was now moving away from the centre of town but still hopeful that the station could be an out-of-town one. It was then that road itself crossed the railway tracks. I slowed to a stop in the middle of the tracks and looked in both directions along the line. They were rusty and overgrown with weeds. Now I'm no expert when it comes to railways but even I can recognise a railway line that doesn't get used much and this most definitely fell into that category.

The truth is that the line was still in use but I could have experienced a potentially lengthy wait, as the trains were very infrequent and, according to those that have used them, they rarely follow the timetable. Although the fares are cheap, the rolling stock (consisting mainly of second-hand locomotives and carriages from the Czech Republic) is falling apart. Many journeys are cancelled because essential pieces of equipment have been stolen for their value as scrap metal. Most Albanians have voted with their feet when it comes to travelling between the towns and cities of their country and most public transport is now in the form of buses, something that I had seen for myself through the large number of buses and coaches on the roads. Lushnja does have a railway station but it can't have been signposted or have looked in away way, shape or form like railways stations should, as I never found it. Back on the ground in Lushnja I was in a bit of a pickle. Dusk had set in, I couldn't find a hotel, the railway track appeared to have been abandoned and I had already cycled 130km to get where I was. This wasn't the kind of place where I would choose to make my first venture into the world of wild camping, so that was off the agenda. There remained just one option and that was to continue cycling. Just to the north of Lushnja, the road that had guided me alongside the railway line joined the motorway and in effect disappeared. It was going to be the SH4 or nothing, so I set aside the arguments that earlier in the day had prevented me from cycling along the motorway and continued. I immediately felt as though I was in a much safer environment. The traffic was not heavy – it was by this point about 7pm on a Saturday evening – but it was of course fast, though not markedly faster than the cars, lorries and coaches that had been zooming past me all day long. There were two key differences: I now had a band of tarmac to the right of the carriageway to myself (it wasn't really a hard shoulder as we know them in Britain, in that it was only about half the width of a normal lane) and the surface of the road was predominantly excellent. Occasionally, the newly lain tarmac had slid away from surface in great folds of black stones and bitumen, but apart from these obstacles it was a case of putting my head down and cycling as fast as I could. It was reassuring to see that, in reality, the Albanian motorway was a little less hermetically sealed than those in other parts of Europe. Where there was land available, enterprising locals had set up stands selling watermelons for the passing motorists to buy and it wasn't uncommon to see the odd chicken wandering perilously close to the traffic. At one point, on the other side of the central reservation, there had been a crash of some description and apart from the firemen and policemen, many members of the public had gathered to watch the rescue efforts. No cones had been set up to warn other traffic and people were milling around in a leisurely way, as if at a social event. The stalls, the chickens and the accident 'party' were all rather reassuring, in that I was clearly not going to be bothered by anyone for having the temerity to cycle along the motorway that evening, and I wasn't.

It had been a while since I was able to cycle consistently fast over a longer period of time, and I was enjoying it as I pushed my speed to around 25km/hr. But where was I heading? The motorway could have taken me all the way to Tirana if I had wanted but I didn't want to be still cycling at 11pm and it seemed unlikely that I would be able to find accommodation in the capital at that time of the night. I passed the towns of Dushku, Rroggozhina and Kavaja without stopping and then, on my map, I could see the town of Durresi. It was at the end of a crescent-shaped bay, and along the shoreline of the bay were a string of small houses marking out the points where I would find hotels. I didn't really need the map to tell me this, as I had now entered the greater urban area of Durresi and there were frequent neon signs advertising hotel after hotel. The only problem that I had was actually accessing the hotels from the motorway, which had now become much more like a proper urban motorway, with high walls and fences preventing me from leaving the road. Finally, a slip road appeared and I cycled towards the large, yellow and blue signs for a Kastrati petrol station (not a place even to consider not paying for your fuel). More enticingly for me, was the building sitting directly behind the petrol pumps: the five storey, three star Continental Hotel. I had found a home for the evening.

To be honest, I was getting a little disgruntled with the Albanians. Antonio back at the *Hamiti Hotel* hadn't been gushing in his enthusiasm to have me as the only guest in his hotel and the guy in the street in Lushnja had just scared me. Apart from the odd exchange required when buying a bottle of water or something to eat, I hadn't had contact with any other Albanians that Saturday but I had spend much of the day deriding their driving habits in my mind. I had occasionally shouted abuse in their direction if they had come too close. The staff of the Continental Hotel were about to bring me back into a world populated by friendly, welcoming and unbelievably kind Albanians. Despite the language barrier, I checked in and was charged €15 for the room.

"*Fifteen euros?*" I queried.

"*Fifteen euros,*" the receptionist replied, after a short pause to remember his schoolboy English.

"*Not fifty euros?*" I suggested.

"*Fifteen euros,*" he repeated and, to confirm it, wrote it on a piece of paper.

The only downside of the hotel was that the restaurant had closed, so I ordered a beer from the bar and bought a couple of packets of crisps. I would survive. Then the owner arrived and the bar staff explained my problem to him. He introduced himself to me and then promptly made a phone call. The phone was then passed to me.

"*Hello?*"

"*Hi. My father is the owner of the hotel. You need food?*"

"Yes, but..."

"Spaghetti? Tomatoes? Onions? Bread?"

"Yes, but..."

"I will deliver in 20 minutes."

The owner's son duly arrived, with an enormous plate of food from his restaurant a few blocks away. He refused my attempts to pay him and was gone as quickly as he had arrived.

It had been an extraordinary day of cycling, adventure, stress, fun, exasperation and just a little fear. But I had found a comfortable bed for the night and was being fed for free. Despite all its problems, I was beginning to like Albania, not just a bit, but a lot.

Sunday 14th July 2013
Cycling Day 12: Durresi to Tirana, 34km

Saturday had been the longest day yet of cycling; Sunday would be the shortest, just 34km from the coast inland to Tirana. Visiting the capital of Albania would be a slight deviation away from my route along the Mediterranean, but it was a city that I was not prepared to miss out on and it would be the perfect place to take a pause from the cycling and have a good rest. My last day off the saddle had been a full week earlier in Olympia and, especially after the 172km of the previous day, I needed another. If I could arrive in Tirana in good time and find somewhere to stay quite quickly, I could extend this rest day to a rest day and a half. There was much to look forward to.

I didn't see much of the kind staff or owner of the Continental Hotel in the morning. They were all busy looking after the bar, which seemed to be a popular Sunday morning destination for the locals. Reggie had spent the night in the underground car park of the hotel and, as I wheeled him past the armed security guard who was milling around the petrol pumps, I gave him a nod of thanks for having guarded my bike as well.

There was no direct route to Tirana from Durresi. Hills prevented that. The motorway took the northern option, heading in the direction of the airport and then back in a south-easterly direction towards the capital. The normal road mirrored the route of the motorway on the southern side of the hills, heading first south-east and then north-east. After my experiences on the motorway close to Durresi on the previous evening, when it had begun to resemble any other motorway in any other country, it seemed best to avoid it, so it was back to cycling on the comically appalling, normal roads for the short morning ride.

And they were indeed comically appalling. Just as potholed and uneven as they had been before I had abandoned them for the motorway en route to Durresi. The drivers were just as fast and ignorant of appropriate etiquette when it came to overtaking a cyclist (that being slow down a little and move away from the bike). The transition between the urban area around Durresi to the countryside was quite quick, but the change back from countryside to the built-up centre of the capital was long and very drawn out. It was almost all uphill but not in any dramatic fashion, just a steady sense of climbing over long distance. This can often be tough cycling, as you can feel your legs working – one pause in turning the pedals would result in coming to a halt after only a few metres – but there are no obvious signs around you as to why this should be the case. The road looks quite flat, so why am I not able to do some freewheeling once in a while? The answer is, of course, that the road only *appears* to be flat and in reality, it contains just a slight gradient that requires you to keep pedalling. It can be just as draining as a much steeper climb, where your mind and body are focussed upon the effort required to make the ascent. On a shallow gradient your subconscious mind doesn't switch into effort mode and as a result it can become a long grind. I took my motivation from one particular donkey (there were many tethered to the spot along the side of the road) that was slowly plodding along in the same direction as me. It was piled high with long, green grasses that had been cut from the fields and its owner was nowhere to be seen. I suppose he might have been hidden somewhere in the load of the donkey, but I reasoned that it was more likely that this was a regular journey for the animal and that it had learnt what to do over many long years of labour. It was the only moving thing I overtook all morning. I did so slowly and by leaving a good distance between Reggie and the grasses piled high on its back. I think my point was lost on all but me. Even the donkey wasn't paying much attention to my worthy attempt to educate the Albanians in how to overtake properly.

One road safety initiative that did seem to have been taken up by the authorities was the building of metal pedestrian bridges that crossed the road high above my head. They were quite substantial constructions, with long flights of steps leading to the top on either side of the road and they looked more than just a little out of place spanning relatively narrow roads, with only room for two cars to pass in opposite directions. You could understand why the bridges had been built as soon as a lorry or bus went under one of them with the speed of a Formula 1 car, but the reality was that nobody seemed to be using them, choosing instead to take their lives into their hands by crossing the road in the traditional way. At least the bridges served the purpose of being somewhere to drape your advertising banner or paint the initials of your favourite political party. I found it rather ironic that one of the adverts contained the word 'funeral' and was presumably for a firm of undertakers. I fear that they have a steady stream of income from those who succumb on the Albanian roads.

Tirana itself was announced with its own overhead gantry. The sign took the opportunity of also reminding car drivers to keep their speed down to 40km/hr and lorry drivers to just 30km/hr. Whether any of the drivers noticed the sign as they whizzed past underneath at speeds of at least double those mentioned, is open to question. Tirana may have been announced but it wasn't obvious where it actually was.

At some point, I expected to see before me a large urban sprawl nestling in the space provided between the mountains, but I never did. Instead the gradual transition continued. Rows of shops started to appear on either side of the road and considering this was Sunday – the day of rest – they were very busy with customers. For many of course, this wasn't the day of rest. The religious make-up of Albania was one of the things about which I was looking forward to finding out a little more on my own rest day. As I had travelled through the south of the country, I had passed many churches in the Greek Coptic style and these had not disappeared. They had been added to, however, by an increasing number of minarets, especially here in the suburbs of the capital. Reinforcing the split between those who take Friday as their day of rest and those who have it on Sunday, I had heard the ringing of bells as well as the call to prayer and walking by the sides of the roads I had seen the hijab being worn as well as nuns in their habits.

The hot, dusty, dry day may have helped but I had a sense of having been transported to somewhere out of Europe: the Middle East perhaps or North Africa. This was certainly the case in the suburbs, where all the activity of everyday life was busy taking place. As I continued to the very centre of the city, things clamed down a little. Here, the offices and the banks were closed, although the shops and food outlets were open for business. I found one such establishment, which I guessed was near the main square – I couldn't see it but my online map told me I was nearly there – and bought a large sandwich and a drink. For more than just a few minutes, I watched the world go by, and yet again I was amazed by how unlike everything was to the picture of Albania I had painted in my mind prior to arrival in the country. Modern cars, old cars, young fashionable people, old men smoking, mothers with their noisy kids, police cars with sirens blaring, people drinking beer, others sticking to coffee. Just like anywhere else in Europe.

After the hectic nature of the previous day, it was nice just to sit and stare but I did eventually turn my attention to finding somewhere to stay. It had always been my intention when staying in big cities like Tirana to push the boat out a little in terms of the accommodation. This occasional extravagance would, I hoped, be offset by more minimal expenditure when I stayed on campsites or indeed in places like the €15 three star Continental Hotel (with free evening meal) of the previous evening. I browsed through the hotel options on Booking.com and came up with a few likely candidates, before cross-referencing them to the comments about them in the guidebook. I discounted everything that was more than a few hundred metres away from the central Skanderbeg Square and was left with three or four options. I was tempted by the *Tirana International,* which in communist times had been the main official hotel for visitors and took up a prominent position in the north-eastern corner of the square. In the free market world of the 21st Century, it had become just another swanky, business hotel and I feared they might turn their noses up at Reggie. In the end I went for the *Vila Alba Hotel,* a four-star 'boutique' establishment tucked away in a backstreet. It had 'interesting' written all over it and for the price of 14,200 leke per night (a very un-four-star £70), it was mine for two. I wasn't able to check in until mid-afternoon so I wheeled Reggie away from the sandwich place and located the main square which, just as I had hoped, was only a matter of a couple of minutes' walk away.

Skanderbeg Square was named after Albania's national hero. His real name was George Kastrioti, but he was renamed by the Ottoman sultan who looked after him when he was a boy and everyone now knows him as Skanderbeg. George Kastrioti Square doesn't quite have the same majestic ring to it as Skanderbeg Square so let's all thank the Ottomans for that. Well, Skanderbeg himself probably wouldn't, as he seems to have spent much of the 15th Century fighting them. He died in 1468 from malaria but as a hero of the nation and the Albanian flag of today (of a black double-headed eagle on a red background) is the flag of the Kastrioti family. It could be seen at various places in the square, most strikingly on a large mosaic above the entrance of the National Historical Museum. Skanderbeg was sitting on his horse at the southern end of the square and I took up my own position under the shade of the grand entrance of the Palace of Culture, where a couple of cafés were open for business. The lucky one got mine and I spent the first of quite a few hours over the following forty-eight knocking back at least two invigorating black coffees, while reading up about the city in my guidebook.

The *Vila Alba Hotel* put the *b* in *boutique.* It had only recently been refurbished and they had clearly seen me coming, as everything that the weary cycling tourist needed was available. A good quality bed, a wet room with showers that pointed in directions you didn't realise showers could point, a laundry service where your clothes were returned after having been washed (in contrast to my experiences at the *Hotel Palma* in Saranda) and most welcome of all, a shady roof terrace, where I spent most of the afternoon catching up on the notes that I hadn't had the time to write over the previous couple of days.

As the evening arrived, I ventured out onto the streets near the hotel but fatigue set in quickly and it wasn't too long before I was back in the café at the Palace of Culture, reading and watching the Albanians go by. I was very much looking forward to exploring more of their capital on the following day.

Monday 15th July 2013
Rest Day 3: Tirana

So far in my journey through Albania, I had felt very much an observer, at times a fairly critical one, as so much of what I had experienced had been tainted by the cycling conditions on the roads. However when I had been able to put that to one side, I had found a country rich in beauty and culture. In the capital, I hoped to be able to see the Albanians at closer quarters and hopefully, if the chance presented itself, get to know some of the Albanians a little bit better than I had up to that point. It wouldn't be an easy task, as one thing that had proved to be a barrier to doing so in the previous few days had been the extent to which people didn't speak English. Apart from the younger generations of Albanians who now learn English as a matter of course in school, there was no reason why anyone older than about thirty-five should speak English in preference to another northern European language. Unlike many other Eastern Bloc countries, the Russian language never had the chance to gain a foothold following the schism that took place between long-standing communist leader Enver Hoxha and the Soviet Union in the early 1960s. More about Comrade Hoxha later, by the way. The only language that did catch on as a popular second language in Albania was Italian. This had nothing to do with it being taught in schools and everything to do with the fact that Italian TV stations could be picked up along the Albanian coast. The communists tried to block the signals (one wonders if it was because of the imperialist western propaganda contained within the programmes or simply because it wasn't very good) but the resourceful Albanians became very good at rewiring their TVs.

I would see what happened. The very helpful receptionist at the *Vila Alba Hotel* spoke excellent English and that was a good start. I had also lined up a meeting with the Albanian-born director of the local British Council office, but that wasn't scheduled to take place until the following morning, so on Monday I would be on my own. I didn't mind in the least; it was actually quite refreshing to be in a country where English hadn't yet bulldozed every other foreign language into submission.

It will come as no surprise that my first stop of the day was at the café in Skanderbeg Square. I now had a more detailed map of the city courtesy of the *Vila Alba,* and I tried to plan a walking tour that would attempt to take in the highlights of the capital. Unfortunately the National Historical Museum – the place with the magnificent communist-era mural above the entrance – was closed. It would have been good to have spent a bit of time filling myself in on the official version of the facts, before trying to figure them out for myself as I wandered around. It looked as though I would have to resort to doing just that.

Guidebook in hand, I set off to explore. The main historical attraction of the square (other than the museum which, apart from being closed, was actually not very historical in itself, having been thrown up in the late 70s) was the Mosque of Et'hem Bey. Built in 1823, it is one of the oldest buildings in central Tirana but to my untrained eye it looked much older. It wasn't a big building, but it was beautifully delicate with large, arched windows on three of its four sides. Filling in the space above the columns of the windows and between each arch, were colourful frescos of winding green flora. Just to the left of the mosque stood a square clock tower. It wasn't as tall as the minaret attached to the mosque and was plain in comparison, but it was just as old, having also been built during the 1820s. It was a comforting thought that, at no point during the nearly two hundred years since the construction of the Christian clock tower and the Muslim mosque, neither community had seen fit to turn on their neighbour and attack the main symbol of their religion in the capital. If they had, it clearly hadn't been successful, and the symbolism of the two structures sitting happily side by side in the very centre of the city was a clear message to any visitor that this was a country in shared religious ownership.

My interest was not primarily focussed upon the 19th century however. I was curious to know more about the country's recent history, especially that of the post-war communist period. Very briefly, the Ottomans were in charge until the start of the 20th century. In 1912, the First Balkan War broke out and Albania came under attack from all sides. It appears that the Ottomans didn't put up much of a fight, or at least if they did, they weren't very good at it, as their army succumbed quite quickly. As history tends to do, it then got very complicated. Later in 1912, a gathering of Albanians from all over the country declared independence in Vlora (the nice seaside town that I had cycled through a couple of days previously) and this was recognised by 'The Great Powers' in 1913. True to form, these stalwarts of global diplomacy (Britain, France, Germany, Russia...) buggered up the whole thing by imposing a German prince – Wilhelm of Wied, who never actually made it as far as Tirana - before falling out with each other and going off to fight World War I. Chaos ensued in Albania until Ahmet Zogu emerged from the fractured mess of the country in the early

1920s. He was an enlightened soul, who was very friendly with the Italians and who crowned himself Zog I, King of the Albanians in 1928. He subsequently gave himself all the powers he needed to extinguish any opposition to his rule, which as you can imagine didn't make him a popular king. In her book *The Albanians: A Modern History*, Miranda Vickers recounts a shooting incident on the steps of the Opera House in Vienna in 1931, which was just *'the first of 55 assassination attempts'*! However, his cosy relationship with the Italians turned sour when, in 1939, Mussolini invaded Albania and took control. Zog fled to Greece and, as is often the case with tyrannical dictators, ended up in Paris where he died in 1961. During the Second World War, things got *really* complicated. Two competing groups fought against Italian rule: the nationalists who were loyal to King Zog and the partisans, who were communists at heart and included our friend Enver Hoxha. When Italy surrendered to the Allies in 1943, their rule in Albania crumbled but this only resulted in the Germans moving into town. The nationalists and partisans were both assisted in their resistance efforts by the British Special Operations Executive (SOE) but over time it was the partisans who gained the upper hand, courtesy of more weapons from the SOE. Towards the end of 1944, the Germans were driven out of Albania and, unsurprisingly, the communists took charge.

Enver Hoxha emerged from the partisan movement as the first post-war Albanian prime minister and he set about nationalising anything that moved (and probably quite a lot of things that didn't). He came to rule the country in the same liberated way as King Zog developing a love of the death penalty to eliminate those he didn't like. He also seems to have had a penchant for falling out with people: first the British and Americans shortly after the end of the war, then the Soviet Union – Albania eventually left the Warsaw Pact in 1968 – and then even the Chinese, although not before adopting the latter's desire to become a haven of atheism. He even fell out with his post-war political ally, Mehmet Shehu, who succeeded him as prime minister during the 1950s but who was found dead (with a bullet in his head) in 1981. Enver himself died in 1985, probably much to the relief of the Albanian population who had inherited from their leader the sorry accolade of being the most isolated and impoverished country in Europe. It must have seemed that things could only get better and in time, they did. Along with the other countries behind the Iron Curtain, liberation from the shackles of communism came in the early 1990s, but life hasn't been a bed of roses in the last 20 years. The understandably financially naïve Albanians were taken in by pyramid investment schemes in the mid 1990s and, when these began to unravel, mass rioting ensued, the government was overthrown and United Nations peacekeepers – Operation Alba – had to intervene. However, things have now settled down and as I strolled off on my walking tour of Tirana, it was hard to believe that I was doing so along roads, which, for much of the previous century, had been places of strife, violence and all too often, death.

I had entered the capital from the west on the previous afternoon through mainly commercial streets lined with shops, food outlets and banks. The area east and south of Skanderbeg Square looked much more appealing, so I headed off along *Boulevard Dëshmorët e Kombit*, which in English translates as *Martyrs of the Nation Boulevard*. If I hadn't been aware that I was in a country with a strong socialist tradition, I was now. At the northern end of the boulevard was a cluster of government buildings, including the parliament building itself. They were easy to identify as they were all festooned in the dark red and black of the Albanian flag, but most lacked the grandeur of their counterparts in London, Paris or Berlin. All, that is, apart from the offices of the president. They were set back slightly from the road and were housed in a smart three-storey building. I poked my nose through the railings and looked towards the two guards who were standing either side of the main entrance. They were both dressed in what appeared to me to be the uniforms of commercial airline pilots, complete with golden stripes on their epaulets and a peaked cap with golden beading around the edge. The only giveaway that perhaps they hadn't been moonlighting on a short-haul flight for Albanian Airways, were their weapons: ceremonial swords swinging from their belts. Between the pilots, sorry, guards and me was a grand staircase, complete with not one but three dark crimson carpets, a large expanse of marble and some fashionable jets of water just a few metres from the gate where I was standing. It was an ordered and serene scene that proclaimed to all observers that stable government was in place, albeit one guarded by airline pilots with swords.

Just a minute or so from the presidential offices was Mother Teresa Square, around which many of the university buildings were located. Mother Teresa had been of Albanian origin (she was born in modern day Macedonia but her parents were Albanian) and she returned for the first time in 1991 to open one of her missions. Tirana's international airport is now also named after the beatified friend of the poor, as is the capital's largest hospital. I can't but think that Agnes Gonxha Bojaxhiu, as she was christened, might have preferred that the time and effort involved in renaming the square, the airport and the hospital had been better spent assisting the less fortunate in society but then again, knowing what we do about King Zog and Enver Hoxha, it's a marked improvement on naming them after those guys.

To the south of the square, a large wooded park extended up a hill and then down again towards Lake Tirana. My guidebook told me that I would find a British Memorial Cemetery in the park but before I found it, I first paused at a similar cemetery dedicated to the German soldiers who died here during World War II. Most of the men named on the dark granite slabs – and there were many - were in their 20s and 30s and every single one of them had perished during that short period between the retreat of the Italians in late 1943 and the victory of the partisans in late 1944. It was one thing reading about history in a guidebook; it was altogether more meaningful seeing the names – Heinz, Walter, Helmut, Peter, Rudolf... hewn into a slab of rock. The British cemetery was just as sobering, although this time there were only forty names to read. Each man had his own gravestone, just like the ones you can see in any of the war cemeteries in northern Europe. Most had been members of the SOE and most, just like the Germans, had been brave young men following orders.

902982 Gunner

A.J.D. Clarke

Royal Artillery

No.2 Commando

9th October 1944 Age 23

From the horrors of war to the horrors of late 20th Century communist architecture. Back on the Martyrs Boulevard, I stopped and wandered around the outside of a building that can have few rivals in the former communist countries of the east in terms of its ugliness. Had Prince Charles been a prince in communist Albania (Okay, I admit that it's an unlikely scenario but bear with me) he would have had to find a word that outdid 'carbuncle' by quite some margin. It was a shocker. Called The Pyramid, it was built in the 1980s at the behest of (you guessed it) Enver Hoxha to serve as a museum all about (well, you probably guessed this one too)... Enver Hoxha. As pyramids go it was a fairly flat one, but it lacked any of the simple beauty of the four-sided pyramids at Giza in Egypt. It consisted of around fifteen slopes built from stone (perfect, I dare say, for the local skateboarding community) with angled walls of glass filling the gaps. All the slopes met at the pinnacle of the pyramid, where there was a flat area just perfect for standing upon and waving at the comrades. It wasn't so much Cheops as Millennium Falcon in desperate need of a service. It will come as no surprise that UNESCO believes that the building should be preserved

'...*as a reminder of what happened*', which is a fair point until you consider that most people who see it on a daily basis – the local residents of Tirana – might not be that keen on being reminded of what happened. If the government do ever get around to renovating the building then I wish them luck. One much more meaningful reminder of recent history was the bell suspended in the garden just a few metres from the slopes of the pyramid. Following the riots of the late 1990s, children collected metal bullet casings and they were melted down to be recast as the bell. The inscription on the bell proclaimed that it would '...*sing for peace and children in the 3rd Millennium*'. Let's hope that it does.

As I returned towards the centre of the city, I began to wander a little more erratically along the streets that took my fancy, rather than in the direction of something worthy to visit. It struck me how colourful some of the residential blocks of flats were. One building had a rainbow stream of colours painted across its façade of white, one sported a grid pattern of wavy green lines and yet another had been covered in large pixels of primary colours. One particularly vibrant gable end to an otherwise drab concrete block had been painted bright pink. I mentioned the buildings to the receptionist at the Vila Alba when I returned to the hotel later in the afternoon and she explained a little about the man of the moment: Edi Rama.

"*He was the mayor of Tirana for about ten years and he encouraged the painting of buildings to make the city look nicer.*"

"*He sounds like an interesting man,*" I commented.

"*Yes, he was an artist and very popular with young people especially but he was not elected again in 2011.*"

"*Would you have liked him to stay in charge?*"

"*Well, there are national elections later this year and he is the leader of the socialist party so...*"

I had noticed lots of political posters in the streets during the day and later in 2013 Edi Rama was indeed elected, along with his socialist party coalition. He was subsequently asked to become Prime Minister and he accepted. A very different character from Enver Hoxha and, should he be able to keep Albania on track to becoming a fully-fledged stable and secure democracy, those painted buildings will hopefully be a much more meaningful and beautiful monument to the new Albania than the dodgy pyramid could ever be for the old one. And he has a cool name.

Tuesday 16th July 2013
Cycling Day 13: Tirana to Ulcinj, 130km

I hadn't finished with Tirana. Not quite yet. Before I cycled off to the border with Montenegro – a not insignificant 100km ride if I made it that far before nightfall – I had an appointment at the British Embassy. I had never before stepped inside anyone's embassy, British or otherwise, so I was looking forward to my little foray into the world of diplomacy. I would never have made a good diplomat; I'm far too impatient, direct and cynical to mix with the Foreign Office crowd. I could quite easily see myself creating more problems than I solved. But perhaps the FCO lot are as impatient, direct and cynical as the rest of us, just better at hiding it. I could probably add two-faced to my list if required so on second thoughts... Mind you, is the life of a diplomat as fascinating and exciting as we think it is? Perhaps diplomats are as bored and frustrated as the rest of us in our jobs. It's just that they manage to get bored and frustrated in exotic locations like Honolulu, Reykjavik and Tirana, while the rest of us have to make do in Halifax, Reading and Telford.

My visit to the British Embassy was not to meet the ambassador. Perhaps I was a little too late in coming to Albania for that. Before setting off on my Mediterranean adventure, I had exchanged messages with cyclist Gav McDonald who had cycled through the country in 2005.

"I called into the British Embassy in Tirana just to say 'hello, I'm passing through'. I was ushered very promptly into a lovely clean room and served up some tea and biscuits. A very harassed looking chap soon appeared and asked 'robbed, lost your passport, no money, which is it?' When I explained I was just passing through and wished to say hello he thawed and smiled and we had a lovely little chat. Apparently nobody pops in for the pleasant things, only the hassly ones."

I suspected things had moved on somewhat by 2013 and that the diplomats were probably far too busy forging ties with the locals for future Albanian membership of the European Union to have time to serve me tea. My contact was the country director of the British Council, which had its offices inside the British Embassy.

The British Embassy was located in a leafy street in the north-west of the centre of Tirana. Opposite was the French Embassy and next door were the Germans. Both buildings were far grander than the two-storey British Embassy which, if you stripped away the high metal fence, metal security gate and the signs, could have passed for a pleasant suburban house in Milton Keynes, albeit one with a terracotta-tiled roof. With my taxpayer's hat firmly on my head, I reasoned that it would at least be cheaper to heat than the French or German Embassies. My contact was Aida, and I had agreed to meet her at 9am. Shortly after 9, she arrived and escorted me inside via several air-locked security doors before we settled down in her comfortable office for a chat over coffee. Reggie was more of an issue for the security guard, who was very suspicious of his panniers but after a few smiles (terrorists don't smile) he was allowed to lean nonchalantly against the wall inside the compound, next to the ambassador's gleaming white Range Rover.

Aida had been a teenager when the communists lost power in the early 1990s.

"What was life like in the communist days?" I enquired.

"I remember having food stamps allocated by the government. Everyone was treated equally. It didn't matter if you were a professor at the university or a factory worker because you got exactly the same allocation. My parents describe the life before 1990 as 'stress free' because everything was provided for you: healthcare, education, housing. There was no private ownership of cars or property. Everyone had a flat for their family," she explained.

I had never before considered life under a communist regime to be *'stress free'* but what she said made logical sense, especially if you weren't someone who ever kicked up a fuss about your life (and let's face it, most of us don't).

"What did you know about the lives of people in western Europe?"

"We knew a little but the communist regime emphasised the inequalities of the system in place in the west; in comparison what we had didn't seem so bad."

"How was the period of transition in the early 1990s?"

"The first thing was that everyone was given their flat but lots of people sold them to speculators too cheaply and they put up the rents. Then the building boom started – it was uncontrolled and it's still continuing."

"Are you hopeful about the future?"

"Edi Rama will probably be the new prime minister. He's a socialist and leads the party that used to be the communist party but the leadership is now very different. He will need to address the

*environmental problems we are facing and corruption continues to be
a problem, especially in the health care and education systems. If you
want better care or a better school, it helps if you know someone you
can pay."*

I then asked her about the image that Albania has abroad. I
mentioned the Top Gear programme and she smiled.

*"You've got to remember that the few thousand people who made
it to the UK in the 1990s were illegal immigrants. They were the
people who were involved in crime in Albania in the first place. In
other countries such as Greece or Italy, where there has been
immigration from Albania over a much longer period of time the
reputation of Albanians is very different, especially as the second
generation start to integrate within society."*

*"How long will it be before Albania is a member of the European
Union?"*

*"We are about to become a 'candidate country' but I think that
joining the EU is more important for the political stability of the
country and for human rights rather than the economy. We look to
Croatia and see what they have managed to do with their tourist
industry. But it's now 20 years since the fall of communism and
people want to see progress. The new socialist government will have
a lot to do!"*

Towards the end of our chat, I asked Aida about the religious mix
in Albania. As far as I could see, it was something of which the country
could be rightly proud:

*"The figure of 70% of the population being Muslim is not correct
– it's much lower. Albania is a secular country and a model for how
religions can coexist in harmony. For most people, religion is not a
big part of their life. My husband is Muslim but we married in a civil
ceremony."*

Just outside Aida's office was a portrait of the Queen (I nodded in
her direction) and a painting of Lord Byron at the Temple of Poseidon.
We had followed similar paths up to that point but we were about to
head off in our own directions: Byron to the south and me to the north.
The former Yugoslavia – the land of the southern Slavs – was my next
destination.

Aida had painted a very full picture of modern day Albania and
she was justifiably proud of the achievements of the post-communist
society that had been created. She wasn't uncritical but could see a
positive future for the country within the greater family of nations that
is the European Union. There was a definite tussle taking place

between the old and the new. As if to emphasise this point, as I cycled north through the suburbs of Tirana my eye was caught by a young man by the side of the road. He was standing in front of a stall where live animals were being sold. In one hand he was holding the scruff of the neck of a goat. The animal was dangling over the gutter in the road. In his other hand he had a large knife which was moving in the direction of the goat's throat. I quickly turned my head away so as not to see what happened next.

The remainder of my time in Albania went very much to plan. After an initial ride downhill towards the coast, the road to the border with Montenegro was as flat as I had expected it to be and I was happy that, although I could see the Albanian Alps to the north-east, I never had to climb any of them. I paused for a bite to eat in Lezhe and smiled at the signs that repeatedly informed me that Puke was only a few kilometres to the east. The fact that there were still plenty of flats, shops and restaurants that were *'shitet'* continued to amuse the juvenile in me. Just to the south of Shkoder, I turned away from the main road to follow the course of a river along a road that was signposted 'Montenegro'. It seemed a very quiet and out-of-the-way place to have a border crossing, but after about 6km the cluster of buildings around the frontier appeared.

The Albanians were happy for me to leave their country with the most cursory of cursory glances at my passport. At the other side of no man's land I was in for more of a grilling:

"Are you travelling alone?" the officer barked. The clear temptation was to glance to either side, raise my eyebrows and give a sarcastic answer. However, even a reply along the lines of *'just me and Reggie'* may have had me in for interrogation more quickly than you can say *'get the rubber gloves Luka'.*

"Yes, I'm travelling alone," I replied and smiled.

"For what purpose are you travelling?" Was he trying to wind me up?

"I'm on a f**king bike travelling with a British passport. What do you think I'm doing? Delivering fridges to the next village?" I thought, but didn't reply lest I find myself back at the embassy in Tirana (although it might have been an opportunity to meet the nice chap who had served Gav MacDonald his tea back in 2005).

"I'm on holiday."

"Thank-you. Enjoy your visit."

I was soon able to forget the disgruntled border guard, as my attention was immediately drawn to the sudden change in my environment. On entering Albania from Greece there had been an abrupt move from lush green to sun-bleached light brown and here it was again in reverse. Not just that, but there was now a road to cycle upon which was as smooth as a baby's cheek. The change was striking. I also sensed a certain calmness on the roads. Gone were loud, revving engines overtaking at speed; they had been replaced by sensible Sunday drivers (which was even more impressive as it was a Tuesday) who gave the distinct impression that they were aware that I was using the road as well.

There was no route finding to do as there was only one road from the border to the coastal town of Ulcinj. I knew very little about the Ulcinj, apart from the fact that it did have at least one campsite and served good ice cream. So said Monica Piercy, a cyclist who had followed a similar route to my own earlier in the year. For a couple of days I would be travelling blind, or at least without the ushering hand of a guidebook. When planning, it had seemed an extravagance to buy a book for a country through which I might only be spending 48 hours travelling. So I was relying upon Monica's word, especially the ice cream bit.

There was a sting in the tail of the cycling in the form of a sharp 100m climb just a few kilometres from the coast, but this was rewarded by an equally sharp descent into the town of Ulcinj. I'll be honest, I was disappointed. Back in Albania there were times (many times) when I felt that I was the only tourist around. In some places I probably was. Ulcinj had hundreds of tourists. Sorry, Ulcinj had thousands of tourists and they all seemed to be making their way, on foot or in their cars, along the main road through the centre of the town. It was all more than a little disorientating. Monica's information about there being a campsite was reassuring, but in the hullaballoo of people jostling their way up, down and across the street (many with inflatable objects in their hands having presumably just come back from the beach), it was difficult to make any sense of the place. I turned to my iPhone in the hope of finding comfort from the online map, only to discover that I had received several increasingly alarming messages from my mobile phone operator.

"You have used 5/10/15... MB of data today. 5MB of data is charged at a rate of..."

What? I was shocked at not just the price but also the fact that I was receiving the message in the first place. I was supposed to be paying £3 per day for the privilege of using my UK contract minutes and data allowance throughout Europe. (I later discovered that Montenegro was one of the few places where the service didn't apply.) I immediately switched off the phone and went to find a town plan. I found one and began to work out exactly where I was. The campsites – there was more than just the one – were on the southern end of town, so off I cycled in the direction of Gjerana.

All along the road were stalls catering to the whim of anyone who wanted to spend time at the beach: food, drink, sun cream, parasols, inflatable animals... but no sign of a campsite. On the left of the road was a large travelling funfair, complete with noisy rides and even noisier, screaming kids. I had inadvertently discovered cycle touring hell. I crossed a bridge and stopped the bike by the edge of a large roundabout to once again gather my thoughts and work out what to do next. Just opposite I could see a holiday village of some description. Could it perhaps have a campsite too?

"You need camping? You need camping?"

"Well..."

"I have campsite. Very cheap. €5. With wi-fi. 2 minutes from here." The man, in his 50s, pointed back across the bridge.

"I thought the campsites were in that direction," I replied pointing further along the road in the direction that I had been travelling.

"It's been turned into a hotel."

"Well, what about the others?"

"They are 4km away and they are dirty..."

I had been found by Ulcinj's answer to Del Boy Trotter. Had he accosted me two hours earlier I would have made my excuses and cycled on, but time was getting on and I'd cycled 130km. I was willing to give this campsite wheeler-dealer the benefit of the doubt.

"Go over bridge and turn right. Camping is after 200m."

A few minutes later, I was standing in front of a small block of flats next to an elevated highway. At the entrance was a handwritten sign with the word 'camping' written vertically. An arrow pointed along the side of the building. A teenage boy appeared and guided me to the 'campsite'. It was just the garden of the apartment block but in fairness it had everything that I needed: green grass, a very small wash block and most reassuringly, a handful of other campers who had no doubt also been lured off the road by Del Boy. It was a pity about the traffic on the road above me, but I was willing to compromise as there was no option B.

Within half an hour I had erected the tent, been back to the shops to stock up on bread, cheese and a €4 bottle of Montenegrin wine and was catching up on my emails via the intermittent wi-fi signal. I slowly drained the wine from the bottle and, as I did so, my willingness to care about the noise from the road seemed to diminish somewhat. The contrast with the boutique hotel back in Tirana with its double bed, pristine white dressing gown, well-stocked mini-bar and wet room was too obvious to be stated, but I was still just as happy. As, no doubt, was Del Boy.

PART THREE: MONTENEGRO, CROATIA, BOSNIA AND SLOVENIA
Wednesday 17th July 2013
Cycling Day 14: Ulcinj to Tivat, 92km

In theory, the third stage of my journey, from Montenegro all the way along the relatively straight Adriatic coast to the border between Slovenia and Italy, should have been the easiest to navigate. I would keep the sea on my left, the land on my right and the road in front of me. I had planned no major deviations away from the coastline, although inevitably I would move nearer and further away from the shore as I saw fit. Estimating distances would also be a piece of cake. Or rather, it would have been if I had had the forethought to bring some kind of measuring device with me. I hadn't, so I improvised by searching online for the dimensions of a mini iPad, which were 20cm by 13.5cm. You can see this is getting technical. Sitting outside the tent in Ulcinj with the map spread out on the grass, I calculated that the distance between Ulcinj and Dubrovnik was two lengths of a mini iPad or 40cm. The scale of my map was 1:300,000 so 1cm on paper was 3km in reality, making the direct, as-the-crow-flies distance some 120km. Although the coastline was quite straight, the winding nature of the road would extend that distance somewhat, so I decided to add an extra 50% of 'wiggle', which made a grand total of 180km from Ulcinj to Dubrovnik or two days of 90km. (For the record, the distance that I cycled would be 203km, but that did include an unmissable detour around a large coastal lake which added about 40km to the distance on cycling day 15, so my estimate was only around 20km over. Not bad for a mini iPad, although I don't think the Ordnance Survey will be calling on my skills anytime soon.)

I wasn't in the greatest of moods as I cycled back towards the centre of Ulcinj heading north. Although I had slept well – no doubt helped by the Montenegrin Chardonnay that I had knocked back the previous evening – I felt decidedly disgruntled by having been taken in by the owner of the 'campsite' that was actually just a patch of grass behind his small holiday apartment block. I was in little doubt that the campsites I had been looking for existed and were most probably pristine establishments worthy of attracting my custom. But this had been denied me by a man who was desperate to rake in a bit more of the tourist cash for himself. Nothing really beats a good camping ground. Although it clearly can't always be guaranteed, they tend to be filled with happy-go-lucky people who are willing to have a chat if you approach them with a question or a request to borrow something. That was something I had missed while staying in the hotels in Albania; asking someone in the room next door if you could borrow their mallet might raise a few suspicions. On campsites there tends to be an open anonymity. You can see the people going about their lives before you pick on one who might be a good candidate for a chat. In Ulcinj, the problem was that there were so few of us in such a small area that it was more like staying in a hotel without walls; an idle exchange with one of the neighbours would have to be continued way beyond its sell by date simply because you couldn't wander off to the bar / wash block / swimming pool etc. It was a bit like going to a party on a small river cruise boat; no escape until the boat decided to dock.

The morning was a series of interesting encounters but not all of them good. The first was at a bakery just south of Ulcinj where I decided to stop for breakfast. I had parked Reggie next to a table on the terrace with the intention of then buying something at the counter and returning to the table to eat it. As I was in the queue waiting to be served, I was rather indignantly instructed by one of the staff to remove my bike. I did so immediately, along with my custom, muttering words of discontent under my breath regarding the long-term economic viability of the establishment. To add insult to injury, or rather injury (almost) to insult, as I was pushing Reggie from the bakery across the pedestrian crossing linking the two sides of the dual carriageway to rejoin the road heading north, I was very nearly flattened by a Serbian tourist who was also attempting to cross from one side of the road to the other in his Mercedes. He seemed to be under the impression that the narrow gap in the central reservation for the pedestrian crossing was also a suitable place for him to do a U-turn. I stared at him in a way I usually reserve for recalcitrant motorists on my daily cycling commute back in the UK, but he barged his way through the gap ignoring the fact that I happened to be in his way. He stared back at me and his gestures suggested it was my fault for blocking his way. His silent protestations – he was enclosed within the air-conditioned bubble of his car - were so convincing that I did stop to ask myself whether it was indeed a crossing for pedestrians. I checked and it was.

My stress levels were climbing at a point in the day where normally I didn't have a care in the world. Fortunately, the Kosovars came to my rescue. The first was a fellow cyclist who joined me for a few minutes as I cycled through the centre of Ulcinj on a long stretch of flat road. He was tanned, fit, young and good-looking and wore his black lycra in a manner about which most of us can only fantasise (although I hasten to add that I do not spend my time fantasising about anyone wearing lycra, not even good-looking men from Kosovo). He was curious about where I was going and where I had been and we chatted amiably as we cycled along side by side. He had a summer job working at a local resort complex looking after children but every morning before starting work, he tried to fit in a 40km bike ride in the local countryside. After a few minutes he waved goodbye and sped off towards the hills and already my blood pressure was beginning to normalise.

Then came Blend. I sill hadn't had breakfast, so paused at a second bakery on a hill just north of the centre of Ulcinj. There was only a limited choice of breads and pastries to choose from and I was served by a boy who was perhaps twelve or thirteen years old. He appeared to be the only person in the shop but he spoke good English so I bought a couple of croissants without much difficulty and went outside to sit at the table next to Reggie. After a few moments, the boy joined me. Unlike his counterpart at the previous bakery, it was not to ask me to remove my bike from the premises.

"Can I sit here?" he asked.

"Yes, of course. You speak very good English. What's your name?"

"Thank-you. My name is Blend Kabashi. I learn English at school but I watch a lot of American films on the television as well."

This explained why his accent was decidedly North American, but he spoke softly as I munched my way through my flaky breakfast.

"One day I would like to visit England. I am a supporter of Manchester United and I would like to see them play."

Blend was a real delight. He went on to explain that his family were from Kosovo but that his father ran the bakery here in Montenegro. Blend worked in the shop when he wasn't at school during the holidays. It was so nice to have met not just one, but two Kosovars in the space of just half an hour. They were both wonderful ambassadors for their homeland, which sits immediately to the east of Montenegro on the other side of the Albanian Alps. The region of Kosovo was probably unknown to most people until the events of the late 1990s. Following the break up of the former Yugoslavia and subsequent failure of the Dayton Peace Accord of 1995 to concern itself with the issue of Kosovan independence from Serbia, the Kosovo Liberation Army started to offer armed resistance to the Serbian and Yugoslavian forces in the region. As the conflict developed into a full-blown war, over half of Kosovo's population of around 2 million people became refugees. Eventually NATO intervened by bombing what remained of Yugoslavia, which by that time consisted of just Serbia itself and Montenegro. I remember the television images at the time depicting long lines of refugees fleeing from the region over the mountains in the middle of winter. It was genuinely shocking seeing people in Europe, at the end of the 20th Century, escaping their homeland because of war. Shocking and tragic. But yet here I was, barely 15 years later, interacting with two young Kosovars who couldn't have been more different from the images I had in my head of what Kosovo's people were like and what Kosovo was. The status of Kosovo remains undecided, with some in the international community recognising it as a country in its own right, others not. When I had spoken to Aida at the British Council in Tirana, she had explained how many people in Albania see the region as part of 'Greater Albania' - *"the Kosovars speak Albanian; they are Albanian!"* she enthused - and she envisaged a future when Kosovo would become part of her own country. But to be honest, I'm not sure whether my lycra-clad fellow cyclist or Blend, the apprentice baker, were too worried about all that. They had clearly seized the opportunity to make a positive future for themselves and it appeared to be working out for them. I wish them continued good luck. My mood had been uplifted, to say the very least, and it was with renewed enthusiasm for life on the road that I continued my journey northward.

Now, you've just had to read through a concise modern history lesson about Kosovo, a country that I hadn't even visited, so it would seem absurd if I didn't fill you in on a few facts about the country through which I was cycling: Montenegro. At the time, I knew little about the place apart from the fact that the eponymous *Casino Royale* in the James Bond film was located in the country (even if none of the filming actually took place in Montenegro). I was aware that it was renowned for its beautiful coastline and, shortly after my arrival from Albania, I had discovered that it was also a member of the European Union. I needed money, so on seeing a cash machine at a petrol station a few kilometres from the border, I had stopped and filled up with Euros. An option for a local currency didn't exist. I had been a little surprised but didn't think too much of it; Montenegro must be one of the 28 countries of the European Union. But it was a fact that was playing on my mind... Cyclists will know that facts that play on your mind can be quite useful, as you have plenty of time to think while sitting on a bicycle. On several occasions, I listed in my mind the 28 countries of the European Union (not forgetting that Croatia had only just joined on the 1st July 2013) and on each occasion I had one too many. Was I going mad? (Come to think of it, was I already mad by being able to come up with a full list of the members on the EU in the first place? Perhaps.)

My head scratching would be eased by Aleksandar, an IT worker who lived in the town of Bar. We had exchanged messages via Twitter earlier in the week and he had invited me for coffee in his hometown. We met next to a rather unconvincing statue of Vladimir The Great, in a large square in the centre of town. Vlad – or Knez Vladimir as he was called on the base of the statue – had lived his life towards the end of the first millennium, so I'm not sure how the figure could have been changed to make him more convincing. He just didn't look very 'great' I suppose. Anyway, Aleksandar turned up on time and we wandered off to a beach bar for coffee and ice cream. I mentioned, in passing, Montenegro's membership of the European Union and he immediately corrected me.

"What makes you think that?"

"Well, you use the Euro."

"OK, but we are not in the EU."

This somewhat illogical position is tolerated by the powers in Brussels and is a consequence of the Montenegrins deciding to adopt the old Deutsche Mark back in the late 1990s. They abandoned their own local currency and when the Germans did the same with the Mark, they duly started using the Euro. It now made more sense.

Aleksandar was an interesting character and he was critical of the NATO bombings that had taken place during the Kosovo episode. This was understandable; he described how, as a young boy, he had been sitting on the harbour wall in Bar with his friends when suddenly fighter jets had started attacking the military installations above the town. It must have been quite a frightening experience. He also expressed his regret that Yugoslavia had disintegrated:

"Yugoslavia means 'southern Slavs'," he explained. *"We are all the same!"*

He expressed no desire to return to the days of communism, but he shattered my pre-conception that everybody in that part of the world was happy for their respective parts of the former Yugoslavia to go their own way. I was only beginning to scratch the surface of the complexities of life in the modern day Balkans, but I was already seeing first hand just how complicated the situation was.

Before we said our goodbyes, Aleksandar made sure I was aware of some of the places that I should visit, if I got the chance, as I cycled along the coastline of his country: Petrovac, Saint Stefan and the beautifully preserved town of Budva. I didn't stop at Petrovac but could admire the tiny island of Saint Stefan from the road. It was crammed with small red-tiled buildings and linked to the mainland by a short raised road. It was also the first thing I had seen that ticked all the boxes of what this part of the Adriatic coastline should be like. The same could be said for Budva and its beautifully preserved old town. I groaned just a little as I approached, as I could feel the tourist crowds beginning to build once again but I persevered and by following the signs for '*stari grad*' (or 'old town') I eventually escaped the hoards and found a quiet, shaded restaurant and ordered a pasta lunch.

"*Is this your bike?*" asked one of the waiters. I was half expecting him to ask me to move poor Reggie but no! He was a cyclist too and wanted to know more.

"*I would like to cycle long distances but there are no places to buy a good bicycle in Montenegro,*" he explained. I found this a little hard to believe. Surely there is somewhere in Montenegro to buy a touring bike.

"*What type of bicycle is this?*"

"*He's... Err... It's a Ridgeback Panorama.*"

He seemed particularly interested and I wrote down the details for him on the back of a discarded receipt.

"*Do you know Yorkshire?*" he asked. (Is Patriarch Irinej an orthodox Christian?)

"*Yes, that's where I originally come from in England.*"

"*I have been to Bradford – it's a very nice city.*"

"*Yes, it's...*" I paused trying to think of an honest yet positive adjective to fill the gap.

"*I want to go and live in Bradford.*"

Sun-drenched, historic town on the Adriatic coast or Bradford? The next time I'm in the northern city I will see it in a whole different light, albeit one that is usually under a greyish sky.

Budva to my destination Tivat was a gradual uphill climb for some 10 kilometres, then an equally gradual descent for another 10 kilometres. The drivers in Montenegro had, up until leaving Budva, been a refreshing delight after the horrors of Albania but the road to Tivat had me thinking again. I am not proud to admit that the middle finger of my right hand saw some serious action that afternoon, along with some Chaucerian expressions that would have given even Chaucer heart palpitations (although were probably lost on the majority of the locals). But I did make it to Tivat in one piece and, after a swift beer to celebrate my survival, I headed to the tourist office for some camping advice.

"Auto Kamp Bova is beautiful. It's on the shore. There is a beach. It's very good indeed," exuded the young guy who dealt with my request. I think he must have been on the payroll of *Auto Kamp Bova*, as when I arrived it was anything but *'very good indeed'*. It consisted of two small fields behind a ramshackle building that looked as though it had been prepared for a Montenegrin remake of *Steptoe and Son*. In fact, it wasn't so much *Steptoe and Son, as Steptoe and Wife*. Mr Steptoe was standing at the entrance of the campsite holding an oxy acetylene cutter in his hand and was in the process of dismantling a car engine. Mrs Steptoe gave me a quick guided tour of the two fields which were packed to the rafters with an assortment of caravans, old mobile homes and the very occasional tent. I seemed to have been suddenly transported back in time to the Kosovan refugee crisis of the late 1990s. In my mind I was thinking *'How can I possibly get out of this place with a diplomatic excuse?'*

"It's a bit too busy for me I'm afraid. Sorry."

And with that I was gone.

Back in the centre of town I returned to the bar where I had earlier had my beer. They had free wi-fi and I logged onto Booking.com in search of a hotel. I chose the Hotel Palma, again. My first night in Albania had been at the Hotel Palma in Saranda. It was clearly a popular name.

If *Steptoe and Son* could have been remade at Auto Kamp Bova, *Carry on Abroad* could have been filmed at the Hotel Palma. I spent the next twelve hours transported back to the early 1970s on a Spanish Costa. After a few more beers, even I was tapping my feet while listening to the resident crooner who was knocking out every classic hit from about 1955 onwards, albeit with a Serbo-Croat accent. It was wonderful:

"Start spreading the news... I'm leaving today..."

But, even more exciting than the prospect of hearing another of Sinatra's best known tunes, was the fact that the following day I would be arriving in the city I had been looking forward to visiting for months: Dubrovnik. Not even Frank could better that.

Thursday 18th July 2013
Cycling Day 15: Tivat to Dubrovnik, 111km

Most hotels were not keen on me taking Reggie into the room at night and the Hotel Palma in Tivat was no exception. The staff at reception had suggested on my arrival that I secure him to some railings, in an area to one side of the building that was used to store sun loungers. By coincidence, my room on the third floor was not only also on that side of the building, but directly above the area where he had spent the night, so when I threw open the pale blue shutters, the first thing I was able to do was check that he was still there. Much to my delight, he was. Without his panniers he cut a slender figure and for a few moments as I breathed in the warm morning air, I reflected upon how such a small and relatively simple machine could transform a journey of many thousands of kilometres into something that almost anyone could achieve. What's more, it was able to complete such a feat with minimal impact upon the environment, or indeed the people who happened to be sharing the space around it. At which point my quiet contemplations were rudely interrupted by the roar of a jet engine, as a plane flew low over the hotel on its approach to the airport some 2km south of Tivat. Clearly, travelling by bicycle was, alas, not everyone's preferred method of transport.

If you were paying attention when you were reading about the previous day's cycling, you will remember that the official Apple distance between Tivat and Dubrovnik was one length of a mini iPad, which equated to 60km plus a bit of wiggle. It could have been just that, but I had other plans. It was never my intention for the cycle along the Mediterranean coast to be a mad dash from one corner of the continent to another. Clearly, I had a limited amount of time – two months - in which to complete the journey and as time passed, it was something that would increasingly play on my mind as I neared the deadline of the 31st August. But if proof were needed that I was still willing to go a little out of my way for the sake of a nice bike ride, cycling day 15 would be the evidence I could submit.

Tivat is not a town on the coast of Montenegro. It is, however, only a few kilometres inland and *is* on the shore of the beautiful Bay of Kotor. The bay has two distinct parts. The larger part (where Tivat is) has direct access to the sea via a narrow channel towards its western extremity. The smaller part of the bay is accessed via an even narrower channel to the north of the larger expanse of water and forms a butterfly-like shape beneath steep-sided hills that surround it. If you

129

have in mind a Norwegian fiord - albeit one where the mountains are not quite mountains - you are doing pretty well. As I examined my map, it was just too tempting a ride to miss. Although there was no bridge that would have allowed me to cross the inlet channel and avoid cycling around the wings of the butterfly lake, I could have taken the sizeable ferry that spent its day ping-ponging from one side of the bay to the other. It was only a journey of about 500 metres and I wondered if perhaps being captain of the ship was part of the training course for one day becoming the master of a great cruise ship. More about these in a few moments by the way.

I estimated that by cycling around the enclosed inner part of the bay I would be extending my journey by some 40km, but that didn't push the distance I would eventually have to cycle to get to Dubrovnik to a level that wasn't comfortably achievable. My decision to add the extra kilometres was a very good one indeed, as I was to be rewarded with one of the most wonderful rides not just of the trip to that point but of the entire cycle from Greece to Portugal. It was far from strenuous cycling, as I simply followed the level road that curved around the shore of the bay. It never climbed more than a few metres above the water level and allowed me to concentrate upon soaking up the views.

The first 20km were along a thin road from which much of the traffic appeared to have been banned. Occasionally a bus would zoom past, but there were only a few cars and I assumed that these were restricted to the people who lived or were staying in the many houses, guest houses and holiday homes that lined the right hand side of the route. Had I been travelling on foot, I would have taken a photograph every few metres. On a bicycle it was difficult to fight the temptation not to do the same and my progress was slowed somewhat by my eagerness to pull on the brakes and find my camera. The water was crystal clear, the houses and their gardens pristine and without much traffic to drown them out, the principal background noise was that of the cicadas vibrating around me. The elegant buildings on the opposite side of the bay stood out clearly, as the white of their stones and orange of their roof tiles contrasted starkly with the green vegetation growing on the lower slopes of the hills behind them. On the water itself, there was a steady stream of boats taking the day trippers from one tip of the butterfly's wings to the other. The scene was crowned perfectly by a cloudless blue sky.

At the town of Kotor the scene became less tranquil as people crowded the cafés and restaurants. Those having chosen to travel there by car or by bus had been joined by tourists who had been delivered by two enormous cruise liners, which were berthed in the town centre. They had seemed large from a distance, but as I cycled past the immense walls of their white super-structures, they were almost as awe-inspiring as the more natural scenery that surrounded them. They resembled incongruously placed icebergs and despite my own distaste for that style of vacation, their presence added a touch of exciting glamour to my cycle through the town. It is often said that some people can walk into a room and people will turn and stare. Cruise ships tend to have the same effect on me, although in fairness they are difficult to miss.

Out of Kotor I cycled north, before turning again to head back towards the body of the imaginary butterfly. This stretch of the road was much busier than the earlier one. Not only was traffic now allowed to travel freely along the shore without restriction, but the cruise liners had started to dispatch their contents in coaches and mini buses heading towards all the outlying settlements around the bay. Each vehicle had a sticker in its windscreen naming the ship and a number. It was the same system that I had seen in action back at Olympia earlier in the month, but at least this time the cruisers were not quite as free to roam as they had been in Greece; I had the sun and breeze on my face but they had to make do with peering at the scenery from behind the laminated glass of their bus. It was a victory, of sorts.

I cycled through a series of shore side villages, each just as beautiful as the previous one, but I chose to stop for coffee at Perast where I sat for an hour or so in the small main square, gazing at the delicate clock tower behind me, the lake in front me and the comings and goings of the other people who were milling around. Whoever they were and whatever their purpose for being there (most were obviously tourists), everyone seemed to have slowed down. This wasn't a place to be frenetic in any way whatsoever. It was a place to sit, stare and in my case sip. Utterly and absorbingly relaxing.

Eventually I moved and completed my circumnavigation of the bay. In this final stretch of my 40km detour the villages had merged into one long strip of shops, souvenir stalls, ice cream kiosks, cafés and restaurants which were all catering for the needs of the families who had turned up to soak up the sun. Although just as great in number as the hoards from the cruise ships, these people weren't going anywhere. They were installed in their positions on the pebble beach for the duration of the day and this lack of movement ensured that there was little distraction from the continued calmness of the water.

It was interesting to see how the local community had managed so successfully to provide for all holidaying tastes around their jewel of a lake, from the exclusive second homes to the busy towns full of cruisers to the western beaches full of families. Even I as a cyclist felt at home. As did the other touring cyclist that I passed. Travelling in the opposite direction to me, he shouted a salutation across the road but I was so absorbed in the sights and sounds of the Bay of Kotor that, to my shame, I ignored him completely. When I realised what I had done, it was it was too late to stop, turn back, catch up and chat. If you were that cyclist, I apologise most sincerely.

When I arrived back at the narrow channel linking the small part of the bay to the larger part, the red and white ferry was loaded and ready to set off on the short trip back to Tivat. I didn't have a gram of regret that I had chosen to take the long route. Indeed, I felt a pang of pity for those who were on the boat in their cars and coaches and who were missing out on one of Montenegro's (slightly) hidden secrets. They would have enjoyed it even more had they been on two, rather than four, wheels.

My sympathy didn't last too long, as I had a new destination in mind. Croatia. Country number four was about to appear and it did so in a stuttering kind of way. I had stopped for a drink at a petrol station on the road leading to the border. Without having access to Google Maps in Montenegro – if you remember, my mobile phone roaming arrangements didn't extend to this little corner of the continent - I was just guessing exactly where I was at any particular moment. It had been an easy job doing that as I cycled around the clearly defined angles of the bay, but back on the coastal road I was a little less sure of my bearings. So, fully rehydrated courtesy of my filling station replenishment, I set off once more for the border which was, err... somewhere in the distance.

But suddenly there it was, just around the corner, barely two minutes of cycling time from my pause for water. I was already at the border with Croatia. Perhaps more accurately, I had reached the Montenegrin border control post so I whipped out my passport, handed it to the chap behind the glass, he stamped it (yes, you did read that correctly; he stamped it – not something that happens very often in modern day Europe) and I cycled off up a steep hill. Normally at border crossings – and this had certainly been the case so far on this trip – there is a small area of so-called 'no-man's land' (I'm sure in reality it does belong to someone) before you arrive at a second building which is the border post of the country you are entering. Initially, that didn't appear to be the case here on the Montenegrin-

Croatian border. Perhaps it was another oddity of Balkan political geography. The road up the hill was beautifully tarmacked and there were three or four abandoned duty free shops sitting empty and forlorn by the side of the road. By the time I arrived at the top, I was out of breath and eager for a short break after having climbed a rather sudden and unexpected 200m. In front of me was another border control post – this time the Croatian one – and a long line of mainly German-registered, Mercedes cars. I joined the queue and tried to think of a good reason why the Montenegrins hadn't built their border crossing post here, or why the Croatians hadn't built theirs at the bottom of the hill. Who did that road actually belong to? Had I keeled over and fallen into a ditch, who would have come to my rescue? The UN? It was all very intriguing.

Equally intriguing was how every car in front of me seemed to be taking an age to have the documentation of its occupants checked. I could understand the Albanian cars getting an extra special once over, but the ones from Germany? Every vehicle was taking at least five minutes to be cleared by the border control. After a considerable amount of time – at least three quarters of an hour – I finally pushed Reggie under the large, protective canopy of the border post building and edged towards the uniformed official. After such a long wait, I was mentally prepared for an interrogation about where I had come from, where I had stayed last night (the Hotel Palma had given me a certificate of some sort to prove that I had played my bit part in *Carry On Abroad* and the receptionist had said that it might be needed at the border) and where I was going. I handed my passport to the woman and smiled. She handed it back and wished me a good journey. *Hang on! What were you speaking to the Germans about? Couldn't you ask me at least one searching question?* (How about the one regarding where I was going, as I had discovered that it was a good conversation starter; most people were not expecting me to say '*Portugal*'.) I find it's like this at the post office or the bank. People in front of me seem to have terribly complicated lives. Mine, in contrast, appears to be boringly simple.

"*I'd like to send this package to Belgium.*"

"*Stick it on the scales... Nothing of value?*"

"*Well, just my very good book...*"

"*That's a 'no' then. £3.74. Stick your card in the machine. Anything else?*"

"*No thanks.*"

"*Bye.*"

Back at the Croatian border control, the woman didn't even stamp my passport. I could have been offended.

The remainder of the afternoon was as normal as my visits to the post office back in Britain. Nice roads, nice views and I stopped a couple of times for refreshments. I have to say that the merits of a late afternoon Snickers bar are much undervalued. There was, as was becoming the norm, a sting in the tail of the day with another steep climb up a hill just south of Dubrovnik, but I was now getting used to such last-minute exertions. Halfway up the climb, I came across my second touring cyclist. After the embarrassment of ignoring the previous one, I made a point of chatting to this guy when he waved and made his way onto my side of the road. The effort required to stop and make conversation was more his than mine, as I was climbing very slowly whereas he had to interrupt a high-speed descent in order to speak with me. I was slightly honoured. He was a Serbian, his name was Svetomir and he was on a Balkan cycling tour. It was quite difficult to understand exactly what he was saying as every few moments another articulated truck thundered past our ears. It's interesting how they seem far more fearsome when you are standing by the road rather than cycling with them but that, I suppose, is Einstein's Special Theory of Relativity for you. (Go look it up; that's why they invented Wikipedia.) Svetomir was very keen for me to sign up to a pan-Balkan cycle tour for 2014 via his Facebook page. I wasn't quite sure what I had committed myself to and it could be that, as I type these words, Svetomir is standing somewhere along the Adriatic coast, tapping his watch and waiting for me to arrive. Apologies if that's the case.

At the top of the hill, I had my first awe-inspiring glimpse of Dubrovnik. As I munched my way through a white chocolate Magnum, I gazed down upon the city that I had been looking forward to exploring ever since coming up with the idea of cycling along the Mediterranean coast. It was a city of some size, with suburbs climbing the surrounding hills but I was interested in the tightly packed centre enclosed within the old walls, which, even from a distance of a few kilometres, could clearly be distinguished. The descent back to sea level took only a few minutes and, following the signs intended for mass tourism rather than a man on his bike, I duly found the Pile Gate, the main entrance to the city.

I still had no accommodation booked, but in order to maximise the amount of time I would have in Dubrovnik I had discounted the idea of camping close to the city. I wanted to spend a couple of nights sleeping within those walls and I had mentally prepared myself to pay for the pleasure. Sitting in the square near the Pile Gate, I was accosted by at least two people offering 'cheap accommodation' even before I had had the chance to whip out my iPhone and start looking on the Internet. *Did I look like someone who did 'cheap accommodation'?* I thought. The answer was probably *'yes'* but I shooed them away dismissively anyway.

The *Antica Ragusa* Bed and Breakfast was perfect and it certainly satisfied every criteria I could think of, apart from 'cheap'. It was centrally located and the owner was as welcoming as she was friendly. As was the English bloke who was sitting on the floor in the reception area, attempting to remove a pedal from a bike.

"*You wouldn't happen to have a 15mm spanner on you?*" he enquired, after hearing me speak English at the reception desk and seeing my cycling attire.

"*Well now you ask...*"

I did have one, as I had needed to reattach Reggie's pedals after the flight from the UK. His name was David and he had flown over from Britain to collect his son who had just completed a cycling trip from Venice to Dubrovnik. We chatted for a few minutes and made tentative arrangements to perhaps share a beer later in the evening but I never saw him or his son again. It was perhaps fortuitous. *'Venice to Dubrovnik? Is that all?'*

135

Friday 19th July 2013
Rest Day 3: Dubrovnik

I do like a city contained within a wall. As a child growing up in Yorkshire, I frequently visited York where walking around the walls was a real treat. City walls provide an immovable historical frame in which can be painted centuries of stories. Although most such walled cities are now cluttered with the modern day paraphernalia of urban life – traffic lights, road signs, refuse bins and the like – it only takes a moment to cast your gaze towards the nearest encircling wall to bring to mind the personal and public dramas that have been acted out in the years since their construction. Dubrovnik's walls are somewhat younger than the Roman walls of York, having been constructed during the twelfth and thirteenth centuries, but arguably more impressive as they tower over the buildings that they contain. At 25m tall and 2km long (without any breaks) they seemed like the perfect place to start my day in the city and so it was that at 8am, I was standing high above the Pile Gate, looking down along the *Stradun* or main thoroughfare of Dubrovnik. The Stradun was almost free of motorised traffic – as was the entire area contained within the walls – but at such an early time in the day it was also mainly free of pedestrians. The walls were equally quiet so, after recording a short video message for my students in the UK wishing them a happy holiday (back at the school where I worked it was the final day of the summer term), I set off in an anti-clockwise direction without having to fight the crowds.

Although obviously a place where tourism is the main source of income, it was quickly evident that much of the old city continued to be a home to those who service the tourist industry. From the vantage point of the southern section of the walls where on one side there was a vertiginous plunge towards the sea, I could peer into the courtyards and occasionally the windows of the local residents. Washing lines abounded, as did the cats lazing in the early morning sun. A group of builders were in the process of renovating a long neglected, shell of a house. Two women stood on a roof top terrace debating the exact position of a table. There was even a school squeezed into the crowded residential area, complete with outdoor sports area painted bright blue and green. In front of a large Jesuit church were large columns, which had toppled over; perhaps it was next on the list for the builders.

The height of the walls was much lower as I approached the old port area and the pleasure boats were already beginning to ply their trade between Dubrovnik and the other towns along the coast. Reading the advertising signs on the stalls, which had been set up on the quay of the port to sell tickets, the main attractions were the Elaphiti Islands, where a 'fish picnic' was on offer and the nearby coastal town of Cavtat, where presumably you would have to fend for yourself if you fancied a bite to eat. Business didn't seem so brisk and one of the salesmen stared up at me while drawing slowly on his cigarette. He was too far away to even attempt to persuade me that what my life was missing was a fish picnic on the Elaphiti Islands.

It was a steady climb around the final, northern section of the walls in the direction of the Minčeta Fortress, from where I was able to look down upon the entire walled city. It was an ocean of orange tiles, with only the odd church tower pushing above its surface. Having spent a couple of hours walking the walls, I was impatient to seek out what lay at the bottom of this stone and terracotta sea, so in I dived in by returning down the steep steps of the Pile Tower, to join the masses who were now wandering the streets of old Dubrovnik.

In the sense that there was little traffic to drown out the background chatter of people, I was immediately reminded of Venice, albeit Venice without the canals. The number of people on the streets was now significantly greater than it had been only two hours earlier, but it was still a calm place to be. The wide *Stradun* east-west axis, from which much narrower streets branched off north and south, provided sufficient space for even the most claustrophobic of tourists to feel comfortable. I found a café (which didn't require too much searching as the *Stradun* was not lacking in establishments offering things to eat and drink) and quickly checked my social networks to see if anyone who had been following my journey online had anything interesting to say about Dubrovnik over and above what I could read in my guide book. A chap called Alan, who went by the name of @alzarni on Twitter, had sent me a series of recommendations;

"@CyclingEurope Now then Andrew, you must go to bar #Buza setting is gorgeous, art cafe head up the road from Pile Gate for about 400yds"

"@CyclingEurope Really quirky, sea kayaking in the evening is good, cable car to look down on #Dubrovnik, restaurant is crap up there tho!"

"@CyclingEurope The guns and mortars were placed where the cable car is, that's where they bombarded the city! Enjoy!"

"@CyclingEurope There's an eccentric artist down one of the side streets whose house was the 1st one shelled, worth having a chat with!"

"@CyclingEurope There's a war photo exhibition on just off the Stradun, really good and thought provoking. Just nimble tho mate, amazing place!"

Nimble?

"@CyclingEurope Bimble! Autocorrect stepped in again! Hope you enjoy the city, it's a truly beautiful place #Dubrovnik"

Bimble? Alan proceeded to send me a definition to explain the meaning of the word: *'to move at a leisurely pace'*. I was up for that. I was also tempted to put my *Rough Guide* in the nearest bin. The Buza bar sounded good but it was still only mid-morning. The art café? I might have been sitting in it already! Sea kayaking? Interesting, but I was happy to stay on terra firma. Cable car? Guns? Mortars? Bombardments? Shelled houses? It was a good job I still had my guidebook. Alan was referring to *The Siege of Dubrovnik* that lasted from November 1991 to May 1992. I had vague recollections but they lacked detail. I could have said something similar about events across the Balkans during the 1990s. It seemed that a visit to the war photo exhibition also suggested by Alan might be a good place to start jogging my memory.

War Photo Limited was the name of the organisation I was looking for and it was conveniently located in one of the streets heading north from the *Stradun*. The exhibition consisted of three galleries, each one taking up a floor of the building. One gallery housed a permanent collection entitled *'Ex-Jugoslavija 1991-1999'*. The other two were temporary; one related to the war-torn *'Land of Cush'* in Africa, the other contained photographs taken by a New Zealand photographer called Wade Goddard and had the haunting title *'Enclave, East Mostar'*.

Goddard was only in his early 20s when he decided to travel to the fragmenting former Yugoslavia of the early 1990s to document what was taking place. The exhibition showed some of the photographs that he took in the town of Mostar and it was a vivid reminder of just how brutal the conflict was. Had they been unlabelled, most of the photographs could easily have been mistaken for pictures taken during the Second World War. The photographer himself noted how, during the siege of Mostar, he was confronted with images that he could only compare with the ghettos of Europe during the 1940s. Some of his subjects were familiar – the famous bridge of Mostar, for example, which had stood for 427 years before being destroyed by mortars – others less so. The exhibition pulled no punches and images of the dead and the dying were commonplace. The physical destruction of the town was alarming. The permanent exhibition showed images from the wider Balkan conflict and was just as harrowing. As war photography should, the images seemed to simply reflect the reality of what was happening. The written descriptions of what each image portrayed were matter of fact and, from the perspective of a man who had literally just walked in off the street, fair and balanced. Near the reception desk of the gallery was a map showing clearly the complex ethnic make up of the land covered by the former Yugoslavia. Beside it was a useful English summary of the events of the final two decades of the 20th century:

"The break up of Yugoslavia was almost inevitable after its economic collapse in the early 1980s. Following Tito's death in 1980 the Communist Party began to fall apart. In June of 1991 Slovenia and Croatia each declared independence. With 90% of its population ethnic Slovenians, Slovenia was able to break away with only a few days of fighting. In Croatia violence between the Croats and the 12% Serb minority, which wanted to stay within Yugoslavia, escalated. By the fall [autumn] the Yugoslav Army had invaded Croatia to 'protect' the Serb minority there and seized a third of Croatia's territory. Following a ceasefire agreement, the United Nations sent a military peacekeeping force in early 1992 allowing the Yugoslav army to withdraw into Bosnia and Herzegovina.

Bosnia was the most ethnically diverse of the Yugoslav republics, with 43% of the population Muslim, 31% Serb, and 17% Croatian. Ethnic tensions strained to breaking point when a referendum in February/March 1992 resulted in a declaration of independence, and Bosnia erupted into war. Serb paramilitary forces supported by the Yugoslav Army launched a land grabbing campaign, accompanied by ethnic cleansing – the forceful displacement of the non-Serb population. Hundreds of thousands of Muslims and Croats were rounded up and taken to prison camps where they were tortured and often killed, many others were bussed out of Bosnia. In November 1995 the Dayton Peace Agreement ended the fighting, but it divided the country into a Serb Republic and a Bosniak (Muslim) – Croat Federation, both with a high degree of autonomy."

It was a cruel, divisive war – as Alan had pointed out, Dubrovnik itself wasn't left untouched – but visiting the area in 2013 showed the extent to which things had recovered so quickly. However, I wasn't sure how much of what I was seeing was papering over cracks that still existed or whether real conciliation had indeed taken place.

The exhibition had provided a much welcome context in which to explore Dubrovnik for the remainder of the afternoon. I stumbled upon the house of Alan's 'eccentric artist' that had been the first to be shelled during the siege. A large photograph outside the entrance to the man's ground floor studio was understandably a much more subjective depiction of events than had been the ones in the War Photo Limited gallery earlier in the day. It was dated '6.XII.1991' and showed the house in front of which I was standing in flames. Windows of the upper floors were labelled '*sestrina soba*', '*mamina soba*' and '*moja soba*', indicating the rooms where his sister, his mother, and he had presumably been sleeping at the time. There was no mention of whether his sister or mother had come to harm. At the bottom of the photograph, in Croatian and English was written "*LEST WE FORGET! On the occasion of the 20 (sic) anniversary of Serbian and Montenegrian (sic) aggression on Dubrovnik*". A small sign attached to the door of the building informed visitors that the man himself had popped out for lunch.

The city was festooned with red and black banners and posters for the 64th Dubrovnik Summer Festival, promising opportunities to see and hear jazz, pop, classical music, theatre, film, opera and ballet. I noticed that Prokofiev's ballet *Romeo and Juliet* was being performed that evening in Bošković Square, just next to the Jesuit Church where I had spotted the discarded stone columns earlier in the day. Or were they? It seemed more likely that they were actually part of the set. The festival office was very close to the *Antica Ragusa* bed and breakfast where I was staying, so I went along and purchased one of the few remaining tickets for the event. Row 13, seat 409 was at the very back of the open air, tiered seating area, so I reasoned that if I became bored with the dancing, I would at least have a good view of the other members of the audience. If they failed to amuse me, I could marvel at the beauties of Dubrovnik at dusk. In the end, I delighted in all three: the stirring music and athletic, yet graceful, movements on stage, the eclectic mix of people in the crowd from the luvvies on the front row to the two middle-aged women sitting next to me (who were locals and couldn't really believe that I was a cyclist), and the stunning views across not only the old town of Dubrovnik but also the placid Adriatic and the craggy coastline to the north. I don't often go to the ballet and I'm certainly no expert in such matters, but I can say without a shadow of a doubt that it was the finest performance of *Romeo and Juliet* I had ever seen.

Saturday 20th July 2013
Cycling Day 16: Dubrovnik to Podaca, 120km

Up until the morning of 20th July, I hadn't felt the pressure of time much at all. Two months. Nine weeks. Sixty-two days. Whenever I considered the length of time I had available to cycle from the Temple of Poseidon in Greece to the lighthouse at Cape St. Vincent in Portugal, it just seemed like a long, almost endless summer. Obviously it wasn't and perhaps that is what was dawning upon me as I lay in bed that Saturday morning in Dubrovnik, trying to count the number of weeks I had remaining. The answer was six. There was an antique map on the wall of the room at the *Antica Ragusa*. I got out of bed and stared at it. I had sufficient faith in the cartographers of yesteryear to determine that Dubrovnik was not a third of the way to my destination - a quarter, perhaps - but not a third. Either I needed to speed up or Europe needed to shrink and even in my dozy half-awake state, I was able to rationalise that the former possibility was the more likely of the two.

The bed and breakfast where I was staying had many things that were commendable (location, comfort, friendly staff...) but it had one thing that wasn't. It didn't actually have breakfast. In fairness to the *Antica Ragusa*, they never described themselves as a 'bed and breakfast', but the online booking service that I used had. Breakfast was available at a restaurant elsewhere, but it did require a not inconsiderable walk along several of the old town's narrow streets to find it. I took with me my Michelin map of Croatia as I needed to set myself some distance targets for the week ahead. The map was so large it could have easily been used as an interesting (if rather expensive and not very absorbent) tablecloth had that been required. It hadn't, so after tucking into a smorgasbord of breakfast delights, I wrestled with its enormity and finally laid it out in front of me to see where I would be heading. Slovenia and Italy did seem an awfully long way away but after a few minutes of tip of index finger to tip of thumb calculations (I had left the iPad back in the room), I reckoned that five days of cycling a minimum of 100km a day would see Reggie and me within spitting distance of Trieste, our first destination in Italy. It would mean dispensing with plans to explore Istria, the peninsula in northern Croatia that people had told me was 'unmissable'. Well sorry folks, I would have to miss it. More disappointingly, I decided that the town of Mostar in Bosnia – the place that had been the subject of the galleries at the photo exhibition the previous day – was just too far out of my way. Croatia needed to be more cycling and less sightseeing.

I climbed the hill out of Dubrovnik to rejoin the main road north and found myself in the port area where another cruise ship had docked. It was the *MSC Fantasia*, all 138,000 of her gleaming white tonnes on view. It was quite a sight and I wasn't the only person who had paused their journey to take a photograph. I could count at least fourteen decks at her highest point around the bridge of the ship (there were actually eighteen so goodness knows where they had hidden the other four). She was capable of carrying 3,900 passengers and I think that during my visit to Dubrovnik I had met most of them face to face. It took me about a minute to cycle from her stern to her bow along the road that was adjacent to the dock. All but two of the balconies on the starboard side of the ship (which was actually next to the port – aren't there laws against that kind of thing?) were empty. On each of the occupied balconies a solitary middle-aged man was leaning against the rail and each of them followed me with their eyes as I cycled by.

"I've always wanted to do a bit of cycle touring," thought one of the men. *"If just once my wife would let me arrange the annual summer holiday..."*

"O.K.," thought the other. *"It's Saturday 20th July: where the bloody hell are we today?"*

The highlight of cycling day 16 promised to be the point at which I entered Bosnia and I could say *'I'm half way to Portugal'*. As we've already seen, this wasn't at all true in terms of kilometres but in one respect it was correct. Bosnia would be country number five after Greece, Albania, Montenegro and Croatia, leaving just Slovenia, Italy, France, Spain and Portugal to conquer. Get out the bunting! As you can see, I'm a glass half-full kind of person and thoughts of being able to celebrate this significant achievement kept me pedalling merrily as the coastal road climbed and then fell, over and over again. It would be like this along the entire coastline of Croatia – I had been warned that it would be tough going – but with regular breaks and the fast descents during which I could relax and cool off, I didn't mind putting in the effort when it was required. After 60km I arrived at the border with Bosnia.

Those of you who are not familiar with the current political geography of the former Yugoslavia may not have been aware that Bosnia actually had a coastline. You probably also didn't realise that Croatia is a country made up of two non-contiguous pieces of land. The one that I had been travelling through since my arrival from

Montenegro, and where Dubrovnik can be found, is by far the smaller of the two. Sitting at the very southern tip of Bosnia, most of it is well under 10km wide and it is all on the coast. The second and much larger piece – it makes up 98% of Croatian territory – is to the north and covers an area that runs along the coastline until Slovenia stops it in its tracks. The capital, Zagreb, is much further inland. Imagine Marge Simpson headbutting Homer: her ever-widening body is the coastal region, her arms (flung behind her by the force of her movement) are Istria, her earring is Zagreb and her long, blue crop of hair, which is in the process of giving her husband what he deserves for being such a dumb ass, is the interior of the country. You can see why I never became a geography teacher. Between these two bits of Croatian territory is a thin strip of Bosnia barely 8km wide that links the bulbous, landlocked mass of the rest of the country to the sea like a very short umbilical cord. (Sacked!)

The border guard at the first frontier between Croatia and Bosnia was far too interested in something on his mobile phone to bother too much with trivialities such as passports. He looked annoyed when I paused and offered him mine.

"Clear off will you! I'm nearly at my Angry Birds high score!"

I don't consider that I have actually visited a country if I haven't managed to do anything meaningful during my stay. I haven't been to Austria, for when I did, it was merely to change trains en route to Prague. That's actually quite meaningful, now that I think about it, for if I hadn't, I would have ended up somewhere in the Alps but you know what I mean. I did want to say that I had visited Bosnia properly and there is nothing more meaningful on a long-distance cycling trip than an extended stop to eat lunch, so that is exactly what I did.

My route along the coast of Bosnia was obviously a short one, so I couldn't be too fussy about which café or restaurant I chose. I could see on my map that there was a town called Neum ahead of me, but I had no idea what kind of place it might be. Logic would dictate that the reason why this little strip of land existed was to ensure that Bosnia had a place from which to export and import its goods. Did I want to have a lunch in a busy, industrial port? A couple of kilometres south of Neum, I found a collection of shops and, on the right side of the road, there were three eating places next to each other. Ignoring the fact that it had the architectural merits of a Portakabin, I pulled up outside the one that had an outdoor seating area, sat down and waited to be served. After a few minutes, I was handed a large, laminated menu that contained lots of photographs and not very many words. Restaurants with large menus should, if possible, be avoided. Those which laminate their menus should be avoided full stop. If you are handed a menu with pictures on it, you have only yourself to blame. I had found a restaurant that gave me all three. And it looked like a Portakabin. I began to have second thoughts about rejecting the port of Neum.

On the plus side, the restaurant terrace was busy and getting busier but I feared that it was more a reflection of the time of day and its prominent location next to the road with plenty of space to park a car, rather than for the quality of the food. Few, if any, of the cars were Bosnian. Most were German or Italian with a few Serbian vehicles and the occasional Montenegrin one thrown in for good measure. With this mix of languages taking place, it was easy to see why the proprietor had opted for a pictorial approach to his menu. I scanned down the long columns of photographs. Had I been a vegetarian I would have been having heart palpitations; every single dish was a celebration of meat. '*Where is the pasta?*' I thought. I narrowed down the dishes to two or three that I thought I could recognise and in the end plumped for a *Wiener schnitzel* and chips.

"*Mit Salat?*" Asked the waiter. Do I really look that German?

"*No, thank-you. Just Wiener schnitzel and chips*" I replied, trying to clip every syllable in an exaggerated English way, which isn't easy when you are trying to say '*Wiener schnitzel*'.

"*Salat ist gut,*" he insisted.

"*I'm sure it is,*" I thought, "*but frankly it's not going to compensate in any meaningful way for the slab of meat is it?*" But I gave in.

"*Ja.*"

I could soon hear the poor piece of meat being hammered into submission in the kitchen. At least they were preparing it fresh, which was good, and my hopes were raised somewhat as to the quality of the salad.

Once eaten, the meal left me very full and the remainder of the day's cycling was completed rather lethargically. Passing through the town of Neum, it was clear that my hasty decision to stop at the Portakabin had indeed been a little premature. It was far from being the industrial port that I had imagined it to be. Instead it was a pleasant seaside resort, full of happy families with their beach paraphernalia and a whole host of different places to eat and drink. I dare say there might even have been a vegetarian restaurant amongst them (although to be honest, I doubt it). You win some and you lose some...

Incidentally, if you are still wondering why there is this quirk of geography that gives Bosnia one of Mediterranean Europe's shortest coastlines, we have the Treaty of Karlowitz to thank for that. It was signed in 1699 and it appears to have been one of the many Balkan land allocation exercises for which the 'great' powers have such fondness. Our old friends the Ottomans were of course involved, as were the Russians, but so too were the Holy Roman Empire and the Venetians. Not to be outdone, the British turned up as 'mediators'. During the days of Yugoslavia, the agreement was meaningless but in the fragmented political situation of the 21st Century, the age-old treaty is clearly once more of relevance. There are plans for Neum to become a viable, commercial port but in the meantime the Bosnians have agreed with the Croatians to continue to use the existing port of Ploce just to the north. That does seem much more sensible, not least because Neum is not a bad little place to visit and if you are not too impatient, find somewhere to eat.

Within only a few minutes, I had crossed back over the border into Croatia after my little foray into Bosnia. It was also a return to country number four on my list, which dented my optimistic belief that I was making good progress.

Prior to my arrival in Croatia part II, I had come across fellow touring cyclists only sporadically. As I headed north from Neum, however, I was to see and occasionally interact with quite a few. First up were a couple of 'too-cool-for-school' twenty-something lads who were heading south. They were each wearing just a pair of swimming shorts and their tanned bodies were clear proof that they hadn't pulled off the rest of their garments just for my benefit. I wondered if my own pale, white skin (which was just as pale as it had been upon arrival in Athens, courtesy of my insistence upon wearing clothes and a developing addiction to factor 50 sun protection cream) might have been equally bronzed if I had taken a leaf out of their books three weeks earlier. I tossed them a merry wave and an even merrier '*Hi!*' but as soon as they saw that I wasn't a blond female who could keep them entertained for a while, they ignored me and cycled past.

Restoring my faith in the youth end of the cycle touring community were the next two cyclists. They were travelling in the same direction as me, and I met them on two or three occasions as we headed north at slightly different speeds and then paused at different places for different periods of time. They had both just graduated from Cambridge University and had decided to come over and cycle in Croatia, after having successfully completed a tour of Italy with a larger group of friends the previous week. They had crossed the Adriatic on a ferry and arrived in Dubrovnik earlier in the day. As we exchanged the stories of our respective trips, it made me wonder whether I should have done something similar upon graduation from university when I was 21. I had travelled around Egypt with a couple of friends from school during the summer of 1990 but not on a bike and the most adventurous thing we did was to use the toilet in the third class carriage of a train en route to Aswan. After having returned to Yorkshire to live with my parents for a few weeks, I promptly went off to London to seek my fortune. After three years working in an office, I still hadn't found the map, never mind discovered the fortune so I threw in my job and headed off to that land of ultimate middle class adventure that is, err... France. Fast forward 20 years, I had somehow found myself acting out long-distance travel experiences on a bicycle that perhaps I should have squeezed from my system a long time ago. When I arrived at the astonishing Neretva Delta, a vast expanse of cultivated flat land just south of Ploce, I dismounted Reggie, sat on a bench and pondered. It was the perfect place to ponder, high above the plain with only the sound of the occasional car passing behind me on the road.

When I finally did get moving again, I turned my focus away from the previous 25 years of my life to the more urgent matter of the next couple of hours. I was about to pass the all-important 100km mark – the goal I had set myself for each day of cycling in Croatia – and once that point had been crossed, I would turn my attention to finding somewhere to sleep. I had high hopes of finding a campsite; the coast on my map was dotted with little red triangles (if such a thing is possible) so I should be able to pick one of them, erect the tent and relax. Much to my delight, that's more or less what happened. The stretch of coastline with all the triangles announced itself on a sign placed high on a corniche road as the *Makarska Riviera* and within 10km I had found the *Kamp Uvala Borova Podaca*. I ate some snacks, drank some wine and went to bed.

Sunday 21st July 2013
Cycling Day 17: Podaca to Stobrec (near Split), 90km

A few months after my first book - *"Crossing Europe on a Bike Called Reggie"* – had been published, a fellow touring cyclist contacted me to say how much he had enjoyed reading it and I subsequently exchanged a few emails with him about not only cycling but also writing. The online conversation culminated in me suggesting to him that he should have a go at writing about his own cycling adventure, to which he replied,

"I would, but nothing particularly interesting happened..."

I thought back to the cycle that I had completed from the UK to southern Italy upon which the book was based. It was packed full of events and stories which by themselves, were of little or no consequence but which, when collated together, suitably linked with retrospective comments, a few historical notes and the very occasional dollop of poetic licence hopefully made for a good read.

When I sat down at the end of cycling day 17 to write up a few notes about the day that had just finished, I thought back to what my email correspondent had said about his own cycling trips and, for the first time, I sympathised with his sentiments. The thing is that I had just experienced a day in which, to be brutally honest, nothing of great consequence happened. Now, I hasten to say, please do not stop reading at this point but please do bear in mind that a long-distance cycle trip is only a microcosm of life in general; there are interesting and exciting bits, but there are also dull bits. Let's see if by adding a few retrospective comments, historical notes and perhaps even some poetic licence, I can make it sound like a more memorable day than it actually was.

Kamp Uvala Borova Podaca had been a great place to spend the night underneath the welcome shade of its pine trees, but when I wandered down to the wash block to shower and generally make myself presentable, I discovered that the water had been cut off. It being a Sunday morning, there appeared to be only a minimal number of staff on site and certainly no one with the authority to sort out the problem. The cleaners seemed happy to down their buckets and brooms and wait patiently while smoking their cigarettes. Did I want to wait patiently? Not really, so I bought a couple of bottles of sparkling mineral water (it was the only sort they had left) from the shop and attempted to wash and brush my teeth in a liquid from '*the finest Croatian springs*'. If you have never attempted to wash your face in

147

sparkling mineral water before I can certainly recommend it. It was the camping equivalent of Cleopatra bathing in asses' milk and I could only imagine that I had been transformed into some kind of George Clooney look-alike as I pushed Reggie to the top of the campsite and prepared to set off. Perhaps. The two cyclists I bumped into at the entrance, who had been out for an early morning ride, ignored me even when I said '*Hi*'. George Clooney clearly isn't a well-known figure in the Balkans.

Just as I was able to do on the previous day, route finding could be dispensed with. Hemmed in between the mountains to my right and the sea on my left, I followed the same coastal road all the way to my destination. What's more, just as it had on the journey from Dubrovnik to Podaca, for most of the day the road roller-coasted its way north, seeing me climb from sea level to 100, 150 and at one point nearly 250m, over and over again.

It being a Sunday, brunch seemed an appropriate idea and, when the smart coastal town of Makarska (from which the riviera had taken its name) came into view, I decided to taken an extended break from the cycling, found a café in the harbour area, ordered a coffee and proceeded to watch the world go by. Of particular interest was an elderly couple, who was sitting doing much the same as me at a table a few metres away. It was only around 10am but she had already launched into a large glass of white wine and he was about to drain the last few sips of beer from a litre glass. Both were smoking Marlboro full strength cigarettes. Perhaps I was still feeling very virtuous after my wash in sparkling mineral water, but I found it difficult to imagine how it would be possible to cope with the rigours (or indeed lack of rigours) of the rest of the day if you consider it appropriate to start indulging at such an early hour. When I lived in France I would occasionally see people (predominantly men) drinking a small beer for breakfast in train stations and, in Britain, some men don't consider that their holiday has begun properly until they have drunk at least one pint of celebratory lager at the bar in the airport before a morning flight. But to do it so publicly and so early in the morning in a smart café in a place like Makarska just seemed bizarre.

Desmond Morris would have been proud of my people watching, but the coastal road beckoned. It was a pity I didn't have the opportunity to stop in every town through which my route passed; each one merited at least a short pause and a period of human observation, but the ticking clock simply wouldn't allow for such leisurely luxuries.

Helping to keep my mind occupied whilst cycling, were the numerous and often epic pieces of football graffiti which covered many otherwise blank concrete surfaces. The word 'graffiti' is perhaps not the best one to choose, as these were precise, planned out and carefully executed pieces of art. All of them were made up of just three colours: red, white and blue – the colours of the Croatian flag – although, as I travelled into and then out of the sphere of influence of any one particular team the name would change. In this stretch of coastline, the team being supported was Hajduk Split. Very often this football related public art would cover the entire concrete surface of a bus shelter, inside and out. At other times long walls would be emblazoned with a football slogan.

"Samo nas nebo rastavit može," read one particularly impressive piece of graffiti, printed neatly along a 50m stretch of wall next to the road and alongside a more comprehensible reference to the football team. It seems to be the name of a popular Croatian song, but as to the exact relevance to a football team, I remain ignorant. Whatever its meaning, it was not only a striking example of the genre but testament to a level of respect between rival fans. If such an epic piece of work were to be found in, say, London or Manchester, I am sure that the supporters of neighbouring teams would have taken the opportunity to deface the message with their own scrawled put-downs, no doubt ending with the word 'off'. As I continued my journey north, I spotted more expressions of devotion to Hajduk Split, including one that had been painted high on a cliff above the road, and others depicting a man with dark sunglasses, long, black hair and a blue and red scarf covering his face. The letter 'h' had been printed on the scarf in reference to the team. Had I not, by that point, worked out the connection between the street art and football, I might have thought it was a symbol of political rebellion. On reflection, perhaps it was that as well.

At Omis, a town about 25km south of Split, I sensed for the very first time a suggestion of the northern Mediterranean. The high street was shaded in ash trees and it was significantly greener than any town through which I had cycled up until that point. The bare, baked earth to which I had become accustomed during the first couple of weeks of travel was gradually being replaced with a continuous strip of vegetation. As I cycled through the town centre, the shade afforded by the ash trees was much appreciated. There was also a hint of something for which I was beginning to yearn: rain. Within a few moments of reappearing from under the leaf canopy into the glare of the late afternoon sunshine, I felt a few drops. The sky had clouded over somewhat and I begged to be doused in a cooling shower of water, but it didn't transpire. I was beginning to look forward to the day when I could cycle through the vertical wall of a Mediterranean rainstorm but it looked as though I would have to continue to wait.

My comparatively uneventful day of cycling started to draw to a close as I approached Split. I was on the lookout for a campsite and found one quite easily, just to the south of the city in a place called Stobreč. The location wasn't so great – it was just next to the busy dual carriageway that was funnelling the traffic towards Split itself – but it did have one promising redeeming feature: it had been honoured with the great accolade of *'Best middle-sized campsite in Croatia in 2012'*, as awarded by the Croatian National Tourist Board. It was clearly a place that would have Alan Rogers quivering with delight (well, it would, if the great man of camping himself hadn't already found his last resting place at the big campsite in the sky back in 2000) and I was looking forward to discovering why it was worthy of such a prize. It might have been the spacious pitches, it might have been its location next to the sea and its adjoining beach (on the opposite side of the campsite to the dual carriageway), it could have been its numerous bars and restaurants or even the campsite-wide cloud of wi-fi under which I could remain connected to the world outside. But actually, I think it was none of these. However impressive they might have been (and they were), the facility that struck me as the one to sway the opinions of the judging panel in 2012, was the ingenious system for making sure that you only had a maximum of three showers in one particular day. (Who needs more than three? I'm usually delighted with just one.) Upon arrival, I was given a rubber wristband and instructed to wear it all the time. Not only did it identify me as a bona-fide camper, but every time I needed a shower I was required to hold it against a panel in the wash block. Once the chip inside the band had been read, I could choose a cubicle in which to shower, select the number on the panel and run off to do the business. Clever, no? Campsite innovations like this never cease to amaze me and this step into the bold new world of the 21st century camping was clearly worthy of praise. In fact, I shall award *Camping Stobreč-Split* the honour of greatest technical innovation during my Eurovelo 8 cycle 2013. Congratulations!

My nourishment that evening would have won no awards whatsoever: a bread stick, cheese spread, a packet of *'Petit Beurre'* biscuits and a mug of red wine. I had been allocated a sandpit kind of area, which was surrounded by a low wall. After having eaten my little feast and drunk a little of the wine I lay back on the thin wall and started to doze. It's amazing just how comfortable a flat concrete wall can be after spending so much time sitting upright on a bicycle. In fact, it was so comfortable that I fell asleep. I was awoken a couple of hours later by the noise of my neighbours returning from an evening out and found myself staring at the black, starry sky above. After the few moments that were required to remember where I was and what I was doing (*What? I'm cycling from Greece to Portugal? Really...?*), I stumbled the few metres to my tent to continue my slumber. Needless to say, my camping mat was nowhere near as comfortable as the wall.

Monday 22nd July 2013
Cycling Day 18: Stobrec (Near Split) to Skradin, 103km

I didn't sleep at all well or if I did I just happened to have some extremely vivid dreams about lying on an uncomfortable camping mat, in a tent, in a sandpit situated within metres of a busy dual carriageway. Where were so many people going at 4am on a Monday morning? I was beginning to re-evaluate my initial agreement with the Croatian Tourist Board's decision to award best middle-sized campsite 2012 to *Camping Stobreč-Split* but, after another high-tech shower, my faith was restored. In a move that would hopefully speed up my departure from the campsite, I had paid a visit to the reception on the previous evening to pay the bill. However, in order for me to keep my rubber wristband overnight and make use of it in the morning, they insisted on keeping hold of my passport. I expected it to be a simple exchange but things are never so simple, certainly not in my life. The reception opened at 8am and I was almost at the front of the queue when the receptionist on the morning shift arrived to open up. In front of me was a harassed looking man in his 50s and I was about to find out why he was looking so stressed. It was horribly complicated but briefly, he was German and had driven down to Split from Hamburg. Unfortunately, his car had broken down some 300km north of Split and it had been transported back to northern Germany. His caravan, however, had not been taken back. Instead, he had asked a friend, who was already staying at *Camping Stobreč-Split*, to drive the 300km to come and collect him, his wife, their several dogs and, crucially, the caravan and bring them all to Croatia. So far, so good. The problem was that he needed a pitch that wasn't just available for the duration of his holiday (which he had already booked), but also for several extra days until such time as the insurance company could come and collect the caravan (which he hadn't booked). What's more, it needed to be close to the pitch allocated to his friend who had so kindly gone to the trouble of picking him up. Negotiations ensued, at length. I could understand all this because the receptionist and the German man were speaking English. Goodness knows how frustrated the people behind me were becoming if they couldn't understand a word of what was being said. At least for me, there was mild amusement in the predicament in which the guy had found himself although, as time dragged on and as my attempts to break into the discussions to point out that all I wanted to do was exchange my wristband for my passport were rebuffed, even I began to lose my patience. I spent much of my time reading the certificates on the wall behind the reception desk;

152

Camping Stobreč-Split had also been named as Croatia's '*most sympathetic*' campsite.

"*I'm so sorry to hear about your cat... He was such a cute little thing... I know... It's a real tragedy... Never mind...*"

"*Can I help you?*" the receptionist asked, and in the process of doing so brought me rather abruptly back into the real world. Some kind of UN-brokered accord must have been signed between the campsite and the carless German. Within seconds I had my passport and I was off.

The plan for the day was just as it had been for the previous two: cycle 100km and then find somewhere to camp. Having spent a decent amount of time in Dubrovnik on the previous Friday, I was willing to forgo the delights of exploring Split (which I assumed, rightly or wrongly, to be a similar city) especially as a visit to the much smaller town of Trogir a little further along the coast had been recommended by my good friend Claus (the one with the psychotic girlfriends for those of you who have read about my previous cycle to Italy). Indeed, so enthusiastic was his advice that it was verging on an order, so I duly put it down as my first destination of the day.

Trogir was about 30km from the campsite but, despite my delays at the reception, I was able to make a relatively early start. This would mean that a late breakfast in Trogir was on the cards, but not before a sharp climb towards Split on the dual carriageway that had kept me awake most of the night, followed by a much more welcome but equally sharp descent away from the city. I was determined to escape the busy coastal road that I had been following for most of the time since arriving back in Croatia after my brief visit to Bosnia, so once I had escaped the suburban claws of Split, I managed to do just that by hauling Reggie over the concrete wall beside the dual carriageway and then opting to take a secondary road that wound its way through a series of pretty (and pretty quiet) towns and villages, before squeezing through the slither of land between the sea and Split Airport. As with many European airports in this age of cheap, budget airfares, Split Airport is quite some distance from Split and should more accurately be called Trogir Airport. In many ways it's a great pity that it isn't, as Trogir itself was a delightful coastal resort with all the charms that you might be seeking in a northern Adriatic port and should you ever find yourself landing at Split Airport, I would certainly recommend that you don't ignore the neighbouring town of Trogir.

The town is actually built upon a small island, attached to the mainland by a short bridge over which I cycled before dismounting and pushing Reggie through the main 'Land Gate' entrance. Within just a few minutes, I had found the main square, balanced Reggie on his stand in the sun and found a chair, table and parasol under which to sit and sip coffee. The square was flanked on three of its four sides by some of the key buildings in the town. Behind me was the Loggia and its impressive clock tower, to my right was the relatively plain town hall and opposite me was the Romanesque magnificence of St. Lawrence's Cathedral. It, too, had a tall tower, but no clock, and many tourists had climbed to its balcony high above the square for an impressive view of not just the square but the whole of the island. I had only been in Trogir for a matter of minutes but could almost immediately see why Claus had been so fervent in his recommendation to visit the town. Unlike Dubrovnik, it wasn't crowded with tourists but inevitably there were groups of cruisers following their leaders who were holding up white table tennis bats with the name of the ship and a number printed on them, just like I had seen in so many other places. Reggie was positioned some four or five metres from where I was sitting and, perhaps because of this distance from his master, several of the men in the cruise groups had the courage to loiter and examine him in great detail. I, in turn, found it fascinating watching them. They seemed particularly interested in the solar panels positioned on top of my rolled up tent on the pannier rack above the back wheel. I was using the panels to help charge a battery pack that was attached to my iPhone. An app on the phone was being used to track my route and without this extra reservoir of energy from the 'PowerMonkey', the iPhone would have run out of juice by early afternoon at the very latest on most days. When full, the battery pack was capable of recharging the phone perhaps three, or even four, times over and as long as I made sure that I had it attached to the phone when it was needed, I was able to keep a record of exactly where I had cycled along the length of my two month trip. The solar panels would never have provided sufficient power by themselves to keep the battery fully charged, so whenever an opportunity arose I made sure that the PowerMonkey was plugged in to mains electricity overnight. However, it did seem sensible to make the most of the almost continuous sunshine that I had been experiencing ever since leaving southern Greece, and by using the solar panels I was doing just that. None of the men (and it was just men) came to ask me any questions about the solar panels or indeed what I was doing and where I was going. Perhaps it wasn't obvious who the owner of the bike was (although there can't have been many people wearing lycra in the vicinity). Or perhaps the men were under orders not to fraternise with anyone who might dent their chances of being invited to sit at the captain's table. Who knows? Just as I had done on seeing the men on the balconies of the *MSC Fantasia*, I liked to think that they were dreaming of escape from the floating open prison that was *HMS Tower Block*, where they were locked up every night.

Following my coffee, I took a leisurely stroll around the rest of Trogir, pushing Reggie through the narrow streets of polished white marble and past the occasional buskers who were merrily entertaining the passers-by. On the southern edge of the town, on the other side of the city walls, was a long promenade where several expensive yachts had been moored, and at the western end of the island I could see the ramparts of a fortress. It was all very beautiful.

If the view of Trogir at sea level had been good and the view from the tower in the main square probably even better, the view from the top of the 300m-high hill that I had to climb just west of the town was spectacular. I was able to look down upon not just Trogir and its attractions, but the whole length of coastline stretching back many kilometres towards Split. Dominating the view, however, was the island of Ciovo, only a hundred metres from Trogir and linked to the town via a bridge. Out of sight of tourists, and hidden from most people's view inside a large bay on the western side of the island, was a rather incongruous oil rig in the process of being constructed. I liked this positive sign that the coastal region had more than just the tourist industry to keep it propped up in difficult economic times.

I had opted to climb the hill, in preference to continuing along the line of the coast, for two reasons. Firstly, I was getting a bit bored with what was essentially the same view. Don't get me wrong; the Croatian coastline was as spectacular as it was beautiful but after several days of experiencing quite similar views, I needed a change. Secondly, unless I intended to explore every nook and cranny of the coast – and I didn't – I needed to ensure that I didn't end up cycling along one of the long, fragmented peninsulas that I could see on my map further north. A move inland by just a few kilometres would ensure that at least I was keeping my options open and I wasn't at risk of cycling along some extremely long cul-de-sacs. The 300m climb was rewarded by a great view but not by an effortless descent on the other side. The road continued to climb, albeit a little more gently, but the wind picked up and as any cyclist will know, wind can turn cycling into trudging. After some 10km of battling both gravity and gusts of air, the gradient did turn in my favour but the wind seemed to more than compensate. Although I could see the road ahead of me, heading downhill my legs were working just as hard as they had been on the long, slow climb up the hill near Trogir.

My intention was to stop for a break in the town of Sibenik, but I was in desperate need of fuel and I gave in as soon as I spotted and could smell a bakery by the side of the road, some 5km before my intended destination. I devoured a large cheese pasty with the table manners of one of the wild boars of which the roadside signs were so keen to warn me. In retrospect it was a good decision, for when I did pass through the centre of Sibenik, it didn't shout *'pause here and eat one of my cheese pasties,'* at least not from what I could see. More hills were waiting north of Sibenik to welcome me and the grind continued for another calf-straining 15km. I estimated that by the time I arrived in a place called Skradin I would have cycled my required 100km and was delighted to see that not one, but three, campsites were advertised on a sign about 5km from the town. Things were finally beginning to look more positive after a long and arduous afternoon battling not just gradients but also the wind.

Or were they? There was *Autocamp Marina* (3km if I turned left), *Autocamp Krka* (at an undisclosed number of kilometres but also on the left) and *Autocamp Cikada* (on the right but again, no distance was given). I discounted this third option as it was in the opposite direction to Skradin, but I remained hopeful about the other two. First to appear along the long straight road was *Autocamp Marina*, but when I glanced down the road I could also see the sign for *Autocamp Krka*. They were just next to each other. There was, however, one problem; they appeared to be in the middle of nowhere. Did I want to spend a night in the middle of nowhere? I was unsure. I looked at my map and noticed that there was a red triangle – a campsite – indicated next to the river, just to the south of Skradin. Should I risk being able to find this as yet un-signposted campsite in preference to the two in front of me, that were both open and could no doubt accommodate me for the night? My GPS cycling app told me that I had only cycled just under 90km and that I was currently at around 200m of altitude. Skradin was at sea level and my online map showed a series of switchback roads just ahead. This meant that if I took the decision to continue to Skradin, it would be one that I wouldn't easily be able to reverse, as I didn't want to end the day cycling back up a 200m high hill. On the other hand I was reluctant to undershoot my 100km target by over 10km. I decided to risk it and cycle on.

The switchback road down the hill to Skradin allowed me to look down upon the town in its wonderful setting. It was quite small, but in the water surrounding it were many lines of white yachts. At the bottom of the hill, a low bridge spanned the river and if my map were to be believed, the red triangle campsite that I had spotted earlier would require me to turn right at the other side of the river. But the road continued to the left. There was no campsite sign indicating anything along the rough walking track to the right. For the time being, I set aside my search for that campsite and headed towards the centre of Skradin, which was now only a couple of hundred metres further along the road. I spotted a sign for not one but two campsites after only a few minutes of cycling. Great! One of them must be perfect, but which one? One arrow pointed up a steep hill, the other one required me to continue along the road on which I was travelling for another undisclosed number of kilometres. Just opposite the hill I would have to climb to the first of the sites, was a car park, which had been set up in a field, and manning the kiosque was a young chap. I asked him which was the best site. He didn't speak any English but somehow managed to communicate that the one up the hill had more shade, so I slowly climbed the road and found the site. It was a rudimentary place without any communal facilities and just a few camper vans parked up and plugged in to the electricity sockets, but I couldn't actually see any human beings so I cycled back down the very steep road and further down the valley to campsite two. I found *Auto Camp Stradin* after about 2km but not only was it devoid of people, it also lacked *any* tents or caravans. It was closed. This was not looking good.

I cycled back towards the centre of town, then to the bridge where I suspected that the campsite that I had found on my map might be. There was a cabin staffed by two young lads working for the Krka National Park.

"There hasn't been a campsite down there for ten years. Camping is not allowed in the national park."

Brilliant. Thank you Marco Polo maps. Why hadn't I stayed at one of the campsites at the top of the hill?

I returned for the third time to the town centre, sat in a café, and went online to see what other accommodation I could find. Booking.com had served me well over the previous few weeks but there was nothing listed as available in Skradin. This was a little double-edged, in that I clearly wanted somewhere to stay but was happy not to be tempted into paying over the odds for another hotel room. I had never before found myself in the situation of having nowhere to stay, neither on this trip nor indeed on the previous trip to southern Italy. Was that night of sleeping rough approaching?

One thing I had noticed since arriving in Skradin were all the signs for '*Sobe/Rooms/Zimmer/Camere*' (I wasn't sure where the French stayed), so I started to knock on a few doors.

"No,"

"No."

Again, my heart was sinking somewhat; Skradin was evidently a popular place to stay and I was beginning to lose hope.

I wandered down yet another back street, following yet another '*Sobe*' sign, pushing Reggie and no doubt looking somewhat disheartened. I noticed an elderly woman sitting on a chair outside her house, whose eyes were following me as I walked. She looked at me invitingly. Did I still have something of the George Clooney about me?

"*Room?*" she enquired.

Phew, that was a relief (in several ways).

"*Yes, I'm looking for a room. Do you have one?*" I responded, but she looked blankly at me. Her English was probably limited to the word on the sign attached to her house.

"*Zorin... Zorin!*" she shouted. Wasn't he a baddie from one of the James Bond films?

Zorin appeared. He looked quite normal, was lacking the evil stare, and wasn't stroking a white cat menacingly.

"*Can I help you?*"

"*Yes, I'm looking for a room. Do you have one?*"

Negotiations lasted about ten seconds (he had the upper hand although perhaps was unaware just how high it was). I had finally found myself somewhere to stay. To say I was relieved was something of an understatement.

Tuesday 23rd July 2013
Cycling Day 19: Skradin to Pag, 128km

It was to be a day of contrasts, and a long chat with Zorin about the realities of life in Croatia kicked it off. Far from being an evil James Bond villain, he was as charming as his English was fluent:

"I'm an engineer and I used to work in a Deutsch Telekom factory near Split but it closed and I've been unemployed ever since. I spend most of my time in Split with my wife – she's also unemployed – and my seventeen-year-old daughter... but during the summer months I come here to Skradin to help my mother rent out these rooms."

It was a bit of a reality check for someone who had been travelling along the coast for many hundreds of kilometres. It was easy to equate busy restaurants and beaches with a booming economy but the high rate of unemployment – it was 17% in July 2013 – was proof that not everyone was benefiting from the tourist cash. Zorin, a skilled worker, was making the most of his situation but he didn't seem positive about the future:

"Yes, we are now in the European Union but what we need is for companies to stop closing factories. I'm an engineer and here I am cleaning rooms for my mother!"

He smiled as he said it, but it was impossible for him to mask his frustrations with not having a job to return to in Split.

I kept thinking about Zorin as I trundled through the first 40km of my cycling day in the direction of Benkovac. It was the kind of ride that I had been hoping to experience on the previous day: pretty countryside, quiet roads gently sloping up and then down and friendly locals who waved at me as I passed (although I think the two blokes who were knocking back beers for breakfast in one particular village would even have waved cheerily at the Grim Reaper had he been passing on his bicycle). It was everything that your average touring cyclist would have wanted and for a few hours it was exactly what I was getting.

Things were, however, about to change. Since leaving Skradin, I had been travelling along a road, which, although parallel to the coast, was around 20km inland. The quiet villages and farmers fields were charmingly rustic, with the occasional tumble down house just waiting for the next property developer to come and snap it up, renovate it and sell it to the highest urban bidder. And then I arrived in Kašić. The first

159

thing I noticed was a derelict house but, unlike the other ruins that I had seen up to that point, this house was not old. Its walls were made from reinforced concrete – I could see bars of metal sprouting from the top of the building – as was the flight of stairs leading down from the first floor of the building. There were large, rectangular holes in the walls where the windows once fitted, but there were also several irregularly shaped holes; this was a building that had, at some stage in the past, been shelled. It was the first physical evidence that I had found in Croatia of the conflict of the early 1990s and I suddenly felt uneasy. I had seen television footage of buildings like this being fired upon; Martin Bell's vivid reports came to mind immediately. It was certainly a place I hadn't wanted to visit when I watched it on TV, yet here I was, 20 years later, with only a few metres separating me and the tangible proof of the events having taken place. I continued to cycle along the road, where I found two more derelict houses. In addition to the shell damage, these two dwellings were both riddled with bullet holes. I felt uneasy about taking photographs in a place like this, so I put away my camera as a mark of respect. Brand new houses had been built in the village, close to the war-damaged ones which had been left untouched. Was it because the previous occupants had been 'displaced' or, to use the expression that we heard so often at the time, the area ethnically-cleansed? Despite the new constructions, there was an overriding atmosphere of sadness in Kašić. Much of the Croatian road network upon which I had been cycling had been recently rebuilt or at least resurfaced. Not in Kašić it hadn't. Potholes were dotted along the crumbling surface. The fields were unkempt, there was rusting farm equipment in the yards and most chillingly, despite the presence of new houses, the village was empty of people. The only sound was that of a distant dog barking.

Just outside Kašić was a memorial containing the names of thirty-five people. They were all male and all had died in 1993, mostly in their early twenties. Their years of birth ranged from 1960 to 1974. Five of the men had, like me, been born in 1969. As a French teacher, I have escorted children to war cemeteries in northern France and Belgium many times over the years and it is sad, very sad to see the lists of names of soldiers who have lost their lives in conflict. But when the list of the dead contains the names of people born in the same year as you, there is an extra special significance. When I had been a baby, they had been babies. When I had been a teenager, they had been teenagers. But when I had left university and was finding my feet in my first proper job, those five people born in 1969 had been killed in a war that was not of their making. I survived the rigours of life as a trainee account in

160

London. They died fighting for their country. The names on the monument were of Croatian soldiers, but there is no doubt another monument elsewhere with the names of soldiers who were killed on the Serbian side of the political divide. All of it had been senseless, all of it so horribly sad. I never shed a tear, either of joy or of sorrow, during my long cycling trip from Greece to Portugal, but I came closest to it at that memorial to the dead in the small village of Kašić.

I spent the next couple of hours in a daze of melancholy, but was cheered somewhat by the realisation that I had covered 70km by the time I stopped for lunch in a non-descript town called Posedarje, just west of Novigrad. It was a supermarket job: bread, full-fat Philadelphia cheese spread (I usually choose the extra low-fat stuff when back at home; it has the taste and nutritional qualities of white mud when spread on your bread), a couple of bananas and one of those 'duo' Snicker things (does anyone actually buy them and think, "*I know what, I'll save that one for later*"?) all munched in the shade provided by the exterior awning of the supermarket. The other customers walked past and looked at me in horror:

"*I can't believe that guy is eating full-fat Philadelphia cheese!*"

My cousin Richard (much more of him when we arrive in Spain) had texted, suggesting that I stay at a campsite on the island of Pag, which he himself had visited a few years previously. He explained that Pag was linked to Croatia via a bridge at its southern end, and that further north I could take a short ferry journey that would bring me back to the mainland. That sounded like a plan. I estimated that the distance from Posedarje to the recommended campsite was about 50km, so after licking the remnants of the cheese spread from my lips, I continued my journey north towards the island of Pag.

I imagine Mediterranean islands to be very green, with vegetation stretching from coast to coast. That said, the only Mediterranean island that I have ever visited is Corsica, so it is perhaps an untenable extrapolation to assume that all such islands are similarly verdant and I was about to be proven utterly wrong in my assumptions. Pag appeared to have been shaven by an extremely fine razor. It was as bald as an island could be. It was rock and nothing else. This was initially a little disconcerting because, well, why would anyone come to spend their holiday on this barren patch of land? Why would anyone set up a campsite? Why would anyone operate a ferry service from here to the mainland? Surely no one lived here, let alone holidayed here. It was a complete contrast to the scenery that I had been experiencing since my arrival in Croatia. But hang on! Wasn't I looking for a change of scenery? The answer was, of course, yes.

The high bridge linking Pag to the mainland spanned a gorge, which, at some point in ancient geology, had created an island out of a peninsula. It was a spectacular setting for a bridge, complete with derelict castle, lofty cliffs... and a fast-food joint. Along with the other sightseers, I stopped and wandered over to the edge of the mainland to gaze across the narrow gap and marvel at how the bridge builders had managed to construct something so strong, yet so elegant. On the other side of the bridge was the moonscape of Pag. I turned to check that Reggie was still standing where I had left him, but my eyes were drawn towards a young couple who had just pulled up in a black convertible Mini. He was balding and quite stout, probably a little older than his companion. She was tall, blond and wearing a short cut-off t-shirt and an even shorter pair of hot pants. On her feet were the tallest black stilettoes that anyone could possibly wear without actually toppling forward. "*This should be fun...*' I thought, as she made her way, very gingerly, towards the stony ground between the road and the cliff edge. Her partner helped support her but I could foresee trouble ahead. She was carrying a large camera which, when they both arrived at the top of the deep precipice, she handed to her friend. He let go of her and she teetered... this could be the end of a beautiful relationship. To my relief (and no doubt that of her boyfriend, although I'm not discounting the possibility of it being part of a scurrilous plan), she regained her balance. He moved away with the camera to ensure she filled the frame and started snapping. It was riveting stuff; one gust of wind could turn their trip into an unforgettable one for all the wrong reasons. My own camera was poised should evidence be later required by the investigating authorities.

Fortunately, she survived to hobble back to the car. I glanced down at the registration plate, which read 'LJ TEXY'. How much must they have wanted to replace the T for a S. As they sped off, they cast a glance at Reggie and me. I looked down upon them for their tacky clothes, her tacky poses by the cliff and the tacky car registration, but it was highly likely that they were also looking down upon me for my scruffy clothes and my own choice of transport. This day of contrasts was continuing.

I crossed the bridge and started the long cycle to the northern end of the island, a journey of around 30km. The road was flat and again, good quality, which made me wonder why the pain in my lower back had returned. Perhaps it was simply that it was being kept rigid in the same position for a lengthy period. Whatever the exact reason, I needed some pain relief and it came in the form of a bus shelter. I remembered the few hours I had spent dozing on the low wall back at the campsite near Split. I needed a similarly hard, flat surface upon which to lie and after passing several deserted bus shelters, I came to the conclusion that they may be the answer to my problems, in the short term at least. So I stopped at the next shelter. It was along a very quiet stretch of the road, although there were a few houses just opposite. I couldn't see a bus coming – there was very little traffic - so I lay down and immediately felt the relief of my back being flattened by the concrete floor. What's more, it was shady and cool. I wondered why anyone would go to the expense of hiring a masseur when all they needed was a concrete bus shelter. It was one of those moments when you don't care what people think, as the relief being dished out was worth any amount of embarrassment. My only concern was whether Miss LJ TEXY might come and join me to get some relief from her high heels. I stayed motionless with my eyes shut for at least half an hour, before eventually returning to the bike and continuing to cycle. My bus shelter therapy had done the trick.

In due course, I arrived at the town of Pag and paused for an ice cream. Croatian petrol stations seemed to be staffed by rather average looking people behind the counter taking the money, assisted by two or three very attractive, and often scantily-clad women in their late teens working the pumps. There's something Freudian in that no doubt. It made me wonder if any spotty, potentially overweight, male Croatian teenager has tested this dubious employment practice used by the petrol retailers in the European Court of Justice. I'm sure they would have a rock-solid case. Anyway, I asked one of the girls at the petrol station in Pag whether she spoke English. She did.

"Are you aware of the fact that your employment here is probably in contravention of some no-doubt complex piece of European Union legislation?" I was tempted to ask, but didn't.

"Which is the best route to continue my journey in the direction of Novalja?" I did ask.

I had noticed from my online map, that although the main road continued all the way to the northern end of the island, there was an alternative route that ran along the eastern side of Pag, before joining up with the main road further north. Staying on the main road would also mean having to climb the not-inconsiderable hill that I could see ahead of me.

"It's very up and down. It would be better to take the main road," she advised.

OK. Local knowledge won out. The town of Pag was the first place for quite a while that had 3G mobile coverage, so I used the opportunity to check Twitter. Fellow cyclist Sean Bennett who was following my GPS track and who had cycled along the same route as me the previous year, had tweeted the following;

"*@CyclingEurope When you reach the town of Pag, don't follow the main road which switchbacks up a hill. Hug the water on the east.*"

"*@CyclingEurope It's a beautiful trail which will take you all the way to about 10km from Novalja.*"

Local knowledge from a teenager who looked good with a hose, or cycling knowledge from a man who had recently travelled my route? I went with Sean.

I missed a subsequent tweet which included the information that there were "*...a few unpacked stretches,*" so set off with high hopes of completing most of the cycle along a track that was free of traffic, had stunning views and would have me merrily whistling all the way to my destination. The track was certainly traffic free and the views were indeed stunning, but I wasn't doing any whistling as my mouth was too busy cursing Sean. Most of the track was made up of large stones, which would have challenged an experienced mountain-biker. Reggie's tyres were sturdy and wider than those of a road bike, but as they ploughed their way through the '*few unpacked stretches*' (which made up around 80% of the journey), my back pain returned with a vengeance as I was thrown in all directions on the bike. I winced at the thought of a spoke snapping. I'd had big issues with spokes on the cycle to Italy three years previously. I didn't want a repeat of those events.

Over 10 bone crunching kilometres later, I stopped to take in the view properly. The route along which I had been cycling had followed a contour perhaps 40m above the shore. I looked down the slope and could see a settlement of some description. I knew it wasn't the campsite recommended by my cousin, but could it be a possible alternative? I had cycled well over the 100km target distance, and for the sake of my lower back needed to stop soon. As I approached – it was about 200m away at the bottom of the hill – I could make out caravans and tents. It looked idyllic. Brilliant! What luck! I began to forgive Sean, as at least his track with its '*few unpacked stretches*' had brought me to a point which otherwise I would have missed. I cycled down the hill towards the campsite.

The reception of *Camp 'Sveti Duh'* (or 'Holy Spirit' in English) was in a caravan, some distance from the campsite itself. On the side was written '*Recepcija Camp Sv. Duh*' so I knew I had found the right place. The caravan dated from the 1970s and was showing its age. The large window on the forward end had been boarded up and an old car tyre had been slung over the tow-bar. I wondered, dubiously, if the site had ever been in with a chance of winning an award from the Croatian Tourist Board. The door was closed so I knocked. There was a sound of movement inside and after a while a bleary-eyed lad opened up. We exchanged a few words, he gave me a ticket and explained that I would need to pay my 40 kuna at the 'spirit bar'. Two days previously, I had paid 138 kuna (around £15) to stay at *Camping Stobreč-Split*. At least it was cheap.

I pushed Reggie along the coast to the point at which the campsite appeared to start proper. A few people were swimming in the sea in the early evening sun, others were wandering in and amongst the tents and caravans. I found the 'spirit bar' at the end of the site. Several scrawny dogs were sitting outside as I tentatively made my way inside. The few men who were smoking and drinking at the bar stared at me in the same dismissive fashion that the dogs outside had done. I showed the piece of paper to the barman and was escorted into an office area round the back, where I paid my money and was given a few instructions by the woman in charge. I couldn't get out of my mind the thought that this place was just masquerading as a campsite and that in reality it was hiding some dark secret. At that point I didn't really want to find out what it was.

I chose the middle of the three fields as a place to erect the tent, mainly because I could see three people who looked vaguely normal in the process of setting up lots of tents similar to my own, in neat rows underneath some netting. I borrowed one of their mallets and they explained that all the tents were for Czech people arriving the following day to attend a music festival taking place the next evening. That was a lucky escape.

It was a warm evening and many people were still wearing their beachwear. The men mainly in Speedos, the women in... hang on. A woman in her fifties was approaching the tent and she didn't appear to be wearing anything. She was carrying a towel and behind her she was trailing a dog on a lead. She smiled as she walked past. Not being accustomed to seeing naked strangers, I didn't know where to look so I kept eye contact and smiled.

Further evidence that I might have inadvertently stumbled upon a nudist colony came in the wash block, which was in dire need of both repair and cleaning. I undressed in the shower cubicle, although my modesty was severely compromised by the 'door' consisting of a small, torn shower curtain. As soon as I had finished my shower and had dressed, I returned to the communal area to brush my teeth only to find Peter Griffin – the lead character in *Family Guy* - naked in front of me. His stomach was so round I could have plotted an around the world cycle trip on it let along one around the northern Mediterranean. He, too, was smiling and looking in my direction. It was all rather disconcerting. I hastily cleaned my teeth with a speed that only the most incompetent of dentists would approve and went to hide in the tent.

Wednesday 24th July 2013
Cycling Day 20: Pag to Novi Vinodolski, 89km

I was making good progress, but at what cost? My body was groaning with the pain in my back and I was feeling tired; the cumulative effect of many nights of fitful sleep was beginning to catch up on me. It had been yet another stuttering night of sleep at *Camp Sveti Duh,* courtesy of the music that was emanating from somewhere along the coast. Was it the music festival that the Czechs were attending? I was under the impression that it hadn't yet started. Perhaps they were practising, but would they be doing so at 4am? I spent a little time in the earlier hours of the morning reading up about the town of Novalja in my guidebook only to discover that *"...it is the 24-hour party destination for young Croatians".* It went on to add that *"...most of the nightlife is based on the beaches of Zrće and Katarelac".* I looked at the map only to discover that I had pitched my tent about 2km from the beach at Zrće. I feared that it didn't require the excuse of a specific music festival taking place; every night was music night. Why had my 50-year-old English teaching cousin recommended such a place? I never had him down as a *'24-hour party'* person. Perhaps his life working at the British Council in Portugal was more exciting than I imagined it to be. In addition to the backache and my general fatigue, I just didn't feel that well, but I got up and made my way to the wash block. En route I noticed that the field immediately behind my tent was strewn with white paper towels. The odour was unmistakeable. Clearly not everyone was willing to walk the couple of hundred metres required to answer the call of nature in a sanitary fashion. Perhaps the proximity of the field to where I had slept was adding to my general malaise.

I packed up the tent and pushed Reggie back along the beach, past the caravan, up the steep lane and after a few minutes of cycling along what remained of the stony track, I turned back onto the main road I had deserted on the previous afternoon. My first destination of the day was the ferry back to the mainland. It would be a cycle of around 10km along the main road and, although that involved a fair bit of climbing, there was no way I would be deviating from the luxurious smoothness of the tarmac. After only a few hundred metres, I spotted something next to the road ahead of me. A dead animal perhaps? As I approached, I noticed that it was indeed an animal, albeit one with clothes. Was he dead? Well, dead drunk I supposed but he was breathing. In fact he was snoring. Lucky bastard! Not only had he no

167

doubt had a good night out on the beach at Zrće, but he was actually now getting in a lengthy and by the looks of it, quality bit of sleeping. I left him to it, while making a mental note to perhaps start attending the odd disco or two to help improve the quality of my own slumber.

The terrain of the island of Pag continued to be just as Martian as it had been on the previous day, in fact if anything, more so. The hill I was required to cross to get to the point where the ferry left for the mainland was the empty quarter of the empty quarter: an expanse of nothing but rock. The small and functional port was the only construction along what was otherwise a featureless coastline and, to my relief, one of the two ferries was about to depart. I bought a ticket, cycled up the ramp, left Reggie to fend for himself on the car deck and went to sit in the sun. The other passengers were mainly people who I assumed had also been partying hard on the island, although they had clearly fared a little better than the guy by the side of the road. Many of them were Dutch and some of the men still found the energy to chat up the local Croatian women. I was happy simply to close my eyes and try and catch up with some much needed sleep.

Unfortunately, the crossing was quite a short one. I could really have done with at least an hour, perhaps even two, but I had to make do with a crossing of just 15 minutes so I was almost as weary as I had been on the other side when I cycled Reggie down the ramp and back onto the Croatian mainland. I was welcomed back by an immediate and blatantly cruel 250m climb in the first 2km, as the road from the ferry terminal at sea level re-joined the coastal road. As some parts of the 2km were relatively flat, other stretches had to compensate and I can only estimate that at times the gradient reached at least 15%, perhaps briefly as much as 20%. It was dispiriting stuff and with my bad back, my lack of sleep and my as yet undiagnosed sickness, I had no choice but to get off and push. Cars zoomed past me in second or even first gear and their occupants stared at me as anyone would stare at a man who had lost all his senses. A few beeped their horns mockingly, encouraging me to keep going. I wasn't impressed. When I finally arrived at the top, I slumped onto the handlebars and read the four letters that had been printed in large font on the road: STOP. The instruction was entirely unnecessary. I staggered across the road to where there was some shelter under the rocks and sat down, exhausted.

What was I doing? Why was I putting myself through this? I still had more than half of the cycle to Portugal to complete! Was it worth it? Just to be able to say that I had really crossed a continent by bicycle? Really? Was that it?

Suddenly there was a whoosh of metal on the other side of the road. I looked up and there were more whooshes of metal. It was a group of touring cyclists and over the course of the following two minutes about ten of them passed me at varying intervals. One of them noticed me and she shouted '*hallo*' across the road. I didn't respond verbally but I did wave half-heartedly. The clues suggested they were also Dutch, although this lot hadn't been partying all night. Apart from looking Dutch and the '*hallo*', they were cycling very upright touring bikes with straight handlebars (although not the butterfly bars I had fitted to Reggie). They appeared not to have a bead of sweat on their bodies. Their backs were straight, their clothes were clean and they had smiles on their faces. What was their secret? I feared that they had just descended a very long section of road, which meant that I was in for a long climb. Just what I didn't need.

It took about half an hour for me to muster the energy – mental as well as physical – to get back on the bike and continue. It was cycling at its slowest and was one of the least enjoyable days of the entire journey. As I plodded further and further north, I tried to work out why I was feeling like I was. The obvious answer would be that I was dehydrated, but I was making sure that I was drinking many, many litres of water. This might be causing other problems however; too much water on its own could mean that I was washing the essential vitamins and minerals from my system. I would try and up my intake of salty foods if possible and when I next arrived at a supermarket or pharmacy I would stock up on some rehydrating sachets. I knew that dehydration could lead to aches and pains in the body and although this might not be the root of my problem with my back, it could be making it worse. I also thought about my experiences in northern Italy in 2010, especially when cycling from Pisa to Siena. I had been badly bitten by mosquitoes and they had given me fever-like symptoms. Although clearly I hadn't contracted malaria, the irritation from the bites had had a negative effect on my well-being. Two things had helped solve the problem: antihistamine tablets and anti-mosquito spray. These flying horrors hadn't been much of an issue up to this point on this trip but I did have one or two bites; it was perhaps time to start using the medication that I had in my first aid kit. I also thought carefully about what I had been eating and drinking; it wasn't always the healthiest of diets as I tried to pack in the calories in preference to my normal five-a-day fruit and veg. But I was consuming large quantities of a liquid that perhaps I shouldn't. OK, far too much beer and wine (which was undoubtedly also a factor) but also sun protection cream. In recent days, I had changed from using factor 50 sun block to factor 30. I had noticed that as I cycled and sweated, the much thinner factor 30 was often dripping into my mouth and I was inevitably drinking some of it. This couldn't be good for me, so for the sake of my stomach I would return to using the very thick factor 50 which was much more enthusiastic about remaining stuck to my skin. I would have to forgo the deep, Mediterranean tan that the vain side of me wanted to show off when I arrived back home.

Most of these were medium-term measures however, and did nothing to improve my well-being in the short-term. More cyclists passed me heading south and every single one of them looked just as fresh and healthy as the Dutch. At around lunchtime, I noticed three cyclists ahead of me who had stopped on my side of the road. Finally, some people who were travelling in the same direction as me! Alas no. They had simply moved over so as to shelter from the sun as they chatted under the rocks. To their credit, they looked slightly more dishevelled than the Dutch although there was still a gulf between their appearance and mine, which was edging further and further to the 'homeless tramp' end of the scale.

"Hi. Where are you going?" I asked.

"We are cycling to India," said one of the men.

"And I'm cycling from Venice to Greece" replied the other.

They were all obviously French – I could tell from their accents – and I was a little embarrassed that I had launched immediately into English without even bothering to ask if they spoke the language. I would have been perfectly comfortable speaking French and felt as though I had pinned another drawing pin in that poster which states that *'the British don't speak foreign languages'*. The couple destined for India were travelling by tandem which had a large trailer attached to the back. It reminded me of the pile of equipment that Jean-François, the French guy whom I had met back in Ioannina, was transporting on his trailer. Perhaps it was the French way of doing things. As I spoke I could hear my voice; I was croaking badly. It was another symptom to add to the list. The guy who was cycling to Greece cheered me up a little by telling me about the long descent that I was about to enjoy – this is the reason why they had stopped for a breather – so my mood was lifted just a little as I allowed gravity to take over, giving me and my muscles a much welcome break.

I hit sea level once again in a town called Senj. It had been one long, continuous downhill ride of about 10km and I had enjoyed every single second. I couldn't get out of my mind, however, the thought that all those fresh-faced, perspiration-free cyclists who I had been meeting during the course of the day had, at some point earlier, cycled up what I had just cycled down. It probably wasn't something to dwell upon, so I turned my mind to something much more important: where was I going to be sleeping?

I was ill. I knew that at least. What I couldn't work out was whether I was getting any better or any worse. I stopped in Senj to consider the options and came to the conclusion that even if I did find a campsite, in the state that I was in, I didn't want to spend the next night sleeping (or more likely, not sleeping) on an uncomfortable camping mat. I opened up Booking.com to see what they had on offer, but all the cheaper options in Senj were sold out and a quick wander around the back streets didn't reveal many, if any '*rooms*' signs. Back on the Internet, there were a few places listed in a town called Novi Vinodolski but that was another 25km north on the coast. Did I have another 25km in my weakened system? I examined the map carefully to see if I could work out if it would be a flat ride and came to the conclusion that yes, it probably was. A few minutes later, I had booked a €50 room at the Hotel Ema. The extra expense would hopefully pay off if my medical condition and morale were lifted by a night that contained that most rare of commodities, sleep.

Novi Vinodolski wasn't a bad little place. I arrived tired but, a little uncharacteristically, not particularly hungry. I put this down to whatever was wrong with me. The hotel, a family run place only a couple of hundred metres from the town centre, was comfortable if a tad dated. Well, more than just a tad. The decor wasn't so much post-modern as post-war and the bathroom had all the charm of the school toilets that I remember from growing up in the 1970s and 80s. It did, however, have one redeeming feature for which my body was yearning: a bed with a thick mattress. I showered, took a quick walk back into the centre of the town where there was a very conveniently located Lidl and stocked up on all the things that my self-diagnosis had told me I required. I returned to the hotel looking forward to getting shot of my ailments and finally escaping the Croatian coastline for the more familiar surroundings of northern Italy the following day.

171

Thursday 25th July 2013
Rest Day 5: Novi Vinodolski

I was being wildly over optimistic about my chances of recovery. Indeed, by the time I had crawled into bed at the Hotel Ema things were getting rapidly worse. Much worse. By the early hours of Thursday, I was making good use of the en-suite bathroom and I didn't care too much about it reminding me of my old secondary school. I shan't explain the ins and outs of my symptoms (they were mainly outs) other than to say they were very unpleasant indeed. I had no inclination whatsoever to continue cycling and decided to take a complete break from the trip. But I needed more than that. I needed a complete break from doing almost anything and rather ironically, by deciding to stay overnight in non-descript Novi Vinodolski, I had found a perfect place in which to do nothing, as there wasn't really much to do.

I did manage to get a little sleep, interspersed between trips to the bathroom, but having decided to stay put for another 24 hours, I needed to make sure that I had somewhere to stay for the second night. I checked Booking.com and it implied that there was no room available at the Hotel Ema for the night of the 25th, so when I heard noises outside I gingerly made my way to the nearby reception to enquire. It was only a few metres from the door of my room, which I left open should I need to rapidly excuse myself and make use of the bathroom once again. The hotel was run by Eleanor and her husband Boris. Eleanor had welcomed me the previous evening but when things had got complicated on a linguistic level she had told me to speak to Boris. I think Boris had let on to his wife that his level of English was better than was the reality, but what he lacked in his ability to conjugate an English verb appropriately (or to use one in the first place), he made up for in his enthusiasm.

"*Boris, I've been quite ill during the night...*" I explained without specifying, lest there be extra cleaning charges "*...so would it be possible to stay for an extra night?*"

I think he already knew the answer but out of courtesy he glanced down at the register and pulled an expressive face that eliminated the requirement to say anything, but he had a go anyway.

"*No possible. Busy, busy. Sorry.*" Then he smiled. "*But I friend... very nice hotel. Not far. €50 for room.*" €50 seemed to be the going rate in Novi Vinodolski.

"*Does it have a private bathroom?*" I asked, for reasons obvious to me if not perhaps immediately obvious to Boris.

"*Of course! Reservation? Yes?*"

"*Excellent. Yes, please.*" I was trying to minimise my own use of verbs in order to help Boris understand.

I returned to the room and packed away my things. I was a little wary of having to move somewhere else; despite the décor I would have much preferred to stay in the same place to ride out my illness. I was also a little uneasy about travelling from the Hotel Ema to the hotel run by Boris' friend. For a certain period of time I would not be within running distance of a convenient toilet. The consequences didn't bear thinking about, so I tried not to.

After about half an hour, a black Mercedes pulled up outside and a woman in her 40s got out. Boris came out to greet her and they exchanged a few pleasantries, which I suspected might have included a few details about my medical condition.

"*Yes, this is the idiot from England who has decided to cycle from Greece to Portugal in the middle of summer... no surprise that he's now suffering! He's very keen on a private bathroom, so you can probably guess what his problem is...*"

The woman's name was Kelly and she was the owner of the second hotel. If she did know exactly what my medical issues were, she wasn't letting on. I arranged to travel to her hotel in her car along with my panniers and I would come to collect Reggie later that morning.

The journey was mercifully short – a matter of a few minutes – and Kelly's 'hotel' was in reality Kelly's house. There was no sign up outside the modern three storey detached building, just a few flower pots hooked along the edges of the balconies. We climbed the stairs running up the side of the house to where there was a small patio next to the kitchen. She asked me to sit down and offered me a drink.

"*Do you want tea? Camomile tea? It's very good.*"

It seemed an appropriate thing to offer an Englishman with a dodgy stomach, so I sat and sipped the tea as we waited for the room to be cleaned. The cleaner was actually Kelly's sister and her name was Sabha. She lived in Germany but had come down to Croatia to help her sister over the summer months. She didn't speak any English but was just as smiley and welcoming as her sister. Once the tea was finished, I was shown the room which was at the very top of the building but which had independent access so that I could come and go as I pleased, although that did seem unlikely in my current state. It was one of three

173

rooms that she rented out and it resembled a suite in a private hospital: spotlessly clean to the point of being clinical, air-conditioned and functionally comfortable. The bathroom was just across the hallway but Kelly explained that, as the other two rooms were empty that evening, it would be all mine. Unlike a hospital, there were no doctors or nurses to tend to my medical needs but apart from that, it was perfect. I thanked Kelly and Sabha for coming to my rescue, closed the door, momentarily forgot about Reggie who was still back at the Hotel Ema, lay on the bed, closed my eyes and relaxed.

The day of complete rest was exactly what my body needed. I'm no medic but the symptoms I had been experiencing and the knowledge that I had been drinking lots of fluid just didn't seem to fit happily with the idea that I was dehydrated. Even if I had been washing away essential vitamins and minerals (which seemed likely), surely my body wouldn't be continuing to get rid of even more fluids in the way that it had during the night. It seemed much more likely that somewhere I had picked up a bug that my body wanted to get rid of as quickly as possible. The prime suspect for a place where I could have picked up such a bug was, of course, *Camp Sveti Duh* where I had stayed on the island of Pag. Apart from my aching back (which had been an on-off problem since climbing the steep hills of Albania), I had felt fine up until my arrival at *Sveti Duh*. Then I had showered in the dirty wash block where I had bumped into Peter from *Family Guy*, I had eaten in the campsite bar, I had pitched the tent next to the field strewn with used toilet paper and I had even had a close encounter with a naked woman's pussy... Any one of them could have been the source of my problems. Well, apart from the last one, which is clearly there for comic effect.

That said, the whole experience had been a wake-up call to think more about prevention rather than cure. I needed regular sleep and I wasn't getting much of that in the tent on my current, ultra-thin camping mat. On arrival in Italy, I would look out for a branch of the Decathlon sports shop and investigate the possibilities of getting hold of something more comfortable. If that didn't work, I would have to splash out a little more often on hotel rooms. The online community had been of particular use when it came to weird and wonderful concoctions for staying hydrated, while at the same time replenishing the all-essential minerals in my body. Some suggestions needed to be set aside; as to follow them would have required visiting a well-stocked branch of *Holland and Barrett* almost every day of the trip but the following recipe did seem to be both practical and sensible:

- 1 litre of water
- 8 teaspoons of sugar (for glucose)
- 1 teaspoon of salt (for sodium)
- 1/2 cup of pure orange juice, not from concentrate (for potassium and taste)
- Shake it well and take it in a period of 2 to 4 hours.

Later in the day, I went back to the Hotel Ema to pick up Reggie and made another trip to the supermarket to buy a small amount of food, including a packet of sugar and some salt. Much of the rest of the time was spent horizontal with my eyes closed, relaxing and occasionally, sleeping. As the hours passed, my trips to the bathroom became much less frequent and by the end of the day my morale was almost back to where it had been pre-Pag. More camomile tea was delivered and consumed and as the afternoon melted into the evening, my thoughts turned to the remainder of the cycle through Croatia and Slovenia. I estimated the distance from Novi Vinodolski to Trieste, just over the border into Italy, to be approximately 120km. Wary of my delicate condition, I wasn't 100% sure that it was attainable in just one day but I was keen to give it a try. Much, of course, would depend upon how I felt the following morning.

I wouldn't be sad to leave the eastern Adriatic coast behind me and move on to Italy. Although there was much that I had enjoyed in Montenegro, Bosnia and Croatia: Dubrovnik, Trogir, the spectacular coastline, the challenging cycling, the glimpse into the history of the Balkans and the friendly people, there were certain aspects of this portion of the journey that I had found much less enjoyable. The scenery had changed only very gradually; I preferred my cycling to be through areas that were much more varied. I had found the language to be almost impenetrable and my efforts to master even the most basic expressions had come to nothing. On a personal level, for much of the time, I had felt alone. The last lengthy chat I had had with anyone was way back in Montenegro when I had spoken with Blend the baker and Alex in Bar. The people whom I had met since then had all been very nice but the situations had been functional. It would be a relief to meet up with old friends and family in Italy, France and Spain, as well as hopefully making some new ones via Warm Showers, the reciprocal accommodation sharing website that I had used from time to time back in 2010. It had many more subscribers in the areas through which I would be travelling in the second part of my trip, than in the first.

After over 2,000km of travelling, I was on the brink of crossing that line between Slovenia and Italy which, for me, marked the point when I would move from the unfamiliar surroundings of the eastern Mediterranean, to the much more familiar regions of the western Mediterranean. I wasn't yet halfway to Cape St. Vincent in Portugal, but I was certainly well on the way.

Friday 26th July 2013
Cycling Day 21: Novi Vinodolski to Trieste, 124km

Upon opening my eyes, I could see an angel dressed in a Persil-white gown with long, blond hair, wings and a shimmering halo above her head. Either my sickness had taken a severe turn for the worse during the night or my head just happened to be pointing at the religious-themed painting on the wall of my room. Fortunately it was the latter. I stared at it for a few moments and couldn't quite work out whether the two small children who were crossing the rickety bridge just underneath the angel were being protected or whether she was having a bad day and was about to push the kids into the raging torrent below. It would be a good way to teach them to swim. I then turned my focus towards my own troubles. How did I feel? Well, not quite fully recovered (as evidenced by a visit to the bathroom), but certainly much improved and without doubt up for the challenge of cycling 120km to Trieste. Well, perhaps.

More camomile tea was served up by the sisters of mercy, Kelly and Sabha, who had been delightful throughout my 24-hour stay in their house. Perhaps camomile tea really did have curative powers. Reggie had spent his restful day on the ground floor of the building and Kelly escorted me downstairs to unlock the door of the room where he had been kept. At some stage in the past it had functioned as a bar; distributed around the room were beer pumps, boxes of glasses collecting dust and at the far end, the bar itself. Kelly explained that her husband used to run the place but that it just didn't pay so instead they had turned their attentions to renting out the rooms, an enterprise that I hoped did make them some money.

As I prepared to leave, an Austrian family pulled up in front of the house; they had a reservation to stay for a few days. The man started to inspect Reggie and asked a few questions;

"Is it a good bike?" he enquired.

"Well, so far I've had no problems, I haven't…"

"You need smaller wheels…" he interrupted *"…and you have strange handlebars."*

"Well, I changed…"

"I have a bike in Austria and I use for cycling long distances. It is very good."

I'm not sure whether he was purposefully trying to provoke me or whether it was just his manner. Either way, I wasn't up for an

177

argument so let him continue for a few moments before turning to Reggie.

"Come on Reggie we need to get moving."

The Austrian looked at me in a funny way, I smiled and cycled off.

I was genuinely excited about my imminent arrival in Italy. I almost felt as though I was returning 'home' after a month abroad. This was bizarre, as I am not Italian and I have never lived nor worked in Italy. I had cycled the length of the country in 2010 on my first transcontinental journey of course (I should have pointed that out to the Austrian; it might have shut him up!) and, on a linguistic level I had a functional, working knowledge of some key bits of Italian. I suppose my feelings simply reflected my desire to spend a bit of time in an area where I could understand signs, buy food in a shop and ask for directions without prefacing every conversation with *"excuse me, do you speak English?"* Perhaps after a week or so in Italy, I would be feeling the same towards arriving in France, a country in which I had not only travelled widely but also in which I had lived for several years and in whose language I was fluent.

However, before Italy (let alone France) I still had a final 100km or so to cycle in Croatia, followed by around another 30km through Slovenia. One of the longest countries would be followed by one of the shortest but I sensed that Croatia wasn't going to let me go without chucking a few final hills in my direction. Perhaps my desire to get to Italy as soon as possible was simply down to the fact that it would be as flat as the Austrian's car tyre if I were ever to bump into him again. The coastal portion as far as the northern Croatian port of Rijeka looked fairly flat but I could see numerous altitude references on my map that reached to over 700m in the portion of the journey where I would move away from the sea to cut across the edge of the Istrian Peninsula. I would just keep thinking about the flat plain of northern Italy.

The main feature along the way to Rijeka, was a large oil terminal just south of the town which necessitated a long, steady climb around an elongated bay that reminded me of the much more picturesque lake around which I had cycled in Montenegro. There, if you remember, I delighted in taking the long route and avoiding the ferry. South of Rijeka, I would have jumped at an opportunity to cut down the cycling but the option didn't exist. The steady climb became a steep one in order to cross the headland where the refinery was located, but then a long bit of freewheeling brought me back to sea level and into the centre of Rijeka itself, where I paused for a drink in a small park near a canal.

Keen to implement my new regime of ensuring that I was replenishing my essential minerals, I had bought a large bag of salted crisps. I sat down on a bench to eat what remained of the contents of the packet but unfortunately this attracted a large number of flying rats or, as I believe they are more commonly known, pigeons. Just what is the point of pigeons? They annoy me in the extreme. OK, I know they are a source of food for larger birds, mammals and probably your cat but couldn't the larger birds turn their attention onto the mammals and perhaps vice versa? As for your cat, well, that's why someone invented Whiskas, no? (We all know that 8 out of 10 cats prefer Whiskas and I'm sure the rest could be persuaded.) I will hear no counter arguments as my point is well-made. They are vermin. Anyway, back to Rijeka. Determined to find a more suitable, pigeon-free location in the centre of town, I reached for my phone to consult an online map, only to notice that I had received a very long text message and a couple of answerphone messages. Something had happened. Even before starting to read, I knew it wasn't going to be good news... The text message read as follows:

"Hi Andrew. My name is Jenny and I live in the apartment below yours. Your flat has flooded as a tap was left on and the water has come through the ceiling into my flat making quite a mess..."

That wasn't the worst news. It continued:

"...The fire brigade broke into your flat and turned off the tap, but the water is still coming in and it's all over your flat. Can you give me a call? Thanks."

Suddenly the pigeons seemed of secondary importance. I'd had illness, now it was flooding trying to put a spanner in the spokes of my trip. What awaited me in Italy? War? Plagues of frogs? My heart sank at the possible consequences of the flood back home in Britain. It was difficult to discount the possibility of having to return to the UK to get the whole thing sorted. How badly damaged was the flat? What had caused the tap to be running? Why would a running tap cause a flood in the first place? Taps do tend to be placed over sinks and plugholes and mine certainly were.

Cycling along the Mediterranean suddenly had to be put to one side as I tried to get the situation sorted from a distance of 1,300km.

Briefly, what had happened was that there had been a cut in the water supply on the previous evening. My lodger, who was continuing to use the flat in my absence and who normally only stayed from Monday to Thursday, had turned on the tap only to find that no water was coming out. As most people would, he had continued to turn the tap so that it was fully on. He reported the problem to the relevant people but crucially he hadn't turned the tap off again. (He had also inadvertently moved the arm of the tap into a position between the two sinks in the kitchen so the water that subsequently came out of the tap hit the strip of metal separating the two sinks.) When the water supply was restored late on Thursday evening, it had started flowing in a torrent out of the tap, much of it hitting the metal between the sinks and flooding the kitchen. This had probably continued for several hours until the fire brigade had had to intervene.

It took around two hours of telephoning, texting and emailing the various protagonists in the little saga for me to arrive at a point where I was happy that, by the time I did eventually return home at the end of August, everything would be in order. It crossed my mind that perhaps my scurrilous thoughts regarding the actions of the angel in the picture earlier in the day might be connected and that it was her way of telling me to jog on. Those who believe, do say that God moves in mysterious ways and it was perhaps also true for his angels. I would have gladly spent the night sleeping in a pigeon loft rather than have to deal with the issue. It wouldn't surprise me if they also had something to do with it. Pigeons certainly do move in mysterious ways; have you seen them walk?

Jog on I didn't, but cycle on I did, and embarked on the long, long climb from sea level to just under 600m where I found the border post between Croatia and Slovenia. I sat for a few minutes on the kerb of a largely deserted parking area next to some souvenir shops and money exchange boxes. They weren't doing much selling and I wasn't doing much buying, apart from a couple of bottles of water to replenish my stocks. In the distance I could see a cyclist and he was heading in my direction. As he got closer I could see he was a touring cyclist, although one who appeared to have hit hard times. My own lycra shorts were a bit faded and my quick drying t-shirt a little moist from the efforts of climbing the hill, so I was hardly in catwalk-ready condition but he had gone for the tramp look and was pulling it off quite successfully.

"*Where are you going?*" I asked after exchanging greetings that implied he spoke English.

"*Don't go to Hungary. Those bastards fined me for cycling on the motorway...*"

Here we go again... He hadn't even bothered to answer my simple question before launching into his tirade against the Hungarian authorities.

"Sorry to hear that," I responded but refrained from asking any more questions that would presumably be ignored anyway.

He continued until he could see that perhaps he hadn't found the most sympathetic ear. I suspected that his story might be leading in the direction of him asking me for money so it seemed best to politely make my excuses and go. He was still muttering as I did so.

"Thieves, all of them..."

Slovenia was pretty and flat and in the late afternoon of a hot day in July, it was a very picturesque and pleasant place through which to cycle. Although linguistically (and probably culturally – I didn't really have the chance to find out) much the same as Croatia, physically, the countryside was more like southern Germany and, I guess, Austria which was only 100km further north. All the fields had been freshly cut and large rolls of hay were strewn across the landscape like discarded Liquorice Allsorts made from Shredded Wheat. In the distance were the hills, carpeted by a continuous cover of dark green trees, which pushed this area to well over 700m above sea level. It was in total contrast to the coastal cycling that I had been experiencing for much of the previous week and it was blinking marvellous.

Just as I had done when crossing the short piece of Bosnia the weekend before, I did want to do something in Slovenia to give me some justification for saying that I had visited the country. I wasn't quite ready for a full-blown meal (Italy could give me that) but a coffee and a snack would have been nice. I passed schools, churches, farms, a pharmacy, several nice country hotels... but no small shops or cafés. What does your average Slovene do when he or she has a sudden urge to consume a tube of Pringles? It wasn't until I was within a kilometre of the Italian border that I finally found a small supermarket where I bought a banana, some cheese, an energy drink (I was starting to get addicted) and a Snickers bar (I already was). I also booked myself a night at the Hotel Milano in Trieste. I think these things combined pushed me over the threshold of being able to say that yes, I had indeed visited Slovenia.

The Italian border was deserted, but it was a real delight to see the familiar signage to which I had become so accustomed three years previously. So happy was I to have arrived in the land of Dante, that I started spurting random pieces of Italian in the direction of anyone who cared to listen (which was fortunately no one).

"Mi chiamo Andrew... Habito in Inghilterra... Amo la mia biciclette... Si chiama Reggie... Dove è la banca?... Vorrei una camera per una notte... Parlo sempre come un idiota..."

181

I was a cycling Berlitz language tape.

The descent into Trieste was payback for the stresses of the previous few days: the dodgy campsite on Pag, the back-breaking, calf-straining, coastal road, the stomach bug, the annoyingly fresh Dutch cyclists, the cynical Austrian, the flood back home, the tramp who hated the Hungarians... 500m in just 10km. The road brought me straight to the door of the *Hotel Milano* and its pink façade in the heart of Trieste. It was a fading, early 20th century place which had been selectively modernised and was full of Chinese businessmen preparing for a night on the town. I would hopefully get the chance to stretch my own legs a little later in the evening, but first it was a celebratory drink of Italian beer in the hotel bar, where I toasted my success in completing the journey from Greece to Italy in one piece. I wasn't drunk on the beer but I was drunk on the emotion of being *in Italia! Saluti!*

PART FOUR: ITALY
Saturday 27th July 2013
Cycling Day 22: Trieste to Caorle, 113km

My job over the few days following my arrival in Trieste – my *Italian Job* if you like – was to cycle across northern Italy from east to west. The distance between Trieste and Nice, the first major town in France and also the place where I was planning to take another day of rest, was around 600km as the crow flies. As the bike cycles, I estimated something nearer to 800km when taking into consideration all the wiggling about. That said, I intended to follow a route that was a straight as I could manage, taking in Venice - where I would be meeting up with a friend from the 2010 cycle and also having a day off - and Verona, before picking my way from town to town in as direct a way as possible in the direction of Cuneo. Cuneo appeared to be a gateway town to the Southern Alps and the nearby Tende pass had been recommended as a possible route into France. From there, I would head back down to the coast at Nice. It would be good if I could arrive in France by the 1st August, but to cycle 800km in just six days did seem a tad over-optimistic, not forgetting of course the day off in Venice, which would cut that down to just five days of cycling. It would require a Herculean 160km per day and that just wasn't going to happen, unless I intended checking into the first hospital I could find in France with exhaustion. I had already had one bout of illness during this cycling adventure and I preferred to avoid a second. I would have to content myself with the knowledge that I would be arriving in France in the first few days of August but certainly not on the first itself, even if that did mean that I was reducing my chances of completing the entire trip to Portugal by the ultimate deadline of the 31st August.

I would worry about all that another day, however. I had made it to Trieste and was delighted to be there. It was so different to any of the places that I had visited up to that point on the trip; Athens had been low level and ancient, Tirana was having a frantic growth spurt, with every entrepreneur in northern Albania jostling for their position in the commercial explosion that was taking place, Dubrovnik was a beautifully preserved, period piece that was trying hard (and succeeding) to please the tourists. Trieste wasn't any of those. It was confident, elegant, a bit rough around the edges in places but happy in its own skin. It was in no mad rush to reinvent itself as something that it fundamentally wasn't; in preference to rebuilding for a new century,

183

it was merrily showing off what it had constructed in the previous two. I was in no particular rush to leave and head off in the direction of Venice, so I spent a couple of hours wandering the streets and taking in several cups of coffee. It reminded me a little of Manchester (albeit a Manchester with an unbroken blue sky and one without everyone calling you 'chuck') and I put that down to the height of the buildings; they were predominantly five or six stories tall, which implied that this wasn't a capital (although low-rise Athens, as mentioned above, had clearly been an exception) but neither was it some irrelevant backwater. James Joyce had liked the place too. He lived in the city in the ten-year period leading up to the outbreak of the First World War, teaching English and no doubt drinking, and his presence was commemorated with a life-size, bronze statue overlooking the *Canal Grande* in the centre of town. I leaned Reggie against his waist and took a photograph. It wasn't such a leap of the imagination to believe that the man who brought us *The Dubliners* and *Ulysses* had taken up cycle touring as well as writing. Perhaps Reggie will one day be honoured in bronze for his passage through Trieste, but as it was only an overnight stay this does seem a little unlikely. I did all my wanderings around Trieste without reference to my *Rough Guide to Italy*, as I suspected that it wouldn't receive a good write-up. I didn't want to be told that it was a city in perpetual decline (as such places are often described if they haven't employed an internationally famous architect to create a worthy, modern-day wonder for everyone to stare at), but when I did reach to open my guidebook over a final cup of coffee, to my surprise, the authors liked it too. They are clearly learning.

The cycling started at around 10am and with an initial climb along the road next to, and increasingly above, the sea heading north-west. There were occasional points at which passers-by were encouraged to stop and take in the panoramic view back in the direction of Trieste and west along the coast towards where I would eventually find Venice. At one of these viewpoints, I bumped into a couple of touring cyclists. They were travelling separately. She was camping nearby and had just come out without her husband for a ride along the coast. I would imagine cycling with another person over an extended number of days could, at times, become a little claustrophobic and I could understand her desire to spend just a few hours by herself on the bike. She was Italian and spoke good English, the language she was using to converse with the other touring cyclist. He was from Germany, sported a pointy beard, white leggings and long black socks. If those weren't sufficient to make him stand out from the crowd, his bike certainly did: it was a recumbent.

For those of you not familiar with a recumbent bike – you may never have seen one as they are quite rare in the UK – they are three-wheelers: two at the front and one in the middle at the back. The rider sits in a central position on the bicycle, not on a saddle, but on what can only be described as a normal chair. Well, with the legs taken off, obviously. The pedals are at the very front of the bicycle and they are turned in the same way that you would turn the pedals on a pedalo boat. The chain is connected to the rear wheel via a subsidiary plate under the cyclist's seat. Get that? If you didn't, pop off to Google and find a picture, as I have reached the end of my abilities to get technical. You might imagine that they are new-fangled inventions – the cycling equivalent of the Sinclair C5 car perhaps – but you'd be wrong. According to William Fotheringham's excellent *Cyclopedia*, they were invented towards the end of the 19th century in Belgium and went on to become popular racing machines in France in the 1930s. They were so effective at beating the normal types of bike that the *Union Cycliste Internationale*, nowadays more commonly known as the UCI, banned them from races. At the risk of alienating any readers who are die-hard recumbent fans, I struggle to see the advantages over what I would call (and most people would call), a 'standard' bike. They look terrifyingly dangerous. Their proponents would argue that they are more comfortable, a point which I can understand, (perhaps I would have benefitted from using one for the sake of my lower back, which was continuing to grumble) and that their lower centre of gravity makes them much more stable machines to control. Well, that and the fact that they have three wheels so they don't topple over so easily. However plausible the arguments of their fans, I can't get out of my head the image of a bus or a lorry squashing the machine and its rider, while uttering those depressingly common words '*Sorry mate, I didn't see you*'. The thing with the recumbent bike is that I do actually believe that the bus or lorry driver might be telling the truth. A word of warning, however. Don't ever enter into a discussion with a recumbent cyclist as to the merits (or lack of them) of his or her chosen form of transport compared to your own. The best thing to do is to simply have a discussion with the person as if nothing is in the least bit puzzling to you. My German friend just outside Trieste was heading in the same direction as me and we chatted about where we had been and where we were going but at no point was the word 'recumbent' uttered. What a nice man (with a curious bike).

After a sharp descent towards the town of Monfalcone, the rest of the day's cycling was as flat as you can possibly imagine. Following weeks of having to confront hill after hill after hill along the coastal roads through Greece, Albania and Croatia, the endlessly flat road heading west out of Monfalcone was much appreciated. In the five or so hours of cycling that remained that afternoon, I was able to maintain a steady speed of around 20km/hr and make good headway towards an as yet unknown destination with a campsite along the coast. However... I am even more reluctant about writing this next bit than I am about having arguments with recumbent cyclists but I'll say it anyway. I don't want to come across as someone who complains about any topographical situation that I find on the roads, but there is, well, a downside to cycling on the flat; it can be hard work because you can never stop pedalling. It's chronic movement of the legs; you never get a chance to catch your breath and let the bike just fall away into the distance. This is what I was experiencing that afternoon in north-eastern Italy. I was also cycling into a slight headwind, which meant that if at any point the gradient of the road did momentarily turn in my favour, it was immediately cancelled out by the strength of the gusts. If I had stopped pedalling, Reggie would have ground to a halt within just a few metres. It appears that I am never happy. Sorry about that.

So my legs were continuing to get a good workout despite the lack of hills and so was my Italian. I paused for something to eat in a small town called San Giorgio di Nogaro, where almost everything was shut. It was a Saturday afternoon and Italian towns do tend to become deserted at that time of the week. From the British perspective, this is of course sheer madness. We live in a shopping-obsessed society which is gradually moving towards the point where everything will be open for 24 hours a day, seven days a week. (What will happen then?) I'm sure the Italians who visit Britain are horrified to see that we have created a leisure activity out of wandering around the aisles of the nearest John Lewis or checking our emails free of charge in the local Apple Store (or is it just me?). My quest to find food in San Giorgio di Nogaro was solved by the *Pizzeria Focacceria Noiar*. The owner had seen the light and decided to keep his shop open. Despite this fact, it was still very quiet and as I waited for my pizza to be prepared we chatted:

"Parla inglese? Non? Sono inglese... Vado in bicyclette di la Grecia in Portugale... Ho fame e sono molto contente que la vostra pizzeria e aperto... Avete de l'aqua? Si? Eccellente!"

My Italian was far from perfect but it was wonderful to be having the bare bones of a conversation with a local who didn't speak any

English. I do like the Italian language; it's like a jigsaw in a way that French isn't. Small morsels of Italian can be pieced together to make coherent sense. Or is it that I am simply more willing to have a carefree attitude towards accuracy when trying to speak Italian? I can hear my errors when I make them in French and it can be frustrating; in Italian I don't hear my errors and plough on regardless. It's what I encourage my pupils to do back at school in Britain and here I was putting it into practice. Communication really is the most important thing.

Buoyed by my mid-afternoon linguistic success, I continued along the SS14, the main road between Trieste and Venice until San Michele Al Tagliamento, at which point I started to edge nearer to the coast where I would hopefully find a campsite. There were various candidates but the place that I chose was the town of Caorle. Unfortunately, it appeared that most of the people who had been travelling on the SS14 had also chosen to head in the same direction as me. That said, after my experiences heading north from Athens, the drivers in Italy did seem to be quite calm and collected. Had it really improved so dramatically since I had last cycled in Italy some three years previously or was it a case of simply everything being relative? I suspected the latter.

Caorle was a busy strip of a town with cars clogging up the main street through the centre. It ran parallel to the beach, which was hidden behind the bars, restaurants, souvenir shops and mini-markets that you find in seaside resorts worldwide. Much to my delight, I spotted a sign for '*campeggio municipale*' or municipal campsite and followed it. At the very western end of the town I finally found what I was looking for. It's difficult to beat to good, council run campsite, which is run for the benefit of the local community. Well, the local visiting community I suppose. Any town in France which is worth its *sel* has one and many in Italy do too. They give you what you need and don't charge you a fortune for doing so. Well, usually.

"*Ventiquattro euros,*" explained the man behind the counter.

"*Ventiquattro euros?*" I repeated as if trying to master the pronunciation.

"*Ventiquattro euros per favore*" he confirmed. My pronunciation seemed to be good. 24 euros was not, however, very 'municipal campsite', but there was little I could do so I smiled and paid up.

The local council was certainly making good money, not just from me but also from the hundreds of holidaymakers it had managed to pack in to its site. I erected the tent and immediately escaped back into the centre of town in search of a supermarket to buy some food. Before

187

I did that, however, I paused at the *Enos Wine Bar*. The name of the bar was written on the awning above my head, in English. If that sounds quite elegant, please bear in mind that if I had chosen to move one table to my right, I would have been sitting under an awning telling me I was in *Enos Snack Bar* which does sound slightly less exotic. As I drained the cold beer from its glass, I tried to take in a little of the atmosphere of Caorle. The buildings were painted in bright colours and the traffic had been stopped for the evening. It gave a feeling of sitting along Main Street at Disneyland, albeit a Main Street without a loud animatronic parade passing by every thirty minutes. In addition, Caorle had an authentic edge to it and people clearly did live behind the shutters; they weren't hiding suicidal 'cast' members knocking back bottles of Johnny Walker and cursing annoying children under their costumes... Or is that just me after a hard day at school?

Eventually I ambled back to the campsite, pushing Reggie by my side and trying to dodge all the tourists who were also heading in one direction or another along the car-free street. I did find a supermarket and bought a few essentials to keep my stomach filled. These included a 25cl Tetra Pak carton of Spar '*vino bianco*' which proudly guaranteed that it was '*100% italiane*'. You may not learn much from reading this book but please take away with you this one, small nugget of knowledge: never buy a carton of Spar '*vino bianco*', even if it does guarantee its Italian authenticity. Should you ever visit the municipal campsite in Caorle, you won't find it difficult to spot the exact pitch that I used that night in July 2013 as it will be the one that is next to the dead tree, killed by the contents of the carton of white wine. It was a lucky escape for me and you have been warned.

Sunday 28th July 2013
Cycling Day 23: Caorle to Venice, 69km

It was a night of camping hell. Nothing to do with the cheap wine (of which I didn't drink more than a sip anyway) or the neighbours (who were a friendly family with a useful mallet), but everything to do with the heat, the camping mat and the sleeping bag. As I perspired, the moisture produced by my body was being soaked up by my down bag (was it the greatest of choices for a trip around the Mediterranean in summer?), leaving me to sleep upon an increasingly damp cushion of moistness. The camping mat had finally given up any pretence of doing its job and was now no more effective at providing support for my body than your average tablecloth. It had clearly sprung a leak but I had no idea where the hole might be and I had no intention of trying to find it. It was clearly a situation that I would have to remedy upon arrival in Venice.

Simone, my friend in Venice, had first contacted me prior to my cycle from England to the south of Italy in 2010. At the time he was living in the town of Pavia, just south of Milan, and he invited me to spend the night in his flat. He also offered to come and meet me in Como and guide me through the suburbs and centre of Milan, which we needed to cross in order to get to Pavia. The following day he cycled with me as I continued my journey and the last time I had seen him was at a non-descript road junction just south of Piacenza. We had kept in contact in the intervening three years via Facebook and when I decided to embark on a second cycling odyssey along the Mediterranean coast, it seemed only natural to meet up with him once again in his new home, Venice. As he had done in 2010, Simone offered to join me on the cycle to where he lived and as soon as I had arrived in Trieste and could say with some certainty when I would be arriving in Venice, we had arranged to meet in the town of San Donà di Piave at 11am. Somewhere.

San Donà di Piave was around 30km from Caorle so I had plenty of time to eat some breakfast in the town centre before heading off across the flat plain for our late morning rendez-vous. In fact, I arrived about 30 minutes early so found a café just off the main square and ordered a drink. I checked my phone to see if there were any last minute messages from Simone and there was one, via Facebook:

Simone: *"I'm now in San Donà, I'm coming toward you on the sp54."*

189

Andrew: *"Ah... I've just arrived in San Donà!!!! STOP! I'm in the café on the pedestrian street just next to the duomo."*

Simone: *"OK. Coming."*

Simone wasn't the kind of person who was happy to laze around in a café and wait for someone to arrive, so he had continued cycling in the hope of meeting me en route. At some point we must have crossed but it was a mystery as to why we hadn't spotted each other. It was Sunday morning and the roads were very quiet. When he did arrive at the café he looked no different than he had three years previously; perhaps we had both had our minds on other things.

His was the first familiar face I had seen since leaving Heathrow Airport exactly four weeks earlier and it was interesting catching up with each other for an hour or so over coffee and water. He had moved to Venice in order to continue his search for a job. He knew the city well as he had been a student there, but he hadn't yet found full-time employment. He was occasionally doing work for the Venice Biennale Festival but apart from that, was still on the look out for a permanent post. Having split from the girlfriend he had been living with in Pavia, he was currently sharing a small house near the centre of Venice with an architect friend and it would be there that I would be spending the two nights I had planned to be in the city. If two nights in Venice wasn't enough to make me smile, the fact that it would be two nights spent not sleeping on the defunct camping mat most certainly was.

We still had much to talk about but the café had been invaded by a loud bunch of pensioners. It was chucking out time at the large church on the opposite side of the road and most of the parishioners had descended upon the terrace of the café to gossip no-doubt about the ungodly goings on in San Donà di Piave. I have no idea what they were talking about of course but there was something about the fervent way in which they were busily exchanging stories that made me think they weren't debating the relative merits of the priest's sermon. So intense was the sound that we decided it would be a good time to complete our cycle to Venice, which was still about 40km down the coast.

This wouldn't be my first visit to Venice. I had flown to Milan in spring 2003, with a colleague from work, to visit my cousin who was living in the city at the time. We caught the train from Milan to Venice and spent a couple of days exploring. It was beautiful; I came away thinking that I had found the most stunning city on the planet. Travelling by train is by far the easiest way to access the islands upon which Venice is built. The 3.6km railway bridge linking the city to the mainland was opened in 1846 but curiously, construction of the Santa Lucia railway station on the eastern end of the bridge didn't begin until 1860. I trust that someone informed the train drivers at least, if not the passengers. Anyway, back to May 2003 when my train did arrive in Venice. Within just a few moments of stepping off the train, you are standing next to the Grand Canal. It's an impressive sight and you are immediately absorbed into the romanticism of Venice. It ticks the boxes of everything that you have heard about the city because you can see it before your eyes: the iconic buildings and bridges, the vaporetto boats and, if you are lucky, perhaps even a passing gondola complete with singing gondolier (no, sorry, that's a television advert).

Arriving by bicycle is a little different. In 1933, Mussolini opened a second bridge – the *Ponte Littorio*, or, as it is now called, the *Ponte della Liberta* – next to the railway bridge. It's a four-lane highway – two in each direction – but there is no special provision for bicycles. A few kilometres before we arrived at the western end of the bridge, Simone warned me to follow him (I had no intention of doing otherwise!) and we proceeded to pick out a route along the horribly busy, convoluted and downright ugly roads which have been built on the mainland in order to guide the hoards of tourists towards the lagoon. Once at the bridge, we moved our bikes onto the narrow pavement, with the low wall of the bridge to our right and a crash barrier to our left, and cycled the 3.6km towards Venice. It wasn't a pleasant experience. If I dared – at times there was a real risk of Reggie's dimensions being wider than those of the hemmed in pavement - I could occasionally look across to the railway bridge and through the window of a passing train to see eager and excited tourists who were about to do what I had done some ten years previously and have a quality arrival in Venice. In the far distance I could see the island – it looked nothing special – and dominating the skyline to my right were a couple of cruise ships. I could also make out what looked like a multi-storey car park. As we neared the end of the *Ponte della Liberta* and it curved away from the railway bridge I could see that yes, it *was* a multi-storey car park. Other modern buildings were strewn along the road and then we came to a large bus station full of noisy coaches. *Was this really Venice?* It was only once we had pushed our bikes over the modern footbridge (which again had no provision for bicycles, just several hundred steps covering every metre of its curved span) that I was finally able to begin to glimpse the picture-postcard Venice that I had in my head. As arrivals go, it was all a little depressing and in stark contrast to my previous visit by train.

In fairness, Venice wasn't built as a place to cycle – it is banned next to the canals – but it might have been nice to have had the opportunity to use a dedicated cycle path along the bridge. Arriving by train, I must have been able to see all the paraphernalia of a modern tourist destination but by being sealed away in the comfort of the carriage I could at least ignore it, in the same way that the Queen can ignore her tradesman entrances, refuse skips and piles of scaffolding which might have been dumped around the back of one of her palaces.

On the other side of the footbridge, calmness and order were restored. One of the great things about Venice is the noise: people chatting, water lapping against the sides of the canals and the occasional water ferry chugging its way past. It wasn't too long before this is all that I could hear; I had finally arrived in the Venice of my memories. The house where Simone was staying was in the Ghetto district, towards the northern end of the city. We pushed our bikes along the busy streets and over a couple more bridges before escaping the crowds and turning down a narrow alley, where a door led us through a thin corridor to a row of low, modern houses one of which belonged to Simone's friend. The location was fantastic and, best of all, it was air-conditioned.

The remainder of the afternoon was spent chatting, doing my washing and, much to my great relief, going on a shopping trip to the Decathlon shop back on the mainland. This was somewhere I could replace my camping essentials but it did require a trek over the bridge once again. Rather than cycle, however, we took the bus to where Simone kept his car in the outskirts of the town of Mestre. Well, kind of. Mestre is actually part of Venice, although from what I could see it was nothing like Venice. The area around the end of the bridge was nothing but a large industrial complex, home to oil storage tanks, disused factories, industrial canals and the odd, modern bit of 21st century, industrial regeneration. It was also home to the out-of-town shopping area, where the Decathlon store was but one of several. Once inside, I purchased a new and frighteningly expensive camping mat. I was willing to fork out the money if it helped me sleep a little easier when I was next in the tent. Instead of replacing the sleeping bag with something equivalent, I bought a sleeping 'liner', which was nothing more than two cotton sheets sewn together to form a lightweight bag. I hadn't really been using my down bag to sleep *in*, rather, I had been using it to sleep *on* in a vain attempt to compensate for the lack of comfort provided by the camping mat. The cheapness of the liner made me feel a little better about the extravagance required for the new mat and I hoped that, combined, they would lead to endless nights of slumber. Sleeping Beauty had better watch her back. Perhaps.

As we drove back through the industrial areas of Mestre, we passed many prostitutes lined up along the road. Some were openly flaunting what they had to offer in none-too-subtle ways. Simone explained that many of the women were from Eastern Europe and that, although illegal, it was usually tolerated. I was to see many more prostitutes as I travelled across northern Italy (clearly not in a professional capacity), some in quite remote areas. I eventually came to the conclusion that I was only shocked by the openness of the industry and that this was probably down to nothing more complicated than the weather. If I were a prostitute in cold, wet Britain, I think I'd find somewhere to keep me warm and I would certainly wrap up. In Italy, where the summer nights are often just as warm as the days, I think I would advertise what was being offered. During the day I would argue that, well, *"I'm sunbathing officer"*. Then again, I probably wouldn't make a very good prostitute, on several levels.

Let's leave the sex industry and get back to the tourist one and Venice. The first thing I did upon arrival back at the house in the Ghetto, was to take my old camping mat and my sleeping bag and dump them in the nearest refuse skip. Shortly after dark we headed out again, but this time only in the local area of the Ghetto. Nowadays, we use the word to describe any area of a town or city where people live in high density in disadvantaged conditions. There is a sense of exclusion about the word and it's likely that the people of 'the ghetto' are predominantly those from a different cultural or ethnic background. The Ghetto in Venice is the original and it is where all the Jews were ordered to live at the start of the 16th century. Subsequent authorities ruled that the height of the buildings in the Ghetto should be much lower than those of the surrounding areas, which resulted in buildings with low ceilings and only added to the sense of claustrophobia. The Jewish community of Venice is now much smaller than it was, but those who remain see the Ghetto as their part of town. I went with Simone to a pizzeria just to the north of where he was living and, wandering through the dimly-lit alleyways, across eerie bridges and beside the quiet canals, there was still a distinctive atmosphere to the place. Having read *The Merchant of Venice* when I was at school (more of my Shakespearean studies when we arrive in Verona by the way), I couldn't help but see and hear Shylock scuttling along behind us.

"I will buy with you, sell with you, talk with you, walk with you, and so following, but I will not eat with you or drink with you..."

Sorry Shylock. You're not invited anyway.

Monday 29th July 2013
Rest Day 6: Venice

Venice is in peril. Apparently. When we emerged from Simone's friend's house in the Ghetto district of Venice for my sixth rest day of the trip, the only evident watery peril was the one falling from the sky. It was raining and with a sky as grey as a non-native squirrel, it didn't look as though it was going to stop any time soon. It was curious how the only rain I had so far experienced had fallen either during the night or, as had been the case on my visit to Olympia and now here in Venice, on one of my days off the bike. During my first continental crossing some three years previously, I had grown accustomed to cycling in the rain to the extent that I occasionally quite liked it. Cycling under endless blue skies was clearly preferable but I really wouldn't have minded experiencing an occasional downpour. Perhaps the inclement, Venetian weather was a sign of things to come in northern Italy and I could look forward to a few cycles in the rain over the course of my week long trek towards the border with France. I was, however, mindful of wishing for something that I might later regret.

But is Venice in peril? You can still buy a Veneziana Pizza ('red onions, capers, olives, sultanas, pine kernels') from any branch of Pizza Express and the price will include '*a discretionary 25p which we will donate on your behalf to the Veneziana Fund'*. In late 1966 Venice flooded on a catastrophic scale. You know when you are in trouble if, within a month of your flood taking place, the director general of UNESCO writes the following:

"During the first days of November, Tuscany and Venetia were devastated by floods of extraordinary magnitude and violence. The damage has been enormous. To the toll in human lives and the loss of property were added the destruction, in Florence and Venice, of creations of the human spirit which made the enchantment of the culture and art of living that Italy has given to the world. In all, 885 works of art of the first importance, 18 churches and some 10,000 other objects have suffered. Seventy libraries and learned institutions have been stricken. More than 700,000 volumes of archives comprising some 50million items, of which 10,000 were of inestimable historical and scientific value, have been damaged. Florence and Venice! The names alone say why Italy's grief is ours. But they indicate also why Italy's resolution to preserve and restore everything that can be saved will be the common purpose of us all. Venice sinking into the waters, it is as if one of the most radiant stars

195

of beauty were suddenly engulfed; Florence bemired, it is the springtime of our hearts which is for ever disfigured. We will not resign ourselves to such disasters."

Crikey. Venice really was in trouble. UNESCO launched an appeal, as did the British, under the leadership of a former ambassador to Rome, Sir Ashley Clarke. Initially known as the '*Art and Archives Rescue Fund*' it wasn't long before the name was changed to the much catchier and donation-prompting '*Venice in Peril*'. In 1977, the founder of Pizza Express, Peter Boizot, decided to create his now famous pizza and the 5 pence pieces started to roll in. Inflation has of course intervened and the donation is now five times greater than it was. It would be interesting to know how many people refuse to pay the '*discretionary*' 25p but, even taking into account those who do, the restaurants have been able to donate over £2million to the coffers of Venice in Peril. Venice has been saved!

According to Pizza Express, Venice is '*famously beautiful... but it's famously sinking*'. That's true (on both counts), but it doesn't really paint the whole picture. According to scientists (and I'm relying upon a certain Dr. Yehuda Bock of the Scripps Institution of Oceanography in California, who produced a piece of research in 2012), during the course of the 20th century, Venice did sink by 120mm. But the waters in the Lagoon which is home to Venice's 117 islands also had a significant part to play; they rose by about 110mm during the same period. The sinking was put down to a combination of plate tectonic geography (the Adriatic plate is 'subducting' or heading underneath the Apennine Mountains to the west), compaction of sediments beneath Venice but, most infamously, the pumping of groundwater from under the city. It's obviously a little tricky to do much about the first two factors, but it was possible to stop the third one and this now no longer takes place. However, according to Dr. Bock (great name - he needs a spaceship, no?), Venice is still sinking at a rate of about 2mm per year and, combined with the rise in the level of the water in the lagoon of an equivalent amount, the distance between the land and the sea is reducing by some 4mm per year. The authorities seem to have done what they can to stop the sinking, so they have now turned their attention to the rising sea levels. In late 2013, the first group of what will eventually be 78 iron floodgates were tested successfully. When complete, the appropriately named Moses Project will form a mile-long barrier blocking off the sea at three entrance points to the lagoon. Over £5 billion has already been spent constructing the barriers and much more will be needed before they are fully operational and Venice is once again safe from flooding. In the meantime, Venice remains in peril so next time you are in Pizza Express, you'd better make it a Veneziana.

During my previous visit in May 2003, Venice had basked under constant, brilliant sunshine and I remember completing the trip with the colours of the city imprinted on my retinas. As we made our way on foot from the northern Ghetto cluster of islands towards the popular central areas, Venice wasn't shining in any way like I remembered. Most tourists were scuttling around under umbrellas and plastic raincoats; my own protection was courtesy of my cycling jacket, which was getting its first outing of the summer. What I hadn't benefitted from some ten years previously however, was a local guide and I was determined to make the most of Simone's inside knowledge of the city. As we meandered from canal to canal, he chatted about his life in the city and the people and places he knew well. From time to time, he would pause to exchange greetings with a fellow resident and, in one or two cases, engage in a little conversation. Simone's English was excellent – he had been a student of Japanese at the university in Venice and clearly had an ear for languages – and he was able to add a detailed narration to the living documentary that I was seeing first hand.

Despite the weather, the gondoliers were out in force either ferrying people from one landing to another or trying to persuade those still on dry land to climb on board. Simone explained a little about the history of the gondolas, how they had first been used over a thousand years ago and how they are all made in exactly the same way and to exactly the same dimensions. One side of each boat is slightly shorter than the other so as to compensate for the weight of the gondolier. It also results in a slightly lopsided appearance on the water. I watched as several gondolas queued to make their way along a narrow canal, their owners expertly manoeuvring the oar so as to successfully navigate their way through an obstacle course of motorised boats covered in tarpaulins, parked against the crumbling brickwork of the *palazzi*. The gondoliers work as part of a guild and at any one time only 425 licences are allowed. It used to be that the licence was passed down from father to son (never, it seems from father to daughter or indeed from mother to daughter), however, more recently stringent training requirements were introduced which dictate that any prospective gondolier must be mentored by an existing member of the guild, practise for four hundred hours and even then pass an exam. But the rewards can be considerable. The prices are fixed and, according to the official website of the guild of gondoliers, a 'standard tour' will set you back €80 for 40 minutes on the water.

Choose to set sail (well, kind of) after 7pm and you'll be forking out €100. Annual income for gondoliers can be over €100,000. In the bold, new world of the 21st century, the once male-only profession has begun (but only just) to acknowledge that women may be equally capable of piloting a gondola and in 2010 Giorgia Boscolo was the first female to be admitted to the guild. That said, she is only allowed to stand in for her male colleagues when they are off sick. It's progress of sorts I suppose.

Our walking tour continued via the Rialto Bridge towards St. Mark's Square, the ornate Basilica, the Doge's Palace and the Bridge of Sighs, at which point we turned to head back north but made a point of trying to avoid the lanes, bridges and alleys that we had used on the trip south. Simone had spent a period of time working for the university on an exhibition of photographs from Iran and we called by the building in which the pictures were still on show. Apart from the images themselves, I found it fascinating to be able to delve deeper into the backstreets of Venice, where no other tourist had trod (well, on that day at least) to explore a quiet corner of Venetian academia. The security guard nodded as we passed him and I nodded sagely at the photos from Iran, while secretly being more enthralled by the views from the windows along the Grand Canal and the chaotic architecture of a building that was never designed to hold the offices of a university faculty of art.

Our penultimate stop was a backstreet café where we ate and drank at prices aimed at the locals rather than the tourists, before dodging a rainstorm under the arcades at the Rialto market. Under the halogen lights of the few stalls that remained open in the late afternoon, the bright red, purple, yellow and green fruit added a little colour to what had otherwise been a visually subdued day, courtesy of the cloudy sky. My guided tour ended close to where it had begun in a large square – the *Campo di Ghetto Nuovo* – just a few minutes' walk from Simone's friend's house. We found a bar and, as I tried to ignore the pigeons, we watched a group of students who had gathered in the centre of the square to celebrate the success of one of their group in achieving her qualification. She was being forced to read from a long text, which had been pinned to a tree, while at the same time being required to drink copious amounts of wine. Her fellow students who were plying her with the alcohol all seemed to be having a great time and as the ordeal continued, her ability to remain standing, let alone continue reading the words gradually diminished. From time to time, an older person would arrive – I assumed him or her to be one of her teachers – to chat to those who were able to string a sentence together.

It was heart warming to see that students were capable of doing stupid things in a place like Venice just as much as they are in Leeds, Manchester, York or London. I just hoped that the woman was suffering for at least a masters or doctorate. It all seemed a little excessive for a mere bachelors degree.

After some time, the conversation focussed once again upon my upcoming cycle across the north of Italy. As I set out my plans, Simone added his own recommendations and observations and, as the evening progressed, a more detailed plan began to coalesce.

The following day, Tuesday, Simone would join me on the cycle to Verona. There was a campsite called the *Campeggio Castel San Pietro* on one of the hills overlooking the town and I would hopefully spend the evening there, making the most of my newly purchased camping mat. I was already looking forward to a night of continuous slumber, hopefully. On Wednesday I would continue alone and I had managed to contact a cycling enthusiast via the Warm Showers website, who lived just to the west of a town called Cremona. I had also sent a message to a second Warm Showers host, who could potentially provide me with a bed on Thursday evening near Voghera. This had not yet been confirmed, so I might have to change my plans depending upon the response I received. As for Friday evening, I had no plan. Asti seemed a possible destination, from where I would start my climb into the Southern Alps towards Cuneo, or perhaps even Limone Piemonte, to spend Saturday night in the mountains. That would leave me to climb to the Tende Pass, before freewheeling back to the coast in Nice and a nice hotel on Sunday. My plan had some meat on it (although it wasn't quite a sirloin steak at this point) and I was already looking forward to arriving in France by the start of the following week. All of the cycles across northern Italy were of the order of 120km, which was above the average for the trip so far, but as most of the cycling would be on the flat at least until I started to climb towards Cuneo, several days of above average distances shouldn't be too much of a problem.

The only black cloud on the horizon was, well, a black cloud. Despite my earlier desires to spend at least a little time cycling in the rain, after the grey day in Venice I desperately wanted a return to the blue skies that had blessed my trip almost continuously up until that point. But things didn't look too promising. As Simone was preparing an evening meal back at the house and I was continuing to piece together the details of my cycling over the following week, outside there were great flashes and cracks of lightning and the ominous rumbles of thunder. I poked my head out of the front door to find that not only had the heavens opened for business but they were putting on some kind of clearance sale.

Tuesday 30th July 2013
Cycling Day 24: Venice to Verona, 136km

I was now into my fifth week on the road and for all of that time I had been travelling alone. I had been in charge of the decision making; I decided when to set off, when and where to turn left or right, when to pause to take a picture, read a tourist information panel, buy a Snickers bar, fill up on water, sit down by the side of the road and stare jealously at perspiration-free Dutch cyclists... You get my drift. Oh, and I was the one who decided when to stop and find somewhere to stay for the night. In the truest sense of the phrase, it was an ego trip. Cycling day 24 would, however, be different. Simone, as already mentioned, had suggested that he accompany me on the ride to Verona and I was happy for him to do so. It would not only ease my passage through the urban sprawl of Mestre but, just as he had been able to do during my day in Venice, he would be able to verbally annotate our journey. The plan was to follow the main road that shadowed the route of the A4 autostrada first to Padua, then Vicenza before arriving later in the day in Verona itself. Simone had a tentative plan to meet up with a friend who lived near Verona and perhaps stay with her. I would hopefully be spending the night at the *Campeggio Castel San Pietro*.

In Venice, I had been sleeping on the sofa at Simone's friend's house. The living room, dining area and kitchen were all part of the same open-plan area, so I did feel a certain obligation to get up very soon after waking up. Mindful of the weather conditions on the previous evening, I was curious to find out if things had improved. The house was almost windowless, save for a couple of skylights in the roof, but even these were covered by blinds so I wandered along the corridor to the front door of the building (come to think of it there wasn't a back door but...), opened it and, much to my delight and surprise, I was immediately basking in bright sunlight. I looked above to the sky and it was blue. It immediately put me in a positive frame of mind about the day's cycle to Verona and I set about packing everything away in the panniers and loading them back onto Reggie, ready for the off. Simone descended from the mezzanine bedroom where he had been sleeping, rustled up some breakfast, packed his own much smaller bag and we were soon pushing our bikes beside the neighbouring canal, back in the direction of the train station, bus station and bridge to the mainland.

The first 30km from Venice to Padua was easy going. Inevitably, there was a slight upward gradient as we moved away from the coast but this was so gradual as to be almost imperceptible. Once we had crossed the strip of predominantly decaying industry that separated Mestre from the sea, the cycling was mainly on cycle paths that were laid out by the side of the roads. Just as is often the case back in Britain, the paths were erratic in terms of surface quality and frequently ended abruptly, only to continue a few metres further along the road. The repeated requirement to judder over the kerb of the road to access the paths as they started and then stopped, was a little annoying but after 36 hours of absence from cycling, I was happy to put up with the inconvenience, for a while at least. Just west of Mestre, we picked up a route that followed the occasionally meandering path of a canalised river and, when this eventually met up with the River Brenta, we headed north following the signs for the centre of Padua which we agreed would make a good place to pause for coffee.

Now I love Italy. Most people do. It's beautiful, the people are welcoming, friendly and laid back in a way that the British, French and Germans aren't, the climate is just wonderful (for most of the time) and the food... The food! What can I say? It's simply a great country in which to travel. However, there is one major problem with Italy and here it is. The Roman Empire finally fell towards the end of the 5th century. We all know just how brilliant the Romans were when it came to organisation: their roads, their cities, their government, their armies, their society, their ability to still have kids around the world anguishing over Latin declensions more than 1,500 years later (that's impressive, no?)... I could go on. We have much to thank the Romans for, from their alphabet, which is helping you read this book, to their architectural style, which might be responsible for your local town hall looking very imposing. Well, unless you live in a place like Reading, but I digress. Back to the point. The Romans were pretty good at 'stuff', especially the 'stuff' that involved organising things. So why is it that in modern Italy, none of these organisational skills have rubbed off on the people who design the roads and especially on those who put up the signs?

"I'm really not sure about where this road is heading Simone."

"Me neither."

"Surely that sign for the centre of Padua – the concentric rings, no? – means that we will have to cycle along that... well, it looks like a motorway to me."

"Yes, it does, but the sign is blue," Simone pointed out, alluding to the fact that in Italy the *autostrada* or motorway signs are green.

Any road that is called the *'Tangenziale Nord'* doesn't exactly conjure up images of rural tranquillity and priests on bicycles merrily pinging their bells at the flock, but failing to spot an alternative, we continued to cycle along the slip road, which then joined the long, dual carriageway bridge over the river. Everything we could see – the two lanes and the hard shoulder, the Perspex walls to protect the locals from the noise of the traffic, the crash barriers, the speed limit signs - would have us believe that this wasn't a road for bicycles but there was nothing stating that fact definitively. It reminded me a little of my experiences of cycling along the motorway in Albania but at least back there I had shared the hard shoulder with many chickens and several pigs. Who would care about a touring cyclist? The only wildlife on this hard shoulder in Italy was of the roadkill variety. Struggling to fathom a way into and then out of the larger towns along our route would become a theme for the day and, at times, my patience with Simone was wearing a little thin, as I'm sure was his patience with me. It was all becoming just a little stressful.

Fortunately our journey was punctuated with some decidedly more relaxing moments, the first of which was our stop in the expansively magnificent, central square of Padua. Well, it was neither very central nor very square but it was very large indeed. My guidebook stated that it *"claimed to be the largest town square in Italy"*. Surely in these days of satellite photography, such potentially tourist-attracting claims to fame could be verified precisely, no? Despite its size, it was mercifully quiet (or perhaps it just seemed that way following the journey that we had to endure to get there) with pretty, pastel coloured buildings on all sides.

West of Padua, we tried our best to keep away from the A4 motorway but it seemed intent upon attracting us, like the child catcher from *Chitty Chitty Bang Bang*. South of Vicenza, we crossed over the autostrada and paused to replenish our stocks of water at a petrol station, where we debated the route to follow for the remainder of the afternoon. I was keen to miss out Vicenza itself, as it would have meant diverting several kilometres north and I wanted to maximise the amount of time I had to explore Verona. Simone was happy with this suggestion but the problem was that we couldn't find any direct way of cycling from one side of Vicenza to the other without going via the town centre. Well, there was one road, or was it two...?

We could see the sign ahead of us. It was blue and listed Verona alongside the road reference, the SS11. Above this in green, however, was the signage for the A4 *autostrada*. More worryingly, on a separate sign just below the first was a list of restrictions, of which cycling was but one.

"That's for the autostrada," I pointed out to Simone.

"No it isn't, it's blue," he retorted.

"I'm a stupid foreigner," I pointed out.

"But I'm not," he retorted.

Examining my online map very closely, it did appear that there were two roads running next to each other: the *autostrada* and another one of the *tangenziale* roads. For a few moments we were silent, neither of us willing to make a decision. I knew that Simone was correct about the cycling restriction being for the *tangenziale* road but I really didn't want to go to the hassle of adding kilometres by an enforced detour to central Vicenza. It didn't seem to make any sense that cycling should not be allowed on the *tangenziale* road. It might have *looked* like a motorway but it *wasn't* a motorway.

"What is the penalty for being caught cycling where you shouldn't?" I enquired of Simone.

"A fine? €100? Perhaps €200? I have no idea."

"We didn't see the sign?" I suggested.

Neither of us spoke for a few moments but then Simone smiled. He started cycling and with my heart pounding just a little bit faster than normal, I followed in his wake. As I had suspected, there were two roads next to each other with the *autostrada* to our left; most of the heavy traffic was using that road rather than the *tangenziale* where we were cycling. But why was cycling not allowed?

After about 5km, the road started to turn to the right. Ahead of us, the *autostrada* and the *tangenziale* disappeared into four holes in the hill. It was a tunnel. That in itself might not be an issue but up until that point we had been safely cycling along the thin band of tarmac to the right hand side of the two traffic lanes. When the tunnel started, the spare bit of tarmac stopped and we would be forced into sharing the road with the traffic behind us, whivh was travelling at over 100km/hr. We paused but didn't speak. The sign informed us that the tunnel would be 553 metres long, so if we could briefly push our speed to 30km/hr we would be out of there in around 2 minutes. The slight downhill gradient would help us. I switched on my lights, hoped for the best and we set off.

I could now fully comprehend why cycling had been banned from that stretch of the road. If knowledge of the fast moving traffic approaching over my left shoulder was frightening enough, with nowhere for it to escape, the sound was terrifying. My heart pumped faster and faster as I tried to cycle as fast as I could but as safely as was reasonably possible. After two minutes, we emerged from the tunnel unscathed and when a second one appeared we could at least see the light at the end – it was a mere 183 metres long – and we survived that one too. It wasn't a pleasant experience and at the first possible opportunity, we branched off the *tangenziale* to search for a more suitable route for the remainder of our journey to Verona.

We had, at least, avoided the long detour and found ourselves in the south-western suburbs of Vicenza. Simone had stopped his bike ahead of me and was taking a photograph with his phone. I turned to my left to see what he was so interested in and saw a large two-storey building on top of which, in curly blue writing, was the word Campagnolo, one of the most mythical in the world of cycling.

Tullio Campagnolo was born in 1901 and by his early 20s had established himself as a competent, amateur-racing cyclist. On 11th November 1924, he was taking part in a race that involved climbing high into the Italian Dolomites. In those days, if you wanted to change gear you had to remove your back wheel and flip it around to place the chain on a different sprocket. But it was November in the mountains, his hands were frozen and he couldn't remove the wingnuts. He didn't win but he was inspired to invent the very first, quick-release wheel. He went on to patent 135 inventions, including the first modern derailleur, the first groupsets (gears, brakes, cranks and sprockets) and, perhaps my favourite, the Campagnolo BIG corkscrew which, according to the company, *"with its maximum precision in removing corks without raising sediments and without shaking the bottle, reflects all the genius of its inventor Tullio Campagnolo, who gave it a self-centring, telescopic bell and a wide, sharp screw in hardened steel to consistently ensure a perfect grip on the cork."* If he could do that for the humble corkscrew, just imagine what he did for cycling.

The company is famously secretive. When the cycling writer Robert Penn turned up at their factory in Vicenza to make his dream bike for the BBC documentary *"Ride of My Life – The History of the Bicycle"*, they wouldn't let him film inside the building, despite the fact that he was willing to shell out €1,800 for their top-of-the-range 'Record' groupset. (He described it as *'the jewellery for my bike'* giving some indication as to just how highly the Campagnolo precision components are regarded.) My own chances of getting to snoop around were clearly non-existent, especially as Reggie was sporting his groupset from Shimano, the Japanese company that nearly put the Italians out of business. Campagnolo has survived, however, with its vision *"to be [the] leader in high end and top of the line cycling applications, with a distinguished brand able to ignite passion."* And open bottles of wine.

Staying well clear of any more *autostrada* or indeed *tangenziale* we spent the remainder of the afternoon on a pleasant, if uneventful, ride to Verona, but from the moment I first glanced across the River Adige towards the historic centre, I knew this was going to be a special visit. I also knew that the bulk of my time spent exploring *'fair Verona'* would have to be the following morning. We made our way to the large square outside the arena and shared a couple of celebratory beers before Simone said his good-byes and I was left to find the *Campeggio Castel San Pietro*. After taking a couple of wrong routes, I eventually found the right one which climbed the very green hill to the north-east of the town. If my first impressions of Verona had been positive, I was about to be blown away by its campsite. Squeezed into a steep corner of land behind the San Pietro castle, I was instructed by the campsite receptionist to go to pitch B2. Can there be a more idyllic and touring-cyclist-friendly place in Italy to spend the evening? I doubt it. Pitch B2 was one of fifteen to be found within a small, walled garden on the southern end of the site. Shade was provided by the vines, which had been trained to create a permeable roof to the area and just next to the garden was a small, terraced area where campers could sit, cook, eat and drink while gazing down upon the town of Verona itself.

After pitching the tent and leaving Reggie to bide his time with the other bicycles in the garden, I ate a pizza in a nearby restaurant which was perhaps a little too upmarket for someone who had just cycled 136km to get there. I scoffed my food as quickly as I could, before returning to watch the sunset from the terrace next to the tent while sipping a cold beer from the campsite bar. At that moment, on that evening, I had but one regret: why had I spent a day off in Venice – a city that I had previously visited – when I could have spent two nights in Verona instead? Was it too late for a change of plan?

Wednesday 31st July 2013
Cycling Day 25: Verona to Cornovecchio (Near Cremona), 146km

The best thing about waking up at *Campeggio Castel San Pietro* in Verona was, well, waking up. It hadn't been one, long night of sleep (I rarely get those back at home in my own bed let alone in a tent) but the periods of sleep that I did experience had definite starts and ends and there had been only three of four of them. This was clearly all down to my wonderful (and wonderfully expensive), new camping mat. It had been a good investment. I did hope that I hadn't just dreamt the entire experience...

So where are you on your travels?

Who said that?

It's Ivan, Ivan iPad.

Oh my... Haven't we taken this personification of inanimate objects a little too far?

As I was saying, where are you?

Ask me for a Shakespearean quote

Err... OK. Andrew, can you give me a quote from Shakespeare?

Yes, I'd be delighted to.

"Two households both alike in dignity, in fair Verona where we lay out scene"

So, you are in Verona. It's a long way to come just to be able to quote from a Shakespeare sonnet that you learnt by heart at school.

How did you know that?

Well, I know how old you are and I know that when you went to school the teachers made you learn stuff by heart. Now they just ask the students to make an interpretive dance out of something. And that's just quadratic equations.

You have a wry sense of humour for an iPad.

We are much underrated as fountains of wisdom and mirth.

Indeed you are.

Back in the real world I couldn't change my plans, however much I regretted my choice of city in which to take a day off. Two in three non-cycling days just wasn't an option if I wanted to be in with a chance of completing the entire trip by the deadline of August 31st. What's more, I had no desire to rearrange the two consecutive nights of

207

Warm Showers accommodation that I had set up for Wednesday and Thursday evening. I would, however, take most of the morning off to explore Verona.

All these arguments aside, it was a wrench to leave the campsite after such a brief visit. I hadn't really engaged in much conversation with my fellow campers – many of them touring cyclists – due to a relatively late arrival and an early departure back into the centre of town. I packed up the tent while most other campers were still sound asleep (well, they probably weren't but that's camping for you...), pushed Reggie up the steep path towards the reception area, where I bought a couple of croissants for breakfast and knocked back a black coffee. At the very top of the site was a terrace – it was actually the flat roof of the reception building – from where I could once again gaze down upon Verona. From that vantage point it appeared even more beautiful than it had done on the previous evening from the lower terrace next to where I had been camping and I took more than just a few moments to stop and stare into the picture-perfect valley.

The main attractions of the city were all to be found within a large bend of the River Adige, which enclosed the area on three of its four sides. I crossed the river via the cobbled and traffic-free *Ponte Pietro*. Most of the buildings on the other side still had their shutters closed against the rising sun, which made their pink, red, brown and yellow walls shine brightly. I retraced my steps from the previous evening and within a few minutes I was back in the square beside the ancient arena. It was the first that I had seen on the trip but over the following few weeks they would become a common feature of most of the towns in France and Spain. Here in Italy however, at least they have the civility to restrict its use to the staging of operas rather than the more brutal attractions that they continue to host further west.

As I drained my second coffee of the day, I sent a couple of tweets. I could see my reflection in the glass of my iPhone and noticed that my hair, after nearly a month on the road, was looking a bit frazzled. I momentarily wondered if I could get a haircut in Verona before turning my attention to other matters, such as where to start my amblings. I followed the curve of the arena and randomly chose a quiet street called the *Vicolo Tre Marchetti* along which to wander. Barely 20m from the arena, I noticed a traditional barber's pole on the wall next to a shop where a vertical sign read '*Parrucchiere per Uomo*'. I knew that 'uomo' was the word for a man so I guessed the remainder of the sign was telling me what the bottles, lotions and creams lined up on the glass shelves in the window were confirming: I had found a barber, already! A white-haired gentleman with an equally white moustache was standing just inside the entrance so I turned to him and said:

"*Posso...?*" Mmm. My Italian had run out after asking simply '*Can I...?*' so I moved my fingers in a snipping movement across my head. "*Si, certo!*" he replied and smiled.

Leaving Reggie unlocked outside, the barber ushered me towards one of the chairs where I sat down and was draped in a gown as white as the gentleman's moustache.

"*Numero uno!*" I declared in the hope that hair lengths were universal and so it appeared to be, as he reached for his shaver and fitted a very short looking comb. As he buzzed around my head, my eyes darted across the room trying to work out why he had so many trophies. If his hairdressing skills had brought him all these accolades, I might be in for a shock when the bill arrived. Once he had finished, I asked him what his name was:

"*Camillo, mi chiamo Camillo*".

I was curious about the trophies so I asked him simply '*Why?*' and pointed;

"*Correre,*" he declared and indicated a picture of a slightly younger looking version of himself in a pair of shorts. The Italian word was sufficiently close to the French word '*courir*' meaning '*to run*' so, putting two and two together I figured, that the trophies were for his running ability, rather than those required to be a barber. That said, he had done a good job and I thanked him in a way that only a man with a limited range of Italian vocabulary can do by repeating the word '*Grazie*' several times. Camillo continued to talk about his running experiences, some of which I understood but much of which escaped me. As we exchanged '*arrivederci*', it struck me that I had probably said more to Camillo on my one visit to his shop in Verona than I had done to my regular hairdresser back home in the UK. I loved how Camillo's establishment was presumably what they used to be like in Britain back in the good old days.

"*Anything for the weekend sir?*" he didn't ask.

"*A couple of opera tickets for the arena would be nice,*" I didn't have the opportunity to reply.

I did, however, like how Verona wasn't crammed full of tourists. The streets were busy, but far from packed and the distance from the coast seemed to have discouraged the cruise ship gangs from descending upon the place. Lots of people had, of course, come to see the balcony where Juliet had wondered "*Wherefore art thou, Romeo?*"

Many, presumably, had done so without necessarily realising that the *star-cross'd lovers* only played out their *misadventured* love in the mind of a playwright from the West Midlands who had famously never been anywhere near Verona. That said, it was difficult not to get just a little bit carried away with all the Shakespearean nonsense and I spent much of the morning dragging up quotes from my own 'O' Level English Literature studies. It was most definitely a city to which I would have to return to in the future.

Exeunt

It was nearly lunchtime by the time I started to make my way out of town and continue my journey across northern Italy. I was heading for Cremona and my first Warm Showers host who lived just to the west of the town. From Verona to Cremona was around 100km, which was an entirely feasible amount of cycling. So I decided, perhaps a little rashly, to extend it somewhat by choosing a more cycling-friendly route, initially heading towards Lake Garda and Peschiera del Garda, the resort that sits at its south-eastern corner. It was a nice spot to choose and I was happy to munch through a few high-class sandwiches (i.e. they were tiny and cost double the price of normal ones) while sipping a cold drink and gazing out across the lake. I seemed to be forgetting that I still had all those kilometres to pedal.

My Michelin map showed a road lined in green heading due south from Peschiera so, posh sarnies eaten, I followed it and, as the green line had suggested, it was indeed a very pretty route - just not a very direct one - so when I arrived at the end of the green line in a nondescript place called Goito and looked at my watch, I was a little concerned that it was already 3pm and the signs were telling me that I had another 64km to cycle before I arrived in the town of Cremona. It was time to set aside sightseeing and begin the hard grind of putting some kilometres on the clock. It involved some very straight roads, a fair number of impatient lorries, a sometimes head-on wind and a good few opportunities for me to stop and snack upon something covered either in salt or chocolate. The one thing I had taken on board from the advice I had received online following my bout of supposed dehydration (it was a bug, I was now sure of that), was that I should increase my salt intake. I could do this by adding salt directly to my water but I didn't find that a particularly appealing option, especially when there was an alternative: eat crisps. It was the savoury equivalent of a spoonful of sugar helping the medicine go down (try saying that without the song coming into your head!) and I was getting into the (bad) habit of doing it every day. My salt levels were, I imagine, wonderful, but it did cross my mind that I might have to enrol on some kind of detoxification programme on my return to the UK.

I had set myself a time of 6pm to arrive in Cremona and I very nearly made it. I had run out of water a few kilometres from the city and was desperate for a drink, so when I spotted a branch of McDonald's just outside the town, I stopped and ordered the largest Diet Coke they could offer me (without ice, which never goes down well with the employees...), along with a small can of Peroni beer to celebrate my success at reaching the town by only ten past six.

My Warm Showers contact in Cremona was called Diego, and he had sent clear instructions how to cycle from the centre of town to his house in the countryside. The first thing I had to do was to follow the signs for Pavia. No problem there, I thought and, to save time, I wouldn't go into the centre, I would cycle around the ring road until I found the appropriate sign. I could feel the warm, early evening sun move gradually across the side of my face as I continued my journey around the town. A couple of drivers sounded their horns and I responded in a suitably belligerent way, fuelled by the one can of beer, which was just beginning to interact with a touch of the bonks (look it up!). Idiots.

After about ten minutes on the ring road, I was overtaken by a police car and the two policemen inside seemed to be overly concerned with something that I was doing or perhaps, something I had done. Was it the tunnel incident from the previous day? Was it the can of Peroni from the McDonald's? The police car didn't stop immediately but continued. However, a couple of hundred metres further along the road, Cremona's finest had indeed ground to halt and it was clear that I was the one they needed to speak to...

I would now love to recount how the two officers leapt out of their high-speed Alfa, crouched behind the open doors of their car, pulled out their weapons and shouted lots of imperative Italian in my direction, along the lines of "*On the floor and spread 'em, buddy*". But they didn't. I didn't even get a flash of the lights that were fixed on the roof of their green and white... Fiat Panda. Their style wasn't so much *Starsky and Hutch* as *Laurel and Hardy*. I later discovered that they were called Alberto and Fabio and it was the former who got out to speak to me first. It was clearly a minor telling-off for being where I shouldn't have been – on the ring road – but before he could get into reading me my rights, I had metaphorically held up my hands to the crime;

"*Mi scusi... Sono inglese... Non parlo molto italiano...*"

211

At which point Alberto started speaking English,

"Where do you need to go?"

I explained some of the directions that Diego had emailed earlier and after a quick consultation with Starsky, sorry Fabio, who was still in the car, they decided to escort me to the correct road. So, although I didn't have a tale to tell of being thrown into an Italian jail for the night, I did have a minor one of having had a police escort, albeit one behind a slow-moving Fiat Panda.

We parted company on very friendly terms, me shaking their hands and them posing for a photograph. They could go home happy and report to their sergeant back at base that yet another potential crime wave on the bypass had been averted by their quick-thinking and decisive action. And, once embellished, I would have a little story for my book. Damn...

It was another 20km of cycling before I arrived at the house that Diego shared with his Argentinian partner Luciana and their very cute two-year-old son, Tiago. But it was worth the time and effort required to get there. Diego - an engineer working on a new mobile phone network for *Telecom Italia* - welcomed me to the family home as if I was a long-lost member of the family, introduced me to his wife and son and plied me with pasta and beer in quantities that can only be appreciated by someone who had just cycled 146km and had a touch-and-go brush with the law (well, that's what I told him). I spent the evening recounting my adventure so far and he gave me a little advice about what was still to come. He talked about his life in northern Italy, his travels, how he had met his wife and his hopes for the future. The physical and emotional struggles of Croatia seemed a million miles away from that house in the Italian countryside and it was a fitting way to end the first of my two months on the road. By the time I headed off to bed, I was well fed, well watered and beginning to believe that yes, my plan to cycle all the way along the Mediterranean coast to Portugal was not just a pipe dream. August? Bring it on!

Thursday 1st August 2013
Cycling Day 26: Cornovecchio (Near Cremona) to Pragate (Near
Voghera), 77km

Although there had been plenty of space to pitch my tent in his garden, when I arrived a little later than expected, Diego suggested that I sleep inside the house in the storage area next to where I had positioned Reggie. It would have been comfortable enough and there was even a shower in the corner of the room. However, shortly after creeping into my sleeping 'liner', I could hear the pitter patter of...

"Don't worry; it's just... What are they called? Little green animals... They live in water and jump," explained Diego after he had noticed that I had switched on the light and was wandering around the room looking anxious.

"Frogs?" I suggested.

"Yes, frogs! They are nothing to worry about."

I wasn't quite convinced that frogs were capable of making the mouse- or even rat-like noises I could hear, so shortly after Diego, Luciana and Tiago had gone upstairs to bed, I crept back into the house and slept on the sofa. Several hours later, I woke to the wonderful silence of the countryside and for a few moments I lay motionless, trying to think of the Italian word for 'rabbit'. I knew 'cane' and 'gatto' and, after the previous evening's events, I even knew 'rana'. I was struggling with 'rabbit' however, so grabbed my phone and looked it up on the Internet.

"Coniglio bianco... Damn! Conigli bianchi."

One white rabbit would have to suffice in bringing me good luck for the remainder of the month. It was August 1st and I had a maximum of 31 days to get to the Cape St. Vincent in Portugal. That would be cutting it quite fine as I needed to be back at work on September 2nd, so 26 or 27 days would be a more realistic target to allow me time to get back to Britain. Today would be cycling day 26, so in that respect I was about half way there and when I looked at the map, I was at least approaching the halfway point of the trip, which I suspected to be somewhere near the border between Italy and France. I also knew that the symbolic crossing point between my 2010 trip from north to south and this trip from east to west was about to take place. I wasn't quite sure where it would be exactly, but I did know that it would happen at some point today. Whichever way I looked at it, I was feeling increasingly confident that I had completed nearly 50% of my journey.

Over breakfast, the carefree chat of the previous evening continued (although frogs, mice or even rats were never mentioned). Luciana was a graphic designer and she gave me a guided tour of her studio, which was crammed full with an eclectic range of things that she had painted, drawn and sewn. She had a distinctive and colourful style that wouldn't have been out of place in a smart designer outlet in London and I made a point of telling her that her creations would fly off the shelves and into the houses of the British middle-classes quicker than you could say 'home counties chic'. I hope one day they get the chance to do just that. Back in the kitchen, Diego called me across to one of the kitchen cabinets. He had a broad smile on his face:

"Andrew, look. I have my own collection..." he explained, before opening two deep drawers *"...of pasta"*. It was indeed an equally eclectic range of about thirty different kinds of pasta.

"I'm impressed!" I explained, in a way that only a man who lives on penne and tagliatelle can be. Diego was an infectiously fun and enthusiastic person to be with, so there was little incentive to gather my things and head off in the direction of Voghera, but eventually I did, waving a fond farewell to this charming and happy little family.

Cycling day 26 was destined to be the equivalent of one of those days when you turn up at work and just potter around doing bits and pieces but never seem to get to grips with the really big issues. Not that I had any pressing big issues to deal with apart from putting lots of kilometres on the clock, but that wasn't even an option. Diego's house had been a little further away from Cremona than I had imagined, so by cycling 146km on the previous day I had dented the distance required to travel to my second Warm Showers host, Carla, who lived some 10km south-east of Voghera, at the top of a hill. More of Carla and her hill in a few moments.

Most of my day would be spent cycling along the SP10 between the towns of Piacenza and Casteggio. At either end of this route was a short 10-15km cycle to get me from and to the homes of Diego and Carla respectively. The initial portion of the ride – from Diego's house to the centre of Piacenza – was the first time since leaving the southern tip of Greece that I had been able to cycle for an extended period upon dedicated and segregated cycle paths. In fact, the whole area had a distinctive cycling-friendly feel to it. There were lots of other cyclists around and about, ranging from the lycra-clad speed merchants to the ordinary folk who were gently rolling from A to B. There was also a cycling-themed piece of modern art. It depicted two life-size cyclists (of the lycra variety) on their racing bikes and was made from plates of sheet metal, which resulted in a work of two rather than three discernable dimensions. There was no risk of this particular interpretation of the cycling world being showered in awards, but in one corner was a small sheet of metal out of which had been cut '70° *Gran Premio Agostano*'. The *Gran Premio Agostano* is a long-standing elite cycle race for under 23-year-olds (so that counts me out, just), which takes place over about 130km in August every year. In 2010 it celebrated its 70th anniversary, hence the piece of modern art. The first race took place back in 1932 and was won by an Italian going by the name of Attilio Pavesi and since then, Italians have won almost all of the races. However, in 2011, the 71st race was won by a fellow Yorkshireman called Joshua Edmondson, who was born in Leeds in 1992. At the time of the 71st *Gran Primo Agostano,* he was cycling as an amateur for an Italian outfit called Team Colpack but he has subsequently gone on to even greater things. In 2012 he competed for the team GB in the Tour of Britain and in 2013 he signed for Team Sky. So, should he ever emulate the achievements of Sir Bradley, well, you read it here first!

As the countryside melted slowly into the city and I crossed a bridge over the River Po just to the north-east of Piacenza, my thoughts turned back to August 2010 and to what I had subsequently written in my first book, *Crossing Europe on a Bike Called Reggie*.

"The morning's cycle was a flat one following the course of the River Po to Piacenza and on arrival, we made our way into the centre of the town along the deserted Sunday morning streets. Although our exertions had been minimal, we did need a top up of food, so we sat under a parasol outside the first café that appeared to be open. Unfortunately it wasn't, even though the evidence in front of us – people sitting outside being served food and coffee by a waiter – suggested otherwise. Simone was just as baffled as me, but it's never a good idea to argue with someone who could potentially be serving you food and drink only moments after having had their illogical argument pulled to pieces, so we moved on and into the very centre of town.

It's said that Italy is home to two-thirds of the world's antiquities and it's easy to believe that statistic when you come to a relatively unknown place like Piacenza. In most other countries, this would be in the top ten tourist destinations in the land with its Renaissance palazzos, its medieval churches and arcaded piazzas. Here in Italy, it was just another living, breathing, beautiful town with buildings that continue to have a functional status way below that which their historic grandeur would dictate: shoe shops, dentists, insurance

215

offices, language schools and mini supermarkets all housed under splendour more befitting of higher causes. We eventually found a café, which was not only open but willing to serve us some food and drink, near the train station. I thought Simone would use the proximity of a direct line back to Pavia to make his excuses and return home from this point but he chose to continue to accompany me as I headed south along the SP6 towards Castell'Arquato."

Fast-forward two years and fifty-one weeks to August 1st 2013 and there I was again. If I had chosen to turn left at the southern end of the bridge, I could have been sitting in the very same railway station café that had fed and watered me in 2010. This was Thursday however, not Sunday, so I thought the chances of there being somewhere in the main square of Piacenza open and willing to serve me a drink were somewhat greater than they had been on my previous visit. After a short cycle into the town centre, I found a suitable café in *Piazza dei Cavalli* and started to reminisce.

Despite what I had written about my first visit to Piacenza, I did come away with the impression that, however wonderful its architecture might have been, it was a soulless place. That certainly wasn't the feeling I was getting now as the square in front of me was busy with the locals going about their daily chores and small groups of tourists posing for photographs on the stage that had been set up between two statues of cavaliers and their horses in front of the town hall. I joined the tourists to take my own photographs and to record a short semi-valedictory video to mark the crossing point of my two cycling trips.

From what I recall of cycling that day back in 2010, I arrived in Piacenza from the west having crossed the Po using one of the three bridges that span the river between Pavia (where Simone was living at the time) and Piacenza. I certainly don't remember swimming across, so it must have been one of them. At the time I was using a satellite tracker that only plotted my route once every 10 minutes and although this would have been sufficiently accurate to tell me which bridge it was, I had not saved my online route for posterity as I was doing during this second trip. It was likely, however, that the crossing point was not one particular place where I could have (had I so wished) put a little cross on the ground, but a stretch of anything between 20 and 35km of road where, if I had decided to put a white line there would have been all kinds of trouble. The Italian police had been kind to me once but I didn't want to risk a second encounter. In light of this leap in tracking technology on my part (if you remember I was now using a cycling app on the iPhone which tracked my route on a more or less continuous basis) compared to my more primitive method in 2010, it was along this stretch of my route of many thousands of kilometres that for some reason the track stopped being made. It could have been that I had switched my phone off and back on again without restarting the app, or it could have been that the phone switched itself off due to overheating (this had happened before but I had stopped and remedied the problem by trying to cool it down before continuing). It could of course be that I am trying to pull the wool over your eyes and attempting to hide the fact that I just got fed up with cycling and hailed a taxi from Castel San Giovanni all the way to Carla's house near Voghera. I didn't do that of course but I've now got you wondering, no? I can't prove or disprove anything as the online track stops at Castel San Giovanni and doesn't start until the following morning when I set off on cycling day 27.

What I can assure you however, is that I did stop at least three, if not four, times along my route from Piacenza to Casteggio. Knowing that I only had a distance of 40km or so to cover made me pleasantly complacent about the job in hand and I was keen to investigate any curiosities I might find along my route, which on other days would probably have been ignored. The first thing to draw my attention was a medieval castle in a small town called Sarmato. It had been heavily signposted on the SP10 for many kilometres, so I was looking forward to something grand and impressive with a few tales to tell. The short deviation of about half a kilometre took me into the centre of Sarmato, but when I found the 14th century crumbling, red-brick structure there was a sign stating that it was *"Privato"* and that I could look and then clear off. Well it didn't but the one word spoke volumes about how welcome I really was. I took a picture and cleared off.

In Castel San Giovanni, I stopped in the main square to inspect a bust of Giuseppe Garibaldi, which had been placed on a tall plinth, and I pondered the ubiquitous nature of such statues in Italy. The plinth carried the date of the 5th July 1908. Now far be it from me to deride a statue of the great man (A.J.P. Taylor, the eminent historian described Garibaldi as *"...the only wholly admirable figure in modern history"* which is quite an accolade) but the date seemed a little out of place. I looked him up online to discover that he was born on the 4th July 1807 and that he died on 2nd June 1882. It could be possible that the bust had been erected to mark the 101st anniversary of his birth but that the local council had been forced to cancel for 24 hours because of bad weather, but that seemed unlikely (it was July; it's always sunny!). I looked up the date of 5th July 1908 and, according to reliable online sources, (well, Wikipedia), nothing of any importance whatsoever

217

happened on this date. Apologies if your granny was born on that day by the way, but with respect, unless you are royalty, it's not that significant in the great scheme of things. I can tell you that on July 6th 1908 the American Robert Peary set sail for the North Pole and that earlier in the week the 'Young Turk Revolution' had kicked off but as for Sunday 5th...

In Stradella, I bought an ice-cream and sat in a park to eat it. A group of old women was sitting opposite me and I listened to them chatter away. I couldn't understand much of what was said but it made me smile when they greeted each other as *'ragazze'*, or 'girls' when one of them arrived or departed. I didn't really need any subtitles for the other things they were saying as their conversation would have been the same in any language: family, friends, gossip with perhaps a few celebrities thrown in for good measure. My final stop was in Fumo where I visited a discount supermarket and for a very reasonable €4.20 I was able to purchase a large bottle of water, two sports drinks and an enormous tube of Smarties. Only the water survived further than the entrance of the supermarket car park. (Come on, the Smarties would have melted...)

Carla, my Warm Showers host, had sent directions and earlier in the day Diego had talked me through where I needed to go. The instructions were clear, however, and I found the house without too much difficulty. The valley leading up to the small settlement of houses and farm buildings was exquisite in the late afternoon sun, with lines of vines running down the hills at slightly different angles. In the final kilometre, the road started to wind up the steep hillside and then there was a homemade sign, in English, stating *"Only Signed Warm Showers"*. It didn't make much sense but it did at least tell me I was in the right place.

Carla, a well-built woman in her 30s was standing chatting to other members of her family at a gate. Her situation in the countryside is very different from that of Diego and his family. She has a smallholding where she grows some fruit and vegetables and rears chickens and geese. Her partner, Luigi, is a nurse in an old people's home in Pavia but he wasn't working that evening and he was busy doing jobs around the house. Neither Carla nor Luigi spoke much English (hence the sign) so my Italian was stretched beyond breaking point, with many sentences started but only a few of them actually finished. My long-practised method of substituting an unknown Italian word with a French word plus a vowel seemed somewhat unsuccessful. Perhaps it always had been. Carla and Luigi didn't strike me as cyclists, which was curious as the Warm Showers principle is one of reciprocity,

218

but asking them why or how they had become involved in the accommodation sharing network was a question that fell victim to our mutual lack of understanding.

Carla produced a simple meal of pasta and tomatoes with the pickings from her own efforts on the land and then the television was switched on and we were joined by her mother who lived downstairs. We were watching an Italian news channel with lots of live reports from different locations around Rome. Silvio Berlusconi's name was being mentioned repeatedly and all three of my hosts were becoming increasingly animated at the prospect of what was going to happen. I carefully studied the scrolling text on screen and eventually worked out that we were about to watch the judgement of the ultimate appeal court relating to one of the ex-prime minister's many tangles with the legal system.

"*E colpevole, è colpevole!*" shouted Carla suddenly. This was sufficiently close to 'culpable' in English and '*coupable*', the French word for 'guilty' for me to realise that this wasn't good news for poor old Silvio. Clearly this was not a household who had ever been great fans of the idiosyncratic politician. A liqueur of some description was produced and we toasted the downfall of an Italian icon. At least, I thought, Thursday 1st August 2013 had a good chance of going down in the Italian history books as a significantly more memorable day than Sunday 5th July 1908. Well, in this little corner of the country at least.

Friday 2nd August 2013
Cycling Day 27: Pragate (Near Voghera) to Cherasco, 146km

The smell of the countryside can be distinctive and the aroma around Carla's house was particularly pungent. It wasn't necessarily unpleasant, but it certainly took a while to become accustomed to breathing it in and when I woke it was the first thing I noticed. I had been sleeping in the spare room, on a mattress that offered the kind of comfort that my camping mat – even the new one – could only dream about giving. I walked over to the windows and opened the shutters. Below me was Carla's plot of land and there she was, tending her vegetables and cajoling her flocks of geese and chickens. It must be nice, I thought, not to have a boss. To be able to wake up and wander outside to farm the land that would produce the raw ingredients for the food that would give you the energy required to once again wake up and farm the land... A nice, neat circle of life. Of course, my romanticised view of what it might be like to lead such a life was horribly inaccurate. Not having a boss might have its benefits, but then again at least he or she provides you with an income to buy all the stuff that makes your life bearable. No doubt it was for this reason that Luigi had a job in the care home in Pavia.

Breakfast was a simple affair, just a few slices of bread, after which I bid farewell to my hosts and freewheeled back along the road that I had climbed the previous evening. It was difficult to decide whether the valley in the low morning sunlight was more or less beautiful than it had been in the low evening sunlight of the day before. Perhaps the slightly fresher feeling gave the morning the edge but it was a close run thing. I marvelled upon just how picture-perfect the valley was, with its jumble of trees, vines, hay bales, farms, clumps of woodland and even a fortified tower on top of one of the hills. The road was almost traffic-free, the sky was appropriately azure blue and it was all unmistakeably Italian. I loved it.

Carla had been a kind and generous host, but I did need a more substantial breakfast than the one she had supplied, so my first stop was in the first town I came to, Voghera, where I found a *rosticceria* (presumably a place where food is roasted) and stocked up with various breads and cakes before spending a little time sitting under a parasol at a café just opposite, watching Italian life pass by. This included a dark blue car belonging to the *Carabinieri*, which pulled up in front of the bank on the other side of the pedestrianised street. The two officers inside the car were a world away from Alberto and Fabio,

220

the friendly and chatty local police officers who had pulled me over on the Cremona ring road a couple of days earlier. The *Carabinieri* both had shaven heads and the one in the passenger seat peered over towards where I was sitting and gave Reggie and me a long, hard stare. I smiled but resisted the temptation to wave lest such an informal gesture be taken in mocking way (which actually, it would have been). Like their counterparts in France – the *Gendarmerie* – the *Carabinieri* are part of the military and I have to say, they come across as a bit scary. I thought back to my adventure on the *tangenziale* road en route to Verona with Simone and through the tunnels where cycling had been banned. Should they have caught us, I can't imagine the two guys who were sitting opposite me in the fast car would have been happy for me to ask their names and take their photo. Mind you, it might have saved me the cost of finding accommodation for the night.

I was hoping for a triple whammy of Warm Showers success at the end of cycling day 27 (which would be just as cheap as a night in a cell but hopefully more comfortable) and had exchanged messages with a woman called Lucia who lived a few kilometres to the north of a town called Cherasco. It would be a return to cycling over 140km after the previous day's rather more leisurely ride, so I couldn't hang around in Voghera for too long trying to look as innocent as possible in front of the military police. From Cherasco I would be able to start climbing towards the Tende Pass so it was starting to feel like the beginning of the end of my cycle across northern Italy. That said, it was still another three days of cycling before I would be fraternising with the French. I had identified a place called Limone Piemonte, which, at 1,000m, was more than half way (vertically) to the pass and what's more, it had a campsite where I would hopefully spend my final night in Italy.

My route to where Lucia lived required me to continue to follow the SR10 as far as Asti then turn south in the direction of Alba and finally (wait for it) Bra. I needed to be a little more careful about being distracted by curiosities along the way if I wanted to arrive in Cherasco in good time. It wasn't really the done thing to simply turn up at a Warm Showers host's house and promptly slope off to bed. Neither was it something I wanted to do; after a long day in the saddle it was always nice to have someone waiting at the other end who was willing to listen and ask a few questions. However, after having cycled fewer than 20km, I was given a very good reason indeed to stop and investigate in the town of Tortona.

Tortona was the first place over the border into the region of Piedmont and it was a pleasant, if unremarkable, small town. I cycled towards the centre along a narrow cobbled street and after a few hundred metres, I arrived in what I assumed was the main square. It was only quite small but the yellow building to my left looked like the town hall and next to it was the tourist information office, which clearly was just that as there was an oversize 'i' next to the door. It was neither of these two buildings, however, that made me stop. It was the benches outside the tourist office. In fact, they weren't so much benches, more sofas made from white concrete. The back of the bench/sofa was curved and the first thing that came to mind was a pair of lips. Having never in my life seen a sofa that was made out of concrete, I was curious as to just how comfortable it was so I stopped, stood Reggie on his stand and sat down. The seat was as comfortable as you would imagine a sofa made out of concrete to be. That said, the thought and effort that had gone into designing this unusual piece of street furniture was commendable and it was certainly worth a few moments of sitting. To my left I could see a statue of a roman soldier, to my right was the tourist office and at the far end of the square was a small bicycle stand. Above the stand was a large, black and white photograph fixed to the wall. It showed a man from the torso upwards holding a pair of sunglasses. He was in the process of breathing onto one of the lenses of the glasses. On his shirt was the slightly obscured word '*arpano*' (I suspected there was more to it than that) and underneath was another word but only the first letter was recognisable – it was a 'C' – as all the others had their bottom two-thirds cut off by the edge of the picture. I stood up and wandered over to inspect the photograph more closely - this guy looked a bit like a cyclist...

There was no plaque to explain who he was or why he had been chosen for this prominent position above err... a cycle rack. After a few moments, I turned and walked past the tourist office. In one of the windows was a large poster advertising a cycling event called '*La Mitica*', which had taken place earlier in the summer on the 30th June. At the top of the poster was written "*Ciclostorica con bici d'epoca per i colli di Serse e Fausto Coppi*". Fausto Coppi? I'd heard about him before. In fact, someone had contacted me earlier in the year pointing out that I would be cycling near to where he had lived. My Italian could just about cope with the poster; it was publicising a historical bicycle race in '*the hills of Serse and Fausto Coppi*'. I wandered inside the tourist office, much to the disgust of the only person working that morning. She had just lit a cigarette and was standing outside chatting to a friend but was forced to put it out and follow me back inside. She observed me like a hawk as I wandered around and examined some of the cycling-related memorabilia.

"Perché tutte le biciclette?" I enquired, but it wasn't really the question I wanted to ask as I already knew why there was a cycling theme to the place.

"Fausto Coppi! Parli italiano?"

"Un poco" I replied. 'A bit.'

She proceeded to write everything she said on a Post-it note.

"Nato a Castellania 1919... Morto a Tortona 1960."

Coppi had been born in the small village of Castellania some 10km to the south but had lived most of his life in Tortona. To say that he was (and still is) an Italian hero is something of an understatement. He is probably up there with Garibaldi (although has yet to receive the ultimate accolade of having a biscuit named after him). His greatest achievements came in winning the *Giro d'Italia* five times – for the first time in 1940 at the age of just 20 - and the *Tour de France* twice (in just three attempts). Had the Second World War not stopped the running of both races for an extended period of time (and had he not been captured by the British in North Africa in 1943), he would have undoubtedly won even more. He was the first cyclist to win both races in the same season in 1949 and then repeated the feat in 1952. His great rival was Gino Bartali and in post-war Italy you were either *coppiani* or *bartiliani*. The rivalry went deep and was just as much political as it was sporting. Towards the end of his career, married Coppi was embroiled in scandal when he started an affair with a woman called Giulia Occhini (or 'the Woman in White' as she was commonly known), the wife of one of his fans. At the time, both adultery and divorce were illegal in Italy and the couple were hounded by the press and prosecuted by the authorities. Even the Pope appealed for him to return to his wife. Both Coppi and Occhini received suspended prison sentences but they did go on to marry. In 1959, he was invited to take part in a cycling event in Upper Volta (now Burkina Faso) where he was bitten by a mosquito and contracted malaria. The disease initially went undiagnosed and he died in Tortona at the age of just 40. His marital indiscretions appear to have now been forgiven as he was voted the second greatest Italian sportsperson of the 20th century. But no biscuit, not yet.

I thanked the woman in the tourist office and she returned to her position outside to finish her cigarette. I glanced back at the photograph on the wall and could now fill in the cropped letters of his name. COPPI. An Italian icon and, for many, a hero.

Back on the road, the cycling continued to be predominantly flat through Alessandra and on to Asti. Between the two towns, near

Castello di Annone, was the strange sight of a group of prostitutes. I wondered why were they there but nowhere else along my route. They were all young, black girls, some of them were sitting in groups of two or three and they were spread out along the road over a distance of about three kilometres. They were mainly sitting on plastic chairs and sheltering from the direct sunlight under umbrellas. These were not the more 'mature' women that I had seen in the industrial area near Venice. Most were very attractive. Just after the town there was one, solitary, white girl who was just as well dressed and attractive as her earlier colleagues but again, clearly selling her body. I wondered what had drawn them all to the little town of Castello di Annone in Piemonte, Italy. I doubted it was the passing trade of touring cyclists.

Asti is the home of Italian sparkling wine. Not that you would really know it, as the town didn't appear to be shouting it from the rooftops. It was in stark contrast to little Tortona, where every opportunity had been taken to build a legacy upon its association with a cycling legend. I was so underwhelmed by the place that I went to the effort of checking online that there weren't two places called Asti in Italy. There weren't. I was, indeed, in the Asti of *Asti Spumante*, they just weren't very good at advertising the fact to casual observers like me. I almost felt a little aggrieved that I had gone to the effort of buying lunch in a town that had taken discretion to an altogether new level. Perhaps I would have more luck in Alba, which was a further 30km down the road.

Several days of predominantly flat cycling across the plain of northern Italy were about to come to an end. Not in any dramatic way, but as I started to cycle out of Asti to the south-west, in the direction of Cuneo and eventually the Tende Pass, it was noticeable that I was beginning to climb. Alba was, thankfully, much more interesting than Asti, with a pretty, central area around which I pushed Reggie and poked my nose into various shops selling cheeses, wines and... lots of jars of Nutella. I picked up one of them up to examine the label and my suspicions of there being a link with the town were well-founded. I had noticed a sweet smell on the cycle into the centre of the town and it turned out that Alba was home to the Ferrero confectionery company. I sat down for a close-to-the-end-of-day, celebratory beer near the *Porta Garibaldi* and looked at a map of the town. The Ferrero factory was just the other side of the road that I had taken to cycle into the centre and it was approximately the same size as the old part of Alba. That's a lot of Nutella and Ferrero Rocher for the ambassador's party.

I must have been in party mood myself, as after the first beer I ordered a second without really considering how much further I had to cycle. My close-to-the-end-of-day, celebratory beers had been a little premature to say the very least as I still had another 20km to cycle to get to Lucia's house just outside the town of Cherasco. It started as a gentle, uphill climb but very suddenly the wilting effects of the beer began to kick in and I was struggling to cycle at any kind of speed. I desperately needed a calorie boost as well as something to soak up a little of the beer; I had the munchies combined with a severe attack of bonking. *Bonking* is the cycling equivalent of hitting the wall in running. I had occasionally experienced mild bonking on the commute home from work, on days when I hadn't really had the chance to eat much. Here in Italy, I had had plenty to eat during the day but the beer combined with the very hot weather had clearly had an alarmingly rapid effect on my body. I looked desperately for a shop of any kind and after about 15 minutes, on the point of exhaustion, I finally found a bakery. I bought some bread and a large bar of chocolate and sat on the step outside chomping my way through both of them. The woman inside must have detected that some kind of crisis was taking place outside on her step, as she instructed one of her a customers to ask me if I needed water. "*Si*" was the answer and she refilled my bottles. Almost ready for the road again but conscious of the time – it was already past 7pm - I set off, but when I arrived at a petrol station just a kilometre or so down the road, I was in desperate need of more calories so stopped again and bought two more chocolate bars. They filled the gap in my stomach somewhat and I continued cycling. It seemed to take a long, long time but eventually I turned off the main road and saw a woman on a bike waving in my direction. My destination had been reached but it had seemed a close-run thing and had given an otherwise fairly standard day of cycling a nasty sting in the tail.

Lucia wasn't a touring cyclist but she had bumped into an Australian cyclist a few years previously as he was examining his map outside her house. He was looking for accommodation and as she had a spare room in her house, she offered him the use of it. She subsequently put her details on Warm Showers and has been welcoming cyclists ever since. She was able to fill me up with pasta and since she spoke only a little English, we chatted in French as I gradually started to feel the effects of over 140km of cycling. After only an hour or so in Lucia's company, I made my excuses, headed downstairs to her spare room next to the underground garage, located and eradicated an annoying mosquito that was intent on my being its main meal of the day, and went to bed.

Saturday 3rd August 2013
Cycling Day 28: Cherasco to Limone-Piemonte, 70km

There wasn't a great deal of natural light penetrating my room within the basement of Lucia's house, so when I woke I couldn't even guess what time it was. Checking my watch I was delighted to discover that it was nearly 8am. This meant that my body had done the right thing and decided to shut down properly overnight (no doubt aided by the darkness of the room) after the exertions of the previous day. I certainly wasn't accustomed to such a late awakening and I most definitely wasn't used to experiencing a continuous night of sleep, especially in the tent. My bonking session of the previous evening had been put firmly and squarely behind me. (I do hope that you have read the previous chapter and haven't happened upon this paragraph at random while browsing in a bookshop. I assure you, it's not the kind of book you might think.)

It was nice to spend some more time chatting with Lucia over breakfast. I was feeling a little guilty about having cut short the previous evening's discussion due to my tiredness and I was able to learn a little more about her life and her family. She explained how she and her former husband used to run the restaurant and bar that was in the building next door. It had become a victim of the economic situation and the place was now empty but she had moved on; she had her family and had found other employment and seemed content with her new life as a single woman. She was very easy-going and it wasn't difficult to sit and chat about our respective lives. It was a perfect and relaxing way in which to finish off my three days of staying with Warm Showers contacts, all of whom had more than met my expectations as generous and kind hosts.

Since leaving Venice, in one respect at least, I had not been travelling light. One of the few bits of forward planning that I had undertaken before flying off to Greece to start the journey along the Mediterranean, was to send Simone my maps and guidebooks for the second half of the journey. I had cobbled together a two volume '*Rough Guide to the Eurovelo 8*' by taking the relevant regional sections from the country guides, collating them into a logical order and then binding them together by drilling a series of holes along the left hand side of the pages and tying the new 'book' together with some shoe laces. My initial attempts had produced a comically thick tome that weighed more than my tent, so I instead I created volume 1 covering Greece, Croatia, Slovenia and Italy (Albania was dealt with in a separate Bradt guide book) and volume 2 covering France, Spain and Portugal. I then posted volume 2 to Simone in Venice, along with the maps that I needed to cover the portion of the trip from Italy to the Cape St. Vincent and had picked up the bundle upon arrival in the city earlier in the week. Whilst in Dubrovnik, I posted home a collection of maps, the Albanian guide and various other pieces of documentation that I had accumulated since leaving the Temple of Poseidon in Greece. However, as I needed the Italian section of volume 1 until the end of my journey across Italy, I had been carrying both volumes 1 and 2 for the previous few days. It seemed a sensible option to lighten the load before starting to climb the mountains, so my first job on cycling day 28 was to do just that at Lucia's local post office. One day I shall donate my guides, maps, leaflets, postcards, campsite bills etc... to the British Library, who will no doubt cherish them in a shoe box labelled *'miscellaneous crap from travel writers who never quite made it...'*

There was a second, practical issue that needed to be dealt with that morning: Reggie's tyres. There was nothing wrong with them but they did need a good pumping. (Insert your own joke.) However, the shenanigans of Athens airport were still relatively fresh in my mind and I really didn't want to start playing around with the dreaded Presta valves again, so I would be on the look out for a bike shop where I could request the assistance of a mechanic. It was all a bit pathetic but I wanted to keep my distance from my own pump, which had been the source of so much anguish in Greece, until such time as I became desperate.

Following the signs for Cuneo, I set off from the post office in a predominantly southerly direction along a series of long, straight roads. The first town I came to was called Fossano and it looked like the kind of place that should have a bike shop of some description. I slowed my cycling to a crawl and as well as examining the shops that were lining the road along which I was travelling, I attempted to peer along the side streets for any tell-tale clues. Fossano had been built on a slope and I was beginning to lose hope as I approached the lower part of town but then, along *Via Matteotti,* I spotted a wheel behind a pane of glass, then a whole bike and then a long line of bikes parked up ready for sale. The awning confirmed that I had found *Marino Cicli.* I pushed open the door and proceeded to guide Reggie into the shop. Everything was neat, tidy and a little worryingly, clean. Cleanliness tends to mean that a bike shop is very good at selling bikes but not that brilliant when it comes to repairing them. But come on, all I needed was a decent pump and preferably someone to operate it (and whom I could later blame for breaking another Presta valve).

"Buongiorno?" The word seemed a little formal for the situation but then again *'Ciao'* implied over familiarity. I didn't want to offend. *"Allo?"* That was French but it somehow seemed more appropriate. After a few moments a man appeared wearing... not overalls. *"Parla inglese?"* But he didn't. *"Posso..."* but then I ran out of words so I bent my back and moved my clenched fists up and own to imitate someone blowing up a tyre. *"Deve andare in montagne,"* I continued explaining that I was heading for the hills.

"Ah, si..." he replied unenthusiastically. I could read his mind which was thinking *"Why is this bloke incapable of pumping up his own tyres? Does he think I've got nothing better to do? Look, there's a mark on the floor and I need to polish it. Hasn't he got his own pump?"*

I winced slightly as it was clearly a bit of a ridiculous situation but whatever he was thinking, it didn't stop him from stretching the hose connected to a source of compressed air towards Reggie and making his tyres as hard as rocks once again.

"Grazie mille" I said. The man looked puzzled but a thousand thank-yous from my perspective did seem reasonable if I wanted to avoid a repeat of the Athens incident.

The climb towards Cuneo was no more strenuous than had been the climb towards Fossano. Over the course of 20km, we knocked another 150m off the eventual ascent of nearly 700m that would be required to get us as far as Limone-Piemonte, but it wasn't really very noticeable, especially given the ease with which Reggie's newly inflated tyres were cutting along the road. It never ceases to amaze me just how big an impact the simple job of pumping your tyres to an appropriate air pressure can have upon not just the comfort of your ride, but also upon the effort required by the rider. Of course, when I say 'simple'... Let's move on. As I closed in on Cuneo, the mountains did begin to loom large on the horizon and I knew that at some point some more strenuous climbing would be involved.

The sign makers of Italy really do need to sort things out. Describing them as a somewhat *'idiosyncratic'* would be like describing Silvio Berlusconi as *'romantic'*. The word is just too polite to describe the reality.

"45km... 35km... Mmm.... Now back up to 38km. Interesting ... And down to 25km. That was quick..."

How difficult can it be to work out the distance from, say, Cherasco to Cuneo or Cuneo to Limone Piemonte? Look boys and girls, here are some simple instructions. First of all, do try to realise that writing signs is fundamentally different from choosing random numbers for the lottery draw. Get in a car and drive between the two places of interest. Take the distance that you noted down at the start of your journey away from the distance that you wrote down at the end of your journey and the number you have calculated is the distance you have travelled. This is the number that should then be transferred to the sign that you position at the place where you wrote down the first number. Once you've got the hang of that, go back and repeat the exercise from the places where you want to erect other signs along the way. A more advanced technique might be to complete one journey and note down the distances at the points where you want the signs to be, but I can quite understand if this might take a few weeks of training on the job. Failing that, use a map. I know it's a tricky concept to grasp but come on, your forefathers built some of the most beautiful and spectacular buildings in the world, they founded an empire that stretched across the Mediterranean basin and beyond, your fellow countrymen at Ferrari make cars that invoke envy in all who see them vroom past on the road and in Alba they are churning out chocolatey rice-crispy thingies that get dished out at diplomatic soirées around the globe! (What do you mean it's just an advert?) OK, your political system is a bit screwed up and we all have a laugh at Berlusconi (you no doubt do the same) but please! Working out the distance between two places isn't akin to painting the Sistine Chapel. (Oh, you did that too by the way.) I'm glad I've got that off my chest.

Was it 45km from Cherasco to Cuneo. Or was it 40? Or indeed 43? Take your pick. The sign makers did. In fairness, I wouldn't like to tar all Italian sign makers with the same brush. There is one master craftsman out there in Italy somewhere who is responsible for introducing the system that allows you to navigate your way easily to a town centre. Just follow the concentric rings symbol on signs and you'll get there, guaranteed. Cuneo loved this system so much that it had two routes available. For me it was a lucky dip so I chose the one that first took me down into the valley bottom and then up the other side. It was a decision I regretted only when I noticed that the other route would have taken me straight across the long viaduct that spanned the wide valley.

Despite its size and importance, Cuneo didn't receive even the slightest of mentions in my *Rough Guide*. Neither did Limone-Piemonte nor the Tende Pass, as the authors had chosen to concentrate their efforts on writing about the Aosta Valley further to the north. Although it would have been useful to have a little background information about the place, it did at least make my decision to post Volume 1 of my Heath-Robinson *Rough Guide* back home an easier one and saved me lugging the book over the mountains. But why didn't Cuneo merit even just a small paragraph? It was quite a substantial place, with a handsome square surrounded by some formidable 19th century architecture and an imposing position at the foot of the Maritime Alps.

I had a leisurely lunch in a café on the main square and then wandered for a while through the cool arcades, along the northern side of the piazza and then down the pencil-straight main street. Built on a grid pattern on an outcrop of rock above the valley floor, I sensed that this had once been a town of military importance in helping keep the troublesome French at bay. In modern times it might have lost its way a little; the French are nowhere near as problematic as they once were and the tourists appear to have bypassed the area, choosing instead to head for the more glamorous attractions of Aosta. It made me wonder: who comes first, the tourists or the guidebook writers?

If the sign on the main street were to be believed, Limone-Piermonte would be 27km away. The same sign also informed me that I was heading in the direction of '*Francia*', which was good to have confirmed (if it was correct). Surely the mountains would now start to kick in big time, no? I was expecting something a little more challenging than what I actually got. If you are able to cast your mind back to 2010 (i.e. if you read the first book) to when I crossed the Alps via the Gotthard Pass in Switzerland, most of the legwork had been done on the previous day, when I had cycled from the valley bottom at Lucerne up to Andermatt. The cycle from Andermatt to the pass was quite tame in comparison. The format of those two days of cycling was clearly not going to be repeated on this journey because although the route did eventually steepen a little in the final 10km, it never quite got to the point where it was painful or, dare I say, strenuous. Indeed, my main preoccupation was yet again whether I should be cycling along the road that I had taken. As the infrastructure of the valley was being squeezed into an ever-narrower band of land, it was difficult to see what alternative route I could have taken so I just plodded on, trying to keep as far away as I possibly could from the lorries and cars that sped past. They were not en route to the Tende Pass but the tunnel, which had been cut out of the mountain somewhere beyond Limone-Piermonte. Many of the drivers seemed very eager to arrive at the tunnel entrance as soon as they possibly could.

A short period of relief from the traffic came when I arrived in the curious village of Vernante. At some point in the past, the SP20 would have continued straight through the centre of Vernante but someone had seen sense and decided to divert the road so that it skirted along the edge of the village. The main street had subsequently been all but pedestrianised, creating cycling conditions that were abruptly and starkly different from those on the main road. But what made this place so curious was nothing to do with traffic management and everything to do with Pinocchio and a man called Attilio Mussino.

Mussino was an artist born in Turin in 1878, who made his name by illustrating a 1911 edition of *The Adventures of Pinocchio*. After his son was killed in the war, he came to spend the last ten years of his life in the village of Vernante and in 1989 two local residents started to paint Mussino-inspired murals in the village depicting the adventures of the little wooden fibber. The result is that Vernante has been transformed from just another pretty alpine village into another pretty alpine village with a reason to stop, admire some artwork and spend money. The shopkeepers and hoteliers have no doubt been rubbing their hands together ever since. The numerous murals depict Pinocchio in various animal-related situations - flying a bird, toying with a very large snake, on horseback pulling a carriage, eyeing up a woman - all of which were presumably not true. But then again, it was fiction. I wonder what he told Giuseppe about the woman. I don't think that part made it into the Disney version.

It was only another 5km to Limone Piemonte, where I easily found the campsite just to the north of the small town and was instructed to pitch the tent in another sandpit, which reminded me of my experiences back in Split. Most of the other campers were in caravans and looked as though they were there for an extended period of time, but for me it was just as useful for an overnight stop. After showering, I cycled into the town centre, which was packed. Some kind of Saturday evening religious festival was taking place, complete with band playing and a procession of the great and good (and no doubt a few who weren't). A biblical scene depicting a man with a halo being given directions by a winged angel was being carried around the main square. I assumed that the man was a saint and that he too was having issues with the Italian signage. It was all utterly bewildering and distinctly alpine. I watched and took some photos, as did the hundreds of others, many of whom were probably scratching their heads just as much as I was. But then again, perhaps they had invested in a guidebook that hadn't erased this small corner of Italy from the map.

Sunday 4th August 2013
Cycling Day 29: Limone-Piemonte to Nice, 121km

When I emerged from the tent, a couple of French mountain bikers were in the process of preparing breakfast next to their car which they had parked just on the other side of the campsite path to where Reggie and I were. I introduced myself and they offered me coffee. Bingo! We started chatting and they explained how they had cycled up the Tende Pass from the French side and down to Limone-Piemonte on the previous afternoon. There was a complicated explanation as to how they had managed to get their car to the campsite, but I was much more interested in their experiences of cycling up and over the pass, albeit in the opposite direction to me. The man explained that the road down from the top was a good quality road and it wouldn't cause me too many problems. He didn't mention the road up to the pass on the French side, but did I really need to ask such a question? If the road on the Italian side was good, it was difficult, if not impossible, to imagine that the French road down the other side was anything other than excellent. Were there to be a road equivalent of the Eurovision Song Contest, France would win hands down every year and the Italians would be left scrabbling for the '*nul point*' alongside Greece and the Albanians. The French woman explained that they were from Fréjus on the south coast and I asked her what she did for a living:

"*C'est le week-end et on ne parle pas de ça!*" she snapped and I took her refusal to answer my innocuous question as clear admission that she worked for the French secret services. It was perhaps the moment to bid them '*au revoir*' and head back into the town centre before she had the chance to silently break my neck and bury my body in the woods.

The main square on a Sunday morning was a much more sedate place than it had been the night before. The saint, his guiding angel and their hundreds of followers were nowhere to be seen. It was an altogether more calming place to be and I spent a good half-hour munching through a continental breakfast, admiring the pretty buildings around the square and gazing towards the mountains that I would soon be climbing. My Michelin map showed very little detail of the route over the pass and it seemed likely that 3G mobile phone coverage for most of the morning's cycling would be thin on the ground, if not non-existent. So, in order to minimise my chances of taking a wrong turn, I carefully studied the online Google map of the area and took a few screenshots to consult later should I need to. After about 7km, I could see that the tunnel plunged into the mountainside and it was after this point that the serious switchbacks started. On the Italian side, there were about a dozen turns in the road but I was a little alarmed by just how frenzied the switchback action became when I examined the French side of the pass. The road flicked backwards and forwards as if it were recording the last gasps of a man in full cardiac arrest. It wasn't an appropriate thought to be having immediately prior to a cycle up a mountain, so I placed my phone in its holder, switched on the tracking app and set off, slowly.

The pass (for those of you who have only scant recollection of your school geography lessons) is the bit of the mountains that sits between the peaks and allows access to the next valley. I had already travelled through several passes since leaving the southern tip of Greece, most notably the one in the Peloponnese that I wasn't expecting (well to be honest, I wasn't expecting the Peloponnese mountains at all) which was at 1,220m and the Llogoroja Pass in Albania at 1,030m. But the Tende Pass at 1,871m was the daddy of them all. It surprised me when I first realised just how high it was; the Gotthard Pass in Switzerland, which I had climbed in 2010, was 'only' 2,091m but it was much further north. The Tende Pass was 30km from the Mediterranean coast and was a clear example of just how far south the grandeur of the alpine range spreads. But before I could enjoy the nearly 2km of vertical descent to the seaside, I had to complete the 900m climb that remained to be pedalled in the other direction.

It would be a journey of around 15km to the pass divided into two roughly equal parts: firstly the cycle to the entrance of the tunnel and then on a smaller road to the pass itself. The switchbacks started well before the tunnel entrance but were significantly fewer in number than during the second part of the climb. There was a long queue of cars at the entrance to the tunnel and I was hopeful that for the remainder of the journey to the pass, it would be just me, perhaps a few other cyclists and the odd fly to swat out of the way. Oh dear. The thin road that branched off the main road to the pass seem to attract the kind of drivers who use their cars as a source of excitement in their lives and there was a steady (and often loud) stream of 4x4 vehicles passing me as I gradually made my way to the top. Then there were the motor bikers, the scramble riders and the people driving quad bikes. In fact, there were no other cyclists and I don't remember having to swat any flies. It seemed highly likely that they had succumbed to the fumes from all the vehicles (the flies, that is, rather than the cyclists, although that wouldn't have surprised me either). I could see no pleasure whatsoever in what they were doing. It required no effort apart from a foot on a pedal and occasionally some braking and I felt pity that they weren't able to experience the sheer joy of achieving a climb to 1,871m as a result of their own human efforts. They, no doubt, had the reverse thought about me as they zoomed their way to the top. When there was a break in the traffic, I paused, dismounted and took in the view. This was classic alpine territory, with a carpet of green vegetation smothering the land save for the high outcrops of rock. The wide meadows near to the road were scattered with specks of yellow, white, blue and purple, where the wild flowers were popping their heads above the less vibrant, green grass. And then another vehicle roared past behind my shoulder.

I am one of life's counters – I do it when climbing stairs and swimming lengths at the pool – and as soon as I had totted up the number of turns in the road when consulting the maps back in Limone-Piemonte, it was inevitable that I would be counting them all the way to the top. So, after I had counted my tenth turn, I knew I was approaching the pass. Or was I? Another couple of turns brought me to a long ridge and in the distance I could see that many of the cars that had passed me were parked up. As I approached them I could see that the road ballooned out into a wider area of land, which again was rapidly filling with cars. On the right was a wooden chalet in front of which were five flagpoles: the French, Italian, Swiss, European Union and British flags were all being held up by the stiff breeze. Nice of them to know that I was coming... But was this the pass? There was no iconic sign covered in stickers from motorbiking groups worldwide to confirm that I had reached the top but I couldn't risk it, so I placed Reggie in front of the flags with a spectacular mountain vista in the distance and took his photo.

At the far end of the car park there were two tracks; the one to the left appeared to lead to a ruined fort of some kind - quite a substantial construction albeit a bit draughty. To the right was a rough track and this looked more promising as it headed further along and up the edge of the mountain, to a point where more cars had been parked. It was difficult to ride upon the rocky, loose gravel so I got off and pushed. After a hundred metres or so, there was a sign warning that people should only continue in 4×4 vehicles. No mention of 2×1 bicycles. I persevered (as did several cars which were more 'hatchback' than '4x4') and after perhaps half a kilometre, I found what I had been looking for: a weather-beaten, wooden sign stating that I had reached the *'Colle di Tenda'*. A few metres away was an equally wooden but much smarter sign, stating that I had also reached the *'Col de Tende'*.

This double certification of my achievement also confirmed that I had, of course, now arrived in France. Country number eight in my list of ten. *Arrivederci Italia. Bonjour la France!*

A shiver of excitement quivered across my body at the thought of finally arriving in my linguistic comfort zone. Or was it that stiff breeze? A few people (and their hatchbacks) were milling around, so after having taken another set of pictures of Reggie next to the sign with another stunning alpine view in the background, I moved to a quiet spot on top of a small mound a short distance away. I peered down the valley into France and my eyes swept backwards and forwards as I attempted to trace the path of the mountain track heading south. I couldn't see any traffic on the road. Was this a good or bad sign? The quality of the road that I could see to my left wasn't brilliant, but as for what it was like further down the valley I could only speculate. What happened to those Eurovision-winning French roads? It was impossible not to cast my mind back to 2010 when, having climbed to the Gotthard Pass in Switzerland, a spoke had broken only a short distance into my descent along the Ticino valley and I was left pushing poor Reggie for many kilometres to the nearest town. Not again, please.

I refocused my eyes upon the activity around the pass. Many people were heading off to wander higher into the mountains. An elderly couple further along the road were sunbathing as if they were sitting on the beach. And one German motorbike rider was taking a piss. Nice touch. It was time for me to head off and down into France.

I made a tentative start to my descent. Well, it was also a tentative middle and a tentative end as well, as I edged my way down from the pass, along the track of loose rocks and gravel. Two mountain bikers informed me it would be like that for about 3km. For them it was perfect but for me, well, I would have much preferred something significantly more stable. There was, however, one saving grace in that I was travelling downhill rather than up. After around half a kilometre, I paused to record a video and was passed by another touring cyclist. I think he was English but it's difficult to say for sure when the only word a person says is '*Hello*'. I asked him where he was going (stupid question, I know, but I meant in the longer term rather than the shorter one) but he ignored me and continued to push his bike up the hill. It only really started to dawn upon me as I continued to edge my way down the mountain, kilometre after kilometre, why he might have been in such a disgruntled mood. It would have been impossible to ride up the road without regularly falling off the bike and perhaps he had arrived at the tunnel entrance in France expecting to be able to cycle straight through, only to be pointed in the direction of the rough track. It was a very, very long way down for me; in the opposite direction the distance must have felt eternal. My own cycle continued, gingerly, and I took several time-outs to gaze admiringly at the scenery and gaze worryingly at Reggie's spokes. By the time I had reached the tunnel entrance, I had re-evaluated the initial impression I had formed of my fellow touring cyclist. For him to have even managed a civil '*Hello*' probably put him in the category of cyclists that I would normally consider to be deliriously happy.

My main gripe (I normally seem to have one, don't I?) as I cycled between the small rocks on the path, was to do with my hands. They were constantly applying the brakes so as to prevent Reggie and me from taking the quick route down to the valley bottom via the steep incline at the edge of the road. On arrival at the queue of cars waiting to head into the darkness of the tunnel in the direction of Italy, I had to stop riding for a good 10 minutes to help them recover. But I was in France! A land where all the signs made sense and so did the people, most of the time. I had a broad smile on my face as I cycled at speed along and down through the deep and dramatic valley that had been carved into the land by thousands of years of alpine river erosion. The first place I came to where I could stop and pause for something to eat and drink, was the town of Tende itself and I sat on the terrace of a busy café, ordered and then demolished a minor feast whilst uploading the video that I had taken earlier to the Internet. The journey after Tende continued in a similarly steep fashion and I occasionally checked the cycling app on my phone to find out how many of the 1,871m I had so far descended. I knew the distance to the coast was around 50km by road and was slightly concerned that I seemed to be using up lots of the vertical metres before many of the horizontal ones had been cycled. It was, however, a nice concern to dwell upon, compared to those of earlier in the afternoon.

I could see on my map that the road split into two near the town of Saorge. If I were to turn right and cycle through Sospel, it would mean a second climb to another, less significant pass but then the route would be a direct one to Nice. If I were to turn left, the road would continue downhill (but for how long?), take me back into Italy before arriving on the coast at Ventimiglia. This was a much shorter route to the Mediterranean but it would then mean that I would have to cycle a good 30km along the coast through Menton and Monte-Carlo, before arriving in Nice itself. In my mind I had images of Cary Grant, Grace Kelly and the French Riviera. I turned left.

Mercifully, there was very little uphill cycling between that point and my final destination in Nice. Numerous, long tunnels did make me question whether (yet again) I was infringing the local traffic regulations, especially in Italy where you can never be quite certain when a road is a road or indeed a motorway signposted like a normal road. When I entered France for the second time at Menton – the once symbolic border post between the two countries having been turned into a rather shabby parking area for motor homes – I smiled again upon realising that I was once more in a country I knew well and in which, for the following week or so at least, I would be fraternising happily with old friends and hopefully a few new ones too.

I tried to stick as close to the Mediterranean as I possibly could as I cycled from the border to Nice and this strategy worked well as not only did it keep me away from the ups and downs of the main road above the towns, but it was just a very interesting ride, especially the cycle through the familiar landmarks of Monte Carlo. I had driven through the town on a couple of occasions previously, but this journey allowed me to inspect the sun-drenched hangout of the rich and famous a little more closely. Away from the main roads, I was pleasantly surprised to find it to be an immaculately tended and decidedly intimate warren of narrow roads. Everyone I could see oozed money and they didn't look the types to ever stick their profile on the Warm Showers website. I did, however, keep an eye out for one man who might have given me space on his lawn to pitch the tent. Earlier in the year, I had seen a picture that had been posted to Twitter by Alan Sugar. It showed the noble lord in full cycling gear on the corniche road somewhere near Monte Carlo. I assumed at the time that he must have a property in the principality but, alas, I never spotted him and I don't have an interesting tale to tell.

The *Promenade des Anglais* in Nice welcomed me with a throng of late Sunday afternoon promenaders. The pebbly beach was still packed but as I had already sorted out my accommodation on the previous day – a nice(!) hotel in the centre - I was in no rush. I sat outside a bar and toasted my arrival. I was now just over halfway to Cape St. Vincent in Portugal. I had been cycling for exactly five weeks and there were another four remaining before I would be forced into abandoning the trip due to lack of time. So, yes, I was a little behind schedule (to the extent that a person without a schedule in the first place can be) but as long as I was willing to put in some serious cycling effort, it might still be possible. One way in which I could make up time would be to reduce the number of rest days. However, ever the man to put off until tomorrow what could be done today (or rather, in this case put off until the day after tomorrow what could have been done the following day), I decided that my day off in Nice was not one that I was willing to sacrifice. So much for will power...

PART FIVE: FRANCE
Monday 5th August 2013
Rest Day 7: Nice

I can't say for sure, but it wouldn't surprise me if some of the greatest works of travel literature have been written up from notes made whilst the author was sitting in a laundrette washing his or her smalls. It's certainly where you would have found me on that first Monday morning of August and that's exactly what I was doing. I leave it for others to debate whether this is a great work of travel literature. But let's backtrack a little. I had decided to forgo the luxuries of a campsite and slum it in a three star hotel in Nice. All in all, Italy had been a cheap country through which to travel. Thanks to Simone in Venice and the three Warm Showers hosts, five of my nine nights in the country had been free. Of the remaining four, three had been under canvas and only the first – the night in Trieste – had been in a hotel. I hadn't needed an excuse to book into a centrally located boutique hotel, but Italy had provided me with one anyway. It made me feel a little more virtuous as I sank my head into the pillows of the *Hôtel La Villa* on *Boulevard Victor Hugo,* rather than the rolled-up jumper I was so used to using in the tent. Perhaps the reason why the *Hôtel La Villa* had yet to achieve its fourth star was because it didn't have the facilities to do its guests' laundry, which is why I was to be found in the *'Top Speed' Laverie Automatique* on *rue de la Buffa* at 8am doing it myself. Should you ever find yourself in a similar situation in central Nice, I can heartily recommend the *'Top Speed'* laundrette. Apart from being spotlessly clean, all the machines around the small room were controlled by one central unit on the wall, which accepted (wait for it...) notes! This is a leap in laundry technology that has passed me by in recent years. The point at which it is no longer necessary to buy an unwanted croissant or packet of Polo mints just for the purposes of receiving the change cannot be far off. I have seen the future and it is on *rue de la Buffa*, Nice, France. Once the novelty value of this realisation had worn off, I settled down to write up my notes about cycling over the Alps the previous day, as my clothes turned the water inside the washing machine an alarmingly dark shade of brown.

There was a distinct risk that by choosing to take a day off in Nice, I would be repeating the error of my rest day taken in Venice. I knew Nice even better than I knew Venice, so would I have been better off waiting until I arrived elsewhere to take a pause from the cycling? Perhaps. But then again, I did need a day without much physical

239

exertion. The day in Venice had been exactly one week earlier and I wasn't a Victorian factory labourer working under the tyrannical regime of a profiteering mill owner. I did need a few days of rest and actually, choosing a place that I knew well could work to my advantage. I wasn't desperate to see anything and was happy to take the day at a very leisurely pace with lots of sitting down and sipping of coffee.

The reason I knew Nice so well was that I had lived in the city for six weeks while training to be a teacher of French. My metamorphosis from graduate with a bachelor's degree in mathematics to fully qualified teacher of French in a British state secondary school had been a lengthy, although rarely arduous. I had stopped studying French formally at the age of 16 when I finished my 'O' level in the subject. At the time (which isn't that long ago), combining the study of a language with that of the sciences was (shamefully) frowned upon, certainly in the school where I was educated. This resulted in my continuing to study the sciences at 'A' level, which had a knock-on impact upon what I chose to study at university. Thinking back, I lacked imagination when it came to my academic choices and I now look with envy at the vast array of courses that are open to prospective university students in the 21st century. But I always considered that whatever I ended up doing in life, a second language would be of use. I still believe that, it's just perhaps a pity that I don't currently do anything much with my language skills apart from trying to teach French to the teenagers of today. My own school French teacher, Robin Barrett (whom I considered to be my only teacher with a skill worthy of my envy and who spent his lunchtimes in the dining hall chatting away in French to one of his language teaching colleagues, much to the bemusement of every pupil and probably most teachers) had faith in my linguistic skills however, and he supported me informally throughout the period of the sixth form with the occasional text, which I would read and return to him. At university, I spent my Wednesday afternoons not on the rugby or football pitches but at the Language Teaching Centre of York University, honing my skills and then, during my failed attempts to become an accountant in the early 1990s while working in London, I attended evening classes at the City Lit College in Covent Garden. After a day in the dusty office of a small-to-medium-sized company trying to work out which ledger was which and not particularly caring whether invoices had been correctly processed, I was in heaven at the City Lit doing something I wanted to do, in an exciting location and with interesting people from all walks of life. It was the highlight of my week for over two years of my life in my early twenties. It was probably also the reason why my score in a professional tax exam was just 13%; I had spent the previous evening not caring a hoot about the fiscal intricacies of taxation policy and everything about the irregular declension of French verbs at one of my lessons. My fellow trainee accountants couldn't understand my folly when I explained to them where I had been the night before, as we queued for the exam outside that bastion of free-market economics, the Trades Union Congress in the West End of London. (It had a large hall.) I knew my days in the world of finance were numbered and had already found a job for the following summer, working on a campsite in France as a courier for a large, British travel company. My employers in the City were only told that I had a 'bad fail' in my exams. The accountancy partner's reaction, when I requested that he *not* give me the opportunity of retaking the exams, was to ask, "*Just how bad can a bad fail be?*" Shortly after my revelation about the percentage score in the tax exam, I was on my way to a more fruitful future where my linguistic talents were prized over my financial ones. After two long, summer seasons working for the camping company, during which I criss-crossed France in a white transit van putting up tents, looking after the British middle-classes and then taking the tents down again in early autumn, I found a job in the Loire city of Tours, teaching English as a foreign language. It would have been easy to spend the rest of my life in Tours; it was a lovely city, I worked with friendly and interesting people, but I became increasingly worried about the prospect of not having a 'proper' job by the time I hit 40. The Internet intervened and one of my first online searches was to find out if it was possible to train as a secondary school teacher in the UK without a degree in the subject you wanted to teach. Much to my surprise, it was, although the choice was limited to just two courses: one at my old university in York and one at the University of Reading. At the time, language teachers in Britain were in short supply and various schemes existed to entice people with the right skills, but not necessarily the academic background, into becoming teachers. I applied to both universities but the York course closed before it started due to lack of interest, leaving me with the option of just Reading. It would be a two-year, postgraduate certificate in education with the first year spent making sure my language skills were up to scratch and the second year the traditional PGCE. And to finally bring our story to the point, as part of my first year, I was required to fly to Nice with my fellow students and spend six weeks experiencing life as trainee teacher in France. It was the least arduous part of all.

We were in the city at the British taxpayer's expense (ironically the very same tax that I had been hopelessly inadequate at trying to work out during my accountancy days) and were accommodated by host families. I had been chosen to stay at the home of Monsieur and Madame Trichet. She was a wonderful cook. He was a politely opinionated, right-wing bigot who made the French National Front's then leader, the hideous Jean-Marie Le Pen, look like a limp leftie. The cooking compensated for the politics, but after a short period of time, I moved into a long-stay hotel in the centre. Nothing to do with the Trichets; everything to do with a fellow student who had also been sent to stay with the elderly couple in their house on the hill above Nice. We didn't see eye-to-eye and the thought of spending six weeks with him in the same house was just too much to bear. I made my excuses and left. Living in the centre of the city was fun and with other trainee teachers not too far away, we spent our time exploring the city, its sights and all too often its bars. One day every week we were required to attend a French international school near Cannes, another day was at the teacher-training institute and another, a cultural trip of some description was organised. The rest of the time was our own. Try not to tell the British taxpayer.

Nice in 2013 was just as bright and welcoming as Nice in 2000 had been. It was, however, a little warmer, as my previous stay had been during February and March. In fact, it was very warm with temperatures pushing to over 30 degrees centigrade. I wasn't accustomed to feeling the full force of the heat on the bike, simply because of the movement of air as one cycles, but in Nice it was intense and whenever I could, I escaped inside the cooling atmospheres of the shops that lined the *Avenue Jean Médecin*, the city's main thoroughfare which cuts a long, wide line through the centre towards the sea. The couple of hours spent wandering the lanes of the old town were not, however, air-conditioned and neither was the old castle, or what remains of it, on the hill on the eastern end of the city. That said, people don't climb the hill to see the castle; they do so to admire the magnificent iconic arc of the *Promenade des Anglais,* which sweeps along the coast as far as the airport in the distance. With so much detail in the view before me - the beachgoers, the water-sports addicts being pulled along by the motorboats, the low flying planes taking off from the airport, the chaotic roofs of the old town and the orderly boulevards of its more modern equivalent - there was little incentive to move away from the viewing platform. In the distance were the hills from which I had descended and which I would once more climb the following day, and beyond them an unblemished, blue sky. This was, unmistakeably, the *Côte d'Azur.*

I returned to the city centre and paused, for the second time, at the *Grand Café de Lyon* on the *Avenue Jean Médecin* to browse the local newspaper *Nice-Matin*. The headline read '*Casse du Carlton: prime d'1 M€ pour un "tuyau"* '. The story related to a jewellery heist which had taken place the previous week at the famous Carlton Hotel in nearby Cannes. Over €100 million worth of precious jewels had been stolen and the insurance company was offering €1 million for '*un tuyau*' - a pipe and what we would refer to as 'a lead'. It seemed a bit modest to say the least, especially if the 'pipe' eventually led to the recovery of the jewels and, in the process, saving themselves a hundred times the value of the reward. That aside, it was the perfect headline to read whilst visiting the French Riviera. Once again, my thoughts turned to Cary Grant and Grace Kelly smooching their way along the Mediterranean coast. I fantasised that the real-life burglar might be just as suave, calm and collected as smooth-talking John 'the cat' Robie, Grant's character in *To Catch a Thief*. It would be a scurrilous thought to imagine that the 2013 Carlton thief was somewhere close, wearing an elegant, cream suit and charming the skirt off a beautiful, visiting American. I don't think I would have turned him in if I had known.

Up until this point in proceedings, I had bided my time visiting old haunts and had enjoyed doing so. But the explorer in me did want to do something different, something new, something that I hadn't done when I was living in the city for the short period during the year 2000. The *Musée Masséna* caught my eye as I was browsing through the pages for Nice in my guidebook. "*The city's local history museum... worth a look to see the sumptuous interior of an aristocratic villa from Nice's heyday.*" The museum was on the western side of the city, in the direction of the airport and just next to Nice's famous Negresco Hotel. According to the *Rough Guide* (bought immediately prior to setting off for Athens), the museum was open '*Daily except Tuesday, 10am-6pm*' and was... '*Free*'. Great. I had nothing to lose. If it was a boring old house with exhibits gathering dust I would make the most of the air-conditioning and then clear off.

Twenty minutes later I was standing beneath the gates of the *Musée Masséna*. It was an imposing, three-storey, white building set back from the road a little and surrounded by a lush Mediterranean garden. A high, metal fence guarded the garden, the building and its contents. Entry was via a small outbuilding where a queue of people had gathered and was gradually edging forward. It seemed strangely slow-moving for a free museum. There was a good reason for this. It wasn't free. By the time I had worked this out, however, there were more people behind me in the queue than in front of me and I was only a few moments from being served.

"Bonjour monsieur."

"Bonjour," I replied, trying not to express my disgust that the pricing policy had changed since the production of my new guidebook. *"It's €10 but the ticket allows you entry to eight museums."* This just made things worse. I had no intention of visiting another seven museums in the time that remained for me in Nice. What's more, why was she speaking to me in English? How could she possibly detect from two syllables – *bon* and *jour* – my nationality? I wanted to insert a long, difficult-to-understand word into my response but the *bon mot* never materialised.

"But I only want to visit this museum, the Musée Masséna," I explained, trying to extract every bit of Frenchness out of the last two words. This wasn't going well.

"It's still €10 sir."

I paid up and I headed off along the curved drive, towards the entrance of the museum proper. It was mildly diverting and recounted the history of Nice, just as my guidebook had *correctly* informed me. The history of the building itself also got a mention. It had been built during the few years straddling the 19th and 20th centuries by Victor Masséna, who lived there until his death in 1910. Seven years later, his son, a certain André Prosper Victor Eugene Napoléon Masséna – how French is that! - flogged the place to the local council, so it was only ever lived in for well under twenty years. But what a period to have chosen: the *Belle Époque*, France's 20th century answer to the renaissance, with a few bottles of Absinthe thrown in for good measure. No mention of wild, alcohol-fuelled parties *chez Masséna* on the plaques in the museum, however. Had I still had one in my pocket, I would have bet €10 they had taken place; I'm sure I spotted a few green stains on those carpets...

I retired to my room at the *Hôtel La Villa* and spread out the impromptu buffet, bought from a nearby supermarket, on the bed. As I fine-dined I lay the maps of France on the floor and started, for the first time, to plot a vague route across the country. I was meeting some friends near *Mont Ventoux* later in the week and I had plans to meet a Warm Showers contact in the Pyrenees. The bits in between were all blank. *Plus ça change...*

Tuesday 6th August 2013
Cycling Day 30: Nice to Castellane, 101km

Apart from not having a laundry service, the *Hôtel La Villa* didn't have a breakfast service either. In fact, I wondered what services it did offer, other than that of providing rooms with beds, clean sheets and bathrooms. Surely for three stars you were entitled to much more, no? The whole place was very beautifully designed and I wasn't looking for a swimming pool or anything like that but a few croissants wouldn't have gone amiss. Five minutes after checking out, I was back on the terrace of the *Grand Café de Lyon* on the *Avenue Jean Médecin*, an establishment that did serve breakfast. How novel.

Nice is a great place to watch people and I do like people watching. From over-tanned women with prune-like skin walking their small dogs, to excessively camp men in brightly coloured tight-fitting shorts that they shouldn't have been allowed to buy in the first place, to the waifs and strays of French society who seemed to have converged upon this southern resort like no other French city I had ever visited. I suppose it makes sense to be homeless and living on the streets in a place like Nice, where the temperature during the summer months rarely drops to a level that could be described as uncomfortable. Spring and autumn are probably bearable and even in winter it must surely be a better place to live on the streets than Paris or Lille or any other northern French city. I wondered what the Médecin family would have thought of this eclectic assembly of modern day Frenchmen and women. The *Avenue Jean Médecin,* where I was sitting knocking back my morning coffee, was named after Nice's dominant political figure of the 20th century and, like his son Jacques who succeeded him as the city's mayor, he was a bit of a right-winger. Médecin senior was the elected mayor from 1928 until his death in 1965, with only a minor interruption during the latter stages of the war. His support for the Vichy régime - the puppet government that collaborated with the Germans – didn't prevent him from being re-elected shortly after the end of hostilities. His son, Jacques, was mayor from 1966 until he fled to Uruguay in 1990, when it became clear he was about to be arrested for corruption. It was Graham Greene of all people who first started to rock the boat for Médecin junior, but alas the British author didn't live long enough to see the former mayor extradited and thrown into prison. On release, he returned to Uruguay where he died in 1998. It will come as no surprise that Monsieur Trichet, the man with whom I had briefly stayed during my previous visit to Nice in the year 2000, claimed to know Jacques Médecin. I have clear memories of him rubbishing the accusations that had been made against his political hero, putting the blame on the Parisian elite. Perhaps Monsieur Trichet was only expressing a more widely held belief amongst the population of Nice, as not only has the *Avenue Jean Médecin* remained just that, but in 2007 Nice's conference centre was renamed the *Forum Jacques Médecin* in 'honour' of the disgraced former mayor.

Jean had his avenue, Jacques had his conference centre and well, we English have the *Promenade des Anglais*, the long, wide crescent-shaped strip of coastal road and pavement which links the centre of Nice to its airport some 5km away. It was also the first stage of my cycle to Castellane. Let's backtrack a little... If you remember (if you can't remember by the way you might have memory issues as it was only two pages ago), I was heading in the direction of *Mont Ventoux*. Earlier in the year, I had escorted a group of children on a school exchange to the small town of Falaise in northern France. Just as the students had stayed with a French family, so too had the accompanying teachers and I was welcomed into the house of Christel, a history teacher, her partner Nicolas, a maths teacher, and their two children Nolwen and Raphaël in Caen. When I explained my cycling plans for the summer, they invited me to visit them at a campsite in Villes-sur-Auzon, where they would be spending a couple of weeks of their own summer holidays. Villes-sur-Auzon is only a few kilometres from the iconic *Tour de France* climb *Mont Ventoux*. Without the intervention of Christel and Nicolas, it is unlikely that I would have deviated so far away from the French coast but this was an opportunity I couldn't, and didn't want, to turn down, despite the mountain being some 80km north of Marseille. The plan was to climb *Mont Ventoux* on my next 'rest day'. Much more of that little adventure later. I had decided that it would take three days of cycling to get as far as Villes-sur-Auzon and over coffee in Nice, had plumped for Castellane as the first overnight stopping point. I still wasn't sure where the second would be but, as ever, I would worry about that later.

Heading back inland inevitably meant a return to some serious climbing and if cycling day 30 required a name, it would surely have to be called *The Day of the Cols* as, over the course of the next few hours I was destined to climb to four of them. But before I arrived at the cols, I needed to cycle to Grasse, which was about 40km from Nice. The first half of the journey to Grasse was flat, even after I turned right at the end of the *Promenade des Anglais* and edged away from the coast. I was following the D6 and D7, roads that took me from the town of Cagnes-sur-mer to La Colle-sur-Loup and then Le Rouret. They were both relatively quiet back roads and for much of the time, I could cycle in the shade provided by the trees that lined the route. Each town, village and hamlet was typically Provençal with pretty fountains, small squares that doubled as meeting place and boules pitch and quaint, red-tiled houses that get snapped up by British investors more quickly than you can say *Peter Mayle*. The final portion of the cycle to Grasse climbed along the D2085, a road much busier than its four-numbered name would imply, but then again it was heading in the direction of the self-styled '*capitale mondiale du parfum*' or 'world capital of perfume'. They do have a good claim to the name as the town does live, breathe and, well, smell perfume. And it's not just marketing hype for the tourists; there are still ten perfumeries in the area around Grasse and many thousands of jobs depend upon its continued success. That said, as I pushed Reggie from the top of town through the narrow streets of small shops, cafés and restaurants, there is no sense of this place having been taken over by big business. There is no Body Shop or Lush (not that I could see), just rue after rue of what appeared to be independent traders selling their soaps, perfumes, bathing salts and whatever else such shops sell (I'm not an expert). After bold, corporate and at times brash Nice, Grasse was a welcome contrast and its count of over-sunned prunes, camp men, waifs and strays was well down on its coastal big brother. What I particularly liked, however, was the system of pipes that had been installed a few metres above the heads of the pedestrians along the hemmed-in streets and which sprayed a fine mist of cool water vapour into the air and down upon the welcoming body of anyone passing underneath. Just like the shower system at the campsite near Split in Croatia, and the laundrette that accepted notes into its machines in Nice, it is an invention that is sure one day to become omnipresent. Perhaps.

It was 64km from Grasse to Castellane. I knew this because the signs told me and, unlike in Italy, I believed them. They were consistent and matched my own calculations. In fact, the French should win some kind of award for their signage. I can't think of another European country that manages their signs so well. They are, as I've just said, accurate but also informative and clear. You are rarely left scratching your head at a junction in France wondering where to go next because the information you need is right there in front of you. And have you ever seen an old French sign? They don't exist. They have all been renewed within the last five years and before you say that there are plenty of old-looking signs out there in rural France, have you considered that there might be a factory (probably state owned) somewhere in France churning out retro signs? This is pure conjecture on my part but I wouldn't put it past them. Full marks to the French sign makers. I write this eulogy because there were some stunning examples of signage that day in southern Provence; every col was noted (enabling me to count four of them), every road clearly labelled (allowing me to tell you about the D6, D7 and the D2085), there were some well-maintained regional cycle route signs (the *'Grand Tour des Préalpes d'Azur'* for example) but the *pièces de résistance* were the signs that told me all about *La Route Napoléon*...

I do love a good sign that stops you in your tracks and tells you about something that happened in the place where you happen to be standing. The detail given on the signs about *La Route Napoléon* was exemplary, but I think it might have been written by a fan as the text started as follows:

"Without a shadow of a doubt, Napoléon 1st is one of the most famous characters in the world... an ambitious and charismatic leader of men, blessed with an exceptional intellect, [he] changed the face of the political world."

La Route Napoléon for modern-day travellers allows you to follow in the footsteps of Mr B., from Cannes on the coast to Grenoble. Napoléon escaped from his island exile of Elba and landed at Golfe-Juan on 1st March 1815. (Isn't that just typically Napoleonic? Who else would insist on starting a great journey on the first of the month? Eh?) By the end of the week, he was in Grenoble and a few days later he was back in charge in Paris. It's difficult not to admire a man who is capable of doing all that. Alas, Napoléon's rebirth as a great leader wasn't to last; he was of course defeated at Waterloo on 18th June 1815 and this time the British were determined to stick him a little further away from French shores than the Russians, Prussians and Austrians had been. Saint Helena is over 8,000km by sea to Cannes. Elba is just 300km.

I would be following *La Route Napoléon* all the way to Castellane - he had lunch there on 3rd March, if you were wondering - and I felt quite proud that after nearly two hundred years of progress, I was able to do in one day on a bicycle what Napoléon and his small army had managed in two and a half. Every col I climbed, they must surely have climbed also but I did have the advantage of being able to freewheel down the other side, an invigorating option that's not quite the same when on a horse or on foot. I don't suppose the French were anywhere near as good at signage back in the early 19th century either, so Napoléon's men would have struggled to tell you that they had climbed to the *Col du Pilon* (782m), the *Col de la Faye* (984m), the Col de

Valferreière (1,169m) or the Col de Luens (1,054m). But I don't. Before I get carried away, the cycling was much gentler than you might imagine, the roads were not punishingly steep (simply steep) and after each *col* I didn't plunge more than about 100m before the next climb kicked in. That said, it was a great work out for the leg muscles and by the end of the day, Reggie and I (and all the equipment, don't forget) had climbed over 1,900m. Napoléon would have been proud! (Had I not been British.)

It was a wonderful day of cycling all round, everything that you might have wanted and expected from a holiday of this type. It wasn't a struggle. It wasn't a chore. It wasn't being done for the sake of crossing a continent by bike. It was thoroughly enjoyable stuff.

Approaching Castellane, the scenery was at its most spectacular. The town sits at the foot of a great edifice of rock rising high into the sky and upon which a church – Notre-Dame du Roc - has been built. The famous Verdon gorge starts in Castellane and I was already considering the gorge as the most likely continuation of my journey for the following day. There were more pressing matters to deal with however; I needed somewhere to stay and in a place like Castellane, which had campsites sprouting from the ground in every direction, that wouldn't be difficult, would it? I picked up an accommodation leaflet from the tourist office and it listed a total of twenty sites of which five were referred to as *'centre-ville'*. I found three of them and each one was packed to the rafters with holidaymakers. This was frustrating as I was only one person with a bike and one small tent. When travelling to Italy in 2010, I found that most sites, especially those in the northern half of my cycle, had a patch of ground where 'free' camping was allowed. You still had to pay of course (!) but you were 'free' to choose where exactly to erect your tent. Some sites even went to the trouble of reassuring potential customers on their website that they would never turn away a cyclist travelling alone. How civilised is that! In busier areas, however, the campsite owners were less liberal in their welcome and if they didn't have a pitch available, they couldn't squeeze you in. That was the situation in Castellane on 6th August, so I went back to the brochure and identified other likely candidates for the honour of accommodating Reggie and me. The two-star *Camping Le Pesquier* came to my rescue, but only just. It was 1km out of town, there was a friendly welcome and at €15 it wasn't expensive. I went to my allocated corner of the site and slumped on the floor prior to putting up the tent. A few minutes later I heard footsteps and a voice.

"*Monsieur... monsieur! Serait-il possible de changer d'emplacement?*" You know you are in trouble if someone uses the conditional form to make a request. It was the woman from reception asking if it '*would be possible*' for me to change my pitch. It became apparent that only seconds after having taken my money, a much larger group had turned up and she was beginning to regret having allocated me to the last decent-sized pitch on the campsite. But being the nice person that I am, I could see that it made sense for a largish family to camp where I was still slumped and I agreed to move.

The 3G coverage wasn't good in Castellane – probably due to the large protruding monolith of rock with the church on top – so as I waited to be served my campsite pizza, I attempted to jump through the online hoops that were required for me to access the wi-fi, which was only available in an invisible bubble surrounding the reception hut. In order to access the Internet, I was required to watch a video advert but something – the lack of Flash? – on my iPhone was preventing that from happening. (How likely was I to buy whatever product they were trying to sell me after a palaver like that? Sorry. I just needed to get those technical issues off my chest.) In the end, I abandoned my attempts to update the website with news of beautiful Provence, sweet-smelling Grasse, Napoleon on tour, the four cols and the campsite hassles. It could wait until the morning. I returned to the tent with what remained of the pizza and slumped once more onto the ground. There are evenings when things conspire to tell you that the best thing you should be doing is absolutely bugger all, so I did just that.

Wednesday 7th August 2013
Cycling Day 31: Castellane To Gréoux-les-Bains, 108km

Most people don't happen to visit Castellane because they have decided to cycle across Europe during their summer holidays. They do so because it's one of the gateways to the world-famous *Gorges du Verdon*. Picture a thick wooden cheese board. Now imagine getting a heavy-duty chisel and hammering a great crack in your cheeseboard. Apart from no longer being on speaking terms with the owner of the cheeseboard, you have something that resembles, very loosely, the *Gorges du Verdon*. It's a monumental crevice in the surface on the Earth which extends well over 20km from the man-made *Lac de Sainte-Croix* in the west to Castellane in the east. At its highest, point the gorge plunges some 700m into the ground and, until the beginning of the 20th century, the deepest gorges were considered to be impenetrable. However, in 1905, the French authorities called upon one Edouard Alfred Martel, who was a skilled speleologist (a caver, to you and me) who subsequently became the first person to complete a full exploration of the *Gorges du Verdon*. Interestingly, he was also the first person to descend Gaping Gill in Yorkshire in 1895, so he was clearly a man on top of his game. Well, I suppose if you're into your speleology it's a good thing to be at the bottom, but you know what I mean. The gorge itself forms a natural border between the French *départements* of *Les Alpes-de-Haute-Provence* and *Le Var,* having been eroded by the River Verdon into the limestone plain of Provence.

That's the end of today's geography lesson, so close your books. Back in the main square of Castellane, I was pondering my route along the gorges and had a choice of either following the shorter road on the northern side of the Verdon or the longer, probably more undulating *'Corniche Sublime'* on the southern side. I asked the girl who was serving me coffee in the bar where I was sitting, which of the two routes she would advise. She provided me with such a diplomatically balanced answer that I came away from our conversation convinced that she had never actually travelled along either side of the gorges or if she had, she hadn't bothered to look out of the car window. She did, however, point me in the direction of a large sign on the other side of the square, which might provide me with a few more answers. Before I did so, I referred to my *Rough Guide*, which gave me an equally (albeit uncharacteristically) balanced description of the two routes. It did warn me that cycling in the area should be reserved for the *'preternaturally fit'*. I sensed this wasn't a good description but looked up the word '*preternaturally*' to have it confirmed that it was used to describe someone whose fitness would be '*out of or beyond the normal course of nature*'. Was that me? Probably not. Anyway, that would be an argument to be had with a doctor later in the day, should I end up being carted off to hospital. My still unanswered question was whether I should cycle along the northern D952 '*Rive Droite*' or the southern D71 '*Corniche Sublime*'. And there I had my answer. How could I possibly not take a road that was described as '*sublime*'? To compete with it, the northern road should really employ an advertising agency to come up with an equally enticing name; '*right bank*' just doesn't cut it.

I could have changed my mind up until the point, 12km from Castellane, where I was required to cross a bridge directing me to the '*Rive Gauche*' or the 'left bank' of the river. Eventually, this would connect me with the '*Corniche Sublime*'. I hoped it would be just that but my lack of preternatural fitness was playing on my mind. Could it be any more challenging than those achingly steep climbs back in Albania? Had I not proved myself by climbing the Alps, not only once in 2010 but just a few days previously in 2013? Should I survive until the end of the day, I would at least have a new word to use on my CV; perhaps any future employer who was not sufficiently impressed by my string of academic qualifications might have their head turned by a prospective employee who was '*preternaturally fit*'.

Apart from its apparent sublimity, the southern route also clung more closely to the gorge itself. That said, after crossing the bridge, I was initially guided well away from the river on a long, steady climb via pretty Trigance, where I paused for a few minutes not only to catch my breath but also to sit and stare along the long, picturesque valley of the Jabron river. On another day, I may have been tempted to climb to the top of the village where an impressive fortified castle was sitting in a dominant position, overlooking the village and the length of the valley. With cycling that required me to put my preternatural body into action, however, I couldn't afford to hang around too long and continued to wind my way through the countryside until, at 1,000m, I was afforded my first spectacular views down into the valley and the *Gorges du Verdon*.

It took me a little by surprise. Although I could see crumbling limestone outcrops in the distance, there were no clues that these formed the very tops of the almost vertical drop on the northern side of the gorge. The first indication that there was indeed something worth seeing was a small car park to the right hand side of the road and a blue and cream plaque from '*Monuments Historiques et Sites*', which displayed a long, thin arrow pointing in the direction of the, as yet unseen, gorge and the words '*Balcon de la Mescla*'. A '*balcon*' or 'balcony' in English, was clearly a point from where it would be possible to peer down into the gorge, so I parked up leaving Reggie alongside an assortment of empty cars and motorbikes and walked in the direction that the arrow was indicating. After a few moments of passing through the shrubs and low trees next to the road, a wide panorama opened up in front of me. I could now see clearly that the outcrops of rock I had noticed from the road didn't just stop at the level where I was standing but they continued downwards for several hundred metres, before meeting the meandering river Verdon in the bottom of the valley. I wandered to the balcony, where several other people were doing what I was about to do myself. The low wall was perhaps a little too low for comfort but I poked my head over the edge and stared into the vertical distance below. The first thing that struck me was the vibrancy of the colour of the water. This being the summer, the river wasn't fast flowing and from the distance of the viewpoint, it was impossible to see which way the water was moving. Indeed, it appeared to be hanging around in large pools, the turquoise of the liquid contrasting starkly with the off-white colour of the limestone bed. Green vegetation covered perhaps three-quarters of the rocky valley sides, which in places were vertical. For the first time, I could really understand why it had taken until 1905 to fully explore the area. Edouard Alfred Martel had done so at a time when maps of the area were presumably scant in their detail and when images from above were still just the fanciful thoughts of Jules Verne and his fellow science-fiction writers. There would have been no '*balcon*' from which to stop and examine the lay of the land and there would have been no road to get you to the viewpoint in the first place. The valley of the Verdon must have seemed as remote and forbidding to Monsieur Martel as do the valleys of Venus from the perspective of the early 21st century.

The only thing that could have made the *Gorges du Verdon* a more impressive sight on that day in earlier August, would have been a bit of sunshine. It had been cloudy all morning since leaving Castellane and although this had made the cycling more comfortable, it had taken away the gloss finish to the otherwise matt views that I was experiencing. This was only a minor complaint, however, and as I continued my journey along the D71, I stopped on several more occasions to admire the views as the road twisted and turned, climbed and then fell, in the direction of the *Lac de Sainte-Croix*. The highest point above the Verdon came after around 50km of cycling, when the

253

road ascended to over 1,200m and once again I stopped to marvel at the gorge where the river was now some 700m below the point at which I was standing. Stupendous. Utterly stupendous. I'm no believer in God, but with the evidence of a place like the *Gorges du Verdon* before your very eyes, it's difficult not to question your belief in the forces of nature that have carved out such a deep path through solid rock. It's only when you consider how our own definition of time is based upon human, rather than planetary, existence that you can really begin to comprehend how such a place was created. If you do believe in God, then you are of course at liberty to believe in your own version of events.

In quite another division of spectacle, although still worthy of a few moments of dropped jaws, was the D71 itself. It had been carved out of the rock to create narrow galleries through which I cycled, and, in places, I paused at points where anyone travelling in a car would have found it impossible to do so without creating a traffic jam. In one such gallery arch, I noticed a plaque high on the wall. It had been put there by the French Touring Club in 1946 and it stated, in French:

"To E.A. Martel who in 1905 discovered and revealed to the French the unique tourist marvel that are the Gorges of the Verdon."

It was good to see that the great man himself had not been forgotten. *Merci* Monsieur Martel for having helped make such an enjoyable journey possible.

Shortly after beginning my descent from 1,200m, something strange happened. The wind started blowing very strongly indeed. I initially thought that it was because of a geographical quirk of the road that I was now descending. It was, after all, at the very end of a deep, narrow gorge which was gradually exposing itself to the wider valley and in such a place, all kinds of mysterious elemental forces must be at work. Whatever was behind the fierce gusts of wind, the result was that it made for very difficult cycling and I was obliged to slow down significantly so as not to go flying (or more likely, dropping like a stone) off the edge of the cliff. I persevered and eventually I arrived in the village of Aiguines, where the wind continued to blow just as strongly as it had during the descent. Perhaps this wasn't some quirk of local meteorology after all. I bought a sandwich from a snack bar just outside the centre of the village, leaned Reggie against some nearby railings and sat down on a bench to eat my lunch. Suddenly there was a great crash of metal being thrown violently against pavement and I turned to see my poor travelling companion lying forlorn, like a stricken horse in the Grand National, on the floor behind me. I picked him up and stood eating what was left of my sandwich, while holding firmly onto the frame of the bike to prevent any more wind-induced tumbles.

Apart from the wind it was getting relatively cold, or at least that was how it felt. After a long, hard cycle in the sun, relaxing and drying off in the very same sun was fine. A long, hard cycle on a cloudy day can leave a cyclist just as moist from perspiration as on a sunny day but once you stop, the evaporation of water from the skin tends to have a chilling effect if there is no compensating sunshine to keep you warm. This is what was happening to me. The temperature had certainly dropped but I was feeling the cold much more as I was drying off. A few shivers vibrated through my body. Was a storm approaching? It certainly felt that way. I bought some chocolate from a small supermarket that had very little on its shelves (my chocolate bar was the last one that they had) and took the opportunity to ask the woman behind the counter if the weather conditions were normal. She explained that they weren't, a response that dashed my theory of it just being an idiosyncrasy of that small area at the end of the gorge. For the very first time since leaving southern Greece, I reached inside one of the front panniers for my raincoat and put it on. After over five weeks on the road, was I finally about to do some cycling in the rain?

Well, no, I wasn't. I was almost disappointed. I descended further into the valley to the man-made lake that plugged the flow of water along the Verdon and the wind continued to rage. It made even cycling downhill a great physical struggle but then, as I moved away from the end of the gorge, the gusts did abate and I was able to return to a normal state of cycling. Then the clouds began to break just a little and on occasions I was able to continue my journey in the sun. It made me wonder if this was going to be one long cycle across Europe that would involve not one moment of cycling in the rain. There had been times during the first cycle from England to Italy when I thought it would never stop raining and I wouldn't have minded just a few showers on this hot and sticky ride along the Mediterranean too. Just not very many.

On the other side of the lake was a short climb in the direction of Moustiers-Sainte-Marie, which was, according to the sign, '*one of France's most beautiful villages*'. That was sufficient enticement to drag me towards the centre of the hillside tourist trap but after fighting with the cars, coaches and pedestrians who were all aiming to do the same thing as me and find out just how beautiful it really was, I lost patience, turned around and headed back to the main road where I continued my journey. The remainder of the cycling on day 31 was all down hill: 30 long kilometres of descent along a wide-open valley that contrasted sharply with the scenery of the Gorges du Verdon. I had initially set my mind upon reaching the town of Manosque but the exertions of the morning and early afternoon were beginning to take their toll on my not-so-preternaturally fit body, so I was on the look out for a campsite almost from the moment of leaving Moustiers.

During the long descent, I was amused by Riez, a village whose name translates as *'laugh'* in English. I can't say I did, but it made me smile as I cycled through the signs that first announced my arrival and then my departure. A second village, called Allemagne-en-Provence, which translates as 'Germany in Provence', also caught my eye. It had a chateau which did look very Germanic and I assumed that this was the origin of the name of the place. When I paused just next to the small town hall, I noticed that many of the streets leading off from the main square were named after resistance fighters who had been executed during the war: *'Rue Félix Arnoux, Fusillé sur la Place, Le 16 Juin 1944'* read one of the street signs. I wondered why the town had kept hold of its unusual name after the end of hostilities. Perhaps, quite understandably, they were of the opinion that their village had just as much right to use the name *'Allemagne'* as their aggressors. That said, there must have been some interesting post-war discussions in the local cafés and bars.

I didn't see any signs for campsites in either Riez or Allemagne-en-Provence, but I did see signs for lots of them as I approached Gréoux-les-Bains. The municipal site was my first target but I couldn't find it, so I ended up crossing the Verdon River once again and following signs to *Camping la Pinède*, a three-star establishment which was populated exclusively with French campers. I pitched my tent for the night on a gravelly corner near the restaurant and bar area, as it was one of only three spaces available and the other two were next to the wash block. The rain started gently at about 8pm and gradually built in intensity as the evening drew to a close but it didn't dissuade the French from continuing to play boules on the gravel outside. I watched from a distance, as I collated my thoughts about my experiences of cycling along the *Gorges du Verdon* and reflected upon my progress to date. In summer 2010, it had taken me thirty cycling days to cycle to Brindisi in the south of Italy from my home in southern England. I had now completed cycling day 31 on this particular trip. On that first trip I had cycled 3,311km averaging 110km per day. I was currently averaging about 108km per day and had cycled over 3,200km. In my defence, the terrain along the Mediterranean in 2013 had so far been much tougher than it had been back in 2010, so I was pleased to be producing statistics that resembled those of the Eurovelo 5 north to south route. It remained to be seen if I could keep up the long distances over the final three and a half weeks of my trip. It also remained to be seen if I could manage to get as far as the Cape St. Vincent in Portugal without some kind of outside intervention. It was beginning to play on my mind.

Thursday 8th August 2013
Cycling Day 32: Gréoux-les-Bains To Villes-sur-Auzon, 129km

When I think of France (and obviously as a French teacher, I tend to do that quite often), it's usually the images of Provence that come first to mind. I can't imagine I am alone. Despite being a large European country that stretches across almost 1,000km from north to south and, at its widest point, the same distance from east to west, and notwithstanding the fact that *'Provence-Alpes-Côte d'Azur'* (or PACA as it is known to the French) is just one of the twenty-two regions of mainland France, for so many people Provence *is* France. Even on the shortest of visits, it's difficult not to fall in love with the place. This is at risk of veering into *A Year In Provence* territory but bear with me. When I look back at cycling day 32 from Gréoux-les-Bains to Villes-sur-Auzon (even those names shout 'Provence!'), one of the most iconic images of the region is foremost in my thoughts. Think France, think Provence, think lavender. Its production makes up for 90% of the land dedicated to the cultivation of aromatic plants in the region. Imagine all that in your granny's bathroom. This was to be a day infused with the aroma of lavender.

That said, there was neither sight nor smell of lavender in my tent at 3am, as a rainstorm to end all rainstorms kicked off. I can't say for sure whether there had been a pause in the downpour that had started on the previous evening, as I had somehow managed to get to the point of ignoring the sound of the raindrops hitting the tent and had drifted off into a state of semi-slumber. But there was no way I could possibly ignore the sounds of people frantically running around outside, repegging tents and making sure that anything that had been inadvertently left outside overnight was safely stored inside. I glanced around the interior of my own tent and, despite the vigorous flapping of material, I still appeared to be in contact with the ground and I couldn't detect any leaks. My concern should have been for poor Reggie, who had been locked to the fence of the children's play area, just opposite my pitch. I zipped open the smallest of holes to peek out and check that he was OK and still rooted to the spot where I had left him. It took only a few moments of thought to realise that, if he were to get carried away in the storm, it was likely that we would all wake up in the Land of Oz. This seemed only a distant possibility, so I turned over, attempted to ignore the kerfuffle taking place outside and tried in vain to fall back to sleep. This was being a trifle over-optimistic, as my success rate in falling back to sleep, even on the stillest of still nights,

258

was hovering somewhere around zero. The next few hours were spent keeping my eyes shut and willing my body to rest. It did, but my brain didn't.

When I emerged from the tent a few hours later, a small part of me was expecting to be confronted by a scene of Biblical destruction that was commensurate with the mad rushing around of people in the middle of the night, but no. Everything was exactly as it had been the previous evening, just a bit wetter. It did, however, seem sensible to try and pack as much as I possibly could into the panniers whilst sitting inside the tent. Doing so outside would inevitably involve my clothing becoming wet on the ground. It proved a rather efficient way of doing things as the limited interior space dictated that whenever I picked something up I was obliged to find a place in one of the bags. In no time whatsoever, I was standing outside the empty tent with four full pannier bags.

I was usually very meticulous in making sure that the tent was as dry as it could possibly be before wrapping it up and setting off to pastures new. Attempting to do this in Gréoux-les-Bains, after having been pounded by rain for most of the night was nonsensical, so I gave the fabric a good shaking (much to the bemusement of a small gathering of children who stood watching the operation), rolled up the tent and prayed for better weather later in the day in Villes-sur-Auzon, where I would lay it out to dry before 'sleeping' in it once again. Hopefully.

Within minutes, I was retracing my journey back towards Gréoux-les-Bains. I crossed over the bridge spanning the River Verdon and climbed the steep hill into the *centre ville*. Few things are more cruel than a sharp climb in the first ten minutes of the cycling day and my body was aching with stiffness until I was able to rejoin the main road and complete the short descent to the end of the valley that I had started the previous afternoon. I then turned right and cycled the 12km to Manosque, where I planned to take breakfast.

There was nothing particularly special about Manosque. It announced itself with a line of out-of-town shops, car dealerships and the occasional dodgy nightclub (no nationality has yet to manage the art of creating the look of a dodgy out-of-town nightclub quite as well as the French) after which there was a gentle climb towards the old town centre. This looked more promising as the entrance was via an ornate medieval gate, but the narrow pedestrianised streets inside the *cité* were crammed full of drab shops. I did find a quiet square where I was able to sit beneath the plain façade of a Romanesque church and order a coffee, which I drank whilst trying to work out a route to get me to the foot of *Mont Ventoux*.

Some days, planning such a route wasn't obvious and the one from Manosque in the direction of *Mont Ventoux* was about as obvious as a win on the lottery. I had exchanged text messages with Nicolas, the friend from Caen with whom I was planning to cycle to the summit of the mountain the following day, and we agreed to meet up in the small town of Sault. That was my destination as far as my planning was concerned. After Sault, I expected that Nicolas would take over the role of chief navigator.

The previous day's cycling had been a strenuous one (even for someone with 'preternatural' levels of fitness like myself) and I was in no doubt about the exertions required to ascend *Mont Ventoux*. So, it was of primary importance to avoid big hills if I could. Would this be possible? Well, my skills as a map-reader, or rather, my ability to read between the lines (surely to read between the contours?) of a map, had become somewhat advanced since setting off from Cape Sounio. In Greece and along the Adriatic coast of the former Yugoslavia I had been straining my eyes (as well as my imagination) using 1:400,000 scale maps. Upon arrival in Italy I had been able to use Michelin maps for the first time and these had a scale of 1:300,000. In Spain my maps would revert to being 1:300,000 but here in France I was luxuriating in the pleasure of having the detail of 1:200,000 scale maps. That said, even this scale left much - especially the topography - down to guesswork. There were clues however... A wiggly road probably meant it was heading uphill or down. A road with a green edge to it was officially a 'scenic route' and again, unless you are very much into flat landscapes (which I suspect Michelin are not, as they no doubt sell more tyres to people who are heading up mountains rather than across flat plains), this equates to hills and climbs. Main roads, however, – the ones in red – tend to have received sufficient amounts of investment in their construction to plough on regardless and have often necessitated great movements of earth in order that their paths are not impeded. As a result, they are usually somewhat flatter or certainly less steep. I know there are millions of exceptions, but these are not bad guidelines to follow when trying to plan a cycling route using just a large-scale map.

There was a main (red) road between Manosque and Forcalquier, which I would follow for a few kilometres before risking it along a short but green-edged, yellow route. From that point, well, there were no main routes, just an irregular web of yellow and white (the most minor) roads to Banon. After Banon, it was a continuation of the same with no route springing out from the map and shouting '*take me for I will sooth your troubled calf muscles*'. What was guaranteed, however, was some beautiful, lavender-carpeted countryside. Perhaps the sight and the smell of that would ease my passage towards Sault.

Manosque to Forcalquier was a pleasantly flat surprise. I couldn't help but thank the quarrying company that was in the process of removing an entire mountain from my path. What was left of the rock edifice was neatly terraced, pyramid style, where successive slabs of stone had been prised away from the hill. Thanks guys. If you keep going for another 300,000 years you will make cycling through the whole of Provence akin to cycling through The Netherlands. That might not be so great for the tourist industry, however.

I took lunch in Forcalquier where I found a beautiful square surrounded by cafés on two sides and a church on a third. It provided a relaxing midday backdrop to sitting down and sipping a cold drink in the sun, which had now reappeared after having been absent for most of the previous 48 hours. Many of the buildings I could see had presumably been built using stone from the quarries that I had passed earlier in the morning. The balance between disfiguring the landscape and providing locally sourced, building material which sits harmoniously in its environment is a fine one, but you cannot have the latter without the former. For every beautiful building in the world, there is a space left empty in the ground elsewhere. I suppose we should only decry the practice if the buildings are themselves an affront to eye. In those cases we have scarred the landscape not once but twice. That certainly wasn't the case in Forcalquier and I was happy that the balance had been maintained.

There was a climb to Banon but it was nothing that could distract from the beautiful Provençal countryside. The landscape was much gentler than I had experienced between Nice and Castellane or along the Verdon gorge: rolling green hills carpeted in sunflowers and, as I edged further west, the lavender fields. When I stopped for a moment, such was the buzz of the bees around the lines of purple flowers that they even began to drown out the ever-present, Mediterranean sound of the cicadas.

I stopped at Banon as my mobile phone needed charging. I had forgotten to ask the campsite reception in Gréoux-les-Bains if I could plug it into the mains overnight and the dribble of energy from the solar panels just wasn't going to keep it alive. Not only was I anxious to keep the phone recording my GPS track as I cycled, I was acutely aware that I was meeting Nicolas later in the day. That would inevitably involve an exchange of at least a couple of text messages, if not a full-blown conversation. Having no battery life left in the phone would have been a nightmare(!). How did we ever manage to lead our lives in the pre-mobile phone era? It is alarming just how wedded to the little black box of communication that we carry around in our pockets many of us have become. It's even more alarming how we react when we are inadvertently deprived of its powers. I think back to being a child and knocking on the doors of friends. *"Is Paul coming out to play?"* was the standard question we asked when parents opened the door. I remember hanging around a meeting point that had been agreed perhaps days earlier, waiting and waiting until it no longer made sense to do so and then returning home. Now it's all different of course. A quick text message or Facebook post. No knocking on doors. No conversations with the parents of friends. We still have to wait around for people but it's not because they have forgotten, it's just that they are late. And then what do we do? Well, we give them an electronic prod via a text message of course. I'm not altogether convinced that progress has been made but would I ever forgo my mobile phone? Certainly not. Back in Banon, so keen was I to replenish the battery of the phone that I was willing to suspend my journey for a full hour. An hour! It wasn't even lunchtime. The price for my addiction to mobile communication? Two coffees in the bar which had agreed to plug my phone into the mains, and from a nearby patisserie, *'un brownie'*. Try saying that in French without sounding like a character from the wartime sitcom *'Allo 'Allo*.

The road out of Banon continued to climb for a few kilometres until it reached 1,000m – the highest point of the day - after which there was a welcome return to cycling downhill. Then, for the first time, I saw it. Far beyond the lines of lavender in the fields, with gently sloping sides, a white cap and a peak that had been artificially elevated by the presence of a distinctive communications mast poking from the summit. *Le Mont Ventoux*. It dominated the view and was to continue doing so almost continually for the next two days.

The cycle to my meeting point with Nicolas in the small town of Sault required another 20km of cycling to be completed, a journey punctuated by frequent pauses to take arty photos of lavender fields in the foreground and the *Mont Ventoux* in the far distance. Upon arrival, I checked my phone for messages and Nicolas had indeed texted to confirm that he had arrived and would be waiting for me in the main square near a merry-go-round. I found him sunbathing on a wall with his mountain bike just to his side and after exchanging a few greetings we made our way to the terrace of a bar to catch up over a drink. I was very keen not to repeat the bonking episode that I experienced in northern Italy so, while Nicolas knocked back a beer, I stuck to black coffee. And there I was, back in the hands of someone who knew the area well. All I needed to do was follow.

Had I been alone, I would have continued cycling along the D1 road. It was the obvious one to choose and even had one of Michelin's green edges, so I would, no doubt, have been afforded some pretty views of the brooding *Mont Ventoux* in the far distance. Nicolas, however, had other plans.

"Do you know the Gorges de la Nesque?" he asked.

I didn't. Another series of gorges? Really? I was a little sceptical as to how spectacular they could be. After having cycled along the *Gorges du Verdon* on the previous day, any other gorge was surely destined to be a little disappointing, no? I was also a little worried that by taking a route which involved cycling through a gorge, it was all but inevitable that a fair proportion of the cycling would be uphill.

"Great idea!" I replied.

I was to be happily proved wrong. The *Gorges de la Nesque* were not quite as deep as the *Gorges du Verdon* but they were just as spectacular and with few tourists on the D942 road we were following – just the very occasional car, a few cyclists and one solitary walker – there was a distinct sense of isolation which had, at times, being missing from the *Gorges du Verdon*. If that wasn't enough, the final 20km of the day, from the start of the *Gorges de la Nesque* to the gate of the campsite in Villes-sur-Auzon, was a continuous, freewheeling, downhill ride. It was perfect preparation for what lay ahead the following morning.

Friday 9th August 2013

Rest Day 8: Mont Ventoux (53km)

This would clearly be a 'rest day' with a difference, but as I would be making no progress whatsoever in my cycling odyssey along the edge of the Mediterranean, it would have been equally nonsensical to refer to it as a 'cycling day'. Some serious pedal action was about to take place, however.

The previous evening with Nicolas, his partner Christel, their three-year-old son Raphael and Christel's fourteen-year-old daughter Nolwen had gone well. We ate, drank, chatted, and laughed. They were in the middle of doing what so many French families do in the summer; they had packed up the car, hooked up the caravan and headed south. When I had visited them in Caen on the school exchange earlier in the year, we had chatted about our respective plans for the summer and a decision was made that we should, if at all possible, meet up. Nicolas had mentioned cycling to the summit of the *Mont Ventoux* in passing, but it wasn't until much later that I realised what a golden opportunity had presented itself.

What did I know about the *Mont Ventoux* prior to Nicolas' suggestion? Not a great deal. I knew that it was one of the most iconic climbs of the *Tour de France* and that it was characterised by bare rock affording cyclists no shade whatsoever in the latter stages of the climb. I was also aware of the story of British cyclist Tommy Simpson who, in 1967 while taking part in *Le Tour,* had collapsed and died en route to the top. But that was about it.

Following a breakfast of black coffee, baguette and Nutella chocolate spread, we set off from the campsite. Nicolas estimated that our ride to the summit would take us around three hours, but we had the whole day in front of us so an early departure time wasn't essential. It would be the first time since leaving Athens that I would be travelling without the panniers and I felt quite sprightly on the bike, as we cycled the first 10km from the campsite in Villes-sur-Auzon to the official start line of the ascent. The campsite was at 300m and the summit of *Mont Ventoux* at just over 1,900m, but by the time we arrived at the point in the road that appeared to have been designated by cycling fans as the official starting point of the climb, we had only ascended a couple of hundred metres. Up to that point, the climbing had been continuous but gentle. It was, however, about to become much steeper.

Whether official or not, the road surface of the D974 just outside the village of Sainte-Colombe had been painted in such a way as to give the impression that it was the starting point. Many roads along the route of the *Tour de France* are painted by cycling fans with images and slogans which, should their favourite team or cyclist manage to see them, would hopefully spur them on to greatness. The roads that guide the cyclists up the most iconic climbs of the *Tour de France* are particularly popular with paintbrush-wielding fans and, as the paint lingers for much longer on the surface of the road than the professional cyclists themselves, the markings have become an all-year-round feature of the *Alpe d'Huez*, the *Col du Tourmalet*, the *Col d'Aubisque*, the *Col du Galibier* and of course the *Mont Ventoux*. And as with all graffiti, the *Tour de France* road 'artwork' comes in many shapes and sizes and of varying quality, ranging from the functionally prosaic '*Allez, Allez!*' ('Go, Go!') to the much more detailed works of art, which can include very accurate representations of the cyclists' faces. They are obviously best seen from the helicopters carrying the television cameras and it's difficult not to admire the dedication of the cycling fanatics who spend hours, if not days, prior to the arrival of the race in their little corner of France trying to make their graffiti stand out from the crowd.

The *Tour de France* had only recently climbed the road upon which Nicolas and I were now cycling and the road surface messages and artwork were almost as vibrant as the day they had been painted. The Team Sky cyclist, Chris Froome, had not only won the 100th *Tour de France* when it arrived in Paris in 2013, but he had also triumphed on the day that it had climbed the *Mont Ventoux* on Bastille Day, Sunday 14th July. It had been stage 15 of the race and a very long 243km cycle from Givors to the summit of the mountain. Froome covered the distance in under six hours and averaged nearly 42 km/hr, cruising past the Colombian rider, Quintana, in the final couple of kilometres of the ascent. It gave him an unassailable lead of four minutes in the overall standings and he never really looked back. Perhaps if he had, he wouldn't have seen the other cyclists anyway.

The meticulously designed markings designating the start of the *Mont Ventoux* climb consisted of carefully aligned rows of hearts, some yellow, some red, some white, some green and some in the three colours of the French tricolore. At the end of the rows of hearts was a starting line, made up of three lines of red, white and blue. A few moments later was a sign informing us that the *Chalet Reynard* – the point after which the trees stop and the accompanying shade disappears – was 12km away and that the summit of the mountain was some 18km up the hill.

From leaving the campsite up to this point, I had not stopped cycling and had yet to put my feet on the ground. I was determined that this was going to continue and that I would be able to say that, not only had I climbed the *Mont Ventoux,* but I had done so without stopping. Was I perhaps being a little over-optimistic? This was, after all, a mountain that had beaten many cyclists in the peak of fitness. I was at least willing to give it a go. It was useful to have Nicolas as my cycling companion, as he was not only able to lead the way and show me where to cycle (although most of the time it was obvious which way to go, as the answer was always 'up'), but he had also had the good sense and forethought to bring with him some energy snacks. Every few kilometres, he would reach into his pocket and pass me another fruit bar of some description, which, once I had managed to remove the packaging (not that easy while ensuring that the bike was still moving in the direction I wanted it to go), was devoured in a few moments of calorific delight.

There are *Tour de France* climbs which require the cyclists to climb to a significantly higher altitude than the *Mont Ventoux* but there is no other mountain which requires the cyclists to do more climbing than when they are attempting 'the bald one'. There are officially 1,639 metres to climb to the summit at 1,911 metres. For those of you who like using imperial measurements, that's a vertical distance of a fraction over one mile. One mile into the sky. Think about it. Visualise a horizontal distance of one mile. It might be from your local pub to your front door (although if you are someone who staggers home you may have to pick something else to visualise) or from one side of your town to the other. In your mind, tilt that distance to the vertical and stare up at it. That is what you need to climb to arrive at the summit of Mont Ventoux. It's a daunting distance and even more daunting when you've just told yourself that you are going to do it without stopping and putting your feet on the ground.

The first couple of kilometres after the village of Sainte-Colombe were fine. Nothing too arduous compared with what had come before and when I turned to the left, I could see the television mast at the top of the mountain. Immediately below the summit, there was a wide band of bare rock and then below that was a wider band of trees. This matched the description that Nicolas had given me of what the cycling conditions would be like: initially in the shade and then, as we approached the end of the ride, in the open, exposed to the sun and potentially, the wind. The weather conditions we were experiencing were decidedly changeable. Much of the sky was covered in cloud and I could already detect that the temperature (compared to what it had been like when we set off from Villes-sur-Auzon) was dropping. If we continued to have cloud cover, then this fall in temperature would surely be maintained and even on the lower slopes of the mountain, I was starting to feel chilly. I asked Nicolas to pass me my sweater, which he was carrying in his backpack and, just as I had done while eating the snacks, struggled to maintain my balance as I pulled it on over my head.

The climbing was relentless. Unlike most roads up mountains in France, the road to the summit of *Mont Ventoux* had clearly been designed by someone who had Albanian blood in their body, as the hairpin bends were nowhere near as frequent as I would have liked. Instead, the gradient was maintained without any break whatsoever. Not at any point between the foot of the mountain and the summit, was it possible to stop pedalling for even just a few moments, relax your leg muscles and freewheel. To have stopped pedalling would have resulted in a very rapid deceleration and would have brought me to an almost immediate halt. Upwards and onwards we continued as the gradient fluctuated between 7% and an occasionally alarming 13%. The average was much nearer the former than the latter but the chronic nature of the climbing made for some very, very tough cycling. However, the longer I succeeded in not stopping, the more determined I was to keep on going. To keep pedalling. To keep moving forward. I didn't care about my speed. As long as I was travelling with a forward velocity sufficient keep me on the bike, I was happy. Happy? Is that the most appropriate word? Perhaps not. This was all about delayed gratification, the knowledge that perhaps within the next 90 minutes, 60 minutes, 30 minutes... the pain would be over and the smile on my face would be as broad as the mountain was high.

We emerged from the shadow of the trees shortly before arriving at the *Chalet Reynard*. I was delighted that not only had we made it two-thirds of the way up the mountain but that we were now able to benefit from the heat of the sun's rays when they were available and not hidden by the large clouds in the sky. The *Chalet Reynard* was a hotel, restaurant and snack bar, according to the words printed on the edge of the awning that was shading the terrace. In front of the chalet, was a large expanse of concrete filled with cars. It was clear that many people had driven to this point, unloaded the bike from the roof rack, climbed on board and started cycling. That's not climbing a mountain! It certainly wasn't climbing *Mont Ventoux*. Would these people consider it appropriate to run the last ten miles of a marathon and then claim a medal for having done so? I looked at them with disdain as they posed in their bright lycra outfits, next to their pristine carbon bikes, for photographs taken by family and friends. Reggie, Nicolas and I were made of stronger stuff. Well, Reggie was made from steel and that's probably not as tough as carbon, but in his soul he was a bike of iron!

The heat from the sun was only intermittent and the compensating effects of the increased altitude made for an increasingly cold cycle as we started to ascend the final 500 metres from the chalet to the summit. The landscape was now utterly different. This could quite easily have been two different cycles, on two different continents. But not only was it the same continent, it was the same mountain. Gone was almost all of the vegetation and what was left was bare, stony ground. Alongside the road, were tall, yellow and black poles that in times of deep snow would allow anyone brave enough to attempt a journey to the summit (not on a bike I hasten to add, although I'm sure that at some point someone has attempted such a feat of folly) to see exactly where they should be heading. In July, they were, of course, redundant but they did allow the cyclists, motorists and bikers so see clearly where the edge of the road was, as it curved off into the distance and around the contours of the mountain. Humans were not alone. There were plenty of sheep grazing on the small patches of grass that had somehow defied the blanket of rocks surrounding them. They looked relaxed and at ease in their surroundings. Not so for most of the cyclists who were gradually making their way to the top. Some were old, some were young, many were middle-aged and in lycra. There were men and women. There was even an occasional touring cyclist who hadn't dispensed of his or her panniers and for whom the cycle to the summit was part of a longer trip from A to B. They had my utmost respect.

On the exposed slopes of *Mont Ventoux,* the wind was now an added challenge. Occasionally the road would approach a ridge in the side of the mountain and at these points it was, more than ever, necessary to pay particular attention to maintaining forward motion on the bike. I still had not stopped and by this point, just a few kilometres from the summit, nothing, not even a sharp gust of wind that had other intentions in mind was going to stop me. On and on we cycled and larger and larger became the iconic television tower on the summit. My eyes were 90% focussed upon the top of the mountain, but I was also on the lookout for the memorial to Tommy Simpson, which I knew was located somewhere near the summit. About one kilometre from the top

I spotted it, set slightly back from the road, at the end of a short flight of stone steps.

Tommy Simpson was a British cyclist who was part of the Great Britain team in the 1967 *Tour de France*. He died on the mountain on 13th July, while attempting to reach the summit. He was just 29 years old. In 1965, he had won the world road race championship and, as a result of this, was a popular figure on the *critérium* circuit of races. These were events in which professional cyclists were paid to take part and they were a good way of earning money. In 1966, Simpson completed forty of them in just forty days, but in order to maintain his presence in such races, he was in desperate need of a good performance in the 1967 *Tour de France*. Stage 13 of the race was from Marseille to Carpentras – 212km – but Simpson never made it to the top of *Mont Ventoux*. The grainy film shows him veering from one side of the road to the other before falling off. He was put back on the bike (although it is widely believed that he never actually said '*Put me back on my bike*') before stopping again and being given emergency assistance. He was transported by helicopter to hospital in Avignon, where he was pronounced dead.

The saddest thing about Tommy Simpson is that the amphetamines he was taking to help improve his performance undoubtedly had a major role to play in his death. They were found in his body, in his luggage and in his pockets. At the time, it seems that most professional cyclists were also taking such drugs; Simpson was the one who was killed. It would be good to look back upon such an event and see it as a defining moment in the sport of cycling which resulted in an end to such abuses, but, as we know, that didn't happen. I have no idea whether any of the 2013 *Tour de France* cyclists were taking illegal, performance-enhancing drugs when they climbed the *Mont Ventoux,* but if there were, I wonder what they were thinking as they cycled past Tommy Simpson's monument. Surely the most fitting memorial to the man would be a definitive end to drug abuse in cycling. Or am I just being too naïve?

The following lines are inscribed on Tommy Simpson's gravestone in the village of Harworth in Nottinghamshire:

"His body ached, his legs grew tired, but still he would not give in."

The only performance-enhancing substances that I had consumed that day were the coffee and Nutella that I had had for breakfast and the regular supply of energy bars from Nicolas. My body was aching, my legs were growing tired but I, too, would not give in. The last few hundred metres were a perfect storm of pain and determination, but after almost three hours in the saddle without once putting my feet on the ground, I unclipped my cycling sandals, pulled on the brakes and stopped. It was a great feeling.

As with all such places, the summit was crowded with those who had earned the right to be up there celebrating (the cyclists and perhaps some walkers) and those who had cheated (the drivers and motorcyclists). We had done it. A celebratory photo at the top next to the sign and a quick snack from the obligatory sausage stall followed, but it was cold, very cold, and very windy indeed. It made sense to make our stay only a brief one before we descended at speed back to the valley floor and the heat of Provence.

We arrived back in Villes-sur-Auzon in the mid afternoon and while Nicolas headed off with the rest of the family to do some shopping and go to the swimming pool, I took the opportunity to visit a bike shop in the village, to give Reggie a quick service. I explained to the guy who ran the place where we had cycled from and where we still had to go. I asked him if he could change the brake pads and to check the spokes very carefully and left Reggie in his capable hands, while I went off to a local café to research the beers of Provence. A couple of hours later, I returned and was somewhat surprised, yet clearly delighted, to be told that my travelling companion was in excellent shape. Nothing wrong with the spokes or the chain or the plates or the gears or anything. I handed over €20 and looked forward to some hopefully trouble-free cycling between the *Mont Ventoux* and Cape St. Vincent.

Saturday 10th August 2013
Cycling Day 33: Villes-sur-Auzon To Nîmes, 115km

A long cycle tour is really only a reflection of life albeit one without the same four walls each night. You can't avoid the chemical imbalances in your body, which, for whatever reason, dictate that today is going to be the day of the week, or the month (or if you are really lucky, the year) that you are going to be grumpy. Saturday 10th August was perhaps destined to be a grumpy day. I can't say with any certainty whether it was because of 'events' or whether it was because of the chemicals swishing around my brain, but grumpy I was. It wouldn't surprise me if the 'events' and the chemicals had planned it that way. Now there's a conspiracy theory for you...

One thing that didn't help was that, in several ways, I was coming down from a high. Climbing the *Mont Ventoux* had been an emotional high as well as a physical one. There had been a great sense of having achieved something worth celebrating (and I seem to remember that back at the campsite that evening, we did). I was also coming to the end of what had been one of the most enjoyable few days of the entire journey since leaving Cape Sounio. Thirty-six hours in the company of friends had lifted my spirits but so had having spent the previous five days in the region of France that so perfectly encapsulates what is wonderful about the country: the scenery, the food, the wine, the climate, the sea, the mountains, the towns, the villages, the flowers, the smells... I've said it before and it's worth saying again: Provence *is* France. Irrespective of what was coming next, perhaps it was always going to be a frustrating day of transition back into the normal world.

Goodness. Anyone would think that I was about to cycle through a post-apocalyptic expanse of ruined wasteland. I was still in Provence and would be for the first half of the cycling day to Avignon. West of Avignon, the plan was to cycle as far as Nîmes. In subsequent days I would continue my city-hopping tour of Languedoc-Roussillon – the region of France that extends as far as the border with Spain – with a second overnight stop in Béziers before heading for Narbonne and then a planned rendez-vous with a chap who lived in the Pyrenees at a place he described as '*The Pilgrims' Nest*'. This was hardly the 'normal' world of a 9 to 5 job. But then again, I was in a bad mood. On the positive side of things, until I reached the Pyrenees I would be cycling once again on the flat. The mere thought of this should have cheered me up, but I don't think it did.

271

I had packed up and was almost ready to go even before Christel and Nicolas had emerged from their caravan next to the tent. I felt a little guilty that they were obliged to get up much earlier than they would normally have chosen to do in order to provide me with breakfast and then bid me farewell, but they seemed just as cheery as they had been the previous two days. It was at least a beautiful morning to be up and around at such an early hour; the cloudy skies of the previous few days appeared to have disappeared for good. We said our goodbyes and I cycled off in the direction of Carpentras hoping that, following my departure, my happy hosts went straight back to bed.

Carpentras wasn't far – perhaps 15km – and the journey was downhill all the way. It was windy but at that point the gusts seemed to be assisting me rather than hindering me. The town was a bit of a disappointment. My guidebook had bigged the place up but compared to the other jewels of Provence I had travelled through earlier in the week, it was merely pretty. In the great scheme of things, that's not too bad as a damning criticism but remember, I was in a grumpy mood. I was keen to locate a quiet place in which I could sit in the shade and catch up on writing about my experiences of climbing *Mont Ventoux*. I found it on the terrace of a café on the western side of *Place Charles de Gaulle,* just opposite the lofty *Cathédrale St. Siffrein.* The clock, however, was ticking and I set myself the challenge of completing my writing and administrative tasks before the sun popped up from behind the roof of the cathedral. I beat the sun but it was a close run thing, requiring a few movements of my chair so as to keep the rays out of my eyes.

The D942 had been subtitled the '*Voie Rapide Avignon-Carpentras*'. When does a '*voie rapide*' – literally a 'fast way' – become a motorway, I wondered? I stuck with it for a couple of kilometres, before bowing to the inevitable and turning due south towards the centre of a small town called Monteux. My sense of direction is usually very good but I struggled to have confidence in my chosen routes for the next hour or so as I attempted to make progress towards Avignon. The normally excellent French signage simply wanted to put me back on the *voie rapide,* but not being a *véhicule rapide,* this was clearly not what I wanted to do. In addition, as the roads began to flatten out as I moved further and further towards the edge of mountainous Provence, the effects of the wind became increasingly apparent. After a second, unpleasant stint on the *voie rapide,* I stopped trying to work out a route using my map and once again headed due south in the hope of finding a second, much quieter arterial road that would take me to the centre of Avignon. It added an extra 5km to my journey but it was worth every single centimetre pedalled.

Never a person to be happy without at least one small thing to grumble about, as soon as I turned to cycle west once more, the wind hit me with a vengeance. I was, of course, coming into contact with the *Mistral*, one of the most potent natural forces at work in the south of France. It blows from north to south along the valley of the Rhone and on the 10th August, it was having a good go at knocking me off the bike. Cycling without any luggage would have been bad enough, but once four flat pannier bags are attached to the front and rear wheels, the fun really does start. As I attempted to cycle west, in a wind that was blowing fiercely from the north, just as much time had to be spent making sure I remained vertical on the bike as it did ensuring that I made progress along my chosen road. My two lurches due south to avoid the *voie rapide* had also been great for avoiding the wind; indeed, as I cycled south, it was helping me keep up a healthy speed, but I did need to make progress west and it was as I did this that the *Mistral* was at its most dangerous. At least by finding a much quieter road into the centre of Avignon, I was increasing my chances of survival should I be blown off, as there were fewer lorries into whose path I could have tumbled. That said, even if the wind didn't get me, perhaps the roads would. Ever since arriving in the Vaucluse *département,* I had noticed a considerable downturn in the quality of the road surface. Once again, just as I had done while climbing the steep roads up the Mont Ventoux, I was reminded of the terrible conditions of the roads in Albania. But this was France, a country whose roads I had openly been applauding even before arriving in the country. The authorities of the Vaucluse were doing a very good job indeed of letting down their country. They have been suitably named and shamed.

Much to my surprise, I survived long enough to recognise the familiar high walls of the papal city of Avignon. This was another place I had visited previously, but it was worthy of an hour of so of my time and after the trials and tribulations with the wind, the road quality and occasionally even the signage, I was ready for a drink. I cast aside my normal reluctance to indulge in a beer before the end of a cycling day and headed for the nearest bar. But not before I was somewhat taken aback to hear the following words:

"Mr Sykes? Mr Sykes!"

Whoever was saying my name was just as surprised to be doing so as I was be hearing it.

"Mr Sykes! I thought it was you. What are you doing in Avignon?"

It seemed a rather redundant question as I was standing next to my bike wearing a t-shirt, lycra shorts and a pair of sunglasses. It was clearly not a business trip. The person asking the question was a former student of the school where I work back in England. Her name is Ellie and she was on holiday with her family and some friends. It did seem bizarre to have bumped into a familiar face, but it made me smile and, as we chatted for a few minutes, I began to forget about the arduous nature of the morning's cycle.

My temporary mood swing was, alas, not to last and after my beer and a lunch consisting of a deeply filled baguette and a small tub of ice-cream, I continued my quest to the west and back into the terrifying power of the Mistral. Could it get any worse? Well... yes, it could.

Earlier in the year I had purchased a book called '*La Route du Sud à Vélo de Menton à Béziers'*. It had been recommended by its author, who had contacted me after reading about my plans online. It was a guide for a cycle route across the south of France from Menton near the Italian border to Béziers in the west. When cycling along the *Eurovelo 5* to Italy in 2010, although there were no signposts or even a detailed description of the route available to follow, it did, at times, piggyback upon national or regional cycling routes that *were* signposted. This hadn't been the case so far with the *Eurovelo 8*. If any national or regional routes I could have followed did exist, I remained ignorant as to where they could be found. Although the route described in the *Route du Sud à Vélo* wasn't an official one, it could, I thought, be extremely useful in making me aware of the best roads to take, or indeed to avoid, if off-road cycling was an option. However, I had then decided to head to Mont Ventoux and most of the book had become redundant. That said, the portion from Avignon to Béziers might be of use, so I started to follow it.

I wish I hadn't. Don't get me wrong, the guide was well researched and well written, with cultural as well as factual route information included. But I had just spent over six weeks working out things for myself, rather than being told what to do. It was a little similar to how I imagine going back to live with your parents would be after many years of living independently. Even if the advice was well intended (and it was), my belligerent streak of independence didn't want to admit that was the case. I was certainly up for taking a route that would see me cycle over the celebrated Roman aqueduct that is the *Pont du Gard*, but did I want to be instructed about every turn? Perhaps not. Having bought the book however, I did feel compelled to give it a go.

Many nooks and crannies of the French countryside later (interspersed with much scratching of the head, attempting to match descriptions given in the book to the reality of what I could see with my own eyes), I sensed that I was finally approaching the *Pont du Gard*. It's not often that you get the chance to see a building that has been standing for 2,000 years and the *Pont du Gard,* with its three tiers of arches, is a stunning example of the 'ancient building' genre. If it weren't for the violence and elitism of the Roman Empire, I'm sure that a competent historian could cobble together a persuasive argument for handing back the reigns of power to the Caesars et al. When you see something like the *Pont du Gard*, which is as beautiful as it is functional, and compare it to some of our utilitarian monstrosities of the modern built environment, it's difficult not to come to that very conclusion. But then again, perhaps the Romans had their own fair share of utilitarian monstrosities which simply didn't survive the cut of history, erased from view by the urban planners of the first two millennia. That's worth bearing in mind the next time you're staring at the excavated foundations of previous civilisations. What once stood in those places were most likely the buildings that never came close to being on the long list for the long list of the Stirling Prize of their day.

When I first visited the *Pont du Gard* way back in 1989 as a student, you turned up, parked in a small car park a little further along the river, walked a few hundred metres and there it was in all its glory. I even remember climbing to the very top of the bridge and spending an hour or so sunbathing on one of the remaining stone slabs covering the aqueduct's water channel. No chance of doing that now. How did the *Pont du Gard* survive for 1995 years without its visitors being funnelled, herded and crucially, charged €10 for the privilege? I was waved down my one of the employees as I approached the barrier for the car park. No provision appeared to have been made for people turning up on one of those strange things called 'bicycles'. I couldn't go through the barrier because I didn't have a car ticket. Instead, I had to haul Reggie up a grass verge towards a path in order to join the other visitors, who were walking in the direction of the bridge. I was hoping to be told off for riding my bike, as I was up for an argument but the attendants stayed well clear. I didn't want to visit the museum or the multimedia exhibition but I still had to help finance them via my €10 investment. For me, it was simply a very expensive toll to pay in order to cross a very beautiful bridge.

Continuing to follow the guidebook, I left the *Pont du Gard* and headed into open countryside. This involved crossing a large military zone that warned me that, should I step foot in the area on either side of the road, there was a '*danger de mort*'. Would doing so be any more perilous than the wind and the condition of the roads? Having successfully dodged any stray bullets or shells and having maintained a predominantly upright position on the bike despite the best efforts of the pot holes and the wind, good news was approaching on the horizon, in the shape of the city of Nîmes. I paused briefly in the north-western suburbs to investigate the exact location of the municipal campsite and was pleased to find out that it was south of the city centre. Or rather, the thing that particularly delighted me was the fact that it was *too* far south of the city centre. I needed a reason to be cheerful and it was called the *Hôtel Impérator*, a four-star establishment next to the canal, willing to sell itself for a three-star price. The great thing about booking a hotel online (apart from being convinced that you really have bagged a bargain even though that isn't necessarily the case) is that the receptionists have no opportunity to examine you from top to toe, consult the computer and pass on the unfortunate information that the establishment is full. I can't imagine that touring cyclists are the most welcome of guests in four-star hotels, but if you've received the golden email saying that you're booked in, there isn't much they can do apart from grin and bear it.

It was a wide grin – far too wide to be genuine – that welcomed me at the reception desk of the *Hôtel Impérator* – but the guy standing outside in a lounge suit, who was much more accustomed to opening the doors of Mercedes and BMWs than he was to escorting travelling cyclists round the back of the building to the garage, made up for his colleague's see-through demeanour. We chatted about where I had come from and where I was going as I secured Reggie to a large pipe in the bowels of the hotel, before he guided me back into the hotel lobby via a series of narrow corridors that were off-limits to all the other guests. He made me feel like a VIP: a very important pedaller.

Sunday 11th August 2013
Cycling Day 34: Nîmes To Béziers, 135km

When I lived in central France during the 1990s, it was possible to keep up to date with affairs back in Britain by tuning in to the variable signal of Radio 4, which faded in and then out on 198m long-wave. It was probably during this period that I became middle-class, as I developed a great love for the *Today* programme, *Woman's Hour* and that ultimate bastion of middle-England, *The Archers* (except for the days when everything had been shifted off the airways to make room for *Test Match Special* with Geoff Boycott et al.). Happy days... Then they invented the Internet and suddenly everything was available in digital clarity everywhere. Perhaps I am looking through the rose-tinted mists of time as I reminisce about my Radio 4 listening experiences, but the ropey signal did make you feel as though you had ventured somewhere far-off, even if it was just across the channel to France. The ubiquity of clouds of wi-fi hovering over campsites and lingering in hotel rooms all along the Mediterranean coast had made tuning into a daily dose of British news on most days of my trip as easy as pushing a couple of buttons on my smartphone. The presenter on Radio 5 Live was talking cycling.

"The Prime Minister has said he wants to start a 'cycling revolution'. Mr Cameron explained that following our success in the Olympics, the Paralympics and the Tour de France, British cycling was riding high and that he now wanted to see cycling soar."

As a glass-half-full person, I do tend to take politicians at their word (they can't all be money-grabbing liars, can they?) apart from when, that is, they talk cycling. A cycling revolution will happen in Britain on the day the country decides to prioritise the humble bicycle to the same extent that it has prioritised the car for the last one hundred years. It was difficult not to be a little sceptical. How about building some high-quality cycling infrastructure Mr Cameron? It's a pity that he wasn't able to join me as I cycled along the coast of Languedoc-Roussillon...

On that quiet Sunday morning in August, bathed in bright sunlight under a cloudless sky, the buildings of central Nîmes shone. I had retrieved Reggie from his underground bunker and set off on a short cycle tour of the city. The centrepiece was the *Maison Carrée*, an astonishing Roman temple that distinguished itself by actually looking like a Roman temple which wasn't in dire need of some drastic restoration. As far as I could see, everything was still there: no missing columns, all the fancy bits sandwiched between the columns and the roof. And the roof! Clearly Lord Elgin never visited Nîmes. Lord Norman Foster had, however, passed this way, as he had been responsible for designing the *Carré d'Art*, a building that now houses the city's museum of contemporary art. The two constructions were separated by a wide road, as well as 2,000 years of time, but complimented each other perfectly. The modern building did not in any way attempt to upstage its ancient neighbour; indeed, its position to one side of the square seemed to emphasise a certain reverence. Goodness. This is beginning to read like an article from *Architecture Today*. Let's cycle on to a café and the second (if that is possible) centrepiece of Nîmes, *Les Arènes*.

I was to see plenty of *arènes* during the course of the following week or so. They are, of course, the local arenas, many dating back to Roman times but others much more modern. Although I had seen the fabulous arena back in Verona, the distinctive thing about these arenas in south-western France was that they were all now used for bull-fighting and they were concrete proof that Spain was just around the corner. *Bull fighting? Really? That's still happening? I thought it had been banned?* Those were my questions too, as I sat under the parasols of *Le Grand Café de la Bourse et du Commerce,* an establishment which distinguished itself not only by having an unfeasibly long name and an astonishing interior but also by its outlook: a close up and personal view of the arches of the two-tiered arena. It was a building that was just as much intact as the *Maison Carrée* had been earlier, although its stones were still sporting the grime of two millennia, the very same grime that had most definitely been removed from the gleaming temple.

Back to the bullfighting. There are three *feria* that take place: one in February, one during Pentecost and a third in September. We will come to the situation in Spain later, but in France in 2012 the constitutional court declared the corridas to be legal after having been requested to make a ruling on the matter by the *Comité Radicalement Anti Corrida*. There's a name to stir the heart of any French citizen worthy of the name! Unfortunately for the people on the committee and their supporters (the majority of the French population according to polls), they didn't stir the hearts of the judges of the constitutional court and in Languedoc-Roussillon, bullfighting remains legal. In addition to bringing in some much-welcome tourist income, its proponents claim that bullfighting is part of the culture and heritage of places like Nîmes. I couldn't help but think that a more appropriate (and more 21st century) approach to grabbing the holidaymakers' cash would be by putting on an opera or two as they had done in Verona.

The *Mistral* wind was still blowing but it was much less fierce than it had been the previous day. I put this down to my movement away from the valley of the Rhone. It was still sufficiently strong, however, to assist me as I cycled the 40km from Nîmes, along the straight road heading in a south-westerly direction towards the coast. My intermediate destination was a place called La Grande-Motte and, with the assistance of the wind on the very gradually descending road, I was able to make good time; my average speed was well above 25km/hr and, on a couple of occasions I noticed that I had pushed my small cycling computer beyond the 40km/hr point, albeit just for a few seconds. Such a speed wasn't sustainable but it was good to know that the wind didn't have anything personal against me (the thought had crossed my mind during the previous day) and was willing to give me a hand from time to time.

I was in good spirits upon arrival in La Grande-Motte. I had grown somewhat attached to seeing the sea since the start of my journey and on the occasions when my route had taken me inland for a few days, it was always good to be reacquainted. That said, the water remained initially well hidden behind the buildings that gave La Grande-Motte its striking architectural style. I can't imagine much of La Grande-Motte existed prior to 1960, as everything that surrounded me shouted swinging 60s or psychedelic 70s. Even the most modern of the futuristic buildings appeared to have been designed by a lover of that distinctive era with their sweeping curves and bright colours painted upon predominantly white-washed walls of plastered cement. I paused for a cold drink in an uncharacteristically drab café near the marina but felt a little out of place surrounded by the happy families *en vacances*.

It was an interesting place through which to cycle but not one in which I would have liked to spend more than half an hour, so I remounted and cycled off along the coast in the direction of Carnon-Plage and Palavas, the two towns that the residents of Montpellier must consider as their own private beaches. For the next 60km, I would be cycling with the Mediterranean Sea to my left and a series of large *étangs* (or lagoons) to my right. Earlier in the day I had, for the first time, used Google Maps to suggest a route for me to follow. Unlike the previous countries through which I had travelled, in France the cycling option on Google Maps was active and I had been suggested a route that followed the thin, at times very thin, pencil of land between sea and lagoons. It continued even when the road didn't. Had I found cycling nirvana?

From La Grande-Motte to Carnon-Plage, I tried to cycle as close as I could to the sea. It was a pleasant 8km ride along what felt like one very long residential street. On both sides there were holiday flats but also a good number of holiday villas, some you might even describe as luxurious (and many more under construction, which were certainly described as luxurious by the hoardings advertising them for sale). The architecture was still very mid to late 20th century and from time to time I wondered what the area had been like prior to the post-war tourism boom.

Well, I was about to find out. After Palavas, the cars of the holidaymakers were funnelled back towards Montpellier by the D986. Having posted an image of my Google Maps planned route on Twitter a few hours earlier, many people had responded with comments along the lines of '*I hope you have brought your wellies...*', I wasn't deterred, however, as the possibility of spending a serious amount of time cycling well away from any motorised vehicles was worth the risk of having to turn back at some point later in the day should my path simply disappear into the water. I was initially led along a rough track that was sitting upon the long, thin piece of land that protected the coastal *étangs* from the sea. It was in such contrast to the built up seaside towns through which I had been travelling: just me and a few other cyclists making our isolated ways along the coast.

After several kilometres of bouncing up and down on the uneven surface of the track, I struck up conversation with a couple of men on bikes. I had already overtaken their wives, who were about twenty metres behind. I tossed them a merry '*bonjour*' and they responded. One of them, seeing the luggage on the bike (and the solar panels which continue to attract more interest than anything else - even if they weren't wonderful at generating power, they were proving to be great at generating conversations with strangers) asked where I was going.

"*Où vas-tu?*" he enquired

I had learnt over the previous few weeks that the best answer to this question was not to say 'Béziers', or whatever destination I was aiming for at the end of the day.

"*Je vais au Portugal*" I responded.

Both men immediately seemed more interested in what I was doing and as we chatted and cycled, I recounted the story of my journey to that point. We stopped at the place where they could turn left towards their regular sunbathing spot and I would continue along the thin strip of land. Their wives caught up and stopped and one of the men explained to them what I was in the process of doing. All seemed suitably impressed. Before separating, we chatted for a few more moments and the men were able to reassure me about the continuation of the track, as well as remind me about the existence of the *Canal du Midi* and the possibilities of following that after the town of Sète. It was always nice to receive the adulation of others but it somehow felt even nicer coming from the French, the inventors of the *Tour de France* and the masters of long distance cycling.

At Frotignan, the path became a signposted cycle path, complete with tarmac surface and even a dotted line encouraging me to keep on the left. It took me all the way to Sète, where I paused for lunch by one of its town centre canals. The high-quality cycling infrastructure continued in the direction of Agde, where cyclists were guided away from the main road along a cycle path by the side of the dunes. I stopped occasionally to follow the short track that crossed the dunes to the beach and take in the expansive views of the sea. The place was so vast as not to be crowded; the sounds were the natural ones of waves gently lapping on the shore, birds in the sky, cicadas in the bushes and Reggie's human-fuelled mechanism; the sun was surrounded by the bluest of blue skies and I was comforted by a gentle cooling breeze. I had indeed found the cycling nirvana that I had earlier dared to think might exist. Everything was coming together to whisper 'Yes, *this is a cycling paradise'*. Wonderful. Wonderful!

As I continued towards Agde, I recalled the Prime Minister's words as reported on the radio earlier in the day. If you want a cycling revolution Mr Cameron (and I don't doubt that you do), come and visit this long corner of Languedoc-Roussillon. Ignore the sun, the blue sky, the cicadas, the lapping Mediterranean... (we don't often get those in Britain). Look instead at what can be achieved if a conscious decision is taken to build a proper, safe cycling environment. Perhaps then, we will have our cycling revolution.

Inevitably, things went a bit downhill just before and after Agde but I didn't mind. The cycle path ended and the road decided to abruptly ban bicycles from continuing, which was a curious contrast with what had come before. A few farmers' fields later, I located the centre of Agde and then the *Canal du Midi*. I don't know why the *Canal du Midi* had not passed through my consciousness in the months of thought about where I would be cycling, prior to catching the plane for Athens or, indeed, as I approached it in southern France. I knew of its existence and a bit of investigating back at home would surely have been time well spent. Clearly I had been too preoccupied with my main hobby of procrastination. (I'm an authority upon the subject.) The *Canal du Midi* is a 250km long body of water that links Toulouse with the sea at Sète. It was the brainchild of a chap called Pierre-Paul Riquet, one of Béziers' most acclaimed sons (I was to find an impressive statue of him later in the day in Béziers). He persuaded King Louis XIV to stump up the cash to build the canal and when completed, it was the high-speed railway line of its day, albeit one without a railway. Ironically, its demise came following the construction of the real high-speed railway of its day (which *was* a railway, although not quite as fast as a modern TGV...). Still with me? Poor Pierre-Paul died six months before the canal was inaugurated in 1681. At least he wasn't around to see the invention of the train. That would have really pissed him off.

I looked at the Google Maps cycle track that had been proposed and yes, the suggested route was indeed to follow the *Canal du Midi*. Two-thirds of my cycle from Nîmes had already been on traffic-free cycle paths. Could the last part of the day from the coast to Béziers also be equally tranquil? My hopes were high as I located and started to follow the canal. But... Unfortunately the authorities that manage the *Canal du Midi* have yet to team up with the authorities that manage the wonderful coastal cycle paths. The ground along the canal was very unsuitable for cycling anything but the most mountainous of mountain bikes. I persevered for a couple of kilometres but eventually gave up, choosing to return to the relatively busy main road. It was a bit of an anti-climax after such wonderful cycling experiences during the earlier parts of the day but upon arrival in the outskirts of Béziers, I was still feeling high after the exhilarating experiences of the cycling day as a whole.

The centre of Béziers was preparing for something. A fun fair was being constructed in the main square (not far from the watchful gaze of Pierre-Paul Riquet), stalls were in the process of being put together for the selling of food and most of the restaurants lining the *Allées Paul Riquet* (who else?) had set up small marquees for their customers along the wide, pedestrianised central area of the street. If confirmation were needed that something big was about to happen, it came in the form of a line of portable loos. The colourful posters that had been plastered almost everywhere confirmed that the *Féria de Béziers* was about to kick off on the 14th of the month. In a large, artistic splat of multi-coloured paint the poster depicted dancers, trumpeters, a horse and (you guessed it) a bull. I wasn't too disappointed to have arrived three days too early.

It had been a long (if admittedly flat) day in the saddle and I had knocked a not-insignificant 135km chunk from the distance that remained between me and the lighthouse at Cape St. Vincent. I am, of course, trying to break the news gently that for the second, consecutive night I reached for my iPhone and booked a hotel online. Curiously, the best bargain to be had was from an establishment called the *Hôtel Impérator,* a hotel with the same name as the one in Nîmes. It was decidedly more run-down than its namesake further east, however, with gaudy, red wallpaper and a bed that could have doubled as a trampoline. Perhaps it occasionally did.

Monday 12th August 2013
Cycling Day 35: Béziers To 'The Pilgrims' Nest' (Near Villardebelle),
98km

The name Eddy Voorspoels conjures up images of the Low Countries. The Pyrenees? Probably not. But that's where I was heading and that's the name of the man who had invited me to spend a little time with him and whoever else there was at the Pilgrims' Rest, his isolated house in the foothills of the Pyrenees about 40km from the coast. It would require a climb from sea level to just over 700m but after a couple of scorching hot days, I was already looking forward to the cool mountain air.

I had eaten a thoroughly French meal on the previous evening at a small restaurant called *Le Vieux Siège,* in the curiously named *Place des Trois Six* or *Square of the Three Sixes,* just opposite the modest (for a French town) *Hôtel de Ville* or Town Hall. *La Place des Trois Six*? 666? That's one hell of a name. I returned to the square on the morning of Monday 12th, as it was the only place I could find a café that was open. The name had me wondering what devilish events had taken place in the very square where I was munching my way through yet another crumbly croissant. It turns out that the square was once home to a market selling *eau de vie,* the clear, yet extremely potent alcoholic spirit. The *eau de vie* needed to be diluted in the proportion of 3 measures of alcohol to 3 measures of water or, as a fraction, 3/6. Hence the name. So no satanic connection unless you consider it to be the demon drink...

It doesn't require a stiff drink to get disorientated in this part of France; the geography of Languedoc-Roussillon is pretty good at doing that all by itself. Without looking at a map, most people would guess that by heading south out of Béziers, you would end up quite quickly in the sea. And so you would. But change your direction by just a handful of degrees towards the west and you will miss the Mediterranean sea completely and be happily skirting your way along the French coast and heading for Spain more quickly than a bank robber on bail. What I'm trying to say is that the French coast was about to complete its 90 degree rotation from being east-west to being north-south and that by cycling off in a south westerly direction from Béziers I would start climbing into the Pyrenees mountains. I got there eventually...

Béziers didn't quite have the gleaming sheen of Nîmes. If the latter was the beautiful girl who sipped champagne with her little finger pointing daintily away from the glass while chatting about the

Molière play she had seen recently, the former was her sister who drank pints, had been around the block a bit but was in a good mood and up for the next challenge that life had to throw at her. I liked them both for different reasons but perhaps because I too was now a bit rough around the edges after so many weeks of cycling, I felt a little more comfortable in Béziers than I had done in Nîmes. That said, my last view of the town as I crossed the bridge over the River Orb was very different from anything else that I had seen during my short visit to the town. I stopped, dismounted and gazed at the beautiful view across the water, over the *Pont Vieux* (or 'old bridge') and up towards the walls, turrets and towers of the *Cathédrale St-Nazaire*. It was an astonishing sight which contrasted with the much less pristine, central part of town. Perhaps it was something to do with the morning light that made the scene sparkle and the stone shine. There was even a hint of pink in some of the buildings that I could see and the ensemble of cathedral, green hill and old arched bridge was mirrored perfectly in the still waters of the river. Perhaps Béziers had a classier side to her after all.

The first 30km was on the flat as I cycled from the *Hérault* department of France and into *Aude* in the direction of Narbonne. After this, there remained just one further department - *Pyrénées-Orientales* – before I would cross the border into Spain for the final slog to the finish line in Portugal. Although I knew there was much cycling still left to do, I could now start to visualise the days that remained and the expanse of land over which I would have to travel. Dare I say that it was the beginning of the end, or was that tempting fate? It would have been dangerous to think that way too much but when my mind's attention drifted away from the scenery that surrounded me, from the towns and villages through which I cycled and from the people I passed, I found it difficult to fight the faint sense of achievement that I was just beginning to feel. I remained determined that the job of crossing the continent would not be celebrated until I could sit on the cliff in Portugal and cast my eyes across the white crested waves of the Atlantic Ocean, but I was feeling just a little excited.

Narbonne was an unexpected delight. The focus of the town centre was a very large square, dissected by a broad canal – the *Canal de la Robine* – and flanked by smart three-storey buildings and a fabulously ornate covered market where, for a few minutes, I wandered to make the most of its relatively cool climate. As I was pushing Reggie along the banks of the canal in the direction of the imposing fortress-like town hall, I bumped into a couple of fellow touring cyclists. They were French and we chatted about our respective journeys. I initially thought they were together as a couple but the woman quickly pointed out my error when I suggested this might be the case. When I thought about it again, they did look like completely different characters; he was a middle-aged man, she was much younger but they had been cycling together without having come to blows for a couple of days. I admired their willingness to set aside differences that I would have found annoying after only a few hours in their company - his flat voice and her laugh being the most obvious traits that would have had me screaming internally should they have chosen to latch themselves onto me. Interestingly, they had both spent some time cycling alongside the *Canal du Midi* further to the north and had found it to be a thoroughly enjoyable experience. I wondered if my own experiences of the previous day had been completely unrepresentative of the rest of the canal. To be honest, I also wondered if I had been cycling along the *Canal du Midi* in the first place. There were plenty of them in this part of France from which to choose.

A subtle change of direction out of Narbonne, along the *Avenue de Bordeaux* marked the start of my long, steady climb into the Pyrenees. After only a few kilometres of cycling, I could see the scenery start to change quite dramatically. Earlier in the day, I had photographed the distant mountain range looking rather small-scale compared to many of the ranges of hills that I had crossed since leaving southern Greece, but here it was getting up closer and more personal. These may have been the 'Pre-Pyrenees', but they would still pose a significant challenge to the calf muscles. The further I travelled, the greener the landscape became. The green also changed from the washed-out faded green of the coastal plain, to a much deeper green more reminiscent of the English countryside than that of the Mediterranean. This sense of being back at home was only compounded by the appearance of cattle that wouldn't have looked out of place in the fields of *Emmerdale Farm,* and a gradual drop in temperature as I ticked off the vertical metres of cycling.

Eddy Voorspoels had supplied me with a rough itinerary of villages through which I needed to cycle in order to reach the *'Pilgrims' Nest',* so the route planning had already been done for me. It was simply a case of ticking off the villages: St. Laurent-de-la-Cabreirisse, Tournissant, St. Pierre-des-Champs, St. Martin-des-Puits, Vignevielle, Montjoi, Bouisse... 3G coverage had now disappeared and for much of the time there wasn't even a standard mobile phone signal, so I had to keep a careful eye out for the small blue and cream signs that pointed me in the direction of where I needed to be. Each village was more

286

remote and more rudimentary, as I climbed upwards into the mountains and further away from the coast. Evidence that I hadn't found an as-yet-undiscovered corner of Europe wasn't difficult to find. The hills were littered with the brooding, ruined castles of the Cathars and the local authority had seen fit to construct large, yellow signs along my route, celebrating the fact that I was travelled along '*Route 20*'. I can only imagine that the person designing the sign was so chuffed with his or her imaginative play on the word French word '*vingt*', that they subsequently ordered a sufficiently large number of the signs to place every few kilometres all the way along '*Route 20*'. Let me explain... I was cycling through the Corbières region of the Pyrenees. Corbières is famous for its wine. The French word for wine is '*vin*' and it sounds just like '*vingt*'. Hence '*Route 20*' being a play on words. But why route 20? This was, after all, the much less pun-friendly D613. Well, the design of the signs attempted to evoke the style of Route 66 across America and at the bottom of each of the panels was the tag line "*En Corbières, on mise tout sur le vin*" - "*In Corbières, we put everything on 20*". It was a roulette thing... The marketing office of the Corbières tourist board must have heard a deafening round of applause when this was revealed. Or perhaps a groan. Who knows? What I do know, is that the signs were a real eyesore.

When I arrived in Bouisse, the final village that Eddy had mentioned in his list, I paused to examine my map once again. It wasn't of great use in these parts, as most of the small villages simply didn't get a mention. An old chap was leaning on his gate and looking at what I was doing.

"*Vous êtes perdu?*" he asked. Was I lost?

"*Non, pas vraiment...*" Not really I explained. I just needed to make sure that I was heading in the right direction. (There is a subtle difference, especially when you are a man.) The man's accent was very strong but I caught a few fragments of what he was saying.

"*...le col de l'homme... je ne vais jamais...*" It was something about the col further up the road and how he never ventured up there.

"*Où vas-tu?*" He had changed from the formal '*vous*' to the informal '*tu*' to ask where I was going. Perhaps he was on my side. Or did he just want to comfort someone who was on a doomed mission into the mountains, along a road that he wasn't that keen to travel up himself. I explained that I was making my way to see a Belgian man who lived just a few kilometres away. He explained that he knew of an Englishman who lived somewhere up there - "*il est un peu bizarre*" -

but nothing more than that. Belgians and Englishman are perhaps fairly similar if you are an old man in the Pyrenees who spends his time watching the world go by from your garden gate.

I thanked him. He shook my hand and wished me well. I felt a little uneasy.

I continued climbing to the *col*. When I arrived, there was a sign, just as there had been at all those *cols* I had passed through in Provence. This one read *'Col de l'Homme Mort'* or *'Dead Man's Pass'*. Was it the effort of having climbed to over 700m that was making my heart beat a little faster than normal, or could it be something else? Ridiculous thoughts started to pass through my head. Had I been lured high into the mountains on false pretences? Forget *Emmerdale Farm*, this was turning into an episode of *Midsomer Murders*.

Reasoning that the name of the col predated the arrival of Eddy by quite some time, I continued and about ten minutes later, I arrived at a collection of buildings with a sign just next to the gate welcoming me to the Pilgrims' Nest. The reassuring presence of a bicycle on a second sign next to the words *'Welcome'*, *'Welkom'* and *'Bienvenue'*, was an indication that this was indeed a friendly place for a cyclist to be and much to my relief, I can reveal that I wasn't about to get murdered.

It was Katrina, Eddy's girlfriend, who initially welcomed me but she was quickly joined by the affable Eddy. We sat for a few moments to chat before he gave me an escorted tour of the buildings and the land around them. As he did so, he talked about his Flemish origins, his life as a bank clerk in Belgium and his time spent running a youth hotel in Antwerp. His experiences as a touring cyclist put my own modest expeditions across Europe to shame; I was particularly interested in what he had to say about Spain, of course, as that was my next destination and he made reference to the *Vias Verdes*. He promised to show me a map later. As we wandered around, Eddy explained his personal philosophy and what he had wanted to achieve by creating the Pilgrims' Nest. It was described on the Warm Showers' website as a place that *"is open to all other pilgrims/travellers/cyclists/wanderers on their individual path of evolution, to let them rest their weary feet, to absorb the transforming energy of this beautiful place, to eat and drink together, and to share of what we all are, and of who we want to be..."*

I was certainly up for a bit of that, so cracked open the bottle of red that I had purchased earlier in the day and offered Eddy and Katrina a glass. The Pilgrims' Nest was very much 'off grid'. Electricity came via solar panels and a small wind turbine, and was stored in a large number of batteries, housed in a small annexe next to the main house. Water came from a local source and fed, amongst other things, the outdoor shower that was to be found next to a fence. Forget your fancy wash blocks with your wristbands, tokens and timed washes; this was showering at its most natural and most wonderful, under the open sky. Not quite open for everyone to see – this wasn't a campsite in Croatia! – but the nearest I had yet come to feeling totally refreshed and relaxed at the end of the cycling day. No cars to be heard, no chatter from the cruisers heading back to their ships, no late-night music from the hotel next door, no shagging students in the adjoining room. Just peace.

After a couple of glasses of wine, my mind and body started to shut down rapidly and I was in no mood to fight the natural urges. The tent had been erected upon arrival and my camping mat inflated when I still had the energy to do so. All that remained for me to do was put them to good use. That night in the mountains, in the darkness, in the silence and in the cool air, I slept. I didn't wake once and much to my relief, I wasn't murdered.

Tuesday 13th August 2013
Cycling Day 36: The Pilgrims' Nest (Near Villardebelle) To Perpignan,
82km

Eddy's mountain retreat was the kind of place where time was very much dictated by the sun. I had gone to bed when I was tired, a moment which handily coincided with it becoming dark. It might only have been 9pm. I got up when the light returned to a level that would minimise my chances of walking into a tree. That may have been as early as 5am. Time, temporarily, didn't seem to have much meaning high in the hills and well away from anyone who required it to be a major factor in their life. The only sounds were natural ones - no refuse trucks emptying bins or early morning deliveries being made to shops and restaurants. Just the birds, tweeting. (Perhaps there was a 3G signal high in the trees.)

Apart from Eddy, Katrina and myself, several other people had stayed the night at the Pilgrims' Nest, but I had yet to meet any of them as they had all been away doing their own thing on the previous evening. I had pitched my tent in a clearing above Eddy's house, a few metres from another tent. It was much larger than my own modest shelter, with a couple of interior compartments and it was bright orange. It was the home of James, an American student who was spending several weeks helping Eddy run the retreat in return for free board and lodgings. Well, free board and tent. I chatted to James over a mug of coffee served by Eddy. He talked about his plans to go travelling around Europe and then his return to the U.S. to study. He had managed to grow an impressive beard during his time in Europe. Apart from reminding me of the Muppets creator, Jim Henson, it also made him look much older than he actually was. Such facial appendages are popular with cyclists who travel around the world spending, many months crossing the mountains and plains of one 'Stan' after another. A few days of stubble was sufficient to annoy me; perhaps that's why I have so far stuck to crossing just Europe on a bike.

I reminded Eddy about the *Vias Verdes* he had mentioned the previous evening and he went off to find the details. He returned a few minutes later and unfolded a large map of Spain on the even larger wooden table where we were sitting, drinking our coffee outside. The network of *Vias Verdes* – literally 'green ways' in Spanish – was quite extensive and covered most regions of the country, although not in any contiguous way. Eddy explained that the routes were disused railway tracks which had been converted to be used by walkers and cyclists.

Why did I know nothing about these routes? Ah, yes... It was because most of the research that I had done prior to leaving home was concentrated upon the first half of my trip. At that time, Spain had seemed a distant portion of the journey that I would sort out when I crossed the border from France. Now it was just around the corner. Many of the one hundred or so *Vias Verdes* routes shown on Eddy's map were very short, some perhaps just 10 or 20km in length. Others, mainly in the south of Spain, were much longer and my eyes were immediately drawn towards two particular *Vias Verdes*: one that started in a place called Albacete – the *Via Verde de la Sierra de Alcaraz* – and a second, just a short distance from the first, that started in Jaén – the *Via Verde del Aceite*. My route through Spain was increasingly playing on my mind and I had all but abandoned any hope of following the coast; it would take up far too much time to do so. The alternative course of action was to stay near the Mediterranean as far as Valencia but then to head inland. The two *Vias Verdes* that I had just discovered were perfectly placed to keep me off the roads for more than fifty percent of the journey from Valencia in the east to Seville in the west. Eddy's mention of the routes in passing had been a moment of stupendous serendipity. After Seville, there were two or three shorter *Vias Verdes*, which may be of use before I crossed over into Portugal at Ayamonte for a final push along the Algarve to my objective, the lighthouse at Cape St. Vincent. Cadiz, the official starting point for the Eurovelo 8, would have to be jettisoned from the itinerary in favour of my more worthy ambition of crossing the continent in its entirety. Time was still a factor, however. It was now Tuesday 13th August. I had under three weeks to finish the French portion of the journey, cross the Iberian Peninsula, arrive at my destination, celebrate, organise the journey home, travel home and then, on Monday 2nd September, be back at work teaching disgruntled teenagers how to speak French. That, I reckoned, was doable (well, apart from the very last bit), especially after having discovered the *Vias Verdes*.

Katrina was nowhere to be seen but Eddy, James and I were joined by a family from Paris: Akiko, Auriella and their children Landry and Ethan. They were paying guests at the Pilgrims' Nest, were all as interesting as their names, and were staying in the large outbuilding that Eddy was in the process of renovating. A sufficient amount of the work had been completed to allow such groups to spend some time in the mountains and the Parisians were loving it, exploring the surrounding countryside, wandering around the small villages and returning to the Pilgrims' Nest each evening to soak up the off-grid lifestyle that Eddy had so successfully created. I admired Eddy for what he had done; I was also a little bit jealous. It must have been a big step moving down to the Pyrenees and sacrifices had most certainly been made, but he gave the impression of being peacefully contented with his lot in life. How many of us can say that?

Although the trek up the Corbières Mountains had been a deviation, it had been well worth it. Not only had I learnt about the *Vias Verdes* (which would hopefully more than compensate for any extra time spent heading inland to the Pilgrims' Nest and then back towards the coast), but I felt spiritually uplifted by the few hours I had managed to spend with Eddy, Katrina, James and the Parisians. I eventually made my excuses at around 11am, when I succumbed to the reality that I still had to cycle as far as Perpignan and that if I left it much longer I risked delaying my arrival in Spain. The following day, I had arranged to stay overnight with fellow Yorkshireman, Dave Cocker and his wife Pauline, on the campsite where they had spent the previous thirty-two summers in their caravan. I somehow sensed that the experience of staying with Dave and Pauline might be a little different from that of staying at the Pilgrim's Nest.

Eddy escorted me to the gate, we shook hands and I cycled back up the hill in the direction from which I had arrived the previous evening and towards the *Col de l'Homme Mort*. I paused at the sign and smiled. Whatever the etymology of 'Dead Man's Pass', I was sure it had nothing to do with my new Belgian friend. I did, however, quite like the thought that the old guy with whom I had spoken the previous evening was continuing to stand at his gate, hinting at nefarious goings on further up the valley. I would never find out, as a few kilometres before his home in Bouisse, I turned off the road, changed direction and started cycling south towards Perpignan.

To a certain extent, it was a reverse of the journey into the mountains, moving from the relatively cool, darkly wooded uplands to the warmer, drier lowlands of the *Pyrenées-Orientales*. That said, whereas the cycle to the Pilgrims' Nest had been one long and increasingly steep climb, the lateral geography of the foothills of the Pyrenees required me to cross two valleys before I would be able to enjoy a lengthy stretch of downhill cycling. It wasn't geography that was uppermost in my mind however; it was food. Eddy, quite rightly, had asked that I bring my own food to eat in the evening and I made sure that I had bought my usual feast of bread, cheese and wine. After the long climb, I had devoured all the food that I had taken up the mountain, leaving me with only half a bottle of wine for my breakfast. Had I been French, this would have sufficed but being from England, a country in which drinking before midday rates alongside violent crime as a serious social *faux pas*, I stuck to the coffee that Eddy had served. The result was that I was very hungry indeed and was keen to find a shop, a *boulangerie* or a café as soon as I possibly could. It was to be a long, frustrating wait.

In the first of the two valleys, the only things I was able to feast upon were the views, which were beautiful. Quaint little villages with red-tiled houses - one with a complete working windmill - overlooked by the sporadic remnants of the hilltop castles... but no shops. What did they do with all the flour from the mill? A nice little bakery serving hungry, passing tourists like me would have been a gold mine, but alas, no. This was clearly a business venture too far for the inhabitants of the *Pyrenées-Orientales*. In the second valley, I had high hopes as I approached the small town of Maury, a place rather unimaginatively named after the river that runs along the valley bottom. Great! A café! Complete with very French-looking waiter leaning against the frame of the door, smiling... But hang on, something was not quite right. This was merely a very elaborately painted and, from a distance, very convincing gable-end *trompe d'oeil*. Further along the road were other painted buildings, attempting to trick the eye into thinking that there was more to this town than there really was. No real café. No shop. One *boulangerie*... but it was closed and wouldn't open until later in the day. I was beginning to grumble as much as my stomach was.

One thing did, for a few tantalising minutes, distract me from my growing pangs of hunger: the weather. Although it had rained overnight on a couple of occasions, I had yet to experience the joy of cycling in the rain. If you have read *Crossing Europe on a Bike Called Reggie*, you may find this comment a little strange, because, back in 2010 I was regularly drenched to the point of starting to rot. One of the principal reasons for choosing the Mediterranean *Eurovelo 8* had been the almost guaranteed good, hot, sunny and above all, dry weather it promised. But after six weeks in the saddle, a little shower would have been quite nice and was it about to happen? The clouds were gathering and the sky was darkening. I felt a drop of rain and a few moments later, another. I stopped, pulled my raincoat from one of the front panniers, put it on and zipped it up. Come on! Give me and Reggie and drenching, just like you did in the good old days when we cycled to Italy. I could have become quite emotional as I reminisced about day after day of cycling through walls of water in eastern France and Switzerland. But no. No more drops of water. The clouds dispersed and the sky cleared. I stopped again and, wiping away one of the few drops that *had* fallen onto my cheek (or was it a tear?), I packed away my raincoat. No rain today. Back to thinking about food.

Next up was Estagel, a much larger place than Maury, full of real cafés, *boulangeries*, a few restaurants and even a hairdresser's. Brilliant! I would finally be able to eat. Err... Not quite yet. The hairdresser's was open, but I didn't need a haircut. Of all the other places, just the *brasserie* in *Place Arago* was serving customers. I sat down and waited to be served.

"Monsieur?" enquired the waitress

"Un sandwich jambon-fromage, s'il vous plait," I requested.

"Je suis désolé monsieur, mais la cuisine est fermée." Really? The kitchen is shut? You need a kitchen to make me a sandwich?

I refrained from offering the young girl my sarcastic yet perfectly reasonable thoughts. I did, however, cancel my order for a drink and moved on. I was, of course, experiencing that quintessentially French attachment to the desire to shut everything down for a long lunch. Unless, that is, you need your hair cut. I had now cycled over 60km and I was famished.

Would Cases-de-Pène come to my rescue? Kind of... The *boulangerie* at the far end of the village *was* open, so I stopped. I had planned to congratulate the owners on being the first *boulangerie* to be open since leaving the Pilgrims' Nest but when I walked in, the rotund owner ignored my presence in the shop and continued to watch the dubbed American film being shown on the television above the counter. After perhaps half a minute – my arrival had clearly coincided with an important point in the plot – the man twisted on his axis and looked in my direction.

"Oui?"

Another candidate for the customer service course I'm thinking of running for the people I meet on my travels. I chose a *'sandwich limo'* which, when it arrived, had few similarities to the image displayed on the menu on the wall. At least the can of Diet Coke and the two *pains au chocolat* looked familiar. Further bemusement was to unfold before me when baker's wife appeared and there was some discussion about taking the daughter somewhere in the car.

"Don't worry, I can manage..." he reassured his wife. She did, however, seem somewhat reluctant. Manage? I was the only one in the shop! Eventually he looked at me, told me the price and I handed over the euros. His wife drove off in the car, I went to sit outside to eat my late lunch and he resumed his position to continue watching the TV.

Three minutes later, she returned at speed and minus daughter, running back into the *boulangerie* to relieve him of his arduous duties serving the non-existent customers. At least I had finally been fed.

Within the hour, I was in the suburbs of Perpignan and cycling past the stadium of the rugby league club Catalans Dragons, the only non-English team in the Super League. It seemed somewhat incongruous to see the words '*rugby league*' plastered on advertising hoardings so far from the sport's (and my) home county of Yorkshire. Perpignan, however, did strike me as the kind of place where rugby league would flourish; it was a grittier, grimier version of Béziers. If you remember, Béziers was the streetwise sister to posh Nîmes. Perpignan immediately struck me as the third sister of the clan and the one most likely to be interviewed at some stage by Jeremy Kyle.

A few blocks after the rugby league ground, I spotted a sign that warmed my heart: *Laverie – Libre Service*. It wasn't quite as well kept as the laundrette I had made use of in Nice the previous week, but it was open so I parked Reggie against the window and went in to explore. Washing machines – tick, driers – tick, suitable coins in my pocket – tick, washing powder... Ah! There was no dispensing machine inside the laundrette to help me out and I didn't want to buy a large box of powder from a nearby shop. Time, perhaps, to put my charm and French to good use. There was one other person doing her washing and she had a large bottle of washing liquid sitting on the top of the machine she was using.

"*Pardon madame... pourriez-vous me prêter un peu de lessive?*" I requested. Asking to borrow some of her washing liquid didn't seem totally appropriate, as she would clearly not get any of it back.

"*Oui, bien sur!*" she replied. Of course I could!

I have been teaching French for a good number of years and many scenarios are imagined; ordering food in a restaurant (despite the fact that most teenagers will do so in a fast food outlet that uses English to describe what it sells), buying a train ticket (despite the fact that the easiest way to do so is via a machine which has an English-language option), booking a hotel room (despite the fact that doing so online in their own language is far easier)... but I have never once either come across or indeed invented a laundrette scenario. It is an under-exploited area of need for anyone visiting France. My requirement to understand and speak the language in order to wash my clothes was far more urgent that my requirement to order a snack, buy a train ticket or book a hotel room. Perhaps its time that we language teachers moved into the 21st century.

Back in Perpignan, the conversation with the woman in the *laverie* continued. It was now time to do some work in return for 'borrowing' the washing liquid.

"Vous pouvez m'aider pour plier les draps?" she asked.

I spent the next five minutes helping her fold her bed sheets as they came out of the drier, chatting about this and that as the neat pile of clean laundry slowly grew beside us. There would, I thought, be enough material here for a whole chapter in my updated French textbook.

Within the hour, I had located the main square in the centre of Perpignan and was to be found sipping a beer while booking accommodation for the evening online. It would be a functional hotel with functional rooms, a functional restaurant and pleasant but functional staff. My time in France was about to draw to a close. A few weeks earlier, it had been a relief to arrive in Italy and be absorbed in a culture and language that was familiar, even more so when I arrived in France. But the adventurer in me now missed the unfamiliarity and, although Spain and Portugal wouldn't quite be a return to Greece, Albania and Croatia, they were countries where I would once again be immersed in a language I couldn't speak and a culture of which I knew relatively little. I was once again feeling excited.

PART SIX: SPAIN AND PORTUGAL
Wednesday 14th August 2013
Cycling Day 37: Perpignan To L'Estartit, 140km

The day started with me sitting in the centre of Perpignan, sipping coffee and pondering which way to cycle to my destination. The word 'Perpignan' could have been replaced with many other towns and cities along my route, but it was a great way to start the day. At 9am I wasn't yet worried about finding accommodation for the evening, I could just revel in the possibility of discovering new, fascinating places (as well as a few that probably weren't). On the morning of 14th August, I didn't even have the distant concern about accommodation to worry about, as that would be provided by Dave and Pauline Cocker in L'Estartit. But how would I get there? There were two obvious possibilities: via the inland border crossing at Le Perthus or via the coast at Cape Cerbère. The former was more direct and wouldn't involve a great deal of climbing as the *Col de Perthus* was only at an altitude of 200m, but I had travelled into Spain many years previously via that crossing and had memories of vast expanses of tarmac in the hills and busy roads. The latter, coastal road seemed a much better option, even though I knew it would not only be a longer cycle, but the craggy nature of the *Côte Vermeille* would inevitably mean a fair bit of climbing. So be it.

Of the eventual 140km to L'Estartit, the first 60km were in France and at times, it was almost as if the French were trying their best to prevent me from getting anywhere near Spain. The busy D914 in the direction of Argelès-sur-Mer was far from cycle-friendly and, if official confirmation were needed to back up this suspicion, I was unceremoniously informed by a sign some 10km into my journey, that I should find another road: *"Cette route vous êtes interdite,"* it instructed. Tractors, mopeds and pedestrians received the same treatment, so I didn't feel too marginalised and anyway, the sign was only making obligatory what I should have had the sense to do voluntarily earlier in the morning by taking some of the back roads in the direction of the coast. However, it wasn't obvious which of those back roads I should be taking, so there followed a hour or so of orienteering across the land that made up this most southerly corner of the French mainland, before I eventually arrived within a few hundred metres of the coast, just south of Saint-Cyprien.

I continued south in the direction of Argelès Plage (the bit of Argelès-sur-Mer or 'Argelès-on-Sea' that *was* actually by the sea – hence the name *'plage'* or 'beach') but didn't stop, as I sensed that there would be greater challenges ahead on the coastal road either side of the border, which would at some point require me to pause for a rest to recover. That was indeed the case, as I embarked upon the twisting, up-and-down road that linked the handful of French towns that remained: Port-Vendres, Banyuls-sur-Mer and then finally, just before the border itself, Cerbère.

Many countries give up when it comes to their frontier towns. It's almost as if those in charge have come to the conclusion that these are places that only exist (or in the case of much of Europe, existed) to stamp the passport of the visitors who happen to be passing through, either en route out of the country or to more enticing destinations within the country. That's not an accusation you can often direct at the French, as their border towns do live up to the generally high standards that most French towns achieve; they are clean, attractive and often merit more than just a fleeting glance from the back of a car as you speed to your destination elsewhere. Cerbère was a good example, so, as it would be the final place on my trip where I would be able to confidently order something to eat and drink in a language that I could speak, I did just that. It wasn't anything grand - just a baguette and a cold drink - which I ate in the shade of the trees, in a small square behind the colourful row of seafront hotels, bars and restaurants. Things had gone very much to plan in France. I had done what I wanted to do, achieved what I wanted to achieve, seen the people I wanted to see and to top it all, I had made good progress along the Mediterranean coast. I wondered if Spain would be so straightforward.

Beyond the large end-of-the-French-railway-line marshalling yard behind the train station, one final sharp climb was required from sea level to just over 150m, where I found the border crossing. The area immediately before the imaginary line in the road was a little unkempt and the large, blue sign pointing out that I was about to leave the country had the word '*France*' scribbled out and '*Catalunya Nord*' written in marker pen underneath instead. It was a reminder that, for many, I was not about to enter Spain, rather the independent nation state that is Catalonia. Perhaps one day. A change in road surface marked the point where I entered Spain and to my right was a small, stone border post building, disused, with its battered wooden door firmly shut and its small windows filled with breezeblocks. Just a few metres into Spain were a series of information panels detailing the importance of the *Coll dels Belitres* (the small pass where the frontier was located) during the latter stages of the Spanish Civil War. Many of the hundreds of thousands of Republican refugees fleeing Franco's

Spain passed this way into exile in France. Behind the border post was a modern, concrete path that led to a memorial to those who had been forced to leave their homeland. Black and white pictures taken in early 1939 showed queues of people waiting to be processed at the border. The now boarded-up building was clearly identifiable in some of the photographs, which all depicted a remarkably different scene to that of 2013. After a few minutes of looking and reading, I returned to the main road and set about cycling across a thankfully much more peaceful country than that of nearly 75 years earlier.

Portbou - the first town in Spain - mirrored Cerbère - the last town in France – in that it was located just a short distance from the border, had been built in a small natural harbour and also had a large railway marshalling yard. But it didn't reflect the colour of its French counterpart an, whereas the beach in Cerbère was populated with a number of sun seekers, there were few people topping up their tan on the beach in Portbou. I cycled straight through the centre, up the winding road on the other side heading south, though a couple of tunnels - one short, one quite long - to Colera and then Llança, where I paused for thought and to try and work out the best route to take from thereon in.

The 1:200,000 Michelin map of French *Languedoc-Roussillon* had helped guide me over the border as far as Llança, but the road along which I was cycling was about to fall off the edge of the page. This wasn't a problem - I had the Michelin map covering Catalonia, of course - but it would mean reverting back to a scale of 1:400,000 and I would need to readjust my perception of distances as represented on the maps. 1cm on the maps of France equated to 2km of cycling. This had now doubled to 4km and the loss of detail was striking. That said, this didn't prevent me from noting that just to the south of Llança was the *Cap de Creus* with the town of Roses at its southern end. I had heard and read very good things about this little piece of land jutting out into the Mediterranean Sea but did I have the time to cycle through it? Google Maps was predicting a 70km journey to L'Estartit on the main roads and, having arranged with Dave to arrive later that afternoon, I didn't want to let him down. I had already put back my day of arrival by at least one day compared to what I had told him when I was in the middle of France. Delaying for another 24 hours wasn't really an option - not only would it be disrespectful to my fellow Yorkshireman (we were part of the same band of brothers, even if I had never met him before in my life) but it would also lead to a very short cycle the following day because I did want to spend the night at the campsite in L'Estartit and soak up a bit of English life on a Spanish *costa*! Taking time to wind my way up the headland of the *Cap de Creus* and passing through Roses would have to wait for another trip to this northern corner of Spain. I reluctantly set off once more along the main road out of Llança in the direction of Figueres.

The N260 proved to be everything that I wasn't looking for: long, straight, boring and hot. I couldn't avoid the heat of course, but I could try to eliminate the first three attributes by simply moving away from the main road. Several kilometres north of Figueres I did just that, turning left to move into open countryside and nearer to the coast. It was a good decision as the roads I was now following were neither straight nor boring. Some were quite long but at least my mind was happily occupied admiring the pretty views, isolated villages and... Stop! I had caught something in the corner of my eye that I didn't quite believe I had seen. It was a sign. I needed to go back and check, so immediately pulled on the brakes and did a U-turn. I was just outside the small town of Castelló d'Empúries. I looked once again at the sign and smiled. It was white with a green border and had the word *'Pirinexus'* printed underneath three images. On the right was a green and blue shape that I didn't recognise, on the left was an image of a person on a bicycle and sandwiched between the two was a blue box with the number 8 inside a circle of yellow stars. This was the official symbol of the *Eurovelo 8*! Remember that? The long-distance cycle path that I was trying (admittedly not too hard) to follow along the coast of Mediterranean Europe? I had cycled a little over 4,000km and through 8 (and a bit) countries to get to this point and, for the very first time, I had been rewarded with an official sign for the cycle route I was travelling along. This was a momentous occasion and photographs were taken. Back in 2010, while following the *Eurovelo 5*, I hadn't come across one single sign telling me I was heading in the right direction. Things were clearly improving!

I was later to discover that the *'Pirinexus'* is a 350km, circular cycle route around Catalonia, the version of Catalonia, that is, which also takes in the southern part of the *Pyrenées-Orientales* back in France (hence the reference to *'Catalunya Nord'* on the sign for France at the border earlier in the day). The easterly portion of the loop is also the *Eurovelo 8* and it was another good example of how much of the *Eurovelo* network piggybacks upon other regional and occasionally national routes. It was good to see that here in Catalonia, the authorities had taken the small but useful decision to include the *Eurovelo 8* symbol on the cycle network signs where it was relevant to do so. It's a pity that others elsewhere in Europe don't always choose to do the same thing.

So, all I needed to do was follow the signs for a while... Well, not quite. I did follow the *Eurovelo 8 / Pirinexus* signs for a few kilometres but, as with many signposted cycle paths, the route took the opportunity to seek out every nook and cranny available. Each village appeared to be tortuously cycled through, even when there were perfectly adequate country lanes to use that were a little more direct. Had I not been keen to arrive in the town of Torroella di Montgri before sunset to meet Dave (we had exchanged text messages and agreed to rendez-vous outside the Carrefour supermarket), I might have been happy to slavishly follow each of the many turns of the *Pirinexus,* but to my shame I gave up after a few kilometres and reverted back to my own version of the *Eurovelo 8.* I preferred it that way. Sorry.

I hoped that it wouldn't be too difficult for Dave Cocker to identify me as I approached the supermarket car park in Torroella di Montgri. After all, I was on a bike laden with four panniers and I hadn't seen any other touring cyclists since arriving in Spain, not even on the *Pirinexus* (for the short time that I had followed it). Dave said he too would be on a bike but, rather than accost any passing cycling Spaniards asking if they were called Dave and from Leeds, I thought it better to simply allow him to make his presence known to me when he saw me. He did, and he waved in my direction from the other side of the road.

Dave had first contacted me via Twitter in 2012, when I had made it known that I planned to cycle around the Mediterranean from Greece to Portugal. On the look out for interesting people to meet, I immediately took him up on his offer to stay overnight with him and his wife Pauline at the campsite where they had spent every summer for the previous three decades. I'll be honest and say it: I cannot think of anything worse than spending every holiday for 33 years in the same place. It must, however, have its attractions, as Dave and Pauline didn't give even the smallest of indications that they may have become jaded with seeing the same views, visiting the same tourist attractions, sunbathing on the same bit of beach and meeting the same people, year after year after year. The pitch at the campsite in L'Estartit was just how Dave had described it in his emails; it consisted of his caravan, to which had been added a large tent extension, and attached to this was a second extension, which had become a semi al fresco dining area. Almost everything that you would normally find in your average British home was also to be found in one of the three living areas of Dave's camping complex, including fridges, a washing machine, wardrobes and a widescreen TV (connected to a satellite dish of course). He even had what he referred to as his 'shed', where he kept an assortment of things that, well, you probably have in your own shed at the bottom of your garden. It was an impressive installation, taking Dave several days of labour to construct each spring before he was joined by Pauline. Indeed, with so many mod cons available in the caravan and tents, it did make me wonder why they ever bothered to return to Yorkshire for the few winter months that remained.

There was room for my little tent to be erected just outside Dave's own construction. What was left of the pitch was used as a parking space for the car (although I suspected that Dave was in the process of drawing up plans for a garage of some description). The car, incidentally, had a personalised number plate very nearly spelling out the name 'D. Cocker' and a sticker in the back window stating '*Love Leeds. Hate Bates*', the Bates in question being Ken Bates, the former owner of Leeds United AFC. To say Dave was a Leeds supporter would be an understatement; it was part of who he was. His father, Les Cocker, had been a professional football player in the post-war period, playing for Stockport County and Accrington Stanley in the days when the footballs were about as heavy as the cows they were made from. He subsequently went on to be a respected coach, not just for Leeds (where he stayed for 14 years until 1974), but also for the England squad during the 1966 Word Cup. He died at the tragically young age of 55. There was a strong emotional attachment between Dave and his team and an even greater one between Dave and his late father. He talked with great warmth about both the team and the man, and he was never short of a story recounting his adventures growing up as the son of a high-profile footballer and coach.

In light of this football connection, it seemed appropriate that the evening should be spent watching some of the beautiful game. England were playing Scotland at Wembley and via Dave's satellite TV, we were able to watch the coverage on ITV. Pauline cooked up a hot meal and a couple of their campsite neighbours - Colin and Dawn (who themselves were parents to a footballing prodigy who had been snapped up to play the game for an American college) - joined us to watch the match. It was all a little surreal and the evening panned out just as it might have done had we all been sitting in the conservatory of a suburban, semi-detached house back in Britain. The only difference being that when we all eventually went to bed (separately, I hasten to add; it wasn't that kind of suburban evening), it was just as warm as it had been when the football match on the TV had kicked off. If I had made an effort to plan an evening that contrasted so starkly with the night spent at the Pilgrims' Nest only 48 hours earlier, I would have struggled to beat the one laid on by Dave and Pauline Cocker. The only thing missing was a large English fry-up to soak up all the beer.

Thursday 15th August 2013
Cycling Day 38: L'Estartit To Barcelona, 156km

In fairness to Dave and Pauline, there were many aspects of Spanish life that they had embraced wholeheartedly. Pauline talked about her regular visits to the local markets and Dave could occasionally be found in the stands of Girona FC, the local, second division football club. To a greater extent, the Spanish language had eluded them, but both had a functional working knowledge, which allowed them to interact with non-English speakers when they needed to do so. They were both very good company, easy-going and had a genuine fondness for the place that had become their home for most of the year. And they even served me an English breakfast of sorts to send me on my way - a fry up consisting of eggs, bacon and beans - which did the job of soaking up some of the previous evening's beer. It was just for my 'benefit' (although the novelty was appreciated) and Dave and Pauline chose not to indulge with me, preferring to brunch later, on something a little more Mediterranean.

As I packed away my tent and readied myself for what I suspected might be a very long day of cycling, Dave introduced me to another campsite neighbour, Angelo. Angelo was Spanish but spoke some English and the three of us debated the pros and cons of my route to Barcelona. It was good to have their local knowledge to factor into my decisions, although the route-planning process for this particular day was never going to be too difficult - for most of the time I would simply need to follow the coast. That said, until coastal Palamós it would be a continuation of the inland route I had been cycling along before I had arrived in Torroella di Montgri on the previous afternoon. I would be following the Catalonian *Pirinexus* cycle route once again, although after my earlier frustrations following its complicated path, I suspected that I might end up just making things up for myself.

I thanked Pauline for her hospitality but not Dave as he was joining me for the first few kilometres of cycling, away from L'Estartit, along a series of rough tracks to the river Ter, where we cycled for several kilometres inland until we arrived back in Torroella, the small town where we had met just over twelve hours previously. As we cycled, Dave regaled me with more mainly football-related stories, including the poignant tale of the campaign that he and the relatives of the other backroom staff who worked with the 1966 World Cup winning team have fought to have them recognised with an official winners' medal. It is now the practice for the winning team to receive

304

45 winners' medals; 23 for the playing squad and the remainder for the coaches, assistants, physios, (person who runs the Twitter account?) etc... This wasn't the case in 1966. Only the players who played in the final were rewarded. In 2007, FIFA decided also to award winners' medals to the players who were in the squad but who didn't play in the final, so the likes of Jimmy Greaves finally received their medals. But it took another two years for the world governing body to decide to give medals retrospectively to the backroom staff. Dave played a key role in the campaign and he is rightly proud of his father's medal which he collected at a Downing Street reception in June 2009. Who would have thought that, on a cycling tour of Europe, I would have come across someone who had been given a 1966 World Cup winners' medal, albeit on behalf of his father? Enough football? OK. Back to the cycling...

I shared a final coffee with Dave in a small village not far from Torroella di Montgri before I continued south and he headed off to the market to buy some fish. Should I attempt to follow the Pirinexus / Eurovelo 8 signs? I had already spotted a few of them before we stopped for coffee but did I really want to focus all my attention on sign-spotting rather than enjoying the cycling? The answer was no, so I continued to do my own thing, picking my way from village to village, along mainly deserted country lanes. I occasionally noticed one of the Eurovelo 8 signs; I nodded in acknowledgement of its presence but tended to ignore the arrow instructing me to turn left or right. After a couple of hours of wonderfully sunny, flat, carefree and predominantly car-free cycling I found myself back on the shores of the Mediterranean in the bustling, but very low-level, port of Palamós.

As I munched my way through lunch in a small, circular park a few metres from the beach, watching pensioners doing exactly the same thing, I was a happy soul. Spain was turning out to be just as rewarding and interesting as my journeys across France and Italy, and so far, I hadn't really had any issues with the language. I hoped it would stay that way. In terms of route as far as Barcelona, things couldn't be simpler: keep the sea on my left, the land on my right and cycle. When I first came up with the idea of cycling along the Mediterranean coast, that's what I imagined I would be doing for most of the trip, but when I thought back over the previous seven weeks of travel, it was only something that I had done quite sporadically. The first couple of days in southern Greece had been like this, then most of Croatia, very briefly the eastern section of the *Côte d'Azur* and again, on and off, south-western France. It total, it had amounted to perhaps only about a quarter of my time in the saddle. I wondered if such a predominantly littoral cycling journey was even possible or indeed desirable. My frequent forays inland had produced some of the most memorable moments of the trip so far and I certainly hoped this would continue to be the case once I turned right at Valencia, away from the Spanish coastline for good. We would see.

I also took a few moments to inspect Reggie and to check that he was OK. There was certainly nothing I had heard which gave me cause for concern; he continued to purr along the roads of Europe like a contented cat. The brake pads, which had only been changed at the foot of *Mont Ventoux,* were fine, the tyre pressure was good (phew!) and none of the spokes had lost their tension. That was about as far as my pit stop examination went. I didn't really know what I would have done had I found terminal problems with the gears, the chain or the frame, so I did the best thing and never checked them. It's a typical man thing.

Practising what I had preached, I set off with the sea to my left and the land to my right, although after only a few minutes I was hemmed in between a row of shops to my left and a row of shops to my right as I fathomed my way out of Palamós. After a couple of kilometres, normal service was resumed and I was soon heading in the direction of Barcelona. Reading between the contours of my map, the journey from hereon in would be split into three: a short, flattish section as far as Sant Feliu de Guíxols, a frenetically twisting, up-and-down section to Lloret de Mar and a third, very long section which would put me in the centre of the Catalonian capital. I say 'reading between the contours', but alas this 1:400,000 map didn't, of course, have the luxury of contours between which I could have read, even if I had wanted to. It simply had shaded patches of green, which hinted at areas that might be a little hillier than those which surrounded it. My tried and tested technique of assuming that a road which was very wiggly and lined with green ink contained lots of ascents and descents (as well as very pretty views) – a tactic that had worked particularly well in Italy – was also being employed to the full. I wanted the nice panoramic views, but on a day that promised to be an extremely long one, I wasn't that keen on all the hills. I wanted to have my cake and eat it but that just wasn't going to happen.

Part one of my three-part cycle was over in no time whatsoever, but as I made my way along the seafront road in Sant Feliu de Guíxols, I knew exactly what was coming. I could also see the coast ahead of me rising out of the Mediterranean. The cycling from here to Lloret de Mar would be through densely carpeted forest but this was now the middle of the day and only the most overhanging of trees gave any shade. They were few and far between. The contrast between the bright green of the trees and the deep blue of the sky was, however, sublime. It was almost as if some higher being had chosen those colours to go together; some believe that to be the case but others, like me, put it down to good fortune. Once I had arrived at the crest of the first headland, I was rewarded with glimpses of why it had been worth the effort taking this route as opposed to anything easier inland. The green trees and blue sky were now joined by the grey-blue sea and the orange rock, which fell steeply away between the road and the unseen beach far below. It was a very limited pallet of colours but each complemented the other in ways that only nature would be able to devise. A few isolated roofs could be seen amongst the trees and bare rock, no doubt protecting exclusive hideouts for the well-heeled. On the water itself were a number of speedboats, racing each other up and down the coastline, marking a long, thin line of white in the water. Had this been an impressionist painting, that line would have been the artist's signature. This could, indeed, have been such a painting and I was sure that somewhere, this was a scene hanging on the wall of an otherwise soulless gallery. I preferred the real thing. The temptation to stop frequently to take photographs or simply to gaze into the distance and soak up the sun was irresistible and time, after time I pulled on the brakes, dismounted and reached for my camera.

Several villages and holiday resorts were dotted along the route: Punta Brava, Canyet de Mar, Salionç, La Pola i Giverola... and their buildings, often replicated in long rows and built at strategic points on the hillside so as to ensure a south-facing frontage, did detract a little from the beauty of the landscape but who am I to dictate that this should only be reserved for those of us who might prefer to spend their holidays sitting on a bike? Under the glare of the sun and had I not had any particular destination in mind, I could quite willingly have stopped and checked in. I might even have been tempted to stay for more than just the night. Goodness! Was I really falling in love with a Spanish *costa*?

At one of the panoramic viewing points towards the end of this second section of my journey, I consulted Google Maps, more out of curiosity than necessity, to see how many kilometres I still needed to cycle before I would arrive in Barcelona. I guessed perhaps thirty or forty. The Internet ticked away for a few moments as the route was being calculated, before announcing that Barcelona was still 95km away. I was a little taken aback by the number so I repeated my request, double-checking that I had provided the correct information. It was still 95km. Bearing in mind that it was now past 2pm, I had already booked a non-refundable hotel room in the centre of Barcelona and I had arranged to meet up with fellow cyclist, Lewis Fox, at the Michael Collins bar next to the *Sagrada Familia* at 8.30pm, I could be in trouble. But there was no point moaning or indeed worrying about it. I simply had to get going.

In light of this revelation, it was good to first arrive in, and then cycle through, Lloret de Mar and finally get onto the long, flat road to Barcelona, where I was delighted to find that I could easily clock up speeds of 30km/hr on the very slight downhill slope of the road. This might mean that I could reach the city before 6:30pm. On and on I cycled and the kilometres were gradually chipped away. Here the scenery was entirely urban, with buildings to my right and, to my immediate left, not the sea, or even the beach but an electrified railway line. I had a sneaking suspicion that a long-distance cycle path (or at least a local cycle path that went on for a very long way) was hidden from view on the other side of the tracks, but did I want to have that confirmed? Time was of the essence and on the road I was making good progress. I wasn't convinced that on a cycle path my route wouldn't be impeded by people, street furniture, junctions and (worst of all) my fellow cyclists out for a late-afternoon potter. Despite the increasingly heavy traffic, I stuck to the road and tried to maintain my speed whenever it was possible to do so.

After the town of Mataró, traffic lights started to hold me up slightly, but they were only once every kilometre or so. Then I arrived in Badalona, the town just to the north of Barcelona and a place that appears to have been built simply to prevent any cyclist from having an easy time reaching the centre of Barcelona itself. The one-way system was hell, throwing me off course and not giving me any alternative other than to join the motorway, which, as I was no longer in Albania, was clearly not an option. I resorted to pavement cycling and eventually made it to the Besòs, the river that separates 'Bada' from 'Barce'. Then the traffic lights started. Can there be any city in the world where there are so many sets of traffic lights? New York, perhaps? My money would still be on Barcelona. And, as Reggie and I made our stuttering progress towards the centre of the city, every set of lights seemed to be red.

On two previous visits to Barcelona I had only ever explored, for a short period, the old part of the city that is clustered around La Rambla. It's how you would expect any historic quarter to be: lots of streets heading off in different directions at nonsensical angles, occasionally interrupted by a square that is anything but square or regular. That's what London, Rome, Madrid and Paris are like. But, as I was finding, not so much Barcelona. Far from it! This was predominantly a planned city on a monumental scale. We have an engineer called Ildefons Cerdà to thank. He first devised the grid plan for the development of Barcelona in the mid 19th century – it was adopted by royal decree in 1860 – and it's still there in its entirety. Block after block of urban planning at its most magnificent, each 'island' measuring exactly 100m by 100m, intersected by two diagonal avenues, the *Avinguda de la Diagonal* and the *Avinguda de la Meridiana*. I was impressed. Or at least, I was impressed by Ildefons Cerdà. It's worth noting that the traffic light wasn't invented until 1868, sometime after Ildefons had come up with his grid pattern. I'm not sure what he would have made of the Barcelona of today, which required me to stop every one hundred metres to wait for the lights to change. I was obviously aware that I was in Spain, a country where the *'mañana'* attitude prevails, but come on! Change! How long does it take someone to cross the road? I wasn't counting but I guess I must have stopped and started twenty, or even thirty times, before finally reaching a point which I assumed was somewhere near the centre of Barcelona (it was actually just around the corner from the *Arc de Triomf*). My self-imposed deadline of 6:30pm for arriving in the city was missed by nearly one hour, despite having arrived in Badalona at well before 6pm. Deep breaths were required...

I located and walked into what I believed to be the *Hotel Granvia*, smiled at the receptionist and informed her that I had booked a room.

"Are you sure?" she enquired in clipped English looking down at my body and clothing that had just travelled 140km to get there.

"Yes, I am sure. This is the reservation confirmation," I clipped back, passing her my phone so that she could inspect the email.

"I'm sorry, this is not the Hotel Granvia. The hotel you want is further along the road."

She seemed somewhat relieved that she wouldn't have to accommodate me (or indeed Reggie) but in my defence, the words *Gran Via* were written large on the large window of the 4 star establishment. That, however, was part of the address, not the name. I did find the more welcoming *Hotel Granvia* a few blocks away, at *Gran Via 642*. When the receptionist at that hotel saw me, he didn't bat an eyelid. He had clearly seen much worse.

If the previous night had been a night out in the English suburbs, the evening in the Michael Collins pub was a night out in Ireland. It was good to swap experiences with Lewis, who had set off on his own trip a few days earlier from Valencia. He had much more cycling to come than me, aiming to arrive in Athens by the end of September before he returned to University in October. Over a pint of Guinness, he revealed that it was his 21st birthday. It would have been rude not to help him celebrate, so we indulged in a couple more. Drinking with someone half your age is never a great idea at the best of times, let alone only a couple of hours after having completed a long cycle journey. My yawns, initially suppressed, seemed a little more frequent than his so after the third pint I suggested we call it a day. He had arranged to meet others from his hostel and I hope he ended his night of celebrations in suitable fashion. As he went off in one direction to find his roommates, I wandered back down the *Gran Via,* pausing only to buy some chocolate in a small shop that sold little else of calorific value. I was feeling tired, very tired. Was that just today? I was beginning to sense that it wasn't and that finally, cumulative fatigue was beginning to catch up with me. Perhaps overcoming that challenge in the final few days of the cycle might be the biggest hill I had yet attempted to climb.

Friday 16ᵗʰ August 2013
Cycling Day 39: Barcelona To Tarragona, 93km

The *Hotel Granvia*, although not quite as upmarket as the first hotel I had attempted to check into further along the street, was still very 'boutique', with an abundance of ornate, white plasterwork, brown sheets on the bed ('boutique' places never seem to opt for plain old white), a mirrored lift that afforded clear views of every bodily imperfection (especially those covered in stretched lycra) and at least one large, flat screen television visible at all times. All these 'comforts' were, however, reserved for just the humans. Reggie had spent the night in a narrow store room near the reception desk where the interior designer had clearly feared to tread; it's plasterwork was decidedly shabby and stained and his sleeping partners had been a selection of old, cracked mirrors and a small collection of discarded electrical equipment. Access to the store cupboard was via a spiral staircase and carrying Reggie back up into the foyer area without any of his greased parts coming into contact with pristine, white plaster was a little like the game which requires the player to move a coil along a twisting piece of metal without the buzzer going off. The receptionist watched me, I perspired a little under the strain of the bike's weight, but there was no buzz.

I made my way into the heart of the old town and found a café serving breakfast, in a large square near the cathedral. It was a return to more continental tastes and consisted of orange juice, coffee, a couple of triangles of toast and a croissant. I opened up the map of north-eastern Spain and followed my route from Barcelona to Valencia. It seemed an extremely long way – I estimated perhaps 300 to 400km – and that would equate to a minimum of three days of cycling, perhaps four if the fatigue that I had been feeling when drinking with Lewis the night before was indeed long term. From what I could see on the map, there were only a couple of large towns between the two regional capitals: Tarragona in Catalonia and then Castello de la Plana in the region of Valencia. Tarragona would be a good destination for the first night of the three-day trek, but it would be a challenge to get as far as Castello de la Plana for the second night. Not that this would really be an issue, as the coastline was dotted with many campsites, even if they weren't really there to cater for a lone cyclist staying for just one night.

Linking all the coastal towns – large and small – was a motorway. This was good news, as hopefully much of the heavy traffic would choose to speed its way south on that road rather than the main road I would be following. I could also see that, at times, there was a secondary road running close to the water and I would keep my eyes peeled for opportunities to branch away from its big brother and make the most of what it had to offer, which I hoped would be fewer cars and better views. Before those joys however, was the not insignificant matter of escaping from Barcelona itself. Would it be another long, stop-start-stop-start traffic light challenge? Well, yes, it would. The previous evening, Lewis – who was travelling in the opposite direction to me of course – had explained that he had been advised to take the train through the southern suburbs of Barcelona and that's exactly what he had done. Following my experiences of the northern suburbs, it wasn't difficult to see why the advice had been given. But, after well over 4,000km of tracing a continuous line of cycling since my departure from Cape Sounio in Greece, there was no way I was going to allow a mere suburb to prevent me from continuing to do so. The River Llobregat appeared to be the main hurdle as the two crossings closest to the city centre were both motorways. Further to the west, however, was the non-motorway C-245. I would aim for this and hope for the best.

It was a long, straight climb out of Barcelona, passing through one set of traffic lights after another, although the repetitive 100m by 100m blocks of 19th century urban planning did stop after only a couple of kilometres, making the distances between red lights a little more irregular. Just after the *Camp Nou* football stadium, the road opened up somewhat to accommodate not just tramlines heading in both directions but occasionally a cycle path, which was segregated from the road. If nothing else, it reassured me that I wasn't the first person to ever consider cycling south out of the Catalonian capital. After nearly 10km, a sharp left turn at a large roundabout ensured that I was not only once again travelling south but also that I had found the C-245. It was also a nice mid-morning bonus to be able to freewheel downhill as the road headed off in the direction of the coast. When I did eventually cross the River Llobregat, it was a merely a meandering narrow body of water, rather than the great navigable waterway I had imagined it to be. I dare say that should I have wanted to (and I didn't), I could have waded through the water like an American Marine, with Reggie hoist high above my head, just as I had done while ascending the spiral staircase earlier in the day. The panniers would have caused all kinds of issues, however, so it's no bad thing that such exploits are left to the military. It's also one of the reasons, perhaps, why countries don't equip their soldiers with bicycles. I digress. Back to Barcelona and my quest to cycle to... Well, where *was* I going? Tarragona was a very tentative destination; it was a big town on my map and happened to be at a distance roughly 100km from Barcelona, but I was eager to get back to the simplicities of a night in the tent. By aiming for the centre of Tarragona, I suspected that it was highly likely I would be tempted once again to reach for my mobile phone and book a night in a hotel. I wanted to avoid that if possible, but knowing how weak-willed I had become with regards to accommodation in recent weeks, the best way not to end up in a hotel, was to find and aim for a campsite. A well-timed text message from my cousin Richard was to come to my assistance.

If you were paying attention when I was cycling through Croatia, you will remember that Richard had been in touch about a campsite on the island of Pag. I never actually made it to his recommended site, opting instead for the 'clothing optional' (or so it seemed at the time) *Camp Sveti Duh.* I subsequently became ill and I began to fall out of love with many things Croatian... Perhaps this time, I should just stick to his advice. It wasn't a campsite he had visited himself, but one that had received a very good write-up in *The Guardian* newspaper. It was called *Camping Trillas* and it was handily located just to the north of Tarragona, so I would be kept well away from the temptations of booking into a hotel in the town centre. Despite the fact that I couldn't get out of my mind images of left-leaning Guardian readers, wearing kaftans with elbow patches (is that possible?), smoking rollies while leafing through old copies of *Down and Out in Paris and London* or *Das Kapital*, I was willing to give it a go. It's perhaps worth pointing out that I am an occasional Guardian reader, don't own a kaftan (with or without elbow patches), don't smoke rollies and haven't read *Das Kapital*. That said, stereotypes are, alas, an easy gag and this one did have me smiling as I cycled south out of Barcelona. (I have read George Orwell's *Down and Out in Paris and London* incidentally, but it was a long time ago, which is probably why I'm only an *occasional* reader of *The Guardian*...)

So, it could be lentils for dinner (shut up!) if I did indeed manage to find *Camping Trillas.* Such exotic foods were a million miles away from the C-245, which was yet another coastal road trying its best to become a motorway, but I persevered (and survived) to be able to cycle through the drab streets of Castelldefels, where I didn't stop hoping for more amiable cycling, along the twists and turns of the corniche road between Castelldefels and Sitges. Alas, it wasn't quite what I was expecting. Although the views were probably equal to those I had experienced on the previous day to the south of Palamós, the nature of the road itself didn't make it easy to enjoy them. It was narrow and busy, and on the left-hand edge – the opposite side of the road to me and the side nearest the sea of course – was a continuous waist-high, concrete barrier. This was obviously great for stopping cars, should the driver experience a momentary lapse of judgement and fancy becoming a little better acquainted with the Mediterranean Sea than he or she wanted, but it was also equally effective in blocking my view. So twisting and turning was the route, that it was rarely possible to see more than just a few tens of metres ahead, so any decision to stop the bike, venture over to the other side of the road and peer over the barrier could quite easily become one that you might live (or perhaps not live) to regret. For much of the time, I had to content myself with a good view of the road, the craggy hill to my right and the blue sky, the sea having been hidden behind the long strip of vertical, white concrete.

I had been told by a Twitter contact that Sitges was a delightful town and I am sure it was, but as with many places along this stretch of coastline where I was keen to make as much progress as possible in as short a period of time as was practicable, I didn't venture off the main road, which was a little way back from the seafront. My reaction to the town was somewhat dismissive but this was, on reflection, far from a fair judgement. I would hate for the places that I know well and that are close to *my* heart to be judged in such a scant way. Sitges was still only halfway to *Camping Trillas,* so I didn't stop, apart from a pause of just a few moments on the outskirts of the town to drink some water and to take a photograph of an abandoned villa which had been extensively and colourfully covered in graffiti. It summed up in one picture what I thought about the town: unkempt and unloved. Perhaps I was simply willing myself to believe that this was indeed the case and, having found the 'proof', I felt compelled to record the fact in a photograph. To Sitges and to all the other towns and villages in this part of Spain, where I couldn't afford to take more than a cursory glance and come to some rather cursory conclusions, I most sincerely apologise.

Vilanova i la Geltru gave the same impression as its northern neighbour: urban, drab, uninteresting. Had I taken the time to venture into its port area, I have no doubt that I would have been proven wrong, but I didn't, and continued on regardless, with my wildly inaccurate assumptions intact. Shortly after Vilanova i la Geltru, I joined the C-31, a road that I slavishly followed for the remainder of the day, despite the fact that this involved some not insignificant detours away from the coast. What was I doing? Was the remainder of my time in Spain going to be spent sacrificing most of the pleasures of travelling just so that I would be in with a shot of actually arriving at my destination? Had distance travelled become my main objective? Was I really so desperate to say that I had cycled from one corner of the continent to another? It had been a good day of cycling (93km was respectable, if not spectacular) but it had been a dreadful day of travelling. Would this continue for another ten days?

The appearance of a sign directing me towards *Camping Trillas* and its pitches packed to the rafters with Guardian readers (perhaps), dragged me out of my melancholic soliloquy and back into the real-world practicalities of finding somewhere to sleep. At some point, the C-31 had upgraded itself to the N-340 and was about to be promoted once again to the A-7. The sign for *Camping Trillas* had been well-placed and I narrowly escaped having to re-plan my end of day route. I climbed the short slip road leading off the N-340 to a roundabout, only to notice a sign on the other side of the roundabout, next to the road leading back onto the road that I had just left, informing me that I was no longer welcome. It had been a narrow escape. The signs for the campsite guided me over the railway tracks and along some back roads, before I was deposited in front of the reception building of *Camping Trillas Platja Tamarit*.

It was a busy place with no obvious Guardian readers to be seen. I waited my turn in the short queue at reception before I got my chance to be served.

"*Sorry, do you speak English?*" was my opening line.

"*Yes, of course I do,*" replied the young guy serving me. His accent was not Spanish, yet a little exotic. I was initially thrown as to where he was from, so I asked him.

"*Are you Spanish?*"

"*No, I'm originally from Newcastle...*" at which point I was able to place the exact exoticness of his accent.

After the formalities, I told him that the campsite had received a glowing recommendation from *The Guardian*. He seemed puzzled and suggested that I might have got the wrong campsite. I later checked and I hadn't. Perhaps the article, which had only been published a week or so earlier, had yet to have the desired effect in attracting the centre-left, chattering classes of Britain in the direction of *Camping Trillas*.

"*Do you sell kaftans in the campsite supermarket?*" I didn't ask.

315

My pitch wasn't the greatest plot of land on the campsite. In fact, it might have been the worst. It was what I had feared would happen on sites like this, which catered for much larger parties staying for much longer periods. The pitch was small, narrow and next to the path leading to the beach but it was big enough for Reggie, the tent and me. Much of the evening was spent strolling around trying to look inconspicuous. I was probably the only single person on that campsite that night and it made me feel a little uncomfortable. In a rural campsite, I would have been fine. In a city centre hotel, I would have been fine. On a coastal campsite, full of families and children, I didn't feel fine. As the sun went down, having failed in my attempt to locate a discarded chair or borrow one from a neighbour, I hid in the tent eating the bread and cheese I had bought in the campsite supermarket, where there was not a kaftan to be seen.

It was Friday night and it hadn't been an enjoyable day in the saddle. However, it looked as though I would just have to resign myself to two more days of the same kind of travelling before I arrived in Valencia on the Sunday evening, from where I could look forward to moving away from the coast on my cross-country trek towards Seville. My mood was low, but I focussed upon the following week rather than the upcoming weekend. What I really needed was a book to read which put everything into perspective; the story of a man, travelling alone from city to city (London and Paris for example), living rough and doing menial jobs to survive. That would make me feel a little happier about my own temporary lot in life. There's never a Guardian reader around with a good collection of George Orwell books when you need one...

Outside the tent, children were screaming, egged on by the parents (or so it appeared from the confines of my windowless tent and from the perspective of a non-speaker of Spanish). The racket continued until midnight, when peace descended upon *Camping Trillas*, momentarily. Within a few minutes of the children being silenced, loud music started playing and continued until around 2am. This really wasn't my kind of campsite.

Saturday 17th August 2013
Cycling Day 40: Tarragona To...

When I emerged from the tent at 7am, after a night of only brief spells of sleep, I stretched in a way that would have any onlookers worried that I might be in the early stages of metamorphosis into The Incredible Hulk. I even gave out a few sounds that would have confirmed their suspicions. Mercifully, with no other campers around to see me, I was saved the indignity of any strange looks. My body ached from a combination of long-term and short-term fatigue, but the stretching did have the desired effect of ironing out some of the more nagging body pains, at least temporarily. I wanted to find evidence of where the annoying children who had kept me awake until midnight were sleeping, but looked around in vain. Toys were strewn on several nearby pitches, but the parents had inadvertently forgotten to put up the sign stating *'the screaming kids you are looking for are in here; please feel free to come over and berate them in a way that we are incapable of doing through our own lack of parenting skills'.* I did look for it.

I packed quickly and by 8am was outside the campsite reception, wondering what the day would bring forth. Before having emerged from the tent, I had consulted the Warm Showers website to see if there were any potential hosts who might be willing to accommodate me, either in Valencia on the Sunday evening or somewhere halfway between *Camping Trillas* and Valencia for that evening, Saturday. I noticed that the distance between where I was standing and the hosts in Valencia was 235km. That was, of course, as-the-crow-flies but when I looked at the map, my route along the coast was a very straight one and had I been a crow, I would have flown more or less along the route that I was intending to cycle. My plan was to continue to follow the N-340 road along which I had been cycling for much of the previous day and which had few twists and turns, so I reckoned that a distance of around 240km to Valencia was a reasonable estimation. Over two days, that would be fine: 120km today, 120km tomorrow. I would cycle the first of those 120km and then look for accommodation. This would be around the area of a coastal town called Peniscola and there were no Warm Showers people listed as living along that section of my route so it would probably be a campsite. There were, however, lots of potential hosts in Valencia. I had a basic plan for the weekend.

I paid the bill when the reception opened at 8am. €22 for the pleasure of being kept awake until 2am seemed a little excessive but in

317

true British style I paid up and, when asked if I had had a nice stay, I lied through my teeth, explaining that everything had been "*perfect... gracias*". With the formalities completed and with only a modicum of enthusiasm, I set off for a weekend of what I fully expected to be cycling drudgery.

Breakfast was in Tarragona, just 10km south of *Camping Trillas*. Having found a small over-the-counter food outlet on the main street into the town, I ordered a couple of pastries filled with a thick, dark meat of some description. They would, I thought, help sustain me through the long ride ahead. Outside the shop, I plunged one of the pastries into my mouth and was a little taken aback; it wasn't meat that I was tasting, it was a rich, dark chocolate. The expectation of savoury and the delivery of sweet was a pleasure in itself and I continued to devour the delicious, calorie-filled snacks with even more gusto than I would have done if they had been what I was expecting. The short experience put a smile back on my face as well as, no doubt, a number of large, brown smudges.

The screaming kids were now well behind me and on the long, straight, flat and surprisingly quiet road I was making good progress. In fact, by 10:30am I had already clocked up some 50km. On a 'normal' day of cycling (if indeed one of those had ever existed), this was a distance that was usually achieved at around lunchtime and I would be considering my options for places to take an extended middle-of-the-day pause and perhaps even a little snooze. It made me wonder, should I be able to maintain the same level of progress, how far I would have travelled by 1pm. When 1pm arrived, I had already travelled just over 100km. I couldn't remember ever having done that before. Indeed, the only day previously when I had been a little taken aback by how far I had cycled in one morning, was back in Croatia. It had been cycling day 19 and as I ate my lunch under the awning of a small supermarket just outside the town of Posedarje I had been delighted that I had already cycled 70km. Such was the exceptional nature of my cycling progress that day, that it had stuck in my mind ever since and had never been surpassed. Until now of course. Over 100km, in just five hours since leaving the reception building of *Camping Trillas*. 50km every two and a half hours, 25km every hour and a quarter. Although most of my distance and time keeping was via the cycling app on my phone, I was also using a small CatEye computer as a back up. It was usually much easier to refer to the CatEye than the app, as it didn't require me to stop, unlock it and then find an angle at which I could actually read the screen in the bright sunlight, which was the case with the phone. When I scrolled through the various statistics on the cycling computer, it confirmed that of the five hours since leaving the campsite, four had been spent moving on the bike and that my average was just over 25km/hr. That was good going! The remaining hour, incidentally, was made up of my breakfast pause, various drink stops and a good number of traffic light halts back in Tarragona.

Enthused by this personal best performance, I chose not to stop for lunch, opting instead to continue grazing when the verdant pastures of a roadside shop or, more often than not, a petrol station appeared. I started to pay much more attention to the distance signs that I was passing; the first one I came to after having realised what astonishing progress I was making, told me that Valencia was 170km away and that I would find Castello (which was now looking a more likely candidate as a place to stop overnight instead of Peniscola) after another 100km. The statistics of possible distances that I could cycle in what remained of the day bounced around my mind like a ping-pong ball on concrete. I should be hitting 150km by 3:30pm and, if I chose to continue, 200km by 6pm. I smiled at the ridiculous nature of such distances being achieved and began to spend just as much time wondering when I would succumb to tiredness and either drag myself into a roadside campsite or reach for my phone and book a hotel room in the next town. Clearly, I would never make it as far as Valencia in just one day of cycling, but where *would* I end up?

It was good to have something to think about, as the area through which I was travelling was far from inspiring. It was turning out to be very much a continuation of what I had experienced for large chuncks of the previous day. For most of the time, the N-340 was keeping me well away from the coast and, when I glanced to my left across several hundred metres of either scrubland or farmers' fields, all I could see was one long line of urban sprawl by the sea. It didn't look in the least bit appealing. From a distance, most things do look much better than when you get up close and personal. (Me in black lycra for example.) Have you ever seen anything or anywhere filmed from a helicopter that doesn't look gorgeous? Back in the 1980s, didn't Britain look like a seamless carpet of beauty from Anneka Rice's seat in the helicopter on 'stop the clock!' Treasure Hunt? Not convinced? How about France when the helicopter lingers over the riders of the *Tour de France*? Undoubtedly France is a very attractive country but not everything matches the pristine beauty of the Tuileries Gardens in Paris. It does from those *Tour de France* helicopters. I would challenge anyone to find the concrete strip of apartment blocks and hotels along the coast between Tarragona and Valencia in any way beautiful, from any distance or from any angle, apart, that is, from a distance where they are no longer visible. They looked horrid from a distance; I had no reason to believe that up close they were any better.

Seeing the sea might have had the effect of softening the hard edge to the monotonous man-made blight along the coast but I wasn't able to spot it very often. I would have to trust the cartographers at Michelin who, via their map, informed me that the Mediterranean was indeed where I assumed it was. To my right, the views were a little more pleasant, since for much of the time mountains could be seen climbing towards the plateau that is central Spain. They reminded me of my decision to turn my back on coastal Spain and to head inland in order to complete the journey to Cape St. Vincent in Portugal. I just needed to get to Valencia first and then head west.

With a reduced amount of time spent stopping, I not only maintained but started to build upon my already excellent progress. I pledged that, should I be able to reach the 200km point before 5pm – probably somewhere around Castello de la Plana – I would continue all the way to Valencia and treat myself with a day off in a city of which I had heard many good things but had never had the opportunity to visit. It still seemed a bit fanciful however until the clocks of this Spanish *costa* struck five and my CatEye cycling computer recorded a distance of 201.5km. This was crazy!

Of the 21 stages of the 2013 *Tour de France*, only six had required the cyclists to cycle over 200km in one day. Now let's not get carried away here. Chris Froome et al were cycling their stages at speeds of around (sometimes well in excess of) 40km/hr. I was 'just' pootling along at around 25km/hr. Indeed, when Chris Froome completed the longest stage of the race, from Givors to the summit of *Mont Ventoux*, a distance of some 242.5km, which included four rated climbs in addition to the final one, he did so by averaging 41.7km/hr. That's impressive stuff! I was cycling along probably the longest, continuously flat section of the entire ride from Greece to Portugal. It does put my own efforts into perspective. But cycling as far as Valencia would stretch my distance to potentially over 270km (or 170 miles). That would be significantly more than the professional slackers of the *Tour de France*! Goodness. Was that really a possibility? It would be the equivalent of cycling from London to Sheffield along the M1 in one day, but I had already arrived in Nottingham, kind of. At least I wasn't having to put up with all those road works around Leicester. (There are always road works around Leicester on the M1, or so it seems.)

It did seem that cycling all the way to Valencia was now a real possibility. I couldn't (and wouldn't) be stupid by straining myself to the point of it becoming dangerous for me to continue, but I felt generally OK. Tired, yes, but not 'bonkingly' tired. My mental resolve to get this whole unappealing section of the trip done and dusted seemed to be countering the arguments telling me I really should call it a day. A case of mind over matter if ever there was one. The final sign that I had made the decision to cycle as far as Valencia would come at the point where I stopped cycling, to ensure that I had secured some accommodation in the city. That moment arrived at around 5:30pm, only half an hour or so after having realised that reaching Valencia was no longer just a possibility but now a real probability. I had thought about the arguments carefully and had come to the conclusion that not to continue all the way to Valencia would no longer be a wise decision, as it would all but eliminate my chances of getting a good day of rest off the bike. Bearing in mind that on the previous 'rest day' I had actually climbed *Mont Ventoux,* the last opportunity I had had to do nothing but wander, snap a few pictures and generally relax had been way back in Nice on the 5th August. It was now the 17th August and I did need to take time out to recuperate and plan for the final push to the finishing line. I pulled out my phone, logged on to Booking.com and found a nice hotel in the centre of Valencia with 'Botanic' in the title. If a hotel has 'Botanic' in its name, it must be a place of ultimate natural relaxation. The booking procedure over, I found a position on the saddle that was comfortable – not easy to do after over 200km and nine hours of sitting on the same thing – and set off for Valencia!

The terrain was just as helpfully flat as it had been all day, but over the course of the next few hours, fatigue did become a factor in my ability to maintain the progress that I had been making up to that point. My average speed dipped somewhat, to well below 20km/hr. I still had another four hours of cycling ahead of me, perhaps longer if my speed were to drop further, but as I no longer had a choice, I continued.

It was almost inevitable that as we got nearer to the greater urban area of Valencia, the road, yes, our dear friend the N-340, ejected Reggie and me. It was just after the town of Sagunt and not wanting to get lost at this late stage of the day, I called upon the directional skills of Google Maps to help me fathom a way into the centre of the city. Curiously, this initially sent me on a 2km trek along the service roads needed to tend to the orange plantations north of Valencia, which, if nothing else was an interesting diversion (probably the first of the day). It did, however, do the job it was designed for and before long, I was once again cycling along... the N-340. The road's foray into the world of motorways had clearly not been a rewarding one and it had reverted back to being a simple single carriageway road. The N-340 just didn't have '*autovia*' in its DNA.

I had thought that 8pm would be my arrival time in the city centre but, yet again, the suburbs of a big city took their toll and traffic light after traffic light (and one level crossing) held me back. By this point, I was now chomping at the bit and simply wanted to eat, drink and be happy in a comfortable hotel bedroom. I paused for some water and to check on progress but when I looked at the screen of my phone I noticed a missed call. Another minor disaster at my flat back in the UK? Please no... The number was prefixed by '34', the international code for Spain and I called them back. It was the *Hotel Jardin Botanico*.

"*Señor Sykes?*"

"*Yes...*"

"*There is a problem with the air conditioning in your room...*"

I didn't believe a word of it. I had, alas, made a sufficient number of these bookings to have worked out the system. Reservation is made online, email is sent to the hotel, room is confirmed, email is sent to customer. But usually, the final confirmation email arrives within seconds of the booking having been made, implying that no double-checking has taken place. On a number of occasions, I had arrived at a hotel only for the person on reception to go looking for the email: "*Ah yes, here it is!*"

To their credit, the *Hotel Jardin Botanico*, where I had been genuinely looking forward to staying as the online pictures depicted as oasis of calm and relaxation, had made a booking on my behalf at an alternative, city-centre '*luxury*' hotel and they were going to pick up the tab. The man on the phone started to list the facilities:

"*Restaurant, fitness centre, free wi-fi, car hire[!], laundry, babysitting[!!], bar, bicycle hire[!!!]...*"

"*OK! Yes, that's fine...*"

I would reserve my judgement as to whether it was indeed '*luxury*' until my arrival.

By the time I had cycled 270km, I was still some way from the city centre, it was past 9pm and it was getting dark. I reached for my lights, clicked them into position and turned them on. The directions, courtesy of my phone, were doing the hard work of making sure that I was taking the correct roads; I was more or less at the point where I would have followed directions into the sea. After many left and right turns, I crossed the *Pont d'Arago,* over a river that is no longer a river (more of that later) and to the doors of the *Hotel Dimar.* It looked OK, even though it lacked the soothing vegetation of the *Hotel Jardin Botanico.*

I smiled with relief and with delight. On most occasions over the previous seven weeks of cycling, when I arrived at my final destination I was happy to leave the statistics to later in the day. Outside the hotel in Valencia, other matters could wait. The statistics told the story of what had been an epic day in the saddle, by far the longest distance I had ever travelled in one day, on two wheels, in my life:

Cycling Day 40:	Tarragona To Valencia
Started:	August 17, 2013, 7:59 AM
Ride Time:	11 hours, 14 minutes, 33 seconds
Stopped Time:	2 hours, 6 minutes, 10 seconds
Arrived:	August 17, 2013, 9:19 PM
Average speed:	24.78 km/hr (15.40 miles/hr)
Distance:	278.54 km (173.08 miles)

(That's just after junction 37 on the M1 by the way, the turn off for Barnsley.)

Sunday 18th August 2013
Rest Day 9: Valencia

If this makes sense, Valencia was always part of the route but never really part of the plan. It was a city that I had certainly been looking forward to visiting but up until only the day before I arrived, I had imagined it would be a case of a quick cycling tour of the place before moving on. This is what I had done in Verona and then in Nîmes, and I had regretted not being able to see more. Finally, circumstances were working in my favour and, courtesy of my epic day of cycling to get there, I had the opportunity to explore an unknown city for an entire day.

I knew little about Valencia before my arrival. It was a name that conjured up images of fashion, style, motor racing and in the back of my mind, I was aware of some spectacular, modern architecture. But that was about it. After breakfast at the hotel, I wandered out onto the street clutching the map of Valencia that the reception had provided. The *Hotel Dimar* had been ringed and it was conveniently located about halfway between the old, historic centre of Valencia to the north and the collection of ultra-modern buildings that made up the *City of Arts and Sciences* to the south. It was my intention to explore both areas, but being the sucker that I am for old, historic city centres, I initially headed north. It also seemed somehow 'correct' to start with the old and to finish with the new; I hoped that the former would put the latter into some sort of context.

Having neatly categorised Valencia into 'old' and 'new', it was slightly ironic that one of the first places I stumbled upon – the *Mercado Colón* – appeared to have fused the two into one sublime building. Perhaps the terms 'old' and 'new' weren't the best ones to use when discussing architecture but then again, this is a book about cycling, not architecture, so I reserve the right to continue using them if need be. The *Mercado Colón* (or Columbus Market in English) was only a couple of blocks away from the hotel but still outside the historic centre, and dated back to the early 20th century, hosting its first market on Christmas Eve in 1916. It wasn't an enormous building – perhaps 50m wide and 70m long – but, as markets go, it was an elegant one, consisting of a roof supported by a delicate structure of metal columns, and two red brick entrances that were detailed with the produce that the market once sold and a colourful, intricate mosaic depicting various figures picking oranges and grapes. Inside there wasn't a barrow boy to be seen nor a man shouting *'three apples for a euro'* to be heard. This was a market that had most definitely moved itself into the 21ˢᵗ century world of 'leisure', with small cafés, bars, boutiques and even a florist having opened up to replace the more traditional sellers of fruit and veg who, by the time the building was beautifully renovated in 2003, had voted with their feet and shut up shop anyway. Below the modern concourse of the market, several levels had been dug out, although the lower three of these were functioning simply as an invisible multi-storey car park, leaving just the one subterranean level for more shops and a few offices. Most of the cafés and bars were open but one thing *was* missing: people. There weren't very many of them around, which, although making for a wonderfully peaceful (and air-conditioned) environment for me and the other Sunday morning strollers, detracted a little from the atmosphere of what a market should be. It was a minor complaint to say the least and it did mean that when I sat down to order a coffee, I was attended to within just a few seconds. It also meant that there was little to distract me from the job of reading up on the city I was about to explore. So what did I learn?

Well, that Valencia – which is Spain's third-largest city - is going through a period of reinvention (I had discovered that for myself already) and is now, in some ways, starting to eclipse its two cultural big brothers of Barcelona and Madrid. It was a city that had been ruled by the Romans, Visigoths and Moors before *Jaime el Conquistador,* the King of Aragon, came along and took over. Much more recently the 32ⁿᵈ and 33ʳᵈ America's Cup events were hosted in Valencia, in 2007 and 2010 respectively and from 2008 to 2012, the streets of the city were home to one round of the *Formula 1 Grand Prix* season. There you have it: the history of a city in one short paragraph. It was time to move on and explore.

The regimented grid pattern of the streets stopped abruptly just one block beyond the *Mercado Colón,* which made for a more interesting and varied cityscape but also made aimless strolling (on which I am something of an expert) a sure-fire way of getting lost. But, as there is no better way to really get under the skin of a big city than getting lost, I was happy for that to be the case. Closer to the centre there was much more human activity than there had been at the market. It was now Sunday lunchtime, so the non-believers had been joined by those who had just come from their weekly pilgrimage to the local churches or the cathedral. The focal point of the old town seemed to be the *Plaza de la Reina,* with at one end a jumble of buildings that together made up one side of the cathedral. On the southern end of the square, tucked round the corner but still clearly visible above the other buildings, were the five storeys of the tower attached to the *Santa Catalina* church. Up until this point, the traffic had become increasingly heavy and the large square – which hadn't been pedestrianised – was an obstacle course of cars, buses, taxis and the occasional bicycle. In the warren of streets to the west of the tower, however, most vehicles had been banished and it was much easier to appreciate the beauty of the buildings, squares, monuments and people. The Spaniards, just like their Mediterranean cousins the Italians, are a beautiful bunch and there were hectares of bronzed skin on display. Despite the weeks of travelling under the Mediterranean sun, my own bronzed skin was yet to appear, having chosen instead to stick resolutely with the reddy-orange look. It also ended at strategic points on my body where my cycling clothing had blocked the passage of the sun's rays. This was not a problem but it did mean that whenever I found myself not cycling, I did feel obliged to wear t-shirts and shorts that extended sufficiently to cover the white skin that had yet to be exposed to the light. I did, however, dread the moment back at home when I decided to go swimming for the first time and my body would be exposed for all to see. Perhaps some kind of modesty-guaranteeing, Edwardian bathing costume might be appropriate.

An open-air bric-a-brac market was taking place in the streets around the closed, covered *Mercado Central*. It would have been nice to get a look inside because, unlike its swish little sister that I had visited earlier in the day, this was a market that still sold fruit and veg. Its exterior was just as colourful and ornate but I would have to console myself with a wander around the stalls in the street selling coins, medals, postcards and old books.

For a time, I did get lost amongst the backstreets and spent a good amount of time admiring the graffiti, the crumbling shop fronts of abandoned buildings, the tiled, hand-painted signs and the occasional, haloed statue perched on top of the many small churches. I was able to regain my bearings when I stumbled into the large *Plaza de la Virgen*, which, apart from accommodating a second side to the cathedral, was home to a large, reclining bronze of a naked, curly-haired man eating grapes. *Was he waiting for his virgin? Was he the virgin? Who knows? Who cares?* The numerous white pigeons didn't seem that bothered. Many of them had taken up a lofty position upon one of his bodily extremities – his head, his raised knee, his bunch of grapes (not a euphemism) – and were using his muscled body as a place upon which to crap.

This was turning into a thoroughly relaxing day. The sun was beating down, I was in no rush to do anything in a manner that was in the least bit earnest and I still had the smile on my face from having cycled all the way from London to Barnsley the previous day. More coffee ensued and I used the opportunity of sitting in a café with descent wi-fi to catch up on writing up my notes recounting the tale of my epic ride. Once done, my focus turned to the modern side of Valencia and *La Ciudad de la Artes y les Ciencias* which would be my destination for the late afternoon.

It was a walk of a couple of kilometres alongside what used to be the bed of the *Rio Turia* to *The City of Arts and Sciences*. The river was diverted away from the centre of the city following devastating floods in the 1950s, but apart from the water, all the other infrastructure remains: the banks, the bridges, the distinctive meandering band on my map now coloured green, indicating that much of the land is landscaped gardens. It's not a bad idea when you think about it. Let's put to one side the useful aspects of having a major river running through your town or city and focus upon replacing it with something else. Here in Valencia, it had, in the main, been turned into a band of open space with parks, a few swimming pools, a running track, cycle paths and, of course, the *The City of Arts and Sciences*. Imagine a city like London suddenly having that amount of green space to play with. You'd have to make sure that the speculators didn't move in, buy up the precious land and build flats on it (and goodness knows what the residents of Oxfordshire and Berkshire would do with all their water), but in principle it's not a bad idea. In Valencia, it became reality and the residents of the city have been benefiting ever since.

The cluster of modern buildings that make up *The City of Arts and Sciences* are primarily the work of local architect, Santiago Calatrava and to say that they are eye-catching would be an understatement of some proportions. They are nothing like anything that surrounds them, predominantly bleached white and surrounded by shallow pools of water. I do like a good quality, modern building that nods to its older neighbours in recognition of their longevity but that doesn't stick two fingers in their direction saying, well, whatever you interpret two fingers as saying. My immediate impression of what I could see as I approached the first of the buildings – the *Palacio de les Arts Reina Sofia* (the Queen Sofia Concert Hall to me and you) – was that these buildings were doing just that. Don't get me wrong, the architecture was simply stunning and I marvelled at how, exactly, such a construction had been assembled. The tapering thin roof was suspended above the main body of the building with support at just one end. *How is it possible to build such a thing?* There was something of Darth Vader about the building (or was it a fish with an open mouth?), but was it aesthetically 'beautiful'? I suppose that depends how you define 'beautiful'. I was troubled that I couldn't make up my mind. My guidebook effused about the place but, in fairness, they were focusing upon what went on inside rather than how it looked from the outside. I never had the chance to witness anything remotely cultural, just the stark lines, curves and monotone colour of the exterior.

I moved on to building number two, the *Museo de las Ciencias Principe Felipe*. It looked as though each member of the Spanish royal household had their own construction. This was a little more to my liking, although it did resemble an airport terminal from the 1970s. Not that I ever went to an airport terminal in the 1970s but you know what I mean. It was a long ribcage of a building housing the city's Science Museum. The structure was essentially the same supporting arm repeated twenty or so times but it had an elongated symmetry that was pleasing to the eye and its squat physique was a little less '*in your face*' than the building dedicated to Felipe's mother had been. I could also imagine it might be a building that would be pulled down in, say, 2050 to make way for something even more grand. I liked the self-deprecating acknowledgement that perhaps it wasn't the best thing to hit the architectural world since the Romans had invented concrete. I couldn't imagine that the *Palacio de les Arts Reina Sofia* would ever be demolished voluntarily. It would take some kind of cataclysmic military action to remove it from its pedestal in the gallery of modern Spanish architecture. The Science Museum was, unlike the Concert Hall, open to the public and I was able to wander through the building although I didn't have time to explore the exhibits. Just as the *Mercado Colón* had been earlier, it was strangely lacking in people.

Neither did I have the time (or indeed the energy) to continue as far as the *Parque Oceanografico* but I did, from a distance, admire the Agora, a more recent addition to *The City of Arts and Sciences*. In contrast to many of the other buildings, its sides were deep marine-blue, and behind the thick suspension wires of the *Pont l'Assut de l'Or*, it looked stunning.

I started to make my way back to the hotel and in doing so, I noticed a young couple who had removed their shoes and had waded into one of the shallow pools surrounding the ultra-modern buildings. They were smiling and holding up their cameras to take a selfie. It struck me as one of the first things that I had seen since arriving at *The City of Arts and Sciences* that encapsulated 'life'. No sooner had this thought entered my mind than a small buggy appeared on the scene and a uniformed official jumped from the cab wagging his finger. I couldn't hear what was said and even if I had, it would have made no sense to me, but the result was that the couple put down their cameras and removed themselves from the shallow pool. It then dawned on me what the problem was: this was a place devoid of energy, laughter, noise, movement, imperfection, irregularity, asymmetry... Everything that makes us human had been clinically removed and that is why, compared to the hustle and bustle of the old part of Valencia, I wasn't a fan. Beauty, unlike my cycling tan lines, is more than skin deep.

Back in my hotel room, I moved all the furniture to one side to create enough space to lay out my three remaining maps, covering the final part of the route from Valencia to Cape St. Vincent. It was now Sunday. I would aim to get as far as Albacete by the end of Tuesday, from where I would pick up the first of the *Vias Verdes* and cycle as far as Peñascosa. It would be back on the roads as far as Jaen, where the second of the *Vias Verdes* started. At some point, I was hoping to be joined by my cousin Richard, who was en route from Britain back to his home in Portugal, but it was still a little uncertain as to where that would be. From past experience, that uncertainty would no doubt remain until the very last minute so, knowing his penchant for procrastination I wouldn't be making any plans which were dependent upon him being at a particular place at a particular time. The town of Lucena would be a good one to aim for by the weekend, leaving a couple of days cycling to get as far as Seville. By that point I would nearly be in Portugal but crossing the border may be an issue; Google Maps was giving me the impression that to cross the *Rio Guadiana* – the border between Spain and Portugal - I would need to deviate some way north to find a non-motorway route. That could be a problem. Once in Portugal, via an overnight stop in Faro, I would be almost there. The finish line was close but I still needed to cross most of Spain and all of Portugal. It wasn't yet a done deal; plenty more cycling beckoned.

Monday 19th August 2013
Cycling Day 41: Valencia To Cofrentes, 106km

About 80km due west of Valencia, there were a couple of elongated reservoirs and my map reading of the previous evening had indicated that there were some campsites a few kilometres further inland, one at a place called Casa de Ves and another at Jarafuel. I would head in the direction of the reservoirs and then make a decision later in the day as to which of the two camping choices to go for. Escaping Valencia was very reminiscent of leaving Barcelona a few days previously, albeit without the slight gradient on the road. I cycled past countless apartment blocks until I crossed a river, after which the urban sprawl of the costal fringe started to fade away rapidly. The CV-405 heading off in the direction of a town called Montserrat was a pencil-thin white road on my map but, in reality, it was a busy dual carriageway for the first 10km before downgrading itself to an even busier single carriageway in the middle of a town called Torrent. As I had done for much of the time since leaving southern Greece, I tried to keep within the narrow band of tarmac to one side of the road. I found it curious that not one local authority, in any of the nine countries through which I had so far cycled, had designated these omnipresent bands by the road official cycle paths. It would have been a very easy and cheap way of suddenly transforming your town or city into a cycling paradise. In Britain where, compared to our continental cousins, we seem to have very narrow roads which, more often than not, terminate abruptly at a kerb or bush situated within centimetres of the white line (if there is one), this is rarely an option. On the mainland of Europe, it *is* an option but one which nobody appears to have taken up.

I stopped in Montserrat, having cycled just 30km. I was knackered! It was strange that my reaction to having cycled 280km from Tarragona to Valencia two days earlier had only now hit me. I didn't feel any after-effects whilst wandering around Valencia the previous day, but now that I had been back on Reggie for a couple of hours, I had been struck down. My legs were tired and stiff and the right one was aching somewhat; they just weren't in any kind of mood for cycling. I found a small supermarket where I filled up on cold water and a minor feast of calories and then massaged my legs by applying a large amount of sun protection cream. I took my time spreading it across my suffering lower limbs, lingering over the parts of my body that didn't seem to have yet woken up. I also found the scissors on my

Swiss Army Knife and removed the elasticated band along the bottom edge of my cycling shorts. For some reason, after so many kilometres of not having been bothered in the least by the figure-hugging item of clothing, it was annoying me intensely. Perhaps it was the heat. Perhaps it was my brain thinking that there must be some reason for the aches in my legs and surmising that it had something to do with what I was wearing. Who knows? What I do know is that I was left with a thin band of white flesh that had not been exposed to the sun for most of the previous seven weeks. It looked somewhat strange and within a few minutes of having removed the second band I was regretting my decision to do so. A few kilometres down the road, so self-conscious did I feel about my two-tone flesh, that I found a deserted corner, removed them, and put on my lycra running shorts. They were just like cycling shorts but didn't have the padded seat; I would now be wearing these until the very end of the Eurovelo 8 trip. I was beginning to feel physically beaten but stopping was not an option, especially when the prize was ever more tantalisingly close. It would have been nice, however, to look forward to an evening in a recuperative health resort, rather than a return to the camping mat. I gritted my teeth, forced a smile, turned towards the mountains in the near distance and set off.

I always knew that when I moved away from the coast in Spain, it would involve a sharp climb and I certainly got one. From more or less sea level in Valencia, I eventually reached over 700 metres as I progressed further and further into the mountains. That said, the hard work was worth every gram of perspiration as I was once again free of the clutter and chaos of the coast. The roads were now almost deserted, save for the very occasional car and just one lorry. It was red. I wondered to myself where the driver was going with his cargo, whatever it was. It was a reassuring thought that, somewhere along the road I was following, there was somewhere meriting the delivery of something; I wasn't just on a cycle to nowhere.

The hills were bare. I initially thought this was just natural but as I climbed higher, it became apparent that this was an area that had recently been the victim of forest fires. The brittle remains of burnt trees were spread across the hills and then there was a sign from the local authorities, indicating that there had indeed been fires in 2012. I think the large panel by the road was also instructing that the area should be left untouched until at least 2014, but I wasn't quite sure. The barren land made this mountainous area feel like a hostile environment and the intense heat seemed to confirm my suspicion. It was surely one of the hottest days I had yet experienced since leaving southern Greece, exacerbated by the lack of cooling air blowing in from the sea. This had clearly moderated the temperature for the first few days of travelling in Spain but as I moved inland, its effects were only now becoming apparent.

Shortly after reaching the 50km point of the cycle, I passed into a new valley. In the far distance I could hear music. After a few more kilometres, I could work out that it wasn't live but recorded music, almost as if one unruly teenager in a nearby village had decided to open his window wide, turn the stereo up to full volume, lie back on the bed and enjoy annoying all his neighbours. I cycled another kilometre or two and gradually the music become more distinct and more echoey. This wasn't emanating from the bedroom of a bored teenager; it was being played through some sort of tannoy system in the street. I looked along the valley and down to my map. I was close to a place called Dos Aguas – 'two waters' – and in this otherwise remote, lifeless valley, something was taking place.

Dos Aguas was a large village. The music that I could hear had now taken on a slight feeling of eeriness, as the street leading into the centre was almost as deserted as the countryside surrounding it. To my left, on a hill, I could see most of the village, which consisted of a tight cluster of white-washed buildings and faded orange roofs. The road along which I was cycling was slightly away from this heart of the village and was lined on both sides by three-storey buildings with balconies, apart from the occasional gap on my left, which afforded pretty views of the rest of the village on its hill. The small apartment blocks on either side of the street were linked by bunting that had been strewn diagonally above my head. The bunting was made up of the flags of Spain and the region of Valencia. There were also a few posters advertising a festival which would be taking place on the 20th August – the following day – and this suggested why the tannoy system was being tested. (*'It's working boys; you can now switch it off!'*)

There were a few shops, although they all appeared to be closed, and at the end of the village was a bar. I needed a break, so I went inside and sat down. It was a rough outfit with a charmless woman serving drinks and snacks from behind the counter and three blokes playing some sort of card game while drinking beer. On the TV was the Spanish version of *Wheel Of Fortune* but no one was watching. I ordered a coffee, bought an ice cream, and went to sit outside on the dirty, plastic chairs that had been set up in the road just outside. There was little risk of being run over as I had yet to see any traffic movement whatsoever. As I drank and ate, I had no choice but to continue to listen to the tinny sound of the music. What a curious, out-of-the-way place Dos Aguas was turning out to be. As I sat, my mind examined the minutiae of what surrounded me: the air-conditioning unit on the side of the bar, the ornate tiles above the fountain on the other side of the street, the green bottle bank, the red lorry parked up just a few metres away... Hang on! Red lorry? That wasn't just any old red lorry; it was the red lorry that had passed me earlier in the morning and which had reassured me that I wasn't on a cycle into oblivion. Having finished my coffee and ice cream, I wandered over to examine the lorry in more detail. I was curious to know what it had brought to the village.

The lorry was parked at the end of what looked like the main street of the village. It linked the road I had used to enter Dos Aguas with the collection of buildings on the hill. Walking along the street wasn't possible, not with Reggie in tow, as a temporary metal gate had been erected just behind the lorry and it spanned the width of the street. The vertical bars painted yellow and red (what else?) were wide enough apart to allow a person to enter, but not a bike with its handlebars sticking out on either side. More gates had also been placed at strategic points along the main street next to doors and windows but sufficient room had been left for anyone to stand between the frame and the door or window. Some people were doing just that. Others were closer to me, on my side of the barrier cutting off access to the street itself. It was difficult trying to work out what was happening or perhaps what was going to happen. Nothing seemed imminent, as there were only perhaps ten or so people around. They did, however, seem to be expecting something to take place.

Suddenly there was a flurry of activity in the distance as people came running down the street being chased by... a bull. It suddenly all made sense. I had stumbled upon a 'running of the bull' event and the lorry that had passed me earlier in the day had been delivering the victim to the point of his demise. I wondered if what I was witnessing was a rehearsal for the real thing on the 20th, the day of the festival itself. The number of people wasn't great – now that the bull was at my end of the street there were still no more than thirty – and some people in the village – the three guys playing cards in the bar for example – were completely ignoring what was happening.

As the bull was teased and tormented, it charged the barriers with considerable force. At one point it came quite close to me, its horns crashing against the metal posts, which were protecting me and those around me from the bull's considerable anger. The forces of inertia projected a considerable amount of bull snot and saliva onto the floor in front of me, as the dazed animal realised that there was no way through. It was exciting stuff but I can't say that I was enjoying it. The

333

crowd consisted predominantly of young men, who were playing up how macho they could be by lying exhausted on the floor after a near encounter with the bull. With the metal frames to protect them, they were at little risk. That said, an ambulance was on stand-by just around the corner. I took some photographs and left, feeling somewhat uneasy about being a bystander at such a distasteful, yet exhilarating event.

Bull running and bullfighting are clearly linked and traditionally, the running of the bulls would take place prior to a fight, as the animals were transported from a holding pen outside the town or city to the bullring itself. It does, however, now seem to have become an attraction in its own right. Examining a map of Dos Aguas, I cannot find anything that resembles a bullring, which suggests that the bull-running incident that I witnessed was the main event. What became of the bull? Did it survive only to be tormented elsewhere? Or was it killed and barbecued? From the perspective of the northern European that I am, bullfighting and bull-running are as anachronistic as the ark, but from the perspective of many in southern Europe, they are part of the culture. I had already seen how in France the practice had been ruled to be constitutional, although it had been outlawed by most of the French regions. Here in Spain, only the region of Catalonia and the Canary Islands have banned bullfighting and it remains perfectly legal elsewhere. For a short period from 2007 to 2012, the Spanish state broadcaster, TVE, stopped showing bullfighting events live on television but they are now once again broadcast for anyone who wishes to tune in and watch. The tide, it seems, has turned against the bull; there are even attempts in the Spanish Senate to have the bans in Catalonia and the Canary Islands overturned.

I continued to climb as I cycled away from Dos Aguas. The bull-running played on my mind; I had enjoyed seeing what I had witnessed but the more I thought about it, the more disgusted I was about the idea of toying with a defenceless animal for pleasure. By the time I reached the high point at the end of the valley, I could still just about hear the music from the village. As I moved over into the next valley, the music disappeared, a new, very different view opened up in front of me, and it was time to think about other things. This new valley was very green in comparison to the one I had just left. Clearly the fires of 2012 had not reached this area, although the shading on my map also suggested that the two areas were already distinctly different, even prior to the fires. The thing that was now on my mind was accommodation. Where would I sleep? I knew about the two campsites – one in Casas de Ves and the other in Jarafuel – but was still undecided as to which I should go for. Upon arrival in the town of Cofrentes, I sat down next to a water fountain to weigh up my options.

Cofrentes had two great edifices to attract the eye: a large (but obviously rebuilt) castle at the top of the town on the hill, and a nuclear power station in the valley. In the town itself there was an abundance of high-quality, sporting amenities and I wondered just how many of them had been paid for to help persuade the local population of the benefits of the power station being built. I also wondered how many of the residents might have been reflecting carefully upon their willingness to embrace the nuclear power station after the fires of 2012.

So, campsite in the west or campsite to the south? For the first time since leaving the greater urban area of Valencia, I had a good 3G Internet access (probably courtesy of the power company) so I logged on with a view to comparing my two options. In passing, I also checked on Booking.com just to see if there was a good deal in or around Cofrentes... and there was. (Damn!) For €50 I could spend the night at a nearby spa resort, the *Hotel Balneario Confrentes*. As soon as my legs were witness to this online revelation, there was no way they were going anywhere else.

The hotel complex was about 5km to the west of Cofrentes and situated away from the road, in a deeply wooded area just next to an unseen golf course. I wasn't quite sure what I was letting myself in for, as I imagined being force-fed a diet of lettuce leaves followed by obligatory gym exercises in the grounds. Mercifully, although the spa dated back to 1905, the modern-day management had dispensed with synchronised group exercise in the communal areas. The range of recuperative facilities on offer was impressive and the buildings and grounds were populated with scores of Spain's more senior citizens, dressed in long, white bathing robes en route to or from a dip in the waters of the spa itself. Despite my aching limbs, I didn't partake, choosing instead to recuperate in my own way, in the open-air bar with a few glasses of San Miguel beer. There was a sense of refined, albeit slightly dated elegance. My room was more a very small house, arranged in a terrace of such houses in the grounds, away from the main buildings. Although built on a slope, lifts had been installed so as to ease the passage from one level to the next. It was all thoroughly relaxing. An evening meal was provided in a large dining hall, where jugs of wine had been set out on each table. I chose a small table to one side of the room and, as no one joined me... Well, it would have been rude not to. I was swaying a little as I made my way back to my room but I had a smile on my face. My body had, after all, found the health resort it had been yearning for earlier in the day. Health resort? Well, think Butlin's for the Spanish superannuated and you'll be very close.

Tuesday 20th August 2013
Cycling Day 42: Cofrentes To Albacete (Twice), 159km

The original plan, as hatched on the floor of the hotel room back in Valencia, was to get as far as Albacete by the end of Tuesday. But when I did the maths, or rather when I let Google Maps do it for me, Albacete was well under 100km from the spa hotel near Cofrentes. I should, I thought, be able to get quite a bit further than that! So I went back to consult the *Vias Verdes* website again. The first of these off-road cycling routes that I was planning to use during my journey across Spain started in Albacete and headed off in a westerly direction. It was called the *Via Verde Sierra de Alcaraz*, was 74km long and, like many of the other *Vias Verdes* across Spain, was a former railway line. The website gave lots of practical information about the route including some suggestions of places to stay. Numerous hotels were listed for Albacete but I was aiming to make at least some headway along the *Via Verde* before the end of the day and the first hotel to be recommended was in a place called Balazote, some 30km from the start of the route. That would make for a cycling day of around 130km, which was above average but well within the range of possibility (a range that had, admittedly, been stretched somewhat by the epic cycle to Valencia at the weekend). The name of the hotel was the *Pensión La Paella,* a one-star establishment and, although it wasn't listed by my favourite online booking site, the telephone number was provided by the *Via Verde* website. I wrote it down and would give them a call when I arrived in Albacete later in the day.

I took breakfast at the *Hotel Balneario Confrentes* with the Spanish pensioners. These included a couple of nuns whom I had seen scuttling around, heads bowed just a little, on numerous occasions during my short stay at the resort. I was reminded of the nuns in the 1980s television drama *A Very Peculiar Practice*, a series that centred upon the (at times surreal) life of a doctor working as a GP on a university campus. The *Hotel Balneario Confrentes* would, I thought, have made a first rate location around which to base a hotel/medical, comedy-drama. *Fawlty Towers* meets *Crossroads* meets *Casualty* meets *Eldorado.* On second thoughts, perhaps not. It didn't prevent me from idling away the few moments I had, as I nibbled through a few croissants and bread rolls, trying to shoe-horn the people who surrounded me into the various roles that might have been required. The Spanish waiter was easy.

337

The morning on the bike went very well. Reggie was continuing to play ball (i.e. he was showing no signs of breaking down anytime soon) and I was beginning to resign myself to creaking through the first 20 to 30km of the day, as my increasingly weary legs took their time to warm up and work effectively. I persevered and, after a steady climb from 400 to over 800 metres, the road began to flatten out and I could look forward with some confidence to a relatively early arrival in Albacete. The good quality, quiet country roads I was now cycling upon gave me the time to feast upon the beautiful (if not necessarily spectacular) scenery through which I was travelling. My cycle guided me along a number of narrow valleys with low hills on either side, covered from top to bottom with dark green trees, the occasional outcrop of light grey rock and, in a nod to modernity, small groups of elegant wind turbines. In the areas on either side of the road were fields, most of which had just been harvested of their crop. Hay bales – one of the few constants along my route since leaving Sounio – were dotted around the swathes of cropped, light brown grass that remained. The sky was blue, there was a gentle breeze to take the edge off the heat and I was a happy cyclist.

Frustrations were, however, about to fall in an avalanche. In the second half of the journey to Albacete, the landscape flattened out to the point where all that could be seen in almost all directions were farmed prairies. Practically everything that was worth seeing was now in the far distance, with just the almost empty road and the featureless fields upon which to gaze. This in itself wasn't frustrating; indeed the grinding monotony of such cycling transported me to North America, Australia or Mongolia. Imagine, I thought, doing this day after day, after day. Perhaps at some point in the future I might find out if my travels on Reggie should ever escape the boundaries of Europe. Frustration number one was not, alas, far off. It concerned those concentric circles that I had admired in Italy and which guide the otherwise ignorant traveller seamlessly to the centre of a town. They had also adopted the same signage practice in Spain but alas, it wasn't working so well. In fact, it wasn't working at all. The problem was that in Spain they seem to have rationed the use of these concentric circles and if you follow them, you just end up somewhere near (but not quite in) the town centre. In my mind, the point that marks the town centre is in the middle of a large square, usually flanked by big, important buildings such as the town hall, the post office perhaps or even the theatre - that kind of thing. (Alas, this no longer actually works in Britain by the way, because so many of the post offices, especially the prettier ones, have been converted into branches of Yate's Wine Lodge and the like. Or is it just in Reading? I've never been impressed with that particular folly of the free market and am now glad I've had the chance to put my opinion in print. Back to the story...) In France, the main square is the centre of the town. In Italy, it's usually the centre of the town. In Spain, it isn't.

In Albacete, as I attempted to fathom my way to the centre by following the concentric circles, I just found dull street after dull street and then the hospital medical school. Not very useful if all you want to do is sit down and have a bite to eat. *'La estación'!* Brilliant, the train station! That's an important building, which in a smallish town can't be too far from the beating heart of the place. I followed those directions but got lost doing that too. After much cycling I eventually found a small, elongated square that at least felt like it was in the very centre of Albacete. I have no idea if it actually was.

In the great scheme of things to come, this was a minor frustration. I found a bar, ordered a drink and something to eat. It was about 3pm. Even after having finished my meal, there would still be plenty of time to squeeze a bit more cycling into the day and those 30km to Balazote and the *Pensión La Paella* would fill the late afternoon gap quite nicely. I found the telephone number that I had written down earlier in the day and gave them a call;

"Hola. Pensión La Paella," confirmed the voice at the other end of the line.

"Hola. Do you speak English?" I enquired.

"-------------," was the reply.

"Hola? Is anyone there?"

Clearly the woman who had picked up the phone had not gone to fetch someone who *did* speak English. She had simply gone.

I would probably have done something similar myself had I received a telephone call from a person whose voice I didn't recognise and who was asking me a question in a language that I didn't understand. But then again, I don't run a hotel where I might expect foreigners to occasionally call and ask a question in a foreign language. Putting this thought aside, I rationalised the situation. The hotel existed: that had been confirmed by the first line of the brief conversation I had just had. It was a Tuesday night in August, in the middle of the Spanish countryside. Unless Balazote was some jewel in the crown of the Spanish tourist industry (which it wasn't, as it got no mention in my guide book), the chances of the hotel being fully booked were minimal. I would risk it and just turn up at the door.

I had already chatted to the waiter about my cycling adventure and after paying the bill, I asked him about the *Via Verde Sierra de Alcaraz* and more precisely, where I would find it. I wondered to myself why I hadn't asked him to telephone the hotel for me but that was now water under the bridge. He showed me on the map where I would need to go. The *Via Verde* started in a corner of a park on the other side of town. I had probably already cycled past it several times when following the erratic concentric circles only an hour or so earlier. Mercifully, I found the park relatively easily and it was, as the waiter had explained, in the furthest corner, next to a canal. This pleased me, as on the website I had been examining earlier in the day, I had been informed that, for the first six and a half kilometres of the route, I would be following the Maria Cristina Canal. (The Infanta Maria Cristina, incidentally, had been the aunt to the now ex-King Juan Carlos of Spain but whereas other members of her family had modern architectural wonders named after them in Valencia, poor Maria Cristina had a canal at the back of a park in Albacete to her name. I hope they broke the news to her gently.)

A sign announced that it was indeed the start of the Maria Cristina Canal cycle route and there were useful symbols to follow. The route was covered in tarmac and for the first few kilometres I made good progress. I had to cross to the other side of the dried up canal once or twice but nothing too complicated. I was then directed to continue my journey by cycling under the main road through a short tunnel. Unfortunately the tunnel had completed silted up. This was not something that had happened overnight. Clearly the canal had been like this for some time but there were no signs indicating where any cyclists wanting to follow the route should go in order to continue their journey via a short deviation. It wasn't an option simply to cross the road above the tunnel since there was a fence, barriers and a central reservation blocking the direct route over the top. So should I turn left or right in my quest to continue following the canal on the other side of the road?

I had seen a cyclist in front of me turn right so I followed him but I had no idea whether he was wanting to continue along the canal or not. He wasn't a touring cyclist and for all I knew, he could simply have popped out for a loaf of bread. After a few hundred metres, there was no indication that this was indeed the correct direction along which to deviate so I turned around, returned to the blocked tunnel and headed left instead. After perhaps 400m, I came to the same conclusion so, once again, I returned to the tunnel and reverted to the initial plan of cycling to the right. I continued until I got to a bridge, figuring out that at least it would get me to the other side of the road where the canal continued. Fortunately, it did but I was now beginning to feel just a little anxious that this whole *Via Verde* thing might not be the walk (or cycle) in the park that I thought it might be. I did, however, manage to relocate the canal as it emerged from under the road and I continued to follow the signs for the canal route. After a few more kilometres, and much to my great relief, the start of the *Via Verde Sierra de Alcaraz* proper was announced with a large sign. At the bottom of the sign it stated "*Prohibida la circulación de vehículos de motor*". After having been instructed by a good number of signs I had encountered since the start of the trip that bicycles were no longer welcome along my chosen path, it was good to find one that was redressing the balance.

I could see the route reaching into the distance, along what was once planned to be a railway track. It never was a railway track because, just before it was put into operation in the early 1960s, the World Bank told the Spaniards that it would be unviable. Everything had been built and installed apart from the signalling. Even the stations, several of which I was to cycle past, had been completed. How crazy is that? Imagine being told that after all the hard work, sweat, blood and tears that go into constructing a railway that actually, it's never going to be a railway. I wondered why the Spaniards (especially bearing in mind that Franco was in charge at the time) didn't just turn round to the World Bank, tell them to shove it and continue with the signalling. They must have been tempted. I almost feel like writing them a letter myself, nearly 50 years later.

It wasn't going to be lack of signalling that would slow me down, however. It would be the surface of the track. It was made up of loose gravel and stones and not the easiest, or indeed the most comfortable, of surfaces upon which to cycle. I thought this might just be the state of the ground for the first few kilometres but it continued and continued. Much of my time since leaving southern Greece had been spent staring at the roads of the various countries through which I had cycled. It's a normal thing to do when you are on a bike, looking out for objects that need to be avoided (more often than not, glass), but usually it doesn't take up almost all of the time on the bike and the rest of the time available can be spent gazing at the view or finding curious things upon which to ponder. I often do the latter, perhaps too much. It had been one of the delights of cycling on the long, flat and quiet roads in the morning; most of my time could be spent looking at things other than the road. So it was with a certain irony that I had now transferred to a track that had been adapted specifically for use by walkers and cyclists, but where I was spending probably 90% of my time looking at the ground trying to avoid larger rocks that could quite easily have thrown me off poor Reggie, rather than appreciating the countryside through which I was cycling. It was all very frustrating but I continued, forcing myself to pause from time to time to appreciate the curiosities presenting themselves along the route, such as the abandoned stations that had never seen a customer in the first place. Does that mean they were never actually abandoned? There's a question upon which to ponder while you are cycling.

It wasn't fun, but it was a little comical that every 100m or so there were signs imploring me to stick to the speed limit of 10km/hr. I tried to do so for a few moments but it was almost impossible, if not dangerous, as the bike required a minimum momentum to carry itself over the rocks on the ground and this wasn't achieved until a speed of well over 10km/hr. The other users of the *Via Verde* were in no danger of being affected by my excessive speeds of 15 to 20km/hr as, err... there weren't any other users. In the 20km that I travelled along the *Via Verde* that afternoon, I passed no one and no one passed me. From time to time, some signage explained the history of the route in Spanish (no translations into other languages) but some of these had been burnt out. To say I was disappointed with what I had found was an understatement. I had specifically changed my route to make use of these *Vías Verdes* and I was increasingly feeling that I would have been better off on the road, enjoying the views on a good surface and knowing exactly where I was, despite the occasional lorry thundering past.

After 20km, the town of Balazote *was* signposted. It was around 6:30pm and I needed to find the *Pensión La Paella*, so I turned off the route, found the main road and then made my way towards the small town of Balazote itself. It wasn't far. The *Pensión* had been advertised as being in Balazote, so I cycled around the town for a few minutes but I couldn't find it. I eventually went to sit in a park to consult an online map but after a few more minutes of peering at the small screen, I was none the wiser as to where exactly the hotel was located. Three old guys were sitting on a bench in the park so I decided to ask them if they had ever heard of the hotel. It wasn't easy communicating with them as I spoke no Spanish and they spoke no English, but between us we did manage to transmit the key facts. I think. If I understood correctly, the *Pensión La Paella* was 5km out of town, in the direction of Albacete. That was the same Albacete I had just come from and it looked as though I would need to retrace five of the twenty kilometres I had just cycled, in order to find a room for the night. At least I would be back on the road. Was there another hotel in the town? The answer from the three wise men of Balazote was 'no'. I think.

I did feel a little annoyed that I had chosen the *Pensión La Paella* as a potential place to stay because it had been a suggestion of the *Via Verde* website, but from what I could see, it was nowhere near the route itself. Users of the track (if there had been any) were walkers and cyclists; at least I was travelling by bicycle and not on foot. That was the very thin silver lining to this frustratingly dark cloud which had suddenly appeared in the early evening sky of blue. I set off back in the direction of Albacete but after 5km, I hadn't spotted the *Pensión La Paella*. After 6km still nothing, nor 7km or 8km or 9km or even 10km. If it was out there somewhere, it was keeping itself well hidden. I was now halfway to Albacete, it was getting quite late so there was no choice but to continue cycling back in the direction that I had come. The only difference was that I was cycling along the road, rather than the *Via Verde*. After 15km I stopped for a drink at a petrol station and went online to book accommodation back in the centre of Albacete, at a hotel just next to the bar where I had earlier had my mid-afternoon snack. Having seen it, I was in no doubt that it actually existed. Feeling somewhat dejected, I arrived in the centre at around 8pm, frustrated and annoyed. For the first time since leaving southern Greece, I had attempted to follow a purpose-adapted cycling track and not only had it turned out to be anything but amenable to cyclists, but for the first time in nearly 5,000km I had been forced to turn back and retrace my steps by some 20km.

The whole experience highlighted a common problem that I see all the time back in Britain. Cycling facilities and infrastructure are all too often conceived, designed and built by people who only ever use them to fill up a few lines on their CVs as wonderful urban planners. The silted-up tunnel: how long had it been in that condition? There were no signs to indicate a deviation. The condition of the surface on the *Via Verde*: had any of the civil servants responsible for the track ever cycled upon it and experienced just how uncomfortable it could be? The information about accommodation on the website: had the webmaster ever thought about the practicalities of what had been written?

It had not been a good introduction to the network of *Vias Verdes* routes. I resolved not to return to the *Via Verde Sierra de Alcaraz* the following day but to stick to the road. I would still be willing to give the second *Via Verde* I was planning to use a chance, but it had better be good. I was in a letter-writing mood but who would I write to first? The people responsible for the *Via Verde* who had created a far from satisfactory bit of cycling infrastructure, or the World Bank who had removed the option of me taking the train in the first place? There's never a relaxing spa resort when you need one and that night in Albacete, I needed one like never before.

Wednesday 21st August 2013
Cycling Day 43: Albacete To Peñascosa, 93km

The *Gran Hotel Albacete* had all the charm of your average operating theatre. The room in which I spent the night had been themed grey. Wouldn't you just love to have been a fly on the wall of the meeting that decided that:

"We'd like to give our hotel a warm, welcoming feel that will help our guests relax after a hard day poring over spreadsheets, tangling with the Spanish language or retracing their steps for 20km after finding that a hotel named after a famous Spanish fish dish doesn't actually exist!"

"Let's go for grey."

"Brilliant idea. I'll order the paint!"

I opened my eyes and for a few brief moments thought that I might have been press-ganged into the Spanish Navy. But surely, even Spanish battleships have a little interior colour, no? I wasn't sailing the seven seas; I was in Albacete, the only place apart from Athens along the Eurovelo 8 (or at least my version of it) that I had managed to visit twice during the trip. In fairness to the Greek capital, the Athens revisit had been planned, albeit at the last minute. My return to Albacete had been forced upon me rather unwillingly.

Rather ironically, given my troubles finding the centre of Albacete on the previous afternoon (during my first visit), I was now starting to feel as though I knew the layout of the place a little too well. I had even mastered the one-way system outside the entrance to the hotel and my bearings weren't thrown by deviating slightly away from the square to find a bakery where I could buy some breakfast. Within a matter of half an hour, I was once again to be found on the N-322, heading in the direction of Balazote. I was a little grumpy to say the very least. Every shop, every café, every petrol station and every farm building seemed familiar. It's amazing how much detail can be retained by the human mind. Not detail that could ever be recalled but detail that was vividly recognisable from the previous evening's cycle. The only point at which I could bring myself to display any kind of joy was when I passed a sign for an out of town 'cabaret'. The large board was attached to the roof of the building and next to a pair of naked female legs it pronounced, in capital letters:

SALA FIESTAS
NUEVO CHANGO

345

SHOW GIRL'S

Show girl's what? I wondered.

Even the faintest of faintest smiles can, however, kindle a more positive outlook on life. Perhaps it was the unintentional comical effect of the addition of the apostrophe by the sign writer that prompted a gradual shift in my mood from one of misery to one of mild contentment. The sun was still shining, I was heading in the right direction once again, Reggie was still in good shape after almost 5,000km, and so was I. More or less.

There was one aspect of travelling along the N-322 that had changed since the previous evening and that was the amount of traffic thundering past my left ear, sometimes a little too close for comfort. In an audacious moment of fickleness that would surely receive at least one nomination at the National Fickleness Awards (which, incidentally, were due to take place in Brighton last year until a last minute change of mind that resulted in a move to Blackpool), I decided to give the *Via Verde Sierra de Alcaraz* a second chance.

"What?!" I hear you cry. *"Are you mad?"*

No, I'm not mad, but I am fickle.

"Ah, I see..." you just said.

In fact, after about only one hour of cycling on the busy road, I actually *wanted* to be back on the annoying gravel and stones of the *Via Verde.* I knew the cycle path was only a few hundred metres to my left and, so desperate was I to make the move, I decided to risk it and take one of the dirt tracks that turned off the N-322 and along the edge of a field, before changing direction to head across a large area of scrubland. It wasn't the wisest of decisions and I never made it as far as the *Via Verde* (although I did manage to prompt almost every rabbit, pheasant and partridge in the vicinity to jump out of their hiding places in the bushes and scarper, as if being hunted by a man with a machine gun and a deep desire for rabbit and game stew). After a couple of kilometres off road, I returned to the 'comfort' of the main road and its traffic.

I made a second attempt to rejoin the *Via Verde,* just before Balazote by retracing my steps from the end of the previous day's encounter with the cycle route, when all I had wanted to do was escape and never see it again in my life. Alas, this plan was also foiled when I discovered that, at the point at which I had abandoned the route voluntarily, I actually would have had no choice, as the next portion of the *Via Verde* was still under construction. Once again I returned to the N-322.

346

My third and final shot at reacquainting myself with the *Via Verde* came a couple of kilometres to the west of Balazote, when the deviation signs instructed me to do just that. Success!

Much to my delight, the track surface was significantly better than it had been on the previous day. Perhaps the closed section of the *Via Verde Sierra de Alcaraz,* which had been out of action and had resulted in the deviation back onto the road, was evidence of improvements being made. I could only hope that this was indeed the case. Although not a smooth surface, for most of the next 40km I was able to stop obsessing about what I was cycling over and spend considerably more time obsessing about the countryside through which I was cycling. The route gently climbed – just as the trains would have had to do if the World Bank hadn't stopped them in their, well, tracks – so for most of the time, the cycling was at the modest end of challenging. Whereas from Albacete to Balazote, the *Via Verde* had followed a dead straight path through an open, flat landscape, after Balazote it entered a more hilly area. But, as this was a train line (which admittedly had never seen nor heard a train), the path burrowed its way though cuttings, along the top of embankments, through numerous tunnels and even along the top of two beautiful viaducts. All of them dug out or constructed in vain. Well, apart from being for my benefit and the benefit of all the other modern day users of the *Via Verde Sierra de Alcaraz* of which there were still... err... none.

Some of the tunnels were lit, others remained in darkness. Sensors detected my arrival at the entrance and in a flicker of fluorescent light, the path ahead of me became illuminated and I was able to continue to cycle without any problem whatsoever. Where no lights had been installed I switched on my own bike light but for some of the shorter tunnels, where I could see the arch at the other end clearly, I continued to cycle, paying particular attention to the only partially visible ground where obstacles may have been lurking. On occasions, I sensed movement around my head. It could have been small birds. It was more likely to have been bats. It wasn't a thought upon which I wanted to dwell, so I tried to convince myself that yes, they were just very agile birds. For some reason, a couple of the tunnels had fences and red and white tape at their entrances. They had been pushed to the floor by previous travellers along the *Via Verde* and, seeing no visible evidence of there being an issue in the tunnel itself, I continued to cycle. As I emerged from one particularly long underground route, I glanced down at the CatEye cycling computer. About 100m earlier in the darkness of the tunnel, something as significant as it was insignificant had taken place. The odometer told me that I had now cycled 5,000.1 km. It was more symbolic than meaningful, as unlike the GPS measurements being recorded by the cycling app on my iPhone, the CatEye device recorded every single movement of the wheel, whether I had been cycling from A to B to C to D during the day, pottering around a town centre in the morning, having a good nosy at the local attractions or indeed cycling from D back to C, as had been the case on the previous evening. Whatever its true 'meaning', it signified that I had moved, with Reggie underneath me or by my side for just over 5,000km. As the crow flies, that's the distance from London to Sierra Leone or Khartoum or Bahrain. It's only 4,300km from the British capital to the North Pole. And let's not forget Barnsley in all this. It's the equivalent of cycling (on a flying bicycle) from London to Barnsley some 16 times. (Just 18 times if you take the M1, but then you've got to consider those road works in Leicester again...)

I paused for lunch in a small, out-of-the-way village called Los Chopses and ate outside the unimaginatively named *Bar Los Chopses* where a cheerfully rotund woman who spoke no English (away from the coast I had met few who did) served me a wonderful ham and cheese sandwich followed by an ice-cream. I was alone outside the bar and I couldn't see inside because the vertical shutters on the windows were closed and a door with hanging beads to prevent the flies from entering also stopped me from attracting the attention of the rather large woman. So, in order to pay for what I had eaten, I pushed aside the beads, entered the building and was surprised to find it packed full of men of all ages, jabbering away and no doubt debating every topic under the sun. It was clear, however, who was in charge; the woman who had served me was giving as good as she got to some poor bloke who was standing at the bar with a glass of beer in front of him. He must have regretted saying whatever he had said. I liked her style and she left me feeling not just fully fed but fully immersed in rural Spanish life.

My opinion of the *Via Verde Sierra de Alcaraz* had been transformed, and so had my mood, which was now in marked contrast to what it had been at the start of the day. When I arrived at the final sign informing me that the route had ended, I consulted the website. It told me that there were plans to extend the 'greenway' for a further 30km through the Sierra de Alcaraz mountains. I dearly hoped that this project would come to fruition but in the economic climate of 2013, it was probably nowhere near the top of the list of priorities of the Spanish authorities. As I turned to make my way across the chunky gravel that joined the cycle track to the road, the gods of the *Via Verde* were keen to punish me for my initial scurrilous conclusions, which had been based upon the first 20km of the route as far as Balazote rather than the excellent 55km that followed. With my cycling sandals clipped into the pedals, I tried to set off, but in the deep gravel Reggie wasn't going anywhere. With no time to unclip myself, I fell – in a manner of which Del Boy would have thoroughly approved - flatly onto the ground with a thud and no bounce. It had been my first cycling accident of the trip but it was more comical than harmful. I unclipped my sandals while still lying on the ground, pulled myself from under poor Reggie, stood up and dusted myself down. A bruised thigh, a slightly dented ego and a small crater in the ground. At least I had left my mark in the *Via Verde*, just as it had left one on me.

It was only 4pm and I considered continuing to cycle along the N-322 towards the *Parque Natural de las Sierras*, its lakes and its campsites. When I realised that I was still some way from my old friend the N-322, however, reason got the better of me. The road that I *was* on climbed a hill to a place called Peñascosa, where my map indicated that there was a campsite, so I decided to bring the cycling day to a close and find it. After only a few minutes of climbing away from the *Via Verde,* the campsite was advertised on a sign by the road and it was a mere 5km away, well before the village itself. Wonderful!

9km later, I arrived at the campsite. If ever I had wanted to be fluent in Spanish it was upon the moment of arrival at *Camping Sierra de Peñascosa*. How satisfying it would have been to make a witty aside to the receptionist about how 'imaginative' their 5km sign actually was. I'm not sure what that witty comment would have been: '*You lying bastards'* would have seen me back on the wrong side of the campsite gate in double quick time, probably after having been chased there by one of the many large dogs that were wandering around the reception building. I chose not to bring up the subject with the woman who was working on reception, opting instead to limit myself to discussion of the less contentious subject of the campsite facilities.

Camping Sierra de Peñascosa was in a secluded, wooded area. It was a little rough around the edges, especially in the area immediately surrounding the reception, where there was a bar and restaurant housed inside a log chalet, and a swimming pool just beyond that. I hoped the barking dogs were a temporary feature. Most of the pitches were to be found on the hill, on the other side of a small river running through the site. I was allocated a plot of gravel next to a number of caravans, most of which were shut up, their owners having been and gone. It was shady and the sound of the river obscured the noise from the dogs. It would suit my purposes just fine.

It was the first time in four days that the tent had been out of its bag and, I was looking forward to enjoying a good erection under the cover of the trees. I glanced around for suitable candidates who might be able to lend me a mallet. I couldn't see too many people who had not only pitched their own tent but who were also loitering outside looking eager to give me a hand. In fact, there was just one: a woman in her 40s who was sitting reading a book and smoking a cigarette.

"Excuse me. Do you speak English?" I asked.

"Yes... Do you need to borrow a mallet?" she replied.

Interesting. Not only did she have magical powers of deduction, but her accent was even more familiar than that of Dave Cocker in L'Estartit.

"Where are you from?" I enquired.

"Originally from Bradford in West Yorkshire..." Bradford? Again? That's the city the waiter in the restaurant in Montenegro wanted to live in. *"...Do you know it?"*

Perhaps her powers of deduction weren't that great after all. Surely 25 years of living away from my home county – the same as hers – had not extinguished all traces of my own West Riding twang.

She introduced herself as Tracey and after a few moments, her husband Ewan appeared. I was offered a beer and the three of us were soon on the road to thick heads in the morning. Tracey and Ewan were both trained linguists and had spent the bulk of their careers working for the RAF, where they were deployed to listen in on the secret communications of the 'enemy' (although I was somewhat surprised to learn who the 'enemy' had been). Ewan had mastered Russian, German, French, Arabic (more or less), Hebrew and Spanish. Tracey was fluent in Russian, German, Serbo-Croat, French, Spanish and Greek (more or less). As a teacher of French - which is admittedly on the thin end of the professional 'linguist' wedge – it was fascinating chatting to two people who had really put their languages into practice, rather than simply teach the next generation how to conjugate them. They recounted tales involving foreign travel and exotic locations, missions flying over war zones and months spent learning new languages that matched the needs of a government that had acquired new enemies. Following retirement from the forces, they had decided to move to the Spanish coast near Marbella where Ewan, a writer, supplemented his income as a teacher (you are not the only one Ewan!) and Tracey put her considerable linguistic skills to good use by assisting others who were lacking in theirs. Unlike many other British people who had decided to settle in Spain, they were fluent in the language and had integrated into their local community in a way that others can only dream about (and some might, sadly, dread). They also served up a cracking spaghetti bolognaise which was washed down with far too much Spanish wine.

The day had started at one extreme of the spectrum of enjoyment and it closed at the other. At least I think it did. The final couple of hours were a little hazy.

Thursday 22nd August 2013
Cycling Day 44: Peñascosa To Ubeda, 139km

The village of Peñascosa, with an altitude of nearly 1,200m, was the physical high point in my journey across Spain. This had been evidenced by a cooler night in the tent and I woke to be embraced by warm, rather than hot, air. Tracey and Ewan provided black coffee, which we all needed, but I passed on breakfast, choosing instead to make an early start in the direction of the small town of Alcaraz.

My plan was to cycle as far as the city of Jaén by the end of the following day, as this marked the starting point of the second of the *Vias Verdes* in which my faith had been restored by the events of the previous afternoon. But as I climbed the short hill away from the campsite and in the direction of the village of Peñascosa, I was still very unsure where I would break my journey overnight. Now, don't get too excited. I wasn't about to repeat the feat of the previous Saturday and suddenly decide to squeeze two days of cycling into one epic journey. My legs were not up to that and neither was my mind. Upon arrival in Tarragona, I had been anxious about the time that remained for me to complete my trek along the northern Mediterranean coast. I was now much less concerned about that, indeed, I was beginning to be able to visualise how the remainder of the journey could be broken down into six or seven days of cycling. Back on the north-eastern coast, the physical environment had been an encouragement to get from A to B, or rather from Tarragona to Valencia, as quickly as possible. I just wanted to escape the urban sprawl that predominated along that part of the shoreline. Here, in the interior, why would I want to push myself to the limit? The views were great, the towns and villages interesting and the people, to the extent that I was able to communicate with them, were charming. As long as I kept cycling in the direction of the south-western corner of Portugal, at some point over the next week or so, I would get there. That was my hope. But in the very short term – i.e. Thursday 22nd August – I still wasn't sure where I would be stopping overnight.

The N-322 connected nearby Alcaraz with Ubeda, a town that my cousin Richard had mentioned. But he also recommended the town of Baeza, just a short distance away. When I asked which one was better, he replied simply that they were *'much of a muchness',* which wasn't a ringing endorsement for either of them. Perhaps it would be better for me to consider moving away from the N-322 and south, towards the *Embalse del Tranco de Beas*, a large reservoir, which, according to my map, hosted at least two campsites with another further along the valley at Cazorla. I wasn't short of options.

It took me just 45 minutes to get as far as Alcaraz, the town from which the *Sierra de Alcaraz* had taken its name and which in turn had gifted it to the *Via Verde Sierra de Alcaraz.* Despite its Spanish origins, the word '*Sierra*' is a familiar one to any speaker of English. There is, of course, the Ford Sierra, and the NATO phonetic alphabet uses the word to represent the letter 's'. I tend to think of spaghetti westerns when I hear it, however, and according to the Internet Movie Database, there are several hundred films and television programmes that have been made which use the word *Sierra* in their title. Many of these are Spanish-language films, but most are in English with titles such as '*High Sierra*' (1941), '*Horsemen of the Sierras*' (1949) and '*The Treasure of Sierra Madrock*' (1966). OK, I admit it. That last one is an episode of *The Flintstones,* but it does sound quite authentic:

"Travelling through the desert on their way to Rock Vegas, Fred and Barney fall prey to con men who have seeded the river with phony gold. When it turns out that the river contains real gold after all, the con men will do whatever it takes to oust the Flintstones and Rubbles from their claim."

Who needs John Wayne and James Stewart when you can have Fred Flintstone and Barney Rubble instead?

Anyway, getting back to Spain and my cycle along the *Sierra de Alcaraz* and potentially the *Sierra de Segura,* if I chose to head in the direction of the reservoir, the word simply describes '*a long, jagged mountain chain'.*

None of this was on my mind as I ate my way through my now usual breakfast feast of pastries, from a bakery on the main street in Alcaraz. I didn't seem to be in a rush and was happy to sit for a while, watching the people go by. They looked back at me, sitting on the step to someone's house, munching through my flaky cakes. Goodness knows what they were thinking. *Is he begging? Is he lost? Why do his clothes look so tatty and washed out? Why is he more red than golden brown like me? What's that curious band of white flesh where his cycling shorts end? Why is he staring at me? His bicycle looks in better shape that he does...*

I knew little about the day that lay ahead, mainly because I had yet to come to a decision as to where I would be going, but one thing I did know: I was about to enter Spain's most populous and arguably most iconic, region, Andalusia. I did so after forty predominantly downhill kilometres. The large, functional sign announced that I was about to enter the '*Comunidad de Andalucía*', as well as the '*Provincia de Jaén*'. It would be the last region of Spain through which I would cycle but it was a big one, stretching some 500km from where I stood next to the signpost in the east, to the *Rio Guadiana* – the border with Portugal – in the west. Vertical geography would be on my side, however, in that the *Sierra Morena* mountains (I could see on my map that they were very long and I imagined that they were just as jagged) had decided to keep themselves to the north of my route, which would be an overwhelmingly flat one as far as Seville, or so I hoped.

Apart from the sign that told me that I had arrived in Andalusia, the only other clue that I had indeed passed from one region to the next was the change in shade of the tarmac below me, indicating the point where one authority had stopped working on the road and handed responsibility to the next. There was no dramatic, or even subtle, change in the scenery. The land sloped away slightly on both sides of the road to form low hills in the near distance and the fields were empty of crops, having only recently been harvested. And so it was to be for many more kilometres to come. Despite the considerable headwind (which was nowhere near as fierce as the *Mistral* that I had fought against back in southern France), the cycling was not difficult. The N-322 remained relatively traffic-free for much of the time, I was making good progress and, well, that was it. There was nothing compelling me to deviate away from its path and I simply continued to pedal. I could see on the map that I was travelling parallel to the *Embalse del Tranco de Beas* but I saw no reason to branch off to the south and climb the mountains to my left, which were considerably higher than the route I was following.

Pain had returned to my lower back. This had first been an issue in Albania, where the climbs had been punishing and the road surfaces somewhat primitive. It had reared its ugly head a little further north, along the Adriatic coast on the island of Pag where, if you were paying attention, you will remember that I stopped cycling for a short period and stretched out along the concrete floor of an isolated bus shelter. As a result of this episode, and having noticed how upright the immaculate, perspiration-free Dutch cyclists that I had seen on the Croatian coastal road had been I had made adjustments to the angle of my handlebars. By tilting Reggie's flat 'butterfly' bars towards me, I forced myself to straighten my back somewhat. It had done the trick. Upon arrival in Italy, where both the terrain and road quality had been more forgiving, my back pain did not return and it had stayed away all the way through France and into Spain. Until Albacete, or more precisely, until I started to cycle along the rocky ground of the first stretch of the *Via Verde Sierra de Alcaraz*. Despite the improvement in the surface of the track for most of the later parts of the *Via Verde*, the pain seemed intent on staying put and it was still nagging away now that I had returned to the good-quality surface of the N-322. I would have to grin and bear it and hope that, as it had done previously, it would go away after a few days of more comfortable cycling conditions. I was, however, acutely aware of the upcoming, second *Via Verde* – the one that would start in Jaén – and if the ground was more mountain-bike than touring-bike friendly, I may have an uncomfortable few days ahead of me. Having never suffered from a bad back before, I was beginning to understand just how excruciatingly painful it could be and in the future I would have renewed sympathy for sufferers. My own pain was, of course, entirely self-inflicted.

After some 50km of cycling, the view began to change. The road from Alcaraz cut a path through countryside that consisted of a jigsaw of large patches of farmed land from which the crops had, as noted above, been recently shaven. But as I edged not just east but also further south, one crop began to replace all others to the point where it came to be the only thing that could be seen in all directions: olive trees. Not just hundreds of them, not even thousands of them, but hundreds of thousands of trees carpeting the landscape as far as the eye could see, all arranged in neat lines, pixelating the brown land and turning it somewhat green. It was astonishing to observe and the further I travelled into Andalusia, the more astonishing it became. This was monoculture on a vast scale.

It must be the mathematician in me – I did, after all, study the subject at university before morphing myself into a teacher of French – but the Andalusian olive industry is one that is, if you pardon the pun, ripe for harvesting a few statistics. Spain is by far the greatest producer of olives worldwide with roughly 50% of world production, and 80% of this production emanates from the region of Andalusia. In terms of trees, there are approximately 250 million of them in Spain. Yes, that's 250 followed by six zeros. So, with 80% of the country's production, it seems logical that there are some 200 million trees in Andalusia. Imagine being given the job of counting them! Production is centred along a fat corridor of regimented lines, stretching from the north-eastern corner of Andalusia as far as Seville. This just happened to be my own passage to Portugal so it was no surprise that my view was becoming increasingly dominated by the olive tree. The province of Jaén itself makes up 50% of the country's production of olives and Jaén was the town I was aiming for at the end of the following day. There was no escaping it; I was about as deep as a person could be in olive oil, without actually jumping in a vat of the stuff dressed as Popeye the sailor!

I grabbed lunch – a simple but delicious *tortilla bocadillo* – in a roadside café in the isolated town of Arroyo del Ojanco, surrounded by workers who were tucking into their own midday feasts. Most of them were washing down the food with a glass of beer but I chose not to join them. The establishment appeared to be run by a boy who could not have been older than fourteen or fifteen. He took the orders, delivered the food and collected the cash, while at the same time ordering a much older woman to do the same. At least that's what it sounded like. For all I knew, he could have been dictating the Spanish phone book. When he worked out that I didn't speak any Spanish (the question '*do you speak English?*' was a bit of a giveaway), he switched to schoolboy English in a way that my own pupils back in Britain would have struggled to do. The other diners congratulated him on his linguistic efforts. Or at least I think they did... As the food was settling in my stomach, I went online to sort out some accommodation in Ubeda, choosing that town over Baeza because it was a little closer to where I was sitting at the time. There was no obvious campsite in Ubeda, so I browsed the hotel options instead. A hotel would also help ease the back pain that was still nagging away and I chose a place called the *Neuve Leyendas* or the 'Nine Legends', for no reason other than it having an interesting name. Well that and the 50% discount.

Many hundreds of thousands – probably millions – of olive trees later, I followed the signs pointing me away from the N-322 and in the direction of Ubeda. First impressions were somewhat subdued. The modern suburbs were just like the modern suburbs had been elsewhere in southern Europe: lots of apartment blocks plastered white or painted pale brown, red or yellow, shops, cars, a bit of graffiti here and there and golden-brown people going about their business in the late afternoon sun. A change from cracked tarmac to cobbles – not the easiest of surfaces upon which to cycle - suggested something a little more interesting was ahead. Following the directions for the centre, it was almost inevitable that I would get lost and I did. I seemed to have missed the area where I would hopefully find the *Neuve Leyendas* and had instead found a road with an ancient high wall to my right and a panoramic view of Andalusia and its olive groves to my left. If I hadn't been astounded by the trees as I cycled through them earlier in the afternoon, the elevated position from the centre of Ubeda was providing me with an incredible vista of green dots, lined up like soldiers, each regiment of several hundred angled in a slightly different way. Stunning.

The high wall was interrupted by a gate through which I cycled, bouncing up and down on the polished cobbles. After a few turns left and right, the road opened out into a medium-sized square. If the view across the countryside only a few moments earlier had been stunning, this was its urban equivalent and it was exquisite.

The *Plaza Vazquez de Molina* was longer than it was wide with, at its eastern end, the intricate façade of the *Sacra Capilla de El Salvador*. On one of the longer sides of the square was the *Parador de Turismo* but this tourist office was housed in a grand two-storey palace that must surely have been a tourist attraction itself. A neat garden of low hedges divided the open space into two, with the large square *Palacio de Juan Vazquez de Molina* at the far end. Opposite it, set slightly back from the square, was a second church, not quite as detailed as the first but just as graceful. The words of my cousin came to mind. '*Much of a muchness*', he had said when comparing Ubeda with Baeza. It seemed strange terminology to have used and I could only imagine that Baeza was of equal beauty. Despite the splendour of its buildings, the square was quiet and intimate, with just a few police cars parked outside what I assumed was one of Spain's most desirable police stations. I really hadn't expected to find this at the end of the day.

I managed to locate the *Neuve Leyendas* in a street very close to the square. If the *Plaza Vazquez de Molina* had been quiet, the 'Nine Legends' was deserted. The building was from the same era as those around the square and a large wooden door gave access to the communal area of the hotel where there was a table, a bar, an office and a staircase leading off to the left. It did feel a little like someone's house, but that's not a criticism. After a few moments of hanging around, a woman appeared and welcomed me. Her English was minimal but we managed to exchange the essential pieces of information. She was very smiley; I think I was the only paying guest and there was, perhaps, a connection. I could only assume that August in Ubeda was not high season and that everyone had headed to the beaches to cool off in the sea.

My room was beautiful, especially for the price that I was paying. I was staying in room four – there were nine in total – and each had been given the name of a legend. Mine was *La Leyenda del Hospital de Santiago*. An explanation of the legend of the Hospital of Santiago was written in Spanish in a frame by the door. It seemed to have something to do with being guarded by a saint with a sword in his hands and, should the sword ever go missing, Spain would once again fall to the Moors. I would keep an eye out.

After a short period of interior rest and relaxation, I ventured outside for more of the same. The sun was setting and the sky darkening. Most of the buildings in the square and adjacent streets were gradually becoming bathed in light. The warm hue of the stone made for some easy photo opportunities and I wandered around the still very quiet streets snapping away as I did. The more I strolled, the more I wondered why I had never before heard of Ubeda. It was a real gem of a town, with architecture equal in splendour to that of Madrid, Valencia or Granada, just more moderate in size. If this had been anywhere near the coast – I was now over 100km inland – it would have been infested with the cruise ship swarms that I had encountered elsewhere. It was great to have it almost all to myself and I sensed that a little digging beneath the surface of the beautiful facades of the buildings might delay my departure the following morning. If, that is, the Moors didn't invade first.

Friday 23rd August 2013
Cycling Day 45: Ubeda To Jaén, 63km

It's usually quite nice being anonymous in a hotel; that way you come and go about your business as you please. Some people, however, need to be noticed and at the other end of the spectrum are those A-list celebrities who book the entire floor of a hotel (I'm sure there have been instances of their taking over the whole establishment) and who demand the attention that they so often crave. Being the only guest in the *Neuve Leyendas* is the nearest I've yet come to being treated like a VIP in a hotel, not just on this trip across Europe, but ever in my life. I hadn't seen much of the owners on the day of my arrival, but in the morning both the woman I had met the previous evening and her husband were there to attend to my every need. They introduced themselves as Begoña and Pedro. They were both in their fifties and originally from the Basque Country in the north of Spain. They had bought the *Neuve Leyendas* some 18 months earlier and had moved to Andalusia for a new life and to hopefully make a successful business out of running the small boutique hotel. It was impossible to fault their attention to their guests, or rather their guest. My laundry had been done overnight (and they never charged me for it), breakfast was included in the price of the room (more often than not, with online 'deals', it wasn't) and they chatted to me as if I was not only a valued customer but also a good friend. Discussion wasn't always easy, as neither Begoña nor Pedro spoke good English and we all know about my inadequacies with the Spanish language, but through a combination of repetition, hesitation and charades, we seemed to manage just fine. I dare say that for fans of Radio 4's *Just A Minute*, there was also a fair bit of deviation, as the topics of conversation followed the direction of understanding rather than perhaps necessity.

It had always been part of the plan (to the extent that I did 'plan') to cycle only as far as Jaén. The second *Via Verde* started in Jaén and it was a mere 60km to the south west of Ubeda - well below my daily average, which was now (according to my cycling app), over 110km. So, when Pedro asked if I would like a private tour of the *Palacio de Juan Vazquez de Molina*, one of the buildings that I had admired upon arrival in Ubeda, including access to areas that were otherwise off-limits to tourists, I was more than happy to abandon an immediate start in favour of a bit of exclusive sightseeing.

The *Palacio* was only a couple of minutes walk from the hotel, so leaving Reggie under the watchful eye of Begoña, Pedro and I set off round the corner to explore. The building was a symmetrical, three-storey edifice and was now the town hall of Ubeda, the *ayuntamiento*. However, it had been built in the 16th century as a home for Juan Vasquez de Molina who was the secretary of state for Charles V and Philip II, but Juan never actually got around to living in the building. Perhaps he couldn't sell his old place, who knows? Instead, it was converted into a convent for Dominican nuns. It was subsequently used as a courthouse before becoming the town hall that it is today. Pedro led the way and I followed: through the main door, up a flight of steps in one corner of the building and then into an office where a couple of women were working away behind computers. Pedro exchanged pleasantries with them – they clearly knew who he was – before he gestured towards the wall on our right where a great mural had been painted. It was dated 1595. I nodded in appreciation without really understanding the biblical scene that was depicted. The lower parts of the painting were obscured by what looked like a set of Billy bookcases from IKEA, circa 2005. Returning to the tiled gallery that looked down upon the square courtyard at the centre of the *Palacio*, my guided tour continued. We climbed a second flight of stairs – a little narrower than the first – into a room lined with more bookcases (pre-IKEA this time) and above which the vaulted interior of the wooden roof could be seen in all its glory. This was the town's historical archive. The man in charge – a bearded chap who wasn't quite at ease meeting strangers like myself (let alone those wearing tight-fitting lycra) – engaged in conversation with Pedro, who in turn translated what he could to me. The archive was the second oldest in Andalusia, holding documents that dated back as far as Valentine's Day 1235. (I wondered if it was a card.) More impressive than any of the dusty documents on the shelves, however, were the views from the oval windows of this third floor of the building, looking down upon the square and the Andalusian countryside beyond. Could there be a more beautiful frame for such sublime views? I doubted it.

As we made our way back to the entrance of the building, Pedro introduced me to a man who I assumed was the mayor of the town. He looked like a man in authority. Just as he had back at the *Neuve Leyendas,* Pedro had managed to make me feel special. Perhaps all visitors to his hotel received the same treatment as me. Perhaps those women behind their computers in the office and the guy looking after the documents on the 3rd floor groaned every time they saw him appear at their door. And perhaps the mayor of Ubeda could have done without being introduced to yet another passing tourist. I was happy to think that this wasn't the case. Both Pedro and his wife Begoña had made me feel especially welcome, not just in their hotel but also in their adopted town.

Looking at the map, I could see that I might have two problems getting as far as Jaén. They were both dual carriageways, along which cycling was presumably banned. Google Maps came to my aid with a motorway/toll-free route which involved a fair bit of twisting and turning, but I did what Mr. Google told me and in the end things turned out just fine. It was a long descent through olives groves – *what else?* – for the first 15km of the 60km that I needed to cycle. The valley flattened out at the point where I crossed the *Rio Guadalquivir,* after which it was a steady climb back up to 700m through (you guessed it) more olive groves. The level of traffic on the road fluctuated between very light and non-existent. There was little fluctuation when it came to the temperature, however; it was perhaps the highest it had been since leaving southern Greece and it was getting hotter as each hour of the day passed. The countryside was isolated and there were few places, if any, where I was able to stop and refill my bottles of water: no shops, no petrol stations, no cemeteries. By the time I arrived in the town of Mancha Real, I was gasping for water and to say that the sight of drinking fountains in the park just outside the town was a relief would be something of an understatement. On a relentlessly hot day, few things can be more satisfying than the sensation of quenching extreme thirst with cool water from a tap. One of life's small pleasures.

Where Ubeda had charm and beauty, Mancha Real didn't. It was a functional outpost in the Andalusian hills, built upon a grid pattern and there was little to see. It was, however, lunchtime and I cycled along one of the long, straight streets in the search of a café or bar that was open. I eventually found one – a sports bar halfway down a pedestrianised road – where I ordered a ham and cheese sandwich and something cold to drink. I wondered if, in places such as Mancha Real, a system existed whereby the local bar owners had agreed some kind of rota to ensure that at least one of their establishments was open at any one time during the day. If no such agreement existed, I could only commend the entrepreneurial skills of the owner who had decided to stay open during the early afternoon, when all but a very small handful of locals and I had hidden themselves away from the searing heat of the day. Before setting off for the final leg of my ride to Jaén, I stocked up on water at an out-of-town petrol station; the sensation of quenching extreme thirst could only really be enjoyed if it was done relatively infrequently.

The cycle from Mancha Real to Jaén was a shorter repetition of the cycle that I had already completed from Ubeda: a long downhill journey to the valley bottom followed by a climb to my final destination. Jaén had been described to me by someone online as a *'dump'* and the *Rough Guide* referred to it as *'an uneventful sort of place'*. I was determined to see a more promising side of the provincial capital. The late-afternoon temperature that was displayed on a green electronic sign just above a pharmacy on the outskirts of town was 39 degrees. I could believe it. This was probably the temperature in the shade and must surely have been even higher when the sun had reached its peak earlier in the day. I had booked a hotel room in Jaén while sipping a late morning coffee back in Ubeda and, whereas I had chosen the hotel in Ubeda because of its name (and the 50% discount), in Jaén I chose the hotel based upon what it looked like in the picture. The online photograph had depicted a modern building which had been painted white. In large, black letters across the façade had been added the name of the hotel, repeated several times in horizontal and vertical directions: *'Europa Hotel Jaén'*. I liked the quirky style, so I booked a room for a value price of €50. It wasn't the easiest of places to find, tucked away in a small square just a few minutes walk from the centre of the city, and required some serious climbing. Jaén was a city on a slope and with four panniers and a tent on board, my calf muscles were once again tested as I rose from the seat of the bike to ensure that we didn't grind to a halt on some of the steep, but mercifully short, backstreets. When I found the small square, it was easy to spot the distinctive 'in-your-face' Europa Hotel. I wondered how such an incongruous-looking building had ever managed to receive planning permission, but I was glad that it had. Every town or city needs its out-of-place oddities and this was certainly one of Jaén's. Once I had registered my arrival at reception, I was able to discover the interior décor of the hotel, which was as quirky as the exterior, and even more vivid. The walls of the corridors on each floor sported a distinctive vibrant colour; the first floor was red, the second violet and the third floor – my floor – was lime green. Yellow and orange made up this mini-rainbow of colour on the fourth and fifth floors. It was a world away from the grey of the hotel back in Albacete and a godsend to anyone with a visual memory.

Determined to find a city that wasn't *'an uneventful dump'*, I set off to explore in the late-afternoon heat. Admittedly, Jaén was a little run-down and shabby and it was certainly no Ubeda (not many places are), but it did have its charms, especially in the older part of town in the area around the 17ᵗʰ century hulk of a cathedral. My guidebook described it as a *'masterpiece of Andalusian Renaissance architecture'* and to the extent that I was able, I agreed. It wasn't so much a church that invited worshippers in, as one that ordered them to do so. There was something distinctly authoritarian about its monolithic design. Banners hanging from the balconies of the adjacent town hall proclaimed that the local authorities were petitioning for the centre of Jaén to be recognised as a World Heritage Site by UNESCO. Perhaps that was just what was needed - a little cultural spotlight to attract investment to help the cathedral and its environs shine once again, just as they no doubt had done back in the 17th century. I had seen many more beautiful places since leaving the southern tip of Greece nearly two months earlier but I had also seen many others that had far less to shout about than the city on the hill that is Jaén.

My evening meal came from a supermarket and was eaten back in the colourful confines of the Europa Hotel. I had forgone my customary habit of dining out in favour of an evening poring over the last couple of maps that remained in my possession: the one of Andalusia and that of the Algarve in Portugal. As I munched my way through a baguette of cheese, a final five-day plan coalesced before me.

Saturday: I would set off from Jaén along the *Via Verde de Aceite* and find an intermediate stopping-off point between Jaén and Seville, perhaps Lucena. My cousin Richard, who had flown to Barcelona a few days previously and who was driving across Spain to return to work in central Portugal, would also be in the area. The plan was to meet up; I would find us some accommodation at an appropriate point, he would join me and we would catch up over an evening meal.

Sunday: Jaén to Seville was about 250km. It would be a challenge, especially in the heat of Andalusia, but if I were able to make it to Seville by the end of the weekend it would significantly increase my chances of completing the entire trip from one corner of Europe to another within fifty days of cycling.

Monday: Well, this was clearly dependent upon what would happen over the weekend, but to be somewhere close to the border with Portugal would be nice. I was still not quite sure how I would cross from one Iberian country to the next. Spain and Portugal were separated by the *Rio Guardiana,* but was there an alternative to the motorway that didn't involve a significant deviation to the north?

Tuesday: Assuming I would be in Portugal, the city of Faro may be my penultimate place of rest.

Wednesday: To the Cape St. Vincent near Sagres, the end of the route.

It was easy to put a plan down on paper. It was more of a challenge making sure that I executed it. Chief amongst those challenges would be the stifling heat of Spain. It was also impossible to ignore the fact that I was feeling increasingly weary. The daily exertions that were required of me were taking their toll; I was feeling dog-tired. But I couldn't stop now. I was so close.

Saturday 24th August 2013
Cycling Day 46: Jaén To Lucena, 103km

I found the start of the *Via Verde del Aceite* at the end of the *Ronda Juez Juan Ruiz*, tucked behind a sports complex on the northern edge of the town at the top of a short hill. I was immediately struck by one aspect of this 'green way' which set it apart from the *Via Verde Sierra de Alcaraz*: it was being used by people other than just me. In fact, I would even go so far as to say that it was busy. Not just with cyclists – mainly on mountain bikes – but also with walkers and a large number of joggers. It was a positive sign that this *Via Verde* might be a little more user-friendly than the one starting in Albacete had been.

The *Via Verde del Aceite* was actually two *Vias Verdes* joined together. The first was the *Via Verde del Aceite I,* and the second was (you guessed it) the *Via Verde del Aceite II*. This second route was, however, also referred to as the *Via Verde de la Subbética,* but for the purposes of this cycle I shall refer to both of the routes as simply the *Via Verde del Aceite. 'Aceite'* is the Spanish word for oil and the oil in question is (you might have guessed this too) olive oil. Just as the earlier *Via Verde* had been, the *Via Verde del Aceite* was a disused railway track although this line did actually see some locomotive action and the World Bank had stayed well clear. Built towards the end of the 19th century, the main purpose of the railway was to transport (you are ahead of me!), yes, olive oil to the port at Malaga. As with many railway lines, it was not a financial success and was taken over by the government in 1936. They kept the trains running – at an average speed of just 30km/hr – until they succumbed to the economic realities of the late 20th century, and the line closed in 1985. The 21st century breathed new life into the route (if not the trains) and it became part of the *Via Verde* network in 2001, open to walkers, runners and of course cyclists like me. My plan for cycling day 46 was to travel along all 55km of the *Aceite I* and then 45km of the *Aceite II,* stopping at Lucena rather than the end of the line destination of Puente Genil, which was a further 20km along the track.

Back to the *Ronda Juez Juan Ruiz* and the start of the *Via Verde del Aceite*. A large sign welcomed me to the route, although my eyebrow was raised just a little by the graphic that had been chosen. It was a Penny Farthing bike. On this surface? Looking down and along the track that headed off into the distance, the ground was again made up of loose stones. Not quite as challenging as they had been along the

365

initial stretch of the *Via Verde Sierra de Alcaraz,* but loose stones nevertheless. Stay positive! This was much better than being on the busy roads. A few metres away was a second sign: *'Normas generales de uso de la Via Verde'.* It was a list of rules and regulations, some of which I could understand but many of which I couldn't. I particularly liked the first one, which I guessed could be translated as *'Respect the rules'.* It immediately brought to mind the *Rules of Cycling* as maintained online by *Velominati* (*"We are the Keepers of the Cog. In so being, we also maintain the sacred text wherein lie the simple truths of cycling etiquette known as The Rules..."*). *Rule number 1: Obey the rules.* Perhaps I also needed to heed *Velominati's* rule number 5. You can look that one up yourself but perhaps it would have stopped me from whingeing about the road surface and just get on with the cycling. As for the other rules and regulations of the *Via Verde*, I would make sure that the ones I infringed would coincide with the ones I couldn't understand. *Los perros atados?*

It was nice to be cycling with other cyclists. This was something that I hadn't done much of at all. Along the Adriatic coastline, I was frequently passed by people on two wheels heading south but had almost always felt alone heading north. It was usually like that on the bike because I didn't tend to see the people either in front of me or behind me, especially if they were travelling at roughly the same speed. Occasionally, someone would whizz past in a flash of muscle and lycra at a speed that only gave me reason to tut disapprovingly. *Who can enjoy cycling like that?* I would ask myself, knowing full well that if I had been capable, I would have been going just as quickly. Outside Jaén, and for the first few kilometres along the *Via Verde,* it was necessary to keep my wits about me. My natural British urge to veer to the left on the single track had to be consciously overcome to avoid the mountain bikers coming in the opposite direction who were more attuned to the continental move to the right. Disaster was avoided and, as the kilometres passed by, the number of other cyclists dwindled considerably. I would never have the route to myself (and that's certainly not what I was hoping for) but the further away from Jaén I travelled, the more 'normal' the cycling conditions became.

The climb to Martos was a gentle one. Most of the railway infrastructure – apart from the tracks themselves – was still in place and, periodically, I was able to pause for a rest at the stations still standing patiently for the trains that would no longer arrive. Most were in good condition, although only a few gave the appearance of being in use. None of the buildings in the first part of the *Via Verde del Aceite* were open for business. Perhaps the passing trade of walkers and cyclists of 2013 wasn't able to sustain a café or a shop or a bicycle-hire shop in the same way that the transporting of olive oil hadn't been able to sustain the railway itself during the 20th century. At least the abandoned stations provided sufficient space for picnic benches positioned under shady trees; they were most welcome as the sun climbed high into the blue Andalusian sky. At several points, a modern road – usually a busy dual carriageway – had been built straight across the path of the old railway line. I could only assume they dated from the period between the closure of the line in 1985 and the decision to turn it into a *Via Verde* at some point during the mid to late 1990s. Rather than sending me on a tortuous detour through the undergrowth of the olive tree plantations, the engineers of the *Via Verde* had done the right thing and built metal bridges to span the flow of cars and lorries. Not only were they of architectural merit but their elevated position over the roar of the traffic gave a sense of travelling superiority. It was a nice touch. Elsewhere, rusting metal viaducts dating from the 19th century were still standing. The wooden planks providing the surface of the bridges made for a rickety ride from one side of a valley to the other. Such was their age and weathered state, the viaducts had become part of the natural environment that surrounded them. Indeed, the regimented lines of olive trees that continued to dominate the landscape appeared much more artificially placed than the long brown constructions of riveted metal. All in all, the day was turning out to be a memorable one in the saddle.

At Martos, I left the *Via Verde* briefly as I needed cash. The town was not dissimilar to Mancha Real, the place where I had paused for lunch on the previous day, except that it was busy with people. And horses. The famous Andalusian horses? Perhaps not. The ones being ridden around the streets of Martos were more working horses than dancing ones. Beautiful, nevertheless and a welcome alternative to the ubiquitous use of the car. After a little searching, I did manage to rejoin the *Via Verde*. The difficulty was that in Martos, the disused railway line had become a suburban street. However, logic dictated that a train would never have been capable of making a sharp turn either left or right, so I simply continued along the curve of the street that I suspected to be the former route of the tracks and it worked. After a few minutes, I was back on the rough, traffic-free *Via Verde*.

Martos had been the physical high point of the route at around 650m. From there until the end of the *Via Verde del Aceite I,* it would be a predominantly downhill cycle but again, as the gradient was sufficiently shallow to allow for the movement of trains, it often felt as though I was cycling on the flat. However the rough surface of the track meant that any pause in turning the pedals would have resulted in the bike coming to stop within metres. It was tiring and was about to become more so.

The point at which the *Via Verde del Aceite I* finished and the *Via Verde del Aceite II* started was marked by a spectacular viaduct that spanned the *Rio Guadajoz*. Or was it the very end of the beautiful *Embalse de Vadomojón*? The two bodies of water seemed to merge into one, not just on my map but also in reality. A sign welcomed me to part II, as did a second, gradual climb stretching over some 20km as far as Doña Mencía. After just a few kilometres, in the heat of the middle of the day, my body was aching and my willpower had been broken. Every turn of the pedal, became a real effort, every jolt over even the smallest of rocks a reason to curse the surface below me. Some respite came in the form of the station at Luque. It was the first one along the route that had been converted into a place to stop, rest and crucially, buy something to eat and drink. It was something of a museum, with old railways carriages standing to one side of the platform (where else?) and the original signage on the walls of the building having been repainted: *almacen* (stock room), *policia*, *sala de espera* (waiting room)... All the stock had gone, there were no policemen to be seen and the only people waiting were the Chinese tourists who had turned up en masse in a coach that was parked nearby. They were queuing at the counter to pay for the souvenirs they had bought from the shop. The owner of the 'station' couldn't believe his luck and was far more interested in tending to their desires than mine. Eventually, once the small swarm had returned to the bus, he approached me and I ordered some much needed food.

I took a long lunch. Clouds of water vapour descended from a sprinkler system in the roof. It reminded me of the network of pipes that had been installed above the heads of shoppers in Grasse in Provence. Here in Andalusia, it wasn't just nice, it was almost essential. Why hadn't the idea caught on elsewhere? I reasoned that the answer to that question was that the people of southern Spain took a preventative rather than curative attitude when it came to the heat; they all went back home and took their *siesta*. The only ones foolish enough to venture out into the midday sun were a mad Englishman like me and a bunch of Chinese tourists.

Having committed myself to meeting my cousin in Lucena, still some 35km further along the track, I did need to move on at some point and eventually I did. The rest, food and drink had boosted me physically and my morale had been lifted but alas it wasn't to last. After barely 5km I once again ground to a halt, beaten into submission by the heat and the track, which had now returned to being rough gravel. I stood next to the viaduct at Zuheros, looked down the stunning valley across the vast expanse of olive trees and, should I have chosen to let my emotions flow, I could have wept. I was feeling a very strange mix of emotions: on the one hand the joy of having very nearly achieved what I had set out to do on the 1st July, on the other, the cumulative fatigue of nearly two months of cycling. I didn't cry. I did the next best thing a 21st century man can do: I recorded a short video and posted it to Facebook;

"I am beginning to feel weary... with potentially four days to go... there is an increasing part of me that just wants to finish... it's becoming more and more difficult, especially in the heat of Andalusia – the temperature is again in the high thirties, perhaps forty degrees – and I am fed up with seeing olive trees! I've had them for three, four days... and they just never stop... I hope the journey to Seville tomorrow is different... no more bloody olive trees..."

The poor olive tree took the brunt of my frustrations.

I did, of course, continue, aided somewhat by the reverse in incline after the *Estación de Doña Mencía*, and I arrived in Lucena, exhausted, in the late afternoon. My cousin hadn't yet arrived. This afforded me the time to sit in a bar and reflect upon the science of cycling long distances on a bike. I wrote the following:

"Cycling day 46 was the big Vias Verdes day and, after the mixed feelings about Via Verde number 1 from Albacete a few days ago, I was hoping for something far better. Did I get it? I suspect that if you'd asked me the question at different points of the day, you would have been given different answers. It all comes down to physics. Yes, physics. The stuff you learnt at school (if you went to school in the days prior to their calling everything 'science') about physical things, and in this case, their movement. Now Newton came up with three laws of motion which, at speeds that are anywhere near the velocity of which Reggie is capable, are true (get nearer the speed of light and that's where Einstein kicks in). For every action there must be an equal and opposite reaction (in other words if you put a piece of bread on the table as I just did in this bar in Lucena, the table exerts an upward force to balance the downward force of the bread and it stays in the same place rather than flying off and hitting the waiter in the eye). If an object is moving in a particular direction it will continue to move in that direction until acted upon by some other force (if I throw the bread at the waiter to grab his attention, it will either fall to the ground due to the force of gravity and miss him or it

will hit him and stop due to the force of his forehead against the bread – I would also experience a force and get kicked out of the bar). Finally, the acceleration of an object is directly proportional to the force that is applied to that object (so if I do get booted out of the tapas bar the speed that I do so will be entirely dependant upon how forcefully the waiter kicks me up the arse). I think that's it.

Now, what has all this got to do with me cycling? (I'm beginning to wonder myself...) Well, smooth surfaces. They are great and it's why the majority of roads upon which you drive are smooth. There is a compromise to be had, however, as a road that is too smooth would have your wheels simply spinning on the ground. So on a micro-level they need to generate friction but on a macro-level they need to be smooth. If you weren't able to drive your car on smooth roads then you would see your fuel prices rocket. Why? Well, because every time your car hits a divet, hole, pimple, undulation..., Newton's laws kick in and the road tries to stop you moving in the horizontal direction you want to move. Your car compensates by applying more force and hence uses more fuel to keep you moving horizontally. In a car, although you feel the physical consequences of being on an uneven road, you only notice the extra energy impact when you pay for your fuel. On a bicycle, it's different. You feel the physical pain in two ways: firstly, the physical movement which has you moving up and down like a whore's drawers (sorry, old joke) but also the extra energy needed to keep moving horizontally is expended there and then. It's bloody knackering! Which is why, on balance, I cannot recommend the Vias Verdes for long-distance travelling cyclists; the ground you are cycling upon is just too uneven. They are great for photos, but for anyone who just wants to enjoy the view and put some distance on the clock, it might be a better option to stick to the relatively smooth roads.

Physics lesson over."

I am torn including these comments in this book, as I believe in every gram of the ideal of having long-distance 'green ways'. I would encourage every single person reading this to get out on their bikes and try them and I would love to be proven wrong. But can I hide the feelings that I had at the time? When I look back through the rose-tinted spectacles of time, I do remember the spectacular views, the tunnels, the viaducts, the isolation, the complete lack of motorised traffic... They were all wonderful things to experience. But as for the physical process of cycling, my reminiscences are less than positive. It is worth remembering that there are scores of *Vias Verdes* in Spain and that I rode along just three. Were the ones that I did experience simply unrepresentative? Or should I just stop complaining and implement cycling rule number 5. What? You didn't look it up? OK, here it is;

Rule #5: Harden the f**k up.

Sunday 25th August 2013
Cycling Day 47: Lucena To Seville, 175km

Lucena, *la perla de Sefarad*, the pearl of Sepharad. The Spanish Jews of the Middle Ages referred to the Iberian Peninsula as Sepharad and Lucena was home to many Jews fleeing persecution elsewhere in Spain. The descendants of the Iberian Jews are the people to whom we now refer as the Sephardi, or more usually the Sephardic Jews. After yesterday's physics lesson, I feel as though I am redressing the balance with a touch of history. Back to the cycling.

Well, before the cycling starts again, a brief summary of the evening in Lucena. After some delay (there usually is), my cousin Richard finally arrived in town in the early evening. I had already booked two rooms in a hotel that was just on the edge of town but when I *arrived* on the edge of town at the place where the hotel was supposed to be, it wasn't there. I asked some passing locals if they knew where it had gone, only to be told that it was several kilometres away up the hill. In my weary state that was the last thing I needed to hear, so I double-checked my facts – yes, the description of the two-star *Sierra de Araceli* stated that it was '...*set in the town of Lucena'* (it wasn't) and the blue place marker on the online map was most definitely pointing at the spot where I was currently standing (but not the hotel). After a stressful afternoon on the bike, I was in no mood for being taken in by an entrepreneurial hotelier who wanted potential clients to think that their hotel was nearer the action of Lucena than it actually was, so I rang Booking.com and demanded an immediate refund.

"Ah yes... I see that you've made quite a few bookings with us recently..."

The woman's tone of voice implied that there was something wrong with this.

"Can I ring you back?"

I reluctantly agreed and spent the next ten minutes sitting on a curb stone on the edge of Lucena under the imaginary blue marker of Booking.com, waiting for them to do just that. They did and I was refunded my money. I continued to sit on the curb stone as I tried again, this time booking two singles at the *Hotel Al-Yussana* which was not only cheaper but also much more central. Why had I not gone for this option in the first place?

372

Once showered and changed, we hit the streets of Lucena. I'm not quite sure that Richard appreciated just how many calories are required by your average long-distance touring cyclist. As we nibbled our way through a series of modest tapas dishes in Lucena's liveliest bar, I began to wish that the arrangement of my paying for the hotel and his paying for the evening meal hadn't been the other way round.

In fairness, I can't have been the greatest of company that evening. I had been travelling by myself for the best part of two months and, although when required to do so I could turn on the charm and be the happy-go-lucky cyclist that I wanted people to think that I was, the isolation of the road had left me out of practice with social interaction. Richard was a relative and I had known him all my life. He would still be my cousin the following day, the following week and at Christmas when I would no doubt see him again. Being with him didn't require me to maintain the pretence that I wasn't tired or indeed that I didn't just want to get the journey finished.

That said, I can't have offended him too much as we agreed to meet up for a second time at the end of cycling day 48, when I hoped that I would have moved on to somewhere near the Portuguese border. I left the accommodation for that evening in his hands rather than mine and he promised to update me accordingly.

I had already worked out that Jaén to Seville was about 250km. Jaén to Lucena had been just over 100km. The 150km that remained would see me return to cycling along the good quality surfaces of the Andalusian roads, rather than the rough tracks of the *Vias Verdes*, but which roads would they be, especially across the slice of land that was to be found to the east of Seville in a triangular segment that was bound by the A4 *autovia* to the north and the A92 *autovia* to the south? Between the two, all the roads on my map (and on Google maps online) ran from north to south; not one of them crossed the area in the direction I wanted to travel. At some point, either a significant dollop of good fortune would have to intervene in the shape of an unmapped road or I would be required to deviate somewhat, either to the north or the south. 150km for the cycle to Seville did seem like a rather conservative estimate.

The best strategy is, of course, to ignore the problem until it actually matters and that wouldn't be until after the town of Marchena. The towns and villages up to that point – Puente Genil, Matarredonda, El Rubio, El Termino and Lantejuela – were all circled on my map and it would simply be a case of joining them up. There was also some good topographic news: Lucena was at 500m and I knew that Seville was an inland river port at sea level, so my journey should be predominantly downhill. That was all theory. Would it be the practice?

Things started well. I made it as far as Puente Genil with no problem. Cycling to Matarredonda wasn't an issue and I arrived in El Rubio with little fuss. On leaving El Rubio, however, I took the wrong road. It left me heading due south and it was an error that I didn't spot until the point where it made more sense to continue and improvise an alternative route than it did to turn back and go along the correct road. That was perhaps not the wisest of decisions - the cycling equivalent of continuing to dig whilst standing in the hole. Unfortunately, no corrective road to the right presented itself, but I knew that if I continued along the SE-727, I would eventually hit the wall of the motorway. This wasn't Albania. Drastic action was needed. Separating me from the road along which I should have been cycling, was a wide (and ever widening) expanse of land. What was covering the land? You guessed. It was time to get up close and personal with the things that I will forever associate with Andalusia: the olive trees. Occasionally, rough tracks that were used to service the trees branched off the road. It was time for an unscheduled return to some very bespoke *Via Verde* cycling. It was a bit of a risk, as I couldn't see where the tracks were leading. My hope was that they would connect with one of the roads that would see me travelling more to the west than the south. For all I knew, however, the unsurfaced tracks might stop in the middle of an olive grove, leaving me with no alternative but to slalom my way around hundreds of trees - not what I wanted to do - or simply retrace my steps back to the SE-727. I wasn't so keen on that option either. Why did I never make life easy for myself by simply spending a little more time planning?

I chose a track and set off, pleased to be heading in the right direction once again, but decidedly nervous about what I might find. The quality of the ride made some of the worst *Via Verde* surfaces seem like a journey in the back of a Rolls Royce. What was perfectly feasible for a purpose-built, agricultural vehicle wasn't necessarily feasible for a touring bike like Reggie. It was a long, tentative ride, trying to avoid the roughest bits of the rough track, but it did allow me to see the olive trees in all their glory. It wasn't something that I had been craving and I would have been perfectly happy keeping them at the distance to which I had become accustomed since arriving in Andalusia earlier in the week. Without any 3G coverage, I couldn't access any satellite images that might give me a little confidence I wasn't on a road to nowhere. And then the dogs started to bark. Not just one, but a whole pack of them. Was this it? After 5,500km, mauled to death by a hungry, potentially rabid gang of canine thugs? *He came, he saw, he was eaten.* I looked up from the surface of the track to see where the barking might be coming from. Ahead of me, I could see two long sheds in the distance. This was doubled-edged news. I had clearly found the location of the dogs (and much to my distress, I couldn't see a fence preventing them from getting at me should they choose to do so), but the significant size of the sheds implied that there must surely be a more substantial road leading away from the buildings on the other side. Perspiring from not only the heat but also from fear, I continued to cycle in the direction of the sheds.

You may have guessed that I survived. The noise of the dogs became louder but I never saw any of them. Better still, the road on the other side of the buildings was of better quality and it did take me as far as the next public road. My plan had worked. Well, kind of. I was now hopelessly lost. I had no idea which road on my map I was on. There was still no 3G coverage to check online. Even the GPS cycling app only provided me with a long track through a sea of blankness because the map couldn't be downloaded. It was time to get down to basics and do a bit of navigation using the sun. Alas, it was now the middle of the day and the sun was of little use. At least I knew the direction I had come from. I would just have to attempt to keep travelling in the same direction.

Buoyed by my first off-road success, I thought I might as well try it again. The track I chose was still as rough as the previous one, but there were no barking dogs. Nothing but olive tree after olive tree after olive tree. It was, however, much longer and, after 7km off road, I finally emerged from the wilderness and back onto a road worthy of the name, and its name was the A-351. Glory be to Heaven! It was a road that was also on my map. I had made depressingly slow progress since leaving El Rubio but I could see light at the end of the tunnel. All I needed to do was cycle as far as El Termino – also on the A-351 – and then turn left towards Lantejuela. I would be in Marchena in no time at all.

Well, it was mid afternoon before I arrived there so I stopped for lunch in a beautiful square surrounded by white-washed buildings. I had cycled just over 100km. Seville couldn't be too far away now.

Two significant things had changed since leaving Lucena. Firstly, the preponderance of olive trees. They never quite disappeared but they had definitely thinned out to the point where they were just one of many crops in the fields. Secondly, the architecture. The style was now very distinct. As far as Lucena, it had only been hinted at by the occasional house or row of houses but since leaving *the pearl of Sepharad,* every town and village consisted almost exclusively of two-storey terraces, painted white with tall windows and doors, bordered with a brightly painted, orange band of ornate plaster. The upper-floor windows all sported Juliet balconies painted shiny black and the windows on the ground floor were mostly protected by their own top-to-bottom railings, also painted shiny black. The contrast of the black and orange against a background of white was as stark as it was attractive and the ensemble of house after house in this style was distinctively Andalusian.

I now had to make a decision about how exactly I would get to Seville from Marchena. Head north-west towards Carmona or south-west towards Arahal? The sensible option was to follow the latter route because the only way from Carmona to Seville was along the *autovia.* Cycling beyond Arahal would at least see me link up with one of the less important arterial routes into the centre of the Andalusian capital. It would inevitably take the number of kilometres to well above the 150 that I had originally hoped for as I first lurched south and then back to the north, but I had no choice. Unless, of course, I fancied some more off-roading but I'd already experienced my fair share of that. For one day at least.

The wind picked up substantially in the late afternoon and it wasn't blowing in a direction that was making life any easier for me on the bike. I did hope that, when I changed abruptly from cycling south-west to cycling north-west and Seville, the situation would be reversed but it was too much to hope for and the long battle of attrition between me and the wicked Iberian wind of the west continued, until my arrival in the very centre of the city.

As with many of the Spanish cities through which I had cycled, Seville was ringed by a wall of almost impenetrable motorway, so once again I called upon Google Maps to guide me to the city centre, which it did, admirably, depositing me at the doors of the hotel that I had booked earlier in the afternoon. It wasn't my first visit to Seville; I had previously spent a warm November day in the city as part of a school trip a few years earlier, so I knew what awaited me and I wasn't disappointed. Both Barcelona and Valencia had, at times, been busy, hectic places full of people doing things. Seville had no intention of being involved in anything so vulgar. It was a city that had taken the chill pill and was full of people who, at the very least, wanted to give the impression that they had little, if anything, to do. I would only be there for a matter of hours but it was my firm intention to join them in doing very little indeed.

Monday 26th August 2013
Cycling Day 48: Seville To El Portil (Near Huelva), 121km

Just to the north west of Madrid is a magnificent renaissance palace called *El Escorial*. It was built at the behest of Phillip II and was completed in 1584. It will come as no surprise to hear that it is Spain's largest building. Royal palaces tend to have regal dimensions and *El Escorial* certainly does. Not to be completely outdone, Seville is home to Spain's second largest building. But it's not a palace, it's a tobacco factory, albeit a royal one, or the *Fábrica Real de Tabacos* as it's known to the locals and, as I was browsing through my guidebook over early morning coffee in the *Avenida de la Constitución,* it struck me as perhaps the most interesting diversion to seek out in central Seville. There were plenty of other contenders for the privilege of having Reggie and me rock up at their gates but it's not every day that you wake up in a city where one of the chief attractions is a factory. So off we pedalled.

We didn't have to travel far although I purposefully took us on a circuitous route so as to at least see some of the other city-centre delights: the *Catedral*, the *Archivo de las Indias* and the *Alcázar* chief amongst them. After perhaps twenty minutes or so of navigating the city whilst simultaneously trying to avoid cycling over the omnipresent cobbles (by teetering on the edge of the narrow pavements), we arrived in front of the two-storey vastness of the Tobacco Factory. Had I not chosen to complete a minor tour of the other delights of Seville, I could have walked there from the café on the *Avenida de la Constitución* in well under five minutes. Cast from your mind any image of a grey and featureless, modern-day factory. This was a factory of the 18th century and built not just to manufacture but also to impress. It could have easily passed as a palace with grand, ornate entrances, upper-floor balconies and countless rooftop statues. From the outside, as I peered through the main door towards the interior of the building, I could see courtyards with elegant fountains, water dribbling from their tiered spouts. When Spain arrived in the Americas in 1492, they started shipping tobacco back home almost immediately and it was to the port of Seville that they brought it. The factory, however, didn't start producing tobacco until 1758, having been constructed so as to ensure that the Spanish state could keep control of the industry and the money it generated. Thousands of men and women – the *cigarreras* of whom Bizet's eponymous Carmen was one – were employed in the

377

factory until the mid 20th century when production ceased and the University of Seville moved in.

There were no apparent restrictions to entering the magnificent edifice and, since the long corridors leading from the exterior to the interior courtyards were simply a continuation of the stone pavement that surround the building, wheeling Reggie by my side, I went in to explore. The paraphernalia of academic life – official notices of exams and their results, posters advertising university events and dozens of homemade adverts for accommodation – abounded, but above all the doors, the original signs remained - *Monta-Carga No.1, Almacen de Elaborado No.2* – just as they had done at the converted railway station along the *Via Verde* a couple of days previously. The very 21st century signs informing students and staff not to smoke – *No Fumar* – made me smile.

The first cycling challenge of the day was to successfully cross the *Rio Guadalquivir,* just to the west of Seville. Once again, for the sake of managing to get to the other side of the river without an excessively long detour, this required me to ignore my suspicion that I probably shouldn't have been on the road along which I was travelling. However, within just a few metres of the western bank of the river, an opportunity presented itself to lift Reggie over the low barrier by the side of the road/*autovia* and join a rough track alongside the busy three lanes, so I did just that. After a few hundred metres, the dusty track took a sharp left turn underneath the SE-30 and I was back into the land of almost traffic-free traveling.

I had been expecting a day of pancake-flat cycling, so was a little disappointed to be confronted with a sharp climb only 10km into my ride. I don't mind the ascents (as the previous two months had proven, with my adventures in the Peloponnese, the Albanian mountains, the Croatian coast, the southern Alps, *Mont Ventoux* and the Pyrenees), but there can be few things worse than even a relatively modest climb, if it is unexpected. It was barely a pimple – just 150m – but my legs strained and I groaned as each metre was pedalled. I wasn't rewarded with any views looking back over the Andalusian capital – the clutter of the suburbs put paid to that and I simply wasn't high enough – but when I looked towards the west, I did see a bright star shining just above the horizon. It was a curious sight that I couldn't quite work out. It wasn't the sun, it wasn't the moon. A point of brightness, hanging low in the sky. How very odd. The three wise men followed their star; I was one man with a lower second-class degree in mathematics, but as my star happened to be in the direction that I was travelling, I would follow it, albeit by default.

The day had started under grey skies in Seville but, yet again, the temperature was fearsome and becoming ever more so as the morning came and went. By midday, the clouds had dissipated somewhat and, for much of the time, I was in the direct glare of the sun, just a thin layer of factor 50 protection cream preventing me from being grilled. I was still following my star. Was I perhaps suffering the ill effects of the southern Spanish climate, imagining things that weren't really there? Cycling out of Sanlucar la Mayor, I began to have a much better view of the star. In fact, one star had become two and I could now see that they were each accompanied by a tall white tower. I had never seen anything quite like this before and my mind was working overtime, trying to work out what was going on. *Was it art? Was it industrial? Was it for the military?* There was certainly something out-of-this-world about what I could see. The closer I became, the more detail I could see and there were, in fact, three bright points of light – one had previously been obscured behind another - and there were three towers. Each tower was slightly different in design, but all three contained a large elongated hole. At the very top of one of the towers was a sign, written in red capital letters: ABENGOA SOLAR. The other two towers had similar signs, although they didn't look identical to the one that was nearest to me. The word 'solar', combined with the numerous pylons that were strewn across the area to the right of the road where the three towers and points of light were located, gave a strong indication that this was some kind of power generation installation. It was a spectacular and beautiful thing to behold.

What I had stumbled upon was the Solucar Complex, owned by the company whose name I had seen on the towers: Abengoa Solar. It's the largest solar-power generation complex in Europe and is capable of generating some 183MW of electricity, an amount sufficient to provide for the needs of some 94,000 homes. What I wasn't able to see from ground level, was the array of mirrors, or heliostats (mirrors that can follow the sun like a sunflower) which reflect solar radiation onto a receiver located at the top of 160 metre-tall towers to produce steam, which in turn is generated into electricity inside a turbine. Very clever. I may not have been one of the wise men myself, but I had little doubt that there were many wise Spaniards working at the power plant just a couple of kilometres from the road. It was astonishing and made it very clear to me that there was another side to Andalusia apart from the primary industry of growing olives.

So it was industrial after all, but it was also something of great beauty and, even after I had passed the complex, it was difficult to fight the temptation to take my eyes off the road ahead, glance behind my shoulders and see if I was still able to see the rays of light being bounced from the ground to the top of the white towers. Until, that is, I had something equally curious to distract me at the end of a very long, straight road through the middle of a vast prairie of prime, Andalusian farmland. *Was it a bird? Was it a plane?* No... It was a bull. I had seen these before, both in pictures and on my previous visit to Andalusia on the school trip, but this was the first time I had been able to get up close and personal with one of them. From a distance of 3km, it looked big: sufficiently large to see that it was indeed a black bull, with two sharp horns and one very dangly bollock. This was not just any bull, however, this was an Osborne bull. They are dotted all over Spain – 91 in total, of which 23 are in Andalusia – and were initially erected as distinctly shaped advertising hoardings for the Osborne company's Veterano brand of spirit. The first incarnations of the bull were made from wood but they are now constructed in metal, weigh some 4 tonnes, are 14 metres tall and cover an area of 150 square metres. The testicle alone must be a good 50cm in diameter. Until 1988, the words *'Veterano Osborne'* were printed large upon the body of the black bull but then a law was enacted banning roadside advertisements. Albania could do with such legislation to outlaw the unsightly and unfeasibly large Vodafone adverts, which I had seen several weeks earlier. They are not even imaginatively mobile-phone shaped, just rectangular. The again, perhaps they are... I digress. Back to Spain. There was a real risk that the bulls themselves would have to be pulled down, but after having been part of the Spanish landscape for over 30 years, a compromise was reached whereby the bull could stay but the letters would have to go. The judge presiding over the case ruled that the Osborne bull had *'exceeded its initial advertising sense and has been integrated into the landscape'.* Even its bollock. Such is the way of our modern world that the Osborne company squeeze the image of the bull dry and you can buy all kinds of merchandise, ranging from earrings to ties to crash helmets to boxes of pencils, all themed with the iconic image of the bull. No bullshit. (That would be going too far perhaps...)

My hopefully pre-penultimate day of cycling was turning out to be an interesting one but between the curiosities I was stumbling upon as I travelled, the cycling still needed to be done. I estimated the journey from Seville to Huelva to be at least 100km and the Osborne bull that I had found wasn't even halfway along that route. I needed to crack on, push my foot down, pull it up and put some distance on the clock. The distractions in the second part of the day were few and far between. I did take a very short detour to cycle through the centre of the town of La Palma de Condado – cobbled of course – where I found the most beautiful square of palm trees with a pristine, white church adorned with colourful decorations. Against the deep blue of the sky – all the clouds having now evaporated under the heat of the sun – it was a wonderfully quiet place to sit and relax. Perhaps a little too quiet. It was, of course, deserted, everyone being at home saving their energy for later in the day. Even the bar was shut so I was left to my own devices for a few moments to sit and stare. One of life's most underrated activities.

Shortly after La Palma, as I was approaching the town of Niebla, I spotted something familiar. Big, black and powerful. It wasn't another Osborne bull but the BMW of my cousin Richard. He had overtaken me a few minutes earlier and pulled off the road in the outskirts of the town to wait for me to catch up. As I approached, he emerged from the air-conditioned confines of the car without a bead of sweat on his body, sporting a Barcelona football shirt, looking refreshed and tanned. I wasn't. I'm not sure whether I was pleased to see him either. I was so close to the end of the road to Cape St. Vincent and, at the risk of sounding cruelly ungrateful for the company, the last thing I wanted was someone interfering with my plans, to the extent that I had any. Then again, on a purely practical level, it would be useful to have someone to travel a little way ahead, who could find a campsite on the coast before I arrived to join him later in the day. Richard had spent the previous evening in a place on the coast, just south of Cadiz called Vejer de la Frontera, which he heartily recommended. I tried to sound interested but, in reality, I just needed to get the cycling done. I guided the conversation around to the camping arrangements and we hatched a plan whereby he would text me a location and I would follow. I couldn't help but think that meeting up with him would have been so much more successful and enjoyable, if it hadn't been at this fag end of the journey, where I was weary, unsociable and eager to finish.

The cycle after Niebla become hellish as the wind picked up and I entered into a steady war of attrition against the force of nature that I, like the majority of cyclists, most detest. The problem was that the wind would, without doubt, be a constant for the remaining two days of the trip. The Atlantic Ocean had started to play a big role in the climate in this corner of Europe and the first effect it was having on me was to try to push me east as I attempted to travel west.

Huelva was modern and horrid. Plenty of places are modern and beautiful. Others are old and horrid but it seems that the modern and horrid ones are the worst. It welcomed me with a smelly industrial plant processing wood and then it was just a series of block after block after block of dull apartments. I crossed the river estuary via a very long bridge, which at least had a segregated bike path. The cycle path – not always expertly signposted - continued and I was able to remain on a traffic-free route all the way to the coast and the campsite that Richard had found, called *Camping Playa la Botta* near the small town of El Portil. After so many days of resorting, perhaps a little too readily, to staying in a hotel, it was good to be back in the tent. The sandy ground made life a little more comfortable, as did the cooling breeze for which I was now grateful.

It would be my final night in Spain of course. The following day – cycling day 49 – would hopefully see me arrive at a point that would be no more than one day of cycling from my final destination, the lighthouse at Cape St. Vincent. Again, as we shared dinner and a bottle of wine in the campsite restaurant, I just wanted to be with my own thoughts, my own reminiscences and my own anxieties. I needed to be with a person who could sympathise with me about what I had gone through over the previous two months of travelling, who could smile when I smiled, laugh when I laughed, cringe when I cringed and get emotional when I got emotional. Alas, the only person who was able to do that was me. I really did need to be alone.

Tuesday 27th August 2013
Cycling Day 49: El Portil (Near Huelva) To Faro, 106km

I woke and peered outside from the confines of the tent. Once again the day was starting with a grey sky, just as it had done twenty-four hours earlier in Seville. The material surrounding me flapped in the breeze. A few metres away was Richard's blue tent, zipped up. I could hear the occasional, faint snore coming from within. My cousin, a man famed within our family for his lack of enthusiasm for any activity taking place before both hands of the clock are almost vertical, was still asleep. I, on the other hand, am most definitely a morning person. I can't imagine how anyone who wasn't a morning person would be able even to contemplate a long-distance cycle such as the one I was about to complete. If I had started each of the previous forty-eight days of cycling at midday, I would have had to continue cycling late into the darkness of the night or simply allow for an extra month to finish the trip. If you really are intent upon embarking upon such a cycling odyssey in some way, shape or form, make sure you are capable of getting out of bed at what I would consider to be a 'decent' hour. 7am is perfect.

I sat down for a few minutes in the fold-up camping chair that Richard had taken from the back of his car. Over dinner the previous evening, we had discussed the possibility of replicating the arrangement of having him drive ahead and me join him later in the day, somewhere along the Algarve. In the fresh light of morning, I was having second thoughts. I had appreciated the help that he had given me finding *Camping Playa la Botta*, but after so many weeks of just figuring the whole thing out for myself, making last-minute decisions, feeling smug when everything went to plan and shrugging my shoulders and moving on when it didn't, I really didn't want the help and advice of anyone, however well-intentioned it might have been.

Everything was packed and on the bike within half an hour or so and the snoring from inside Richard's tent had been replaced by movement. A few moments later, he appeared, bleary-eyed. We exchanged a few pleasantries but it didn't seem an appropriate time to break the news that actually, having slept on it, I was going to do my own thing for the remainder of the trip, so I didn't mention it. I shamefully waved him good-bye, shouting the deceitful words *'see you later'* as I pedalled off in the direction of the campsite reception. Later that morning, I would send him a text, diplomatically retracting my words.

The border between Spain and Portugal – in the middle of the *Rio Guadiana* – was around 40km along the coast from the campsite. Faro – my likely destination for the end of the day – was another 50km along the coast into Portugal. Faro to Cape St. Vincent on the following day – hopefully the final day - would be well in excess of the 110km average I had continued to maintain crossing Spain, but nowhere near the excessively long cycle to Seville of 175km, let alone the epic 279km required to travel from Tarragona to Valencia. I was feeling quite confident that, just as I had 'planned' during my pre-trip preparations, I would arrive at my destination after fifty days of cycling.

"5,500km? 50 days? 110km per day... that sounds doable."

I grabbed an impromptu breakfast at a bakery in nearby El Portil and plodded steadily along the well-maintained, if rather narrow, coastal road. The wind was continuing to blow and my average speed was pegged well below 20km/hr. After 10km, I was forced to move inland quite considerably, thanks to the *Rio Piedras*. The authorities had never seen fit to construct any kind of bridge over the river in the final 10km of its journey towards the Atlantic Ocean. I thought back to all those beautiful, yet massively under-used, roads in the Greek Peloponnese, financed by European Union infrastructure funds. A slice of the cash might have been better invested here to save me the effort of a sizeable detour. I would write to my MEP immediately upon my return home... The move inland required me to rejoin a more major road, which weaved its way through much less attractive countryside and several towns, with what appeared to be complicated one-way systems. They probably weren't; it just felt that way.

When I arrived in the centre of the final Spanish town, Ayamonte, courtesy of the detour, I had actually cycled nearly 50 rather than the expected 40km. But at least I was there. The final place in the last but one country. The town of Ayamonte was a little disappointing. I had been expecting a fishing village with cliff-plunging vistas looking west along the Algarve. What I found was a flat town, strangled to the point of carbon monoxide poisoning with cars, trucks and buses and filled with tatty tourist shops, food outlets and small supermarkets. I couldn't see any obvious reasons why such a place was so busy. There was no physical crossing point into Portugal – the first bridge across the river was 5km upstream – and there didn't seem to be a cute historic part of the town where people could sit, wander and admire the beauty of the place. Perhaps everyone was using Ayamonte to stock up on their holiday essentials before escaping back to the prettier, quieter parts of the coast a few kilometres away. Could it be that the ferry would merit such a large number of cars? Richard had assured me that it existed and if I were able to find it, it would mean that I wouldn't have to venture north to the first non-motorway crossing point into Portugal. But would I find it?

I spotted a sign but following its directional arrow only led me along some backstreets to the south of the port area, where there was nothing resembling a ferry. Logic dictated that ferries require water upon which to float, so following the path of the river from the south of the port in a northerly direction should surely bring me to the point from which the ferry departed across the river to Portugal. It eventually did. Bobbing up and down in the river was the *Virgen de los Milagros* (goodness knows who had thrown her in there) beside a sign saying '*Portugal Por Ferry*'. Without the sign, the *Virgen* could have passed as a spruced up fishing trawler. With space for only a handful – perhaps four or five – cars, it certainly didn't resolve the puzzle as to why Ayamonte was such a busy little place.

I was expecting a hefty, tourist-inflated price for the one-way crossing of the *Rio Guardiana* to Portugal and I had paused earlier at a cash machine to ensure that I had a sufficient number of Euro notes to cover all but the most exorbitant of eventualities. I stood in front of the guy selling tickets in the ferry office next to the river, clutching a €50 note, hoping for the best but fearing the worst.

"€2.80"

I was somewhat taken aback by the low cost and my mood changed abruptly from one of expecting to be fleeced to one of being embarrassed that I only had a very large denomination note. Depriving him of a large proportion of his change, I apologised, albeit in English. I stowed away the notes and coins that I had been given and pushed Reggie down the gang plank and onto the boat where we, too, bobbed up and down for a few minutes on the water, waiting for the ferry to depart. I was more interested in looking across to the last of my ten countries on the other side of the river than I was at looking back at country number nine. The river was wide – perhaps half a kilometre – but everything that I could see in Portugal was very low level. There were no high-rise apartment blocks, no riverside dock buildings, just a line of white constructions, most of them not immediately opposite where the ferry was berthed but further south, nearer to the mouth of the river.

The wait for the ferry to set off wasn't long and the trip itself was quite short, perhaps just ten minutes. Considerably more time was spent filling the boat with passengers than in crossing the river itself. As I suspected, we headed south towards the low line of buildings that were a couple of kilometres nearer to the Atlantic Ocean. Our destination was the town of Vila Real de St. Antonio. Upon arrival, there were of course no border formalities. The smart, one-storey building with a pristine, red-tiled roof and freshly painted, white walls had, I assumed, in the pre-Schengen era, acted as the border post. It had now been converted into a small welcome centre. I cycled past the building and, within seconds of having disembarked from the ferry, was standing next to the main port side cobbled road opposite, err... Cliff Richard?

"Hi Cliff," I said out loud, as I raised my hand in response to his welcoming gesture. He was looking fit and healthy and was holding a bottle of wine in his right hand. He was, however, looking very thin: very two-dimensional. I took his picture and the convincing cardboard cut-out smiled back.

"I'm off to my own high cliff at Cape St. Vincent," I quipped. He continued to smile, clearly appreciating the joke.

As first impressions go, Vila Real de St. Antonio was giving me some good ones. It was everything that Ayamonte wasn't. Pretty, well-kept and there were interesting buildings clearly dating back some way, not too many cars on the streets and a lovely, relaxed atmosphere. I would even forgive the local council for having covered the town in cobbles, although I suspected that all they had done was to preserve – very well - the cobbles laid down by their predecessors. I had never given a second thought to the first town I would pass through in Portugal, so all this was coming as a very pleasant surprise. The original Vila Real was destroyed by the famous earthquake of 1755 that also flattened much of the Portuguese capital, Lisbon. The town was subsequently rebuilt in a grid pattern in just five months and the fruits of the construction workers' rather rapid 18th century labour are still there to be appreciated today. So very often along my Mediterranean adventure, the area immediately around the border between two countries was something of a let down. Ayamonte had been a good example. Vila Real de St. Antonio was, quite admirably, bucking the trend. It had even installed a septuagenarian crooner to welcome me as I stepped off the ferry. *Bem-vindo a Portugal!*

Cycling out of Vila Real, I was brought back down to earth with a metaphorical, if not literal, bump. When the cobbles stopped, the tarmac started and the ride quality was more reminiscent of certain stretches of Albanian road than the better maintained roads of Italy, France and Spain. I shrugged my shoulders – there was only a day and a half (plus the hour that I had just gained by putting my watch back) of Portuguese road to put up with – and carried on. Until, that is, an elderly couple, who had been waiting for an opportune moment to overtake us, drove past Reggie and me at close quarters, shouting what seemed to be abuse in our direction. They appeared very insistent upon making sure that their message – whatever it was – had been heard. Somewhat taken aback, I responded in universal sign language. They drove off, at speed. I was left none the wiser. What I hadn't realised at the time is that, until recently, it was illegal in Portugal for a cyclist to use the road when there was an alternative cycle path available. This had certainly been the case on leaving Vila Real where just to one side of the main road was a segregated cycle route. Alas, as is often the case, it required frequent pauses when a road or driveway crossed the path, and the surface quality made that of the adjacent road look like a brand new Grand Prix circuit. I had attempted to use it but had abandoned the idea after just a couple of hundred metres. Unfortunately, travelling as I was during the summer of 2013, I had been ahead of my time. The law was changed on the 1st January 2014 and now, using the road is permissible if the cyclist considers it to be *'more advantageous'*. There you go: a practical nugget of information about travelling from one corner of Europe to another on a bike. I hope it was worth the wait.

Much of what remained of that first day of cycling in Portugal wasn't pleasant. There was too much traffic, there were too many bumps in the road and there was too much wind. And not only was the wind blowing in what I considered to be the wrong direction, it was cold. Yes, cold. Not even cool. Cold. I had, of course, the Atlantic Ocean to thank for that. Perhaps when cycling from Seville towards Huelva on the previous afternoon, the gusts had had a little time to warm up as they blew across the arid pastures of south-western Spain, their large metal bulls and heliostat mirrors. Here in Portugal, close to the coast, the wind was coming straight from the sea and, at times, it was sending shivers through my body. I couldn't really do much about the wind, but the traffic and perhaps even the bumps could have been dealt with. At the bottom of my map, I had written the words *'Cycle path along the Algarve'*, but had chosen not to follow it. Known as the *'Ecovia litoral do Algarve'* in Portuguese, it links, continuously, the town of Via Real de St. Antonio with Cape St. Vincent and it would have kept me away from the busy N-125. My only reason for not making use of it was my (perhaps misguided) desire to get to the end of the journey before sunset on cycling day 50. Had the route been anywhere else, I would have at least given it a try. Should I ever find myself cycling along the Algarve coast again, I would certainly follow it from beginning to end.

An opportunity missed. Perhaps there was something in the pre-2014 legislation after all.

Faro came to my rescue. In many ways it was very similar to Vila Real: low level, whitewashed, pretty, well-kept with a good dose of history. It was also extremely photogenic and after having found my hotel – a shamefully overpriced establishment near the port, where service came without a smile – I spent the few remaining hours of the day wandering around the compact old part of the town, putting my skills as an amateur photographer to good use. I was particularly appreciative of the 'new' things I was seeing, which were different from those I had encountered in Spain: the blue and red post boxes, the swirling patterns in the cobbles, the French-looking street signage, the sun setting magnificently over the sea. OK, this wasn't unique to Portugal but it was something that I had never encountered during my cycle through Spain, cutting off, as I had, the entire coastline between Valencia and Huelva. It was worth waiting for, however, and I watched the golden sun slowly descend beneath the horizon from the terrace of a quiet, port-side restaurant where I ate and drank well. It would probably be my last opportunity to do so before I returned home to the UK. Tomorrow – cycling day 50 – would see me back in the tent, at a campsite in Sagres that I had been looking forward to visiting for several years, not because of what it was, but because of where it was, just 5km from the end of the long cycle path from one corner of the continent to the other. The journey was nearing its end; the lighthouse at Cape St. Vincent was calling and, should all go to plan, I would be sitting in its shadow in less than 24 hours' time. Well, if I had a plan worthy of the name in the first place...

Wednesday 28th August 2013
Cycling Day 50: Faro to Cape St. Vincent, 126km

It wasn't a great start to the final day of the trip. The receptionist on duty at the *Hotel Santa Maria* was a different one from the previous evening and he was at least pleasant. That was the good news. The bad news was that when I went to find and unlock Reggie, he wasn't where I had left him. Upon arrival, Mr Misery had instructed me to put the bike in the narrow corridor to one side of the hotel. It ran from the street, where there was a locked door, to the kitchens and the staff used it to avoid having to traipse through the foyer of the hotel. Mr Smiley, the new receptionist, handed me the key to the door and I made my way to the corridor to retrieve my constant travelling companion. I opened the door and looked down the dimly lit corridor. He wasn't there. Deep breaths...

Even though when I found Reggie I was relieved (he had been moved further along the corridor out of view of anyone standing at the doorway on the street), I was a little disgruntled that he had be placed (I'm being diplomatic here; he could easily have been thrown) on top of the refuse bins. I have no idea at what time the Faro dustbin men arrive to collect the rubbish, but I was simply happy that I had beaten them to it. Having used the D-lock to make moving Reggie more difficult (there had been nothing in the corridor to which I could have attached him), I feared the worst. Broken spokes were upper most in my mind. I lifted him from the top of the bins – not an easy job and only furthering my suspicions that he had been thrown there – unlocked him and examined him carefully. Everything appeared to be in order. More deep sighs of relief...

Faro was a small town with big infrastructure, or so it seemed. My impression upon arrival had been of an intimate, compact place on the coast. Venturing to the western side of the town centre, I realised that my initial impressions had been somewhat misplaced. Faro Airport dominated. As with most airports, it was difficult to see much of what was located within the perimeter fence, but its impact upon the local environment was considerable. In the sky was a steady stream of aircraft, many heading back to the UK, and on the ground, the N-125 – the road that I had been following since my arrival in Portugal the previous day – was linked to the airport by a busy motorway on this side of town. Had I known (and it was entirely my own fault for not having found out in the first place), it would have been preferable to retrace the route on the eastern side of Faro along which I had arrived, towards the N-125, but I didn't. Yet again, but hopefully for the final time, I was instructed to leave the road upon which I was travelling and was left to my own devices to fathom a route that would have me cycling merrily along the road to Sagres and Cape St. Vincent. After a considerable amount of to-ing and fro-ing along the most minor of minor country lanes, I found the N-125 again and started to make headway to the west. The cycle path along the Algarve might have slowed me down, but it would surely have kept things simpler.

Clearly, cycling day 50 was all about the destination. Just as I had been on cycling day 49, I was willing to put up with the poor quality road and the traffic, as I had a greater objective in mind. I never really felt as though I was travelling along the Algarve. For me, the Algarve was a place that remained hidden behind the three or four kilometre wide strip of land to my left. I had glimpsed it in Faro while eating in the port-side restaurant but would I see it again? My initial plan was to venture back towards the coast at the towns of Albufeira and Portimão but when I arrived in the vicinity of both of these places, their distance from the N-125, combined with my eagerness to get to Cape St. Vincent as soon as I possibly could, doused any enthusiasm I had for doing so. Shortly before Portimão, the wide estuary was spanned by a low but impressive suspension bridge and I was able to see the urban sprawl of the town. The view only confirmed that I had made the correct decision in carrying on and not stopping. If it had charms, those of Portimão remained very well hidden behind the mass of buildings to my distant left. I chose instead to replenish my stomach and fill my bottles of water in one of the frequent BP petrol stations that were strewn along my route.

By 2pm, I was approaching the town of Lagos and here things were very different. I had no choice but to pass through the town centre because that was where the N-125 led me. I was not complaining, however; I was sick of the busy road and needed some proper food to fill me up. In addition, time was on my side; the Cape was only 30km from Lagos as the crow flies. Sunset would be at around 8pm, so I had six hours to cycle what remained of my route, find the campsite, erect the tent and then locate the lighthouse. I could afford to spend an hour of so of that time in Lagos, having a good lunch and contemplating the final afternoon of the journey along the Mediterranean (and, admittedly, a bit of the Atlantic Ocean as well). It was a busy, bustling town in a way that neither Vila Real nor Faro had been. A healthy mixture of locals and tourists also made it quite authentic. In a tourist brochure, that would probably equate to 'scruffy' or 'run down', but it wasn't at all. Perhaps not quite as pristine as its distant neighbours along the Algarve, but attractive nevertheless. I cycled along the long road beside the port, where private yachts – nothing too garish – mixed with a handful of fishing boats and a good number of small pleasure-cruise boats. Employees of the cruise boats were lined up along the quay, trying to entice potential customers to sign up for their grotto trips, barbecue cruises or fishing trips. I was happy to remain on two wheels but it didn't stop a few of them trying to persuade even Reggie and me to set sail. It could, perhaps, have been the start of a whole new adventure.

A great pile of pasta was presented to me at the *Oceano* restaurant in a small square just to one side of the sea front. After getting on for 6,000km, I was in no mood to start counting the calories so I tucked in, washing the whole ensemble down with a couple of glasses of beer. No one was going to stop me indulging on my final day. The downside of the food and beers was, inevitably, a rather lethargic cyclist climbing the road that curved along the cliff above the centre of Lagos. 30km remained to be cycled – minimum – it would no doubt be much more along the increasingly twisting road to Sagres and the Cape. Lethargy and a strong headwind are not good bedfellows but they were sleeping together in what remained of the day. After an hour or so, I was back into my usual cycling stride, but so was the wind, ever eager to ensure that I would be challenged to the very end.

Those final 40km were some of the toughest yet. My mind had informed my body that the end was nigh and it responded by celebrating a little too early. Each incline became a mountain and there seemed to be a countless number of them as we passed through Espiche, Almadena, Budens and Raposeira, before turning left at Vila do Bispo and embarking upon the last 10km stretch to Sagres itself. The landscape of those 10km felt very edge-of-continent. Had you erased my memory of what had come before, blindfolded me and placed me in that land on that afternoon, I could have told you that this was the end of something. I wouldn't have known that it was the edge of Europe, let alone the edge of Portugal, but it was a landscape that oozed finality. The trees had never grown, the buildings had never been constructed and the people had never come here to live. This was a place most certainly at the end of something. I knew, of course, that it was the end of not just a continent, but also the end of a long journey. Nearly.

The '*Vila de Sagres*' announced itself in the customary way, with a rather mundane sign at the top of a long, straight hill that would eventually finish in the centre of town. I was much more interested in finding the campsite, however, which I knew to be somewhere on the right of the road, so I took my chances and ventured off along one of the minor roads in that direction. Following my intuition rather than any signs, I cycled along several rough tracks before arriving, rather miraculously, at the entrance of the *Sagres Parque de Campismo*. Result! It almost seemed a little too easy. I presented myself at the reception desk and, after a few formalities, was invited to camp wherever I pleased. This generosity was more down to the number of campers who were currently resident at the large out of town site rather than anything else. We were few and the tents were far between. I chose a small plot of sandy ground, unburdened Reggie of my chattels and duly set to work setting up camp. My timing couldn't really have been better even if I had planned it that way (and clearly, I hadn't). It was 5.30pm and with all but the bare essentials needed for the short 5km cycle to the Cape St. Vincent – a bottle of water, my cameras and some money - I set off.

Just as it had been for almost all of the time since leaving Cape Sounio, the sky was blue. The sun was low but there still remained a good couple of hours' worth of sunlight in the day. The road was quiet - certainly much quieter than it had been for most of the time since arriving in Portugal - but it was far from being deserted; every ten or twenty seconds, a car drove by in one direction or the other and at one point I passed a man, waving his arms in encouragement. I thought it strange; did he do that for all cyclists? The man later tweeted me revealing himself as Peter Lewis; he had been following my cycling adventure online since my departure from Greece and my arrival in Portugal had coincided with his own annual holiday to the area. He'd made the effort to come along to the Cape to cheer me on. It was a nice thought and I felt a little guilty for having ignored him.

For this final stretch of my journey along the Algarve, my route had coalesced with the route of the Algarve cycle path and occasionally the iconic outline of a bicycle had been painted on the road. I was the prodigal son returning to the security of the fold. To my right was the seemingly endless cable hoisted high above the road by a series of wooden poles. It was reassurance that I was not on a mission to nowhere; there was something at the end of that line which was worth telephoning. As the cables transferred from my right to my left, for the first time, I could see it. In the far distance, sticking out of the ground above a high wall, was a lighthouse. Not just any lighthouse, of course, but the lighthouse at the Cape St. Vincent - the lighthouse that marked the beginning of land for the sailors and ships it was built to protect but that, for me, marked the end of an epic cycle across a continent.

The side of the road was now lined with cars. Had any of them crossed a continent? Had any of their occupants ever considered doing so? A sign announced my arrival at the end of the '*Rota S. Vicente*'. A few stalls had been set up to sell souvenirs, and plastic chairs arranged around tables next to vans selling fast-food. People browsed, trying to choose the ideal trinket, and queued, waiting to order the burger or beer of their choice. They ignored me and I ignored them. They were on their mission, I was on mine.

The lighthouse was located inside a small complex of buildings protected by a high wall but there was free access via a gate. I stopped, dismounted and pushed Reggie under the gate, weaving around the tourists in their flip-flops and sun hats. Once inside, I could quite clearly see the lighthouse. It was a modest construction - on such a high cliff there was no need for it to be excessively tall - surrounded by white buildings and, of course, cobbles. They were shiny and flat. I was happy and beaming. The job had been done, finished, completed, ticked off... This time I really had crossed Europe on a bike called Reggie.

Distance cycled: 5,665 km

Ride time: 291 hours, 17 minutes

Ascent: 51,763 metres

Descent: 51,989 metres

Calories: 185,496

Average distance: 113 km

Average ride time: 5 hours, 50 minutes

Average speed: 19.5 km/hr

...plus Mont Ventoux.

I celebrated my arrival with a couple of (what else?) Sagres beers within the confines of the lighthouse complex. I took pictures of a very dusty bike and a very weary cyclist, before realising that to truly appreciate the moment, I needed to move away from the crowds, away from the lighthouse and watch the sun set over the Atlantic Ocean. I chose my position well, on rocky ground just a couple of hundred metres east of the cape. The sun was now almost touching the top of the lighthouse. All I could hear was the crashing of the waves at the foot of the cliff below where I was sitting.

"*...Cape Sounio in Greece does seem a long, long time ago... I think about the countries that I have cycled through and the places that I have visited: Greece, Albania, Montenegro, Croatia, Bosnia,*

Slovenia, Italy, France, Spain, and finally Portugal... It's been a long, long journey: nearly 6,000 km. I've enjoyed most of it... It's difficult to enjoy rides on busy roads with lorries thundering past, but thinking about all the memorable places that I've been to and the people that I've met, it's been a worthwhile and thoroughly enjoyable adventure. I'm tired, very tired, although sitting here, looking at the sun set over the lighthouse I don't feel it...

I've now got the small matter of trying to get back home before next Monday when I'm due back at work. That might be an epic journey in itself..."

Heading home

It didn't take long for the practicalities of life on the road to kick in after my arrival at Cape St. Vincent. Even as I was reflecting upon my continental journey from my position high on the cliff top, my eye was on the clock. I knew that the campsite supermarket closed at 9pm and as I didn't fancy venturing into the town of Sagres to celebrate – I didn't have the energy - it was a deadline I just had to meet! Further celebrations would have to wait until I arrived back home in Britain.

But how would I do that? Fanciful options had crossed my mind from time to time, involving the ferries from northern Spain back to Portsmouth or a few more days in Portugal before flying back to the UK from Lisbon or Porto but the obvious solution was to fly back from the nearest and most accessible airport and that was Faro. I had seen the Ryan Air and Easy Jet planes fly low over the town earlier in the week so I knew they were a possibility. The problem was that low-cost airlines are not low cost if you buy your ticket on the day of travel. The Ryan Air website, with all its boxes to tick to confirm that '*no... I don't want to purchase travel insurance for my granny's dog...*' (etc, etc...) and pages of adverts, was unfathomable on the iPhone, whereas Easy Jet's was the epitome of simplicity. They got my business irrespective of the price. So I booked and I left Portugal, just before 8pm on Thursday 29th August, Gatwick bound.

The 30km cycle back to Lagos was a drag (and far further than I can ever remember 30km feeling on any one of the fifty cycling days of the trip) but as the train pulled out of Lagos station, destination Faro, I could finally sit back and relax. It was time for someone else to be in charge and I was happy to relinquish the responsibility.

Andrew and Reggie will return...